FOOD IN HISTORY

FOOD IN HISTORY

REAY TANNAHILL

STEIN AND DAY/*Publishers*/New York

For M.E.

First published in 1973
Copyright © 1973 by Reay Tannahill
Library of Congress Catalog Card No. 75-160342
All rights reserved
Printed in the United States of America
Stein and Day/*Publishers*/7 East 48 Street, New York, N.Y. 10017
ISBN 0-8128-1437-1

Contents

[5]

PART FOUR: *Europe,* A.D. *1000-1500*

PART FIVE: *The Expanding World, 1490-1800*

PART SIX: *The Modern World, 1800 Until the Present Day*

MAPS

Preface

Food in History is a pioneer work on a deceptively simple theme. Its purpose is to examine the forces which have shaped the nature of man's diet throughout the course of thirty thousand years, and to show, without special pleading, something of the way in which the pursuit of more and better food has helped to direct—sometimes decisively, more often subtly—the movement of history itself. To demonstrate, in effect, that in some senses at least food *is* history.

As far as I am aware, this type of panoramic view has never been attempted before even on a national, far less on a world scale. Nor do I know of any other work which has tried to correlate the information revealed in recent years by new disciplines in archeology and anthropology, in biology, ecology, economics, technology, and zoology. Such material is diffuse and often narrowly technical, but much of it throws valuable light on the role of food in the past.

Many problems confront the writer of this kind of book. It is easy, for example, because of the danger of overestimating the importance of the subject in a given historical situation, to underestimate it instead. It is easy, too, to give undue weight to material which has emerged from particularly awkward or complex research. But it is not at all easy to compress thirty thousand years into 398 pages.

It need scarcely be said that ruthless discrimination has had to be exercised. Each section of the book is prefaced by an introduction describing the general course of events during the period under discussion; this is designed mainly as a sheet anchor for the reader, and some of the information will already be familiar. Otherwise, however, I have chosen to deal briefly with matters which I take most readers to be acquainted with, or which are satisfactorily documented elsewhere. There is no real justification in a book such as this for going into detail about the development of English food and diet since the Middle Ages, which is dealt with in exemplary fashion in *The Englishman's Food* by J. C. Drummond and Anne Wilbraham, and (for the period after 1815) in *Plenty and Want* by John Burnett; the growth of the United States cuisine, very adequately covered, in its social context, in J. C. Furnas's history *The Americans;* or the history of food in France, which can be found at sometimes over-eloquent length in Dr. Alfred Gottschalk's *Histoire de l'Alimentation.* Nor have I done more than touch in passing on subjects which are strictly marginal to the main theme (the evolution of restaurants, for example), while I have virtually ignored such matters as religious food taboos, the unifying influence of the family meal, and the political nuances of hospitality, all of which are, in the last analysis, more closely related to social psychology than to food.

On the whole, it has seemed more valuable to devote space to such topics as the earliest cultivation of plants and domestication of animals. To a study of the special ingredients used in Roman cooking. To the diet of the Central Asian nomads (who drank blood), and of the Arabs in the great days of the caliphate (who preferred almond milk). To the development of the sacred cow cult in India, the horizon-expanding effects of the spice trade, the way in which a new method of crop cultivation gave a new dynamism to the people of the "Dark Ages." To early convenience foods and the special cooking techniques they required. To the growth of mass production in the nineteenth century, and the Green Revolution in the twentieth.

At certain periods it has been necessary to fill in some of the gaps in the historical record by indulging in informed speculation as to the *probable* course of developments—a custom deplored by many academic historians. But this book is not designed for academic historians (although I have read their own works with profit, sometimes even with pleasure). It is meant to be a coherent and, I hope, stimulating introduction to a vast and fascinating subject.

It would not be possible for me to list all the people who have answered my questions on food, history, anthropology, nutrition, ecology, and a variety of other subjects over the past six years, and invidious to name only a few of them. A list of notes on sources and an annotated bibliography of published works will be found at the end of this book. I would, however, like specifically to thank the staffs of the Reading Room, Print Room and Manuscript Room of the British Museum, London; Mrs. R. J. Brine, formerly Miss Vilia Neilsen of the Royal Asiatic Society, London; and the staff of that unique institution, the London Library—all of whom have been consistently helpful and courteous to me during the course of my researches.

PART ONE

The Prehistoric World

INTRODUCTION

The Course

of Prehistory

Until about 10,000 B.C. man was little more than a successful predator who lived according to the law of the jungle and survived because he was well adapted to it. He knew how to fight, how to make tools and clothes, how to paint pictures on the walls of his caves, even how to cook, but he had no more influence on the outside world than the lion, wolf, or jackal. What self-preservation and the quest for food had done during millions of years of evolution had been to transform a particular type of ape into a two-legged super-animal—man. But when the neolithic revolution began, when man at last discovered how to grow plants and tame his fellow animals, he took a divergent course which was ultimately to change the face of the earth and the life of almost everything upon it.

Although there is comparatively little unequivocal evidence about the world before 10,000 B.C.—before, in fact, 3000 B.C., the approximate date of the first written records—archeologists have dug up tools and food residues which make it possible to sketch in a necessary picture of the diet of prehistoric man. Necessary, because what man ate during the long millennia of the paleolithic era was to have a seminal influence on the neolithic revolution and on the course of much subsequent development.

In the very earliest days of human evolution, food helped to make man. It was roughly four million years ago [1]—some authorities say thirty million—when the ape-into-man transmutation

[12]

began, and it is generally accepted that the change was set in motion by a shortage of eggs, nestlings and fruit which drove the ape down from his familiar habitat in the trees to forage in the grasslands. He found lizards and porcupines, tortoises and ground squirrels, moles, plump insects, and grubs, and took to them with such enthusiasm that, in time, he almost wiped out a number of the smaller species.

During the next three million years of development, he learned how to kill larger animals by hurling rocks at them—a hunting technique which required him to move on three or, ultimately, two legs instead of four. His wits became sharper as he competed with the lion, hyena and saber-toothed cat who shared his hunting grounds. His teeth, no longer needed for fighting, changed shape—and human speech began to develop. His forefeet adapted themselves into hands, and these hands proved capable of making tools.

So far, the food quest had helped to transform ape into ape-man. Now, as the seas and the earth cooled off at the beginning of the Pleistocene era about a million years ago, storms, rain and biting cold forced ape-man to develop more rapidly than before, to adapt himself not only to new, icy climatic conditions but to accompanying changes in his food plants and animals.

By half a million years ago, ape-man—*australopithecus*, more ape than man—had become *homo erectus*, more man than ape.

Peking man, the first real personality in history, dates from about this time. He still looked very much like an ape, although he had developed the broad nose and high cheekbones which have characterized the Mongoloid and north Chinese races ever since.[2] Though only five feet in height, he was prepared to take on such antagonists as the tiger, the buffalo and the rhinoceros. Their bones litter his caves. So, too, do the bones of the otter, the wild sheep, and the boar. But seventy per cent of his diet consisted of venison. Though Peking man's most enduring claim to fame lies in the fact that he was probably the first to make use of (though not necessarily to *make*) fire, and though he had almost certainly discovered that animal bones could be used as fuel, he probably had not yet begun to roast his food. Like his predecessors, he went to the trouble of splitting particularly juicy bones to get at the marrow [3]—which he need not have done if he had

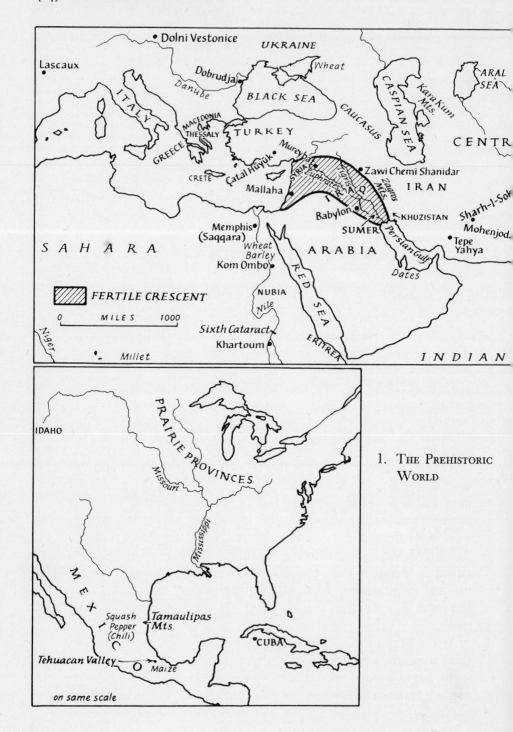

1. THE PREHISTORIC
   WORLD

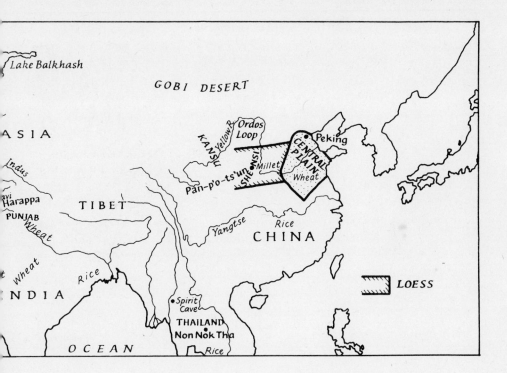

known how to cook. The marrow can be extracted without difficulty from a bone still warm from the fire.

As time passed, other men in other parts of the world also discovered the uses of fire. Light and warmth within the cave must have had a powerful effect on the humanizing process, especially during those millennia when the ice sheets advanced—as they sometimes did—as far south as present-day New York, London and Kiev.[4] With fire as his ally, man did not have to retreat precipitately before them, but could remain close to the fringes, making adjustments to his hunting techniques and diet, eating the meat of such large, cold-resistant animals as the woolly mammoth.

At the beginning of one of the cold spells in about 75,000 B.C., there appeared upon the prehistoric scene a race of *homo sapiens* —the larger-brained successor of *homo erectus*—known as Neanderthals, famous today less for their anthropological interest than because they have become a twentieth-century cartoon cliché.

Whether Neanderthal man's clumsy figure represented physiological adaptation to climate, or was—as some authorities suggest—a sign that he suffered either from the vitamin D deficiency
disease of rickets [5] or from congenital syphilis,[6] he had become
a skilled hunter, had evolved his own rites and rituals, perfected
a primitive surgical technique, and begun to care for the sick and
aged. Like his predecessor at Peking, Neanderthal man regarded
his fellow men as acceptable food when other meat was scarce.

It is only after the disappearance of Neanderthal man from
history in about 30,000 B.C. that it becomes possible to treat developing food habits less summarily. First, however, the reader
may find it helpful to be reminded of the main course of the
events which form the background to the first two chapters of
this book.

After the Neanderthals came a more advanced breed of men
who, in a temporarily mild climate, were able to develop refined
tools which gave the late paleolithic craftsman more scope than
ever before. With bone and horn he made new lightweight hunting weapons, fishing hooks which were more reliable than the
thorns that had been used of old, needles which could sew up
a fitted garment that allowed him to outface the elements when
next the glaciers advanced.

In about 11,000 B.C., however, the ice began to retreat for the
last time (so far). The climate mellowed. Man, animals and
vegetation all began to adapt themselves yet again—and this time,
man's technology was far enough advanced for his adaptation to
take a more radical form. Already, food had played its part in
the making of man. Now, it was to make history, and never more
decisively than in the millennia between 10,000 B.C. and 3000 B.C.,
the gestation period of modern civilization.

As the ice shrank toward the north, vegetational patterns began
to alter. Reindeer—and the peoples who depended on them—
followed the mosses and ferns which grew around the fringes of
the ice. Other animals remained behind, the smaller ones flourishing on the margins of the forests which began to spring up.
Under the influence of warm winds, great fields of wild grain
appeared in various areas of the Near East.[7] Formerly, man had
been a hunter, not a herdsman, a plant-gatherer, not a grower.

But by just over two thousand years after the ice retreat, the deliberate cultivation of plants and domestication of livestock had begun, and the first villages had been established. Slowly, knowledge of agriculture percolated to many parts of Europe, Africa, and western Asia.

In time, farmers in the Near East learned that the type of agriculture they practiced soon turned fertile land into desert. When the solution to this problem—controlled irrigation—was discovered, it was to have an almost incalculable effect on the future of mankind, for although irrigation produced richer and finer crops than ever before, only flat lands near fresh water were suitable for it. After about 5000 B.C., villages began to cluster ever more closely together,[8] all dependent on the same rivers, sometimes fighting for fair shares of the water, sometimes cooperating in the construction of ditches and canals. At last, inevitably, an administrative system came into being. Equally inevitably—as it now seems—the administrative center developed into a town, and then a city, with all a city's characteristic needs, specialized personnel, and formalized institutions. Civilization had been born.

When the ice sheets first advanced a million years ago, it is estimated that there were about half a million ape-men on earth. By 10,000 B.C., the eve of the neolithic revolution, *homo sapiens* numbered around three million. By 3000 B.C., after seven thousand years of farming, the world population was to explode to reach the hundred million mark.[9]

1.
Food and Cooking
Before 10,000 B.C.

Life was short in prehistoric times. During the Neanderthal period, for example, less than half the population survived to the age of twenty, and nine out of every ten remaining adults died before forty.[1] Vitamin deficiencies, seasonal malnutrition, plant poisons, and contaminated food all combined to ensure that anyone who actually achieved the age of forty looked (and no doubt felt) like a centenarian. The lives of these people were, throughout much of the early world, geared to hunting, fishing, and collecting plants.* A small community or clan would make its permanent home in a suitable cave or group of caves—occupied year after year by generation after generation—and scour the surrounding countryside for its food and other needs. In some regions, summer *and* winter quarters were necessary, as certain animals —deer, sheep and goats, for example—preferred the shelter of low-lying ground in winter, but in summer moved gradually toward the uplands and the lush new mountain pastures.[2] The dwellings of the clans had to be carefully sited to fit in with these migrations. Where animals found food and water, so too did man.

* Although hunting-fishing-gathering communities were probably in the majority in paleolithic times, in some parts of the world the economy of the population was based almost entirely on a single kind of animal. In France toward the end of the period, for example, the life of many clans virtually depended on the reindeer. Long after this, in the grasslands of North and South America, the bison and guanaco (a type of humpless camel) were so important that their migrations shaped the calendar of the hunter's year; within the limits of the ecosystem (or territory preferred by the herds), his life was largely nomadic. Later still, the Eskimo ordered his life to suit the habits of sea mammals and the caribou.

Prehistoric man may sometimes have trapped game in enclosures, as the Cree Indians were to do in the nineteenth century.

HUNTING

Though extreme youth or old age might be no barrier to fishing or plant collecting, only the most active and wide-awake members of the community made successful hunters. In a clan of perhaps forty people, consisting of half a dozen related families, no more than ten males would be equipped for the task, and the youngest of these would be mere apprentices. There seems, however, no reason why the younger women should not have had a part to play, in communal hunts at least.

The prehistoric hunter was undoubtedly skillful. Sending a wooden or stone-tipped spear straight through his quarry's eye into the brain, homing a missile on the lethal spot on its skull, crippling it by slashing the heel tendons with a flint knife—these were techniques which demanded swift reaction and absolute coordination of hand and eye. Generally, the hunter may have preferred to kill an animal which was not alert to danger—not only because it was safer and surer that way, but because he may well have observed from experience what science was later to confirm, that an animal which is placid at the moment of slaughter provides better meat than one that is frightened or exhausted.*

* An animal's muscular tissue contains a small amount of glycogen, which breaks down at death into other substances, including the preservative lactic acid. But physical or nervous tension before death uses up much of the glycogen and so reduces the amount of lactic acid that can be produced.

A recent intensive study of seventeen sites in the Zagros mountains of Iran—which cover a period of more than thirty thousand years, beginning at 50,000 B.C.—has produced six thousand identifiable animal bones, mainly from wild goats and red deer, but including hare, fox, leopard, and wild cattle. Though the number of bones may at first seem scanty in the context of such a long period, it still implies consistently good hunting, for the population of Iran in 40,000 B.C. has been estimated as averaging out at only one person to every thirty-one square miles.[3]

How much game did a clan's ten hypothetical hunters have to bring home? No one knows. But assuming, conservatively, that two pounds of boned meat per person per day would represent a minimum ration in an icy climate when other types of food were scarce, the total would come somewhere in the region of 150 pounds live weight every day. The hunters would therefore have to kill the equivalent of at least one, perhaps two, adolescent wild cattle every week. If they were able to choose their prey, would they go for a tender, two-year-old bull, or a larger, tougher (and tastier) eight-year-old? The more mature beast, weighing as much as 2500 pounds on the hoof, would mean at least a fortnight's freedom from worry about the food supply.

Killing his prey may have been less of a problem to the hunter than carrying it or conserving it. A really sizable animal—and the mammoth, the musk-ox and the bison found during the colder spells of the Pleistocene era were extremely large—would have to be carved up on the spot into portable pieces. But there must have been times when it would have been suicidal to hang around dissecting it, with four-legged predators in the vicinity only too anxious to join in the feast. Although there is no surviving evidence to prove that paleolithic man used any other form of transport than his back, arms and head, it is difficult to believe that his ingenuity stopped short of devising some kind of litter made from uprooted saplings and interlaced grasses or brushwood.

Two or three mammoth carcasses would provide a community with plentiful meat for eight to twelve weeks. But a kill of such size may have been something of an embarrassment. Though one mammoth every three weeks would have been an excellent arrangement, this kind of regular marketing was rarely possible. A herd of great beasts might appear in the hunters' neighborhood, and as many as half a dozen might be butchered before the herd

The black bull of prehistoric times.

moved on. The entire community, infants and ancients included, would be enlisted to strip the carcasses and carry the flesh back to camp. No easy task, when each animal probably represented over a ton of meat.

After a few weeks, however, the store cupboard would begin to smell rather high, and though prehistoric man seems to have had no particular aversion to decomposing meat, there must have come a time when he began to connect it with a sudden increase in the family mortality rate.

There is no way of judging when the earliest preservation processes—freezing and drying—were discovered, but conditions during the glacial periods were certainly favorable. The hunter was often drawn a long way from base, perhaps because game was scarce locally, perhaps because such animals as the deer can cover several miles of territory even after they are, technically speaking, dead. Prehistoric man developed his own system of *pied-à-terre* accommodation consisting of caves strategically situated around the periphery of his hunting area. These gave him shelter when he needed it, provided a secluded spot where he could butcher his kill and discard the heavier bones, and acted as a cache for surplus meat when there was too much to be carried home all at once. Delay in making the return trip would teach the hunter, first, that meat was a great deal tenderer if *rigor mortis* was allowed to wear off; if, to use today's phrase, it was "well hung." In bitter weather, he would find the meat frozen or, at the very least, well chilled, and from this he would learn the preservative effects of extreme cold. Dry, flaying winds swept over much of the northern hemisphere in the period between 30,000 and 20,000 B.C., and it may have been at this time that man discovered the keeping properties of dried meat.*

FISHING

When prehistoric man was within range of the sea coasts, he made considerable use of shellfish of all kinds. Inland, he took a club or spear to such large basking fish as the pike, or trapped smaller,

---

* Alternatively, the discovery of drying may not have come until much later, and may have been made in the hot, arid regions of the ancient world, perhaps during the neolithic era in Arabia or Egypt.

migratory fish by damming their streams with upright stakes or laced branches.

It may have been the hunting technique of laying bait to attract animal quarry which first suggested the idea of trying to lure fish to bite on the end of a line. Certainly, by 25,000 B.C., Frenchmen in the Dordogne region had developed the "fish gorge." [4] This was a short, baited toggle with a line attached. When the fish took the bait, the fisherman pulled the line taut and the gorge became wedged at an angle in the fish's jaw. Thorns were sometimes used as hooks at this time, but improved techniques of working with bone and horn soon led the community craftsman to invent a tough yet flexible fishhook.

In France and Spain by about 12,000 B.C., harpoons had been added to the fisherman's armory, and soon afterward the introduction into Europe of the bow and arrow (invented, probably, in Central Asia in about 13,000 B.C. or even, new discoveries suggest, in Africa as early as 46,000 B.C.[5]) gave fishermen as well as hunters a valuable new weapon. It was not only the power and range of the bow which were revolutionary, but the number of arrows that could be carried—allowing the early sportsman to attempt difficult shots on which he would not, before, have dared to risk a harpoon or spear.

Systematic fishing around the coasts, providing a large enough haul to feed a number of people, had to wait until fishermen were able to venture safely on the sea or, at least, close to the river mouth. The dugout canoe and the reed raft of prehistoric times were of no use in deep water until, during the neolithic era, oars were developed. By about 8000 B.C. inshore fishing may have begun in some places; certainly, by that time, fishing nets made from twisted fiber, hair, or thongs, had been invented.[6]

GATHERING

While the men and boys went hunting and fishing and the elders of the tribe occupied themselves with making tools, brewing medicinal potions, and instructing the children, the women and girls set out on their own special food-gathering tasks, looking for edible roots, greenstuffs, nuts and berries, and any small fauna which might present themselves.

Root vegetables, protected by the soil from the worst ravages of the weather, must always have been important. Turnips, onions, and a large type of radish almost certainly date back to prehistoric times in Europe. Within the period of recorded history, the roots of the lotus, asphodel, and Solomon's-seal, and the rhizomes of the canna lily, have all been eaten with evident relish, and there is no reason why such flower bulbs should not also have played a part in the diet of prehistoric man.

In the Americas, root vegetables may even have saved many of the early inhabitants from starvation. Man did not spread over the Americas until about 20,000 B.C.—some authorities say nearer 10,000 B.C.[7]—by which time his weapons were of advanced design. His spirited pursuit of game soon led to the extermination of a number of indigenous species, and changes in climate did the rest. In about 7000 B.C., the retreat of the glaciers opened up a north-south corridor over the country which exposed lands formerly protected by the ice mountains to a searching wind direct from the Arctic. In the prairie provinces, the horse, camel, giant bison and mastodon fell victim to the sudden drop in temperature.[8] The combined depredations of man and nature left the Americas with only a handful of food animals. With limited access, therefore, to the meat which supplied the basis of man's diet elsewhere, many early Americans had to rely on such substitutes as the yam, the potato, and the sweet varieties of manioc.

Above-ground vegetables whose history in Europe and Asia stretches back into the most distant past include the various members of the cabbage family. Prehistoric housewives may also have gathered willow and birch shoots, young nettles, ferns and waterweeds, while moist and shady situations would provide mushrooms and other fungi. In some regions these may have been of as much importance as they later were in Russia, or in nineteenth-century Tierra del Fuego, when the naturalist Charles Darwin reported that the people were largely dependent on one particular type of fungus, which they ate raw and in large quantities. "With the exception of a few berries, chiefly of the dwarf arbutus," he recorded, "the natives eat no vegetable food beside this fungus."[9] In Central America, the gourd and squash can with certainty be dated back to prehistory.

Though many vegetable foods leave no archeological traces,

there is evidence that beans, lentils and chick peas, in various wild forms, were favored in the Near East, Central America, and parts of Europe, and that the seeds of a number of grass-like plants were gathered for use as seasonings. Mustardseed, for example, was chewed with meat from an early stage in recorded history, while toasted seeds of the primitive wheat and barley grasses gave a pleasantly nutty flavor when sprinkled on other food.

Woman's second task was to collect any small animal life that came her way. When the men's hunting was successful she may have turned a blind eye to such delicacies as snails, but in the Near East in about 20,000 B.C. there seems to have been a population increase which began to put pressure on resources which had formerly seemed abundant. Excavations indicate that the tribes were soon forced to gather a greater variety of foods than before—not only snails, but river crabs, fresh-water mussels, and small turtles, as well as acorns, pistachio nuts, and other plants that had normally been used only in emergency. They learned, too, to trap partridges and migratory water fowl.[10]

THE EARLY DEVELOPMENT OF COOKING

For hundreds of thousands of years, the human race ate its food raw. But at some time between the first taming of fire in about 500,000 B.C. and the appearance on the prehistoric scene of Neanderthal man, cooking was discovered. This helped to make a number of formerly indigestible foods edible. It also increased the nutritive value of others, since heat helps to break down fibers and release protein and carbohydrate. The result may have been improved health and longer life for developing man. The distinguished American anthropologist Carleton Coon has even suggested that "the introduction of cooking may well have been the decisive factor in leading man from a primarily animal existence into one that was more fully human." * [11]

* Although, to the food historian, this is a tempting proposition, it is based on the premise that man could not get down to work on developing a "culture" until he was released from the need to spend hours every day chewing tough meat— whereas any deskbound sandwich-eater today knows that working and chewing tough meat are by no means mutually exclusive occupations.

To date, little is known about prehistoric cooking. In fact, what happened in the kitchen between the first culinary use of fire and the evolution of pottery containers tens of thousands of years later is almost entirely open to conjecture.

Roasting—probably the first method used—may have been discovered when someone accidentally dropped a cut of meat in the fire and was unable to retrieve it until the flames died down. But however palatable roast meat proved to be, and however welcome a *hot* meal in ice-age conditions, the technique was wasteful because of the shrinkage inevitable with high-temperature cooking. At some stage, however, the prehistoric cook discovered that meat done in the embers lost less weight than it did when tossed on a blazing fire.

Cooking tough roots in the embers—a logical next step—may sometimes have been productive only of charred ruin. On a flat stone next to the fire, however, turnips and onions could be baked in their jackets with a fair measure of success.

But what happened next? Did cooking development stop dead at this stage for tens of thousands of years? Archeology says it did. There are, however, many ways of cooking which would leave few, if any, distinctive archeological traces.

True pottery was not evolved until almost 6000 B.C., but its earliest ancestor might well have put in an appearance when man realized that the caked and dirty piglet he had so carelessly laid down in a patch of mud produced a much more succulent roast than its cleaner kin. In areas where vegetation was lush, a wrapping of large leaves could be used to protect meat from the flame. Spit-roasting would be a discovery made, perhaps, by hunters far from base—hungry, in a hurry, and observant enough to have noticed that small pieces of meat cooked more quickly than large ones.

A curious sidelight on early man's progress came to light some years ago during excavations at Dolni Vestonice in Moravia. Here, dating from about 25,000 B.C., an oven was found which still contained over two thousand lumps of fire-baked clay—tiny models of animal heads, bodies and feet.[12] Nothing suggests that the oven might also have been used for baking food. The French prehistorian, André Leroi-Gourhan, however, believes that special types of food oven did exist, at this time or before, in the form of small pits which have been found around the hearths of dwellings in the Ukraine.[13] Of much the same shape and size as cylindrical beanpots, these tiny pits were presumably lined with hot embers or pebbles preheated in the fire. The food put to cook in them would be wrapped in—and perhaps covered with—several layers of leaves or, near the coasts, seaweed, and would emerge moist and savory, more steamed than baked.*

Pit cooking is certainly of considerable antiquity, and it may have evolved during early tribal migrations over open terrain. Welcome though a roaring campfire might be in exposed conditions, a roaring cooking fire would have less to recommend it, and the solution of digging a pit for the cooking fire so as to control the flames may well have led to the discovery of the pit-cooking technique.

But how the process of boiling was discovered—as it appears to have been long before the invention of pottery or the development of metalworking techniques—is a much more difficult problem. Fire may turn up by accident, and roasting may be the equally accidental result. But hot water is a rare natural phenomenon, and cannot be produced either accidentally or intentionally without containers which are both heatproof *and* waterproof.

It is usually argued that food in prehistoric times was boiled by the following method. A pit or depression in the earth was first lined with flat, overlapping stones, to prevent seepage, and then filled with water. The water was brought to the boil by heating other stones or pebbles directly in the hearthfire and manhandling them (by some unspecified means) into the water. While the food was cooking, more hot stones were added to keep the water at a suitable temperature. In fact, this pit method sounds like a late development, a mass catering technique designed for large social gatherings which may have been spread by migrating tribes of advanced peoples. These, passing through the territory of backward communities, would repay their hosts by giving a feast. The backward peoples, impressed by the new boiled food, would imitate the method—and continue to imitate it—because it was the only one they knew. 5000 B.C. appears to be the earliest date at which there is proof that the technique was used.

* This cooking technique still survives, on a somewhat larger scale, in the American clambake.

Long before this, however, many widely scattered peoples had their own more logical and far less tiresome ways of boiling meat, making use of pre-pottery containers which not only allowed them to use water in their cooking but may even, in some cases, have inspired the idea—either because without some form of liquid the food would stick to the container, or because food cooked in them produced its own moisture in the form of juices or steam.

In many parts of the world, for example, large mollusc or reptile shells must have been used, as they still were on the Amazon in the nineteenth century, when the naturalist Henry Walter Bates sampled a dish made from the entrails of the turtle, "chopped up and made into a delicious soup called *sarapatel*, which is generally boiled in the concave upper shell of the animal." [14]

In Asia, that productive tree, the bamboo, was probably used. A hollow section stoppered with clay at one end, filled with scraps of meat and a little liquid, then stoppered again at the other would answer the purpose well. The method is still used in Indonesia today.

In Central America, in the Tehuacan valley near the southwestern corner of the Gulf of Mexico, the people who lived in rock shelters around 7000 B.C. and gathered wild maize for food had begun to use stone cooking pots. [15] It seems likely that a pot, once made, was sited in the center of the hearth and left there permanently. It would be very heavy, suitable for use only when a community was firmly fixed in its abode or willing to fashion a new pot each time it moved its cave.

Before the advent of pottery and bronze, there was at least one type of container which was widely distributed, waterproof, and heatproof enough to be hung over (if not in) the fire. This was an animal stomach. In paleolithic times, the hunter, having killed his prey and carved up the flesh for transport, rewarded himself with a banquet of the more perishable parts—the heart, the liver, the brain, the fat behind the eyeballs, and some of the soft internal organs. Like twentieth-century Eskimos, [16] he may have regarded the partially digested stomach contents of his kill as a special treat.* It would be a logical development, as his liking for

* In cud-chewing animals, digestion begins in the rumen, the largest of four stomachs (honeycombed with muscle, and familiar in the kitchen as "tripe"), where partial fermentation takes place—a process that may help to account for the popularity of the stomach contents.

cooked food became a habit, to cook the contents *in* one of the stomach bags, and finally to use the same container for other dishes, some of them not too far removed in their finished effect from the modern casserole.

As late as the fifth century B.C., the nomad Scythians still cooked their food in a stomach bag when they had no cauldron available. "They put all the flesh into the animal's paunch," said Herodotus, "mix water with it, and boil it like that over the bone-fire. The bones burn very well, and the paunch easily contains all the meat once it has been stripped off. [The rumen of a twentieth-century cow has a capacity of thirty to forty gallons]. In this way an ox, or any other sacrificial beast, is ingeniously made to boil itself." [17]

In the eighteenth century A.D. the system still had its uses. The American explorer Samuel Hearne found that a dish called beatee was "handy to make." This was "a kind of haggis made with blood, a good quantity of fat shred small, some of the tenderest of the flesh, together with the heart and lungs of the animal, cut or torn into small shivers, all of which is put into the stomach and roasted by being suspended before the fire with a string. . . . It is a most delicious morsel, even without pepper, salt or any seasoning." [18] It was important not to overfill the stomach, otherwise it might burst during cooking. By about 13,000 B.C., leatherworking techniques had improved so much that skins came to replace many of the older containers.[19]

THE MATERIALS OF REVOLUTION

By about 10,000 B.C., in both the Near East and southeast Asia, man knew a great deal about animals, woman about plants. Indeed, it seems clear that woman's appointed task of gathering seeds, vegetables and fruits had taught her that some plants could be persuaded to grow where she wanted them instead of simply materializing at apparently random locales.

The discovery may have been made first in the case of root vegetables. Sometimes surplus roots would store well, sometimes they would shrivel and become uneatable. Did it occur to someone, some day, that they might keep better in conditions similar to those in which they had been found? Given the right time of year and a modicum of good luck, woman would find that a turnip or radish put back in the ground would continue to grow. Better still, one shallot would obligingly multiply into a cluster. With other kinds of plant, the annual routine of those hunting-fishing-gathering groups which moved from lowland caves in winter to upland caves in summer may have thrown light on the growth of plants from seed. Returning to the hills in early summer, such peoples must have noticed, year after year, the luxuriant young growth capping the previous years' refuse piles—which were, in effect, natural compost heaps. It was only necessary to find one stray seed which, deep in a hillock of earth, dung, and ashes, had been slow to sprout and still held the seed casing around its infant head, and the discovery would have been made that new plants grew from old seeds that had been dropped or discarded.

At first, the refuse heap may have been regarded as possessing magical properties—which, in a way, it did—and early experiments may have been restricted to raising a few medicinal or especially favored herbs. But the essential point was that woman almost certainly *knew* the basic facts about plant cultivation.

Man, too, had embarked on the animal-taming process which was to be the complementary development of the neolithic revolution. In parts of Europe, before the retreat of the glaciers, he had begun to come to terms with the reindeer, which had pro-

On a staff shaped from reindeer antler, a prehistoric artist engraved this scene of deer crossing a stream.

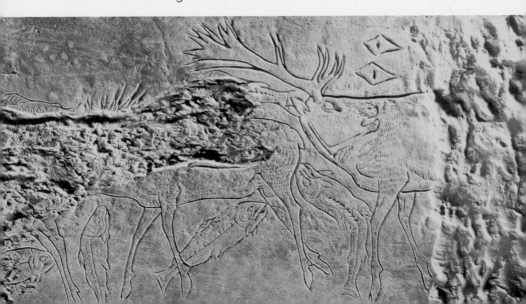

vided him not only with meat, but with the bone and horn he used for his tools. The reindeer fed on the mosses and rich ferns that grew on land watered by melting ice. But animals which depend on snow water suffer from a lack of salts, and have to make periodic expeditions to the seashore or to inland "salt licks." Where human beings congregated, however, it was discovered that the reindeer would accept human urine as a source of salt.[20] With this bait, man succeeded in enticing reindeer to the vicinity of his camps and in building up that interdependence which was to play such a crucial role in the subsequent domestication of animals. Ultimately, the reindeer—like the gazelle in regions farther east —proved resistant to true domestication, but man's experience with it taught him that it *was* possible to achieve a measure of rapport with certain members of the animal world.

One animal *was* to be domesticated in the millennium before the neolithic revolution, an animal which—being a meat-eater, and a man-eater when opportunity offered—would ordinarily have seemed a natural enemy of man. This was the small Asiatic wolf. Until the age of about six weeks, however, the wolf cub is apparently a gregarious little beast who responds readily to friendly approaches. It seems certain that the Asiatic wolf was brought under human control by as early as 11,000 B.C. (although the earliest known relics, from Idaho, are provisionally dated at 8420 B.C.).[21] In later history, it was to be known as the dog.

Though his ancestors had served man as food animals and though his successors were frequently to do so, too, the dog was to prove more useful to the hunter alive than dead. His speed, hearing, and sense of smell supplemented his master's skills and increased his efficiency. And certainly, without the aid of the first sheepdog, man's early experiments in the herding of other animals might, for a very long time, have proved abortive.

2.

Changing the
Face of the Earth

The neolithic revolution—the change from a primarily hunting-fishing-gathering existence to one in which man became a settled farmer and stockbreeder—took place at different times in different parts of the world, but until the improbable day when the entire surface of the earth has been excavated, no one will ever be sure of where or when it really began. The generally accepted view, for example, that there were two clearly defined heartland regions—one to the west and southwest of the Caspian sea, the other in Central America—was seriously challenged in 1970 by publication of the preliminary findings of a University of Hawaii expedition at "Spirit Cave," near the Burmese border of Thailand. There the seeds of peas, beans, cucumbers and water chestnuts, of a size and type which suggest that they may have been cultivated by man, have been carbon-dated at roughly 9750 B.C.— almost two thousand years before true agriculture can be *proved* to have begun in the Near East or in Central America.[1]

Another recently challenged theory is that man only gave up living in small, widely scattered cave communities after he discovered that tilling the land and herding flocks required a sizable labor force; and that this was what led the clans to converge into larger groups and to found villages. Now, it seems likely that in the Near East—archeologically, the world's best documented region—villages sprang up before either farming or stockbreeding began.[2]

THE NEAR EAST

It was not fields of cultivated grain that brought villages into being, but new and abundant fields of *wild* grain. The mellowing climate of the Near East as the glaciers retreated resulted in conditions which favored fast-growing plants. In winter, cool moist air from the Mediterranean helped to stimulate early growth, while summer brought hot, dry, parching winds from Eurasia and Arabia. Grassy plants which could grow, mature, and seed themselves before the hot weather flourished at the expense of slow developers, and rippling fields of wild wheat and barley soon materialized on suitable land.[3]

Even today there are fields of wild grain as dense as cultivated ones. In the mid-1960s, the archeologist J. R. Harlan set out with a flint-bladed sickle to discover what a prehistoric family in Turkey could have expected to harvest if they made an intensive effort. In an hour he gathered enough to produce over two pounds of clean grain—which was, incidentally, twice as rich in protein as the domesticated variety. In a three-week harvesting period, he concluded, a family of six could reap enough wild wheat to provide them with just under one pound of grain per head per day throughout the year.[4]

Early man, anxious to reap such a harvest of free food, had to be on the spot at the right time. One of the characteristics of wild grain is that the ears shatter as soon as the plants reach maturity, spraying the edible seeds out to burrow in the earth for protection until the new growing season. Sometimes, if the summer is hotter than usual, a mature field of grain can turn to a field of barren stalks in as little as a week.

Settlements would, therefore, naturally grow up around the fields, not only in readiness for the moment of harvest but also because, after it, a return to distant caves would hardly be practicable for a family encumbered—in days before either draft animals or the discovery of the wheel—with a commissariat weighing over 2,000 pounds.

By about 9000 B.C. there were established villages in such places as Mallaha in northern Israel which relied on a combination of

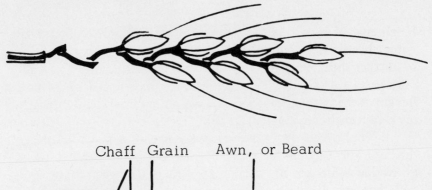

Chaff   Grain   Awn, or Beard

Primitive wheat. As cultivation techniques improved, the ear became shorter and more compact. In some types, the awn disappeared entirely.

hunting and intensive gathering. By almost imperceptible stages,
gathering developed into cultivating. First, the villagers would discover that if they were too efficient at harvesting the wild grain
the next year's crop would be drastically reduced. Then they
would learn to leave some of the ears on the stalks, with better
but patchy results. When they took the next logical step and distributed the seeds evenly by hand, they ceased to be merely gather-
ers—and became farmers.

EARLY GRAIN COOKING

Mankind's sudden and extensive dependence on grain, whether
from wild or cultivated fields, raises at least one interesting question which usually goes unanswered. What did the people of the
early neolithic do with it all?

First, of course, they had to separate the edible part of the grain
from the roughage surrounding it. This was a time-consuming
process. The desirable part of wheat and barley consists of an
embryo (the nutritionally valuable "germ") embedded in a starchy
mass known as the endosperm. Firmly attached to this is a thin,

tough coat of bran, and the whole seed unit is encased in a harsh outer sheath, the chaff. Tufts of the sheathed seeds, protected by further shells of chaff, make up the ear of grain.

It was a feature of wild grains that the seed and chaff were reluctant to be parted, but man seems soon to have discovered that the outer chaff became brittle and easy to detach if the ear was slightly toasted. At places such as Mureybat in Syria, early villagers threshed the ears in pits floored with heated stones.[5] It seems likely that a fire was lit on the floor, allowed to burn for a while, and then raked out; the stones would retain the heat for some time.

But however efficient the threshing, the individual casing of chaff and the inner coat of bran still clung to the seeds and had to be laboriously removed by hand. Rubbing the grain back and forward between two stones helped to split the chaff and scrape off some of the bran. At Kom Ombo in Egypt,[6] in the Sahaba aggradation of the Upper Nile,[7] at Mallaha in the Jordan valley,[8] and at Zawi Chemi Shanidar in Iraq,[9] very early mortars and rubbing stones have been discovered which were probably used for this purpose. The final state of the grain depended very largely on the skill and patience with which the rubbing process was carried out. A careful worker might manage to produce whole, clean wheat, but more often the result would be a coarse residue of groats, spiked with chaff and speckled with bran.

Clearly, early neolithic man was prepared to go to a great deal of trouble to prepare his wheat and barley. Raw grain and the human digestive system are, however, incompatible. He must therefore have evolved some satisfactory method of cooking it. The question is—what, in pre-pottery days, was the method?

Prehistorians are notably reticent on the subject, but the orthodox view is that the pit-boiling method (as described on page 27) was the one used.

Even by neolithic standards, pit-boiling must have been irksome and inconvenient, especially if it came as a climax to the exacting process of rubbing and pounding. Nevertheless, the alternatives at first glance seem even less likely. Such containers as shells, leather buckets, and animal stomachs, though useful on occasion, had too short a life to make them practical for constant use. Tiny particles of wheat could hardly be tossed straight on the fire to cook. And the hot hearthstone would not accommodate more than a handful or two of seeds. But there was one way of cooking grain which would bypass the whole problem of containers, would involve no extra labor, and must have been discovered in the very earliest days of bulk grain usage. This was to heat the threshing floors to a temperature high enough to roast the grain at the same time as it splintered the chaff. Most archeologists believe that the floors were heated only enough to make the chaff brittle, but that —temperature control being erratic—overheating sometimes occurred and a whole batch of grain might be roasted, even charred, by mistake. If, however, it could be established that roasting was in fact commonplace (and so, probably, intentional), then it would become possible to build up a more rational and coherent picture of the early history of grain usage.

Grain roasted on the threshing floor would be divested of its chaff in the usual way, and pounded in a mortar. The resulting coarse groats, needing *no further cooking* to make them digestible (and having an excellent flavor), would of course be far too dry to swallow. The simple solution would be to add a little water and knead the mixture to a stiff paste. This would be roughly similar in taste to the Greek *maza* and Roman *puls*—grain-pastes which were to be standard items of diet in classical times (see page 79) —and, in texture, to the *tsampa* still favored today in Tibet. André Migot, the twentieth-century doctor and traveler, has described in vivid terms how Tibetans prepare the dish, using toasted barley flour (*tsampa*) and, as the liquid ingredient, tea—which is drunk thick and black in Tibet, flavored with salt, and enriched with a lump of potent yak butter.

"You leave a little buttered tea in the bottom of your bowl," he says, "and put a big dollop of *tsampa* on top of it. You stir gently with the forefinger, then knead with the hand, meanwhile twisting your bowl round and round until you finish up with a large, dumpling-like object which you proceed to ingest, washing it down with more tea. The whole operation demands a high degree of manual dexterity, and you need a certain amount of practical experience before you can judge correctly how much *tsampa* goes with how much tea; until you get these proportions right the end-product is apt to turn into either a lump of desiccated dough or else a semi-liquid paste which sticks to your fingers. . . . The whole process, in a country where nobody bothers much about washing, has the incidental advantage that, however dirty your hands may be when you embark on it, they are generally quite clean by the time you have done." [10]

However unpalatable it may sound, the grain-paste would be an epoch-making discovery in prehistoric times, enabling man—despite the limits of his technology—to make a quantity of solid food out of tiny, insubstantial seeds. It was portable food, too, which could be carried on a journey either readymade or in the form of groats to which liquid would be added when required.

The first unleavened bread may have been invented when man discovered that a piece of grain paste laid on the hot stone next to the fire developed an appetizingly crisp crust. Or it may have been the result of a more deliberate experiment with dough made from water and the flour of raw grain. Either is possible, though the second is the more generally accepted view.

The plain flour-and-water flatbread still survives in many parts of the world, sometimes improved by the addition of a little fat, usually seasoned with salt. The Mexican *tortilla* and the Scots oatcake, the Indian *chapati* and the Chinese *pao ping*, the American Indian johnnycake and the Ethiopian *injera* are all direct descendants of neolithic bread, utilizing virtually the same balance of materials. It is mainly the difference in the basic grain—maize, oats, wheat, or millet—which makes the end products seem so dissimilar.

Early flatbreads probably had one disadvantage. Appetizing when fresh and hot, they would become heavy and indigestible when cold. For this reason, perhaps, the ordinary unbaked grain-paste—which had excellent keeping qualities—held its own against cooked breads for a very long time. Even after the development of wheats and barleys which could be threshed without the aid of heat, many people toasted grain at home so that they could continue to make grain-pastes.

Before the days of pottery, there were two other ways in which grain could have been used. In neither of them was it necessary for the grain to be cooked, and both were possible within the terms of early neolithic experience.

The first method would make use of unroasted, partially threshed grain. If wheat or barley seeds are moistened and left to germinate, they produce crisp, nutritious little stalks rather like Chinese bean sprouts. In the process of germination, too, the starch content of the seed—indigestible in dry, raw grain—is converted into digestible malt sugar. It seems legitimate to doubt, however, whether a neolithic family would have been prepared to swallow a ton of wheat sprouts during the course of a year, and this method would have the further disadvantage of pre-empting a large number of as yet scarce waterproof containers. Sprouted grain was, however, to play an important part in the later discovery of beer (see pages 63-64).

The disadvantage of the second method would be that *whole, untoasted*, chaff-free seeds would be needed. Whole wheat, soaked in hot water at the side of the fire, after some hours swells and gelatinizes into a delicious kind of spangled white aspic. A dish of this type crops up in later times everywhere from India to Cuba, from China to England (where it is known as frumenty, fermenty, fromity, or furmity). It may—possibly, if not altogether probably—have been invented as early as the neolithic period.

When pottery at last came into use the cook's horizons expanded. A regular supply of fire and waterproof containers, easily breakable but easily replaced, made it possible to boil grain in a lot of water; to simmer it in a little water; to produce meat and grain stews; to make better-baked flatbreads; to invent a number of new dishes and improve on a number of old ones. And when pottery was succeeded by unbreakable metal containers, the development of modern cooking had begun.

THE DOMESTICATION OF ANIMALS

The fields of wild grain which sprang up in the Near East twelve thousand years ago did more than help to feed mankind. They also attracted a number of those smaller animals which had begun to multiply in the open shade around the margins of the forests. In the early part of the growing season the raids made by wild goats and sheep on the new grain sprouting in the fields must have been a serious threat to the villagers' future food supply. They had three options—to exterminate the flocks, to defend the

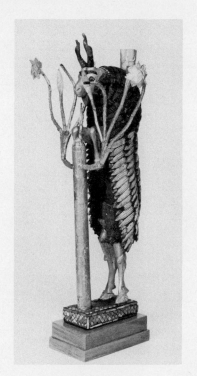

This model—"The ram caught in the thicket"—probably represented not a ram but a goat eating the leaves off a shrub.

fields, or to bring the animals under control (which had the overriding advantage of ensuring the meat as well as the grain supply).

Domesticating the sheep and the goat may have been a comparatively easy task. Both were gregarious; where one led, the others would follow. In some villages it may have been commonplace to adopt orphan baby animals as pets, and a hand-reared ewe allowed to mate with a wild sire would, in the course of a few years, help to establish a village flock.

Whether the sheep or the goat was the first animal to be domesticated remains an open question, though the balance of probabilities favors the goat—an animal which has been greatly maligned through the ages, for its destructive browsing habits as well as its pungent smell. But during the early expansion of farming, in areas where scrub had to be cleared to make way for cultivation, its talent for killing plants by defoliation may have made the goat a useful agricultural laborer.

In the case of the sheep the first stages in domestication had certainly taken place by about 8920 B.C. at Zawi Chemi Shanidar in Iraq,[11] and at Dobrudja in Rumania.[12] But such dates and places are not necessarily definitive. The sheep may originally have been tamed by hunters in cooler regions such as the Kara Kum, east of the Caspian. Long before spinning and weaving were invented, it was possible to make wool into a warm natural felt which was invaluable in a cold climate. A single sheep, however, can eat a hundredweight of greenstuff in a week, and the earliest herdsmen must have been kept constantly on the move in search of new grazing lands. Many would tend to move west, towards the lush pastures of Iraq, and it may have been from such nomads that the peoples of newly settled villages like Zawi Chemi Shanidar learned the techniques of sheep herding.

The pig arrived third in the barnyard, although the occasion seems to have been delayed until about 7000 B.C. One of the reasons may have been that the pig, unlike ruminant animals —goats, sheep, cattle, reindeer, and camel, for example—cannot digest straw, grass, leaves, or twigs. Pig-rearing, in fact, could not be embarked on until man was prepared to invest some of his *own* food—nuts, acorns, meat scraps, cooked grain—in the enterprise.

The last major food animal to be domesticated was the cow, not apparently in the heartland areas of the neolithic, but (depending on the outcome of a current archeological controversy) either in Çatal Hüyük in Turkey or Nea Nicomedia in Macedonia, at some time between 6100 B.C. and 5800 B.C.[13] The task may have been postponed because of the difficulties involved. Though the ancestral type of the domesticated breed died out in the seventeenth century, attempts have been made in Munich and Berlin in the last twenty years to re-create it.[14] If the fiery and agile modern version is anything to go by, neolithic man must have had his hands full with the original. Once brought under control, however, cattle were reduced to submission by poor feeding, close penning, hobbling, and usually, in the case of the bulls, castration.

Since his hunting days, man had known that, in addition to meat, the goat provided glossy waterproof hair, and a skin which made a first-class water container; that the sheep supplied wool, and substantial quantities of fat, useful not only for cooking but as an ingredient in medicinal salves and as tallow for rushlights and lamps; that the pig's bristles were as valuable as its lard and its skin; that the cow's hide was tough and strong, and its dung an excellent fuel for the fire. But, almost certainly, it was only after the first of these animals had been domesticated that man learned about milk and the numerous ways in which it could be used and preserved. This new foodstuff, which was to become of the greatest importance to later generations, was one of two unlooked-for benefits of domestication. The second was that the goat, sheep and ox could be pressed into service as agricultural laborers, made to sow seeds, pull the plough, and thresh the ripe grain. The barnyard animal became, in effect, man's first power tool.

THE EXPANSION OF AGRICULTURE

Slowly and irrevocably, knowledge of plant and animal domestication spread throughout the Old World. Sometimes, the knowledge may have been carried by migrating clans, complete with a baggage train of livestock, seed grains, and domestic impedimenta, sometimes by a few stray wayfarers who did no more than stimulate the minds of those they met by telling what *could* be done.

As the first emigrants from the heartlands—children of the population explosion which inexorably resulted from a guaranteed expansion of the food supply—moved, settled, and then in turn sent out secondary waves of emigrants to even more distant lands, they had to adapt to new conditions. Sometimes their seeds would scarcely grow in a different soil. Sometimes their livestock sickened and died.

About the livestock, they could do little except wait for them to become acclimatized. In the case of the crops, they found that in warm, lowland regions wheat was strong enough to defeat the particular types of weed which invaded its fields, but that in cooler areas or at higher altitudes the weeds flourished. Ultimately, farmers were reduced to harvesting the weeds rather than the wheat. One of these weeds was rye, later to become a staple grain in northern Europe. Another was oats. In Central America, the tomato—a weed of maize and bean fields [15]—was to prove an extremely valuable nutritional supplement.

A dairy five thousand years ago. Cows were still milked from the back—like sheep and goats—instead of from the side.

The early millennia of the neolithic were years of discovery, expansion, and destruction. Great fields of sprouting grain encouraged the multiplication of insect pests. Silos of dry grain stimulated a population explosion among the smaller rodents. Agriculture itself was concerned simply with taking all that it could from the soil, and gave nothing in return. It needs only two or three years to exhaust a patch of earth, as much as fifty years for that earth to regenerate itself. In the heartlands of the neolithic, earth which had first been stripped of trees and scrub, then overworked and overgrazed, began to turn to desert. Cultivable land became progressively more scarce. The neolithic revolution laid the foundations, not only of modern civilization, but of many of the pressing ecological problems which bedevil twentieth-century man.

At some time after 5000 B.C., farmers who had strung out their settlements along the banks of streams in the region now known as Khuzistan, at the head of the Persian Gulf, evolved a technique of breaching the banks so that water flowed out and bedded itself down into tiny canals.[16] This primitive system of irrigation could be used to water fields for as much as three miles on either side of a river.

Gradually, the farmer learned how to improve and expand his irrigation techniques. There were three direct results. The first was more and richer crops. The second was the genesis of a water-administration system which was to help to lead to the growth of towns and the birth of such civilizations as that of Sumer. The third was a return to the desert—for, unless there is perfect drainage, constant irrigation leaches out of the earth salts which destroy fertility. In the Near East, the wheat began to fail, then—though it was more resistant to salinity—the barley. The states which had been built on irrigation were forced to look beyond their frontiers toward new lands which could redress the deficiencies of the old. Irrigation, which had helped to found cities, also helped to precipitate the first tentative attempts at imperial expansion.

The *shaduf*, an early aid to irrigation. Water was raised from rivers and natural reservoirs by means of this counter-balanced bailing bucket (sometimes called a swape) and tipped into adjacent irrigation channels.

The *shaduf* in use in nineteenth-century India.

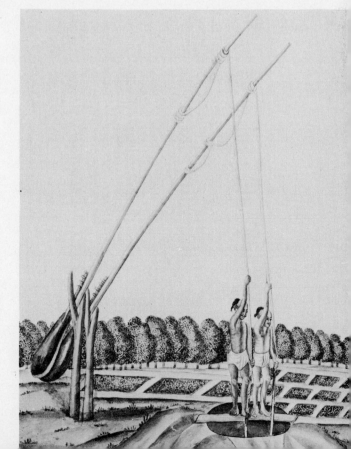

BULLS OF HEAVEN AND GODS OF THE EARTH

Despite—perhaps because of—his now considerable technological expertise, man became ever more aware of how little he really knew about the forces of nature. Long before the neolithic revolution he had summoned up gods whose existence would explain the inexplicable—gods of air, fire, earth and water, friendly deities whose worship brought food in abundance, unfriendly ones who called down scarcity, drought, pestilence or plague. But it may only have been when he took to farming that the annual death and rebirth of the soil began to haunt his imagination and cry out for explanation.

The soil fertility legends which lie at the core of the world's oldest religions have acquired so many political, social and historical accretions over the centuries that they are now almost unrecognizable. But in the mythology of Sumer, the earliest in recorded history (c. 3500 B.C) the message is still clear. Inanna, the tempestuous goddess of love and war, sets off to conquer the nether regions. While she is away, the earth remains infertile, "the bull springs not upon the cow . . . the man impregnates not the maiden." [17] But after many adventures, including a form of death, Inanna at last returns to earth and the world comes to life again.

This, with regional variations, is the essence of most of the fertility myths. In Egypt, it was the god Osiris who died and was resurrected; in Greece, Persephone spent six months of each year in the underworld; in Canaan, Baal was below ground for seven whole years during which drought and pestilence reigned on earth. Even the Jesus of the New Testament, dead, then resurrected, echoes the early farmer's need to know that death was not the end, either for nature or for mankind.

As the gods who represented those unseen forces which man still did not understand grew in power and importance, a number of the gods whom he had worshiped in earlier times declined. Long ago he had been awed by the commanding figures of the animal world, by the wild majesty of the bull, the towering might of the bison, the feline strength of the lion. But domestication of animals began to usher in the decline of animal worship. The lackluster inhabitants of the barnyard inspired no awe, no admiration.

For a time, however, man saw in the rampaging wild bull the epitome of all the qualities he had drained out of the domesticated breed. The great Bull of Heaven, worlds away from the patient castrated beast who drew the plow, for thousands of years continued to play an important role in man's mythology. Sometimes the role was symbolic, as in the Zoroastrian creed of Persia, where the original war between good and evil, light and darkness, was fought between cattle and wolves; sometimes more tangible, as in Egypt, where a live domesticated animal was chosen to represent Apis, bull incarnation of the god Ptah. Sometimes the bull himself was immolated on the altar of greater gods, as in China, where the king sacrificed a red bull to the Sovereign on High in spring and, later in the year, one black bull to the Sun and another to the Ancestors. Sometimes, the bull's worshipers turned memories of human sacrifice into a sport, as with bull-leaping in Minoan Crete. Only once, it seems, did the patient ox triumph over his more dynamic brother—when Saint Luke was represented in the symbolism of the Christian church as a winged ox (an image which was to survive until as late as the fifteenth century).

But domestication, in the end, conquered the animal gods. Only in India, where religion, politics and economics brought to bear an almost irresistible combination of pressures, was the domestic cow—the great provider—to be accorded love, gratitude, and a peculiarly egalitarian kind of worship.

THE NEOLITHIC REVOLUTION IN AFRICA

Although it now seems that the people of the Upper Nile had learned how to grind wild grain at least as early as—if not before —the peoples of the Near Eastern heartland,[18] the discoveries of the neolithic revolution spread from that heartland across the isthmus of Suez into Africa, probably during the fifth millennium B.C.

The new knowledge could scarcely have arrived at a more propitious moment. The drift sands of the desert were closing in on the communities which fringed the Nile valley in Middle Egypt,

Cattle trod the grain at harvest time to separate the wheat from the chaff.

forcing them toward the flood plains. When cultivators with neolithic tools and knowledge moved down to clear the valley floor, the sequel was dramatic. They found that the Nile itself did the farming for them.

Rising in mid-July, the Nile waters reached their fullest extent in September. When they retreated they left behind them a coating of rich black earth deposits (nowadays trapped behind the Aswan High Dam) from the Ethiopian plateau. As Pliny later recorded, it became the custom "to begin sowing after the subsidence of the Nile and then to drive swine over the ground, pressing down the seed in the damp soil with their footprints . . . This is done at the beginning of November, and afterward a few men stub up the weeds—their name for this process is *botanismus*— but the rest of the laborers only visit the fields a little before the first of April, taking a sickle with them. The harvest is completed in May." [19]

Wheat and barley flourished and the population multiplied more than a hundredfold in the course of only a few centuries. [20] By just over a thousand years after the first crops were planted in the Nile valley, a whole new civilization had appeared and Egypt had entered upon its first dynastic period.

It has been estimated that, in the third millennium B.C., the Egyptian peasant was capable of producing three times as much food as he and his family needed to sustain them. [21] Much of the surplus was used to feed workers engaged on flood control projects, on great public buildings, or on the majestic tombs which were designed to ensure that great nobles and dignitaries would be welcomed with due deference in paradise.

It was the travels of early Egyptian traders which helped stimulate cultivation and domestication over a wide area of Africa. From about 3000 B.C., Egypt was in regular contact with Eritrea and Somalia, which produced the incense so much valued in the early dynastic period. Knowledge, seeds, tools and domesticated animals were transmitted to the south in exchange for frankincense and myrrh.

From the easternmost point of Africa, the knowledge and the tools filtered south and west through much of the continent. Animal domestication was adopted wherever the fauna were amenable, but the wheat and barley of the Nile would not grow in many parts of Africa. Cultivation techniques had to be adapted to suit other crops—millet in the light woodland belt south of the Sahara, "red rice" in the great hook of the river Niger. In Kenya, "finger millet" was harvested, while in the Congo basin there are suggestions of a primitive cultivating society which was only to burst into full, influential flower when new and suitable plants were introduced directly from southeast Asia toward the beginning of the Christian era.

THE AMERICAS

Although domestication of plants in the New World may have been almost contemporary with that in the Old, comparatively little is yet known about the progress of the neolithic revolution in the Americas.

By some time between 7000 B.C. and 5000 B.C., however, it is clear that the inhabitants of a group of caves in the Tamaulipas mountains of Mexico, although they still gathered wild plants in the form of runner beans and the agave, or American aloe, had begun to domesticate a number of others. Among these was the summer squash, which provided both a flesh and a seed food; the chili pepper, then as now a much-used seasoning in Central America; and the bottle gourd, whose young fruits could be used as a vegetable, but which was probably more valued for the dry, hard shell of the mature plant, which made a useful water container.[22] Further south, in the Tehuacan valley, there are signs that one of the most important plants of later times, maize, or Indian corn, was brought under cultivation between 6000 and 5000 B.C.[23]

In South America, in the Ancash department of Peru, beans were being grown in about 5680 B.C., and by 3000 B.C. the people of the region had succeeded in domesticating the potato plant.[24]

Because of the diligence of paleolithic hunters and the climatic changes at the end of the ice age, animals suitable for domestication were rare. Indeed, animals in general were rare. Some kinds of seafood, too, were gathered so energetically that they became extinct. Shell remains excavated at Catalina island, California, show that in the fourth millennium B.C. man gorged himself on abalone,[25] and only turned to the mussel tribe when the abalone colonies had been almost wiped out.

The destructive nature of early American hunting and seafood-gathering may be partly explained by prehistoric man's inbred taste for flesh food. But fortunately, even with meat, fish and seafood in short supply, there were insects he could fall back on. An analysis of digestive remains from a prehistoric site in Mexico suggests that early man there was not averse to a meal of grass-hoppers, ants or termites.[26] Indeed, there is no good reason why he should have been. Several insects were considered delicacies in classical times in Europe, and a number are still eaten with pleasure in China, Africa and Australia today.*

At some stage in history, the people of Mexico succeeded in domesticating the turkey, and began to raise dogs for the table; the Aztecs were to favor a special hairless breed, a larger ancestor of the modern Chihuahua.[28] In Peru, the only domesticated food animal seems to have been the guinea pig. The llama and the alpaca were also partially tamed, the first because it was a valuable draft animal, the second for its wool, but both were members of the camel family, slow-breeding, and unprofitable to slaughter for the pleasure of a few good meals.

ASIA

If the progress of the neolithic revolution in the Americas is scantily documented, in Asia it is scarcely documented at all. A

---

* Insects can form a useful protein supplement. The locust, when dried, gives as much as seventy-five per cent protein and twenty per cent fat, as well as a number of vitamins; the termite thirty-six per cent protein, forty-four per cent fat, and some valuable phosphates.[27]

few animal bones, including those of "possibly domesticated" sheep, have been found in the Adamgarh hills of central India and carbon-dated to about 5500 B.C.[29] Two archeological expeditions have reported "probably cultivated" peas, beans, cucumbers and water chestnuts at "Spirit Cave" in Thailand, dated at 9750 B.C., as well as proof of rice cultivation at another north Thai site, Non Nok Tha, in about 3500 B.C.[30] The rest is silence—as far as food is concerned. (Tools and pottery, of course, have as always been subjected to much more intensive study.)

The lack of information about prehistoric Asian food is particularly unfortunate in the cases of India and China, where the great civilizations of the Indus valley and the Yellow river valley materialize with spectacular abruptness on the historical scene, fully developed, yet apparently without antecedents, their food habits established, but not explained.

Harappa and Mohenjodaro, the great cities of the Indus valley, show every sign of having been built to a preconceived plan. Elaborate and curiously uniform, they were provided with markets, granaries, dockyards, temples, public and private baths, and a drainage system of considerable sophistication. Clustered around the cities were smaller farming settlements whose agriculture depended on the river Indus. Controlling the river seems to have involved no major works of the kind used in the Tigris-Euphrates or the Nile valleys. All that were needed were dams and canals small enough to be engineered and serviced by a handful of local farmers.[31]

The people of the Indus valley ate wheat and barley and the field pea, cooked their food in sesame oil, and seasoned it with mustard or, possibly, turmeric or ginger. They ground their grains into flour, made use of ovens and spice-grinding stones. Melons and dates, coconuts and bananas, pomegranates and, perhaps, lemons and limes all figured in the diet. Sheep, goats, buffalo and pig, the elephant and the dromedary were all common species, and it was the people of Harappa who domesticated the Indian jungle fowl, later to become the world's "chicken."

Such a homogeneous civilization cannot have evolved from nothing, but whether it grew out of some earlier, as yet undiscovered Indian culture, or whether intruders from the west or north —emigrants from the Near East, perhaps, or groups of those peri-

The humped zebu bull, and the flat-backed *primigenius* type with an incense burner or manger before it, as shown on Indus Valley seals.

patetic Indo-Aryan herdsmen who ranged Central Asia and far beyond—arrived equipped with all the latest expertise, remains an open question. Certainly, by the time the Indus civilization came into being in about 2300 B.C., the cities of the Tigris-Euphrates valley were well established, while new discoveries in southeast Iran suggest that there may have been another great contemporary civilization centered on Tepe Yahya and Sharh-I-Sokhta—even closer to the Indus than either Sumer or Akkad.[32]

In the context of food history, this question of the origins of the Indus valley civilization is by no means as academic as it might appear. In fact it may be integral to the birth of the sacred cow cult.

Among the archeological relics of the Indus valley civilization are almost two thousand trading seals, miniature wads of clay impressed with a pictorial image and a short legend in a script which has not yet been deciphered. Most of the images represent animals—symbols, perhaps, of various clans or craft units—and among the most frequently shown is a bull. If the bull were always of the indigenous Indian humped type (the zebu), then the matter might simply be allowed to rest there. But, in fact, the foreign flat-backed breed—*bos primigenius*, from which the domesticated cattle of the West are descended—appears with far more frequency, and is usually depicted with what is taken to be a standard or incense-burner before it.

One implication of these seals is that the non-native type of bull may have been the symbol or totem animal of a group of foreigners who were in the process of being assimilated into the society of the Indus valley. If such immigrants had brought with them their own breed of cattle, and if these cattle were responding badly to the climate, the emblems of respect and worship which accompany their images on the seals might be partially explained; nothing would have been more rational than to protect the survivors by emphasizing their value in semi-religious terms which no contemporary could fail to understand.

But whether or not this is the truth behind the Indus valley seals, such an interpretation would be in keeping with the later history of the cow in India (see pages 154-58). However casually it might be treated in normal times, whenever the cattle population was under threat the sacredness of the cow was emphatically restated.

Chinese civilization, as it emerged at roughly the same time as that of the Indus valley, took a rather different form. The well-organized farming communities were similarly in evidence, but not the great cities.

Like the Nile, the Yellow river ("the Father of Floods") carried a rich sediment down on its waters to the valley. In China, the soil came from a plateau to the west, whose fine loess dust of clay, sand and limestone, formed by erosion into natural terraces, was highly fertile and, by its very nature, self-regenerating. The central plain, in contrast, was waterlogged.

The archeological record suggests—rather improbably—that the early farmers of the Yellow river valley appeared from nowhere, in large numbers.[33] In fact, the country probably had a sizable and scattered population which began to draw together after the first experiments in agriculture in the easily worked loess highlands were followed by a move to the plains. There, because of the need for drainage and flood control, farming was possible only with a large and disciplined work force. Certainly, from the middle of the third millennium B.C., the heart of the Yellow river valley seems to have been densely populated. Villages were many, the houses crowded close together, their conical roofs almost touching.[34]

The most important food crop raised in these early days was the small-seeded "foxtail millet," but a small amount of wheat was also grown, possibly from the seeds of plants which had originated in the West and spread from village to village across the lands of Central Asia. Prehistorians are reticent about the date at which these may possibly have reached China.

Rice was originally cultivated not in the well-populated northern areas of China, but south of the Yangtse—a foreign land, wooded, marshy, peopled by nomads of a different race. The beginnings of rice cultivation remain obscure. Some experts claim that there is no evidence for it even on the Yangtse until just before 1650 B.C.,[35] others that it had already reached northern China by as early as the third millennium B.C.[36] If, however, rice was grown in Thailand as early as 3500 B.C., as recent research suggests,[37] it is perfectly feasible that seeds and techniques should have been transmitted to China soon after, as well as to India during the following millennium.

On the loess plateau, sheep and goats appear to have been domesticated at an early stage, and a small breed of pig peculiar to China was developed. At the only village which Western experts know to have been satisfactorily excavated—Pan-p'o-ts'un in Shensi province (whose probable dating is between 2000 and 1500 B.C.)—pig remains were found in every hut. Both socially and gastronomically, it is interesting to note that most had been slaughtered at less than a year old.[38]

This prolific little pig was an ideal food animal in the context of China's developing social system. A large population working a restricted area of land may be able to feed a few draft animals, but to raise grazing stock for food is unrewarding.* The Chinese pig, however, was small enough to be kept indoors with little trouble, was able to feed itself on scraps at practically no cost to the owner, matured at the age of one year, and produced two bountiful litters a year from then on, each consisting of up to a dozen piglets. It was hardly surprising that, in China, the words "meat" and "pork" were to become synonymous.

---

* Cattle, for example, were always to be expensive in China, a capital investment to be worked for many years. Indeed, by the early Han period (the last two centuries B.C.) a contemporary history estimated that a man who could raise and sell two hundred and fifty cattle a year would be as rich as the head of one of the great hereditary families.[39]

PART TWO

The Near East,
Egypt, and Europe
3000 B.C.–A.D. *1000*

The Background

Out of the neolithic era were born the first great civilizations. In the Americas they evolved at a leisurely rate, but in the Near East, Egypt and China—where man seems very soon to have discovered a flair for advanced technology—development was piled on development, invention on invention, with purposeful speed.

Among the most striking features of these swiftly maturing societies were discipline and organization, which were to be agents of change in many ways but particularly in relation to trade. Growing populations with ever more elaborate needs could not afford to rely on the casual commerce of the past, and in Sumer and Egypt in about 3000 B.C. was laid down the pattern for that methodical, long-distance trade which was to have such a continuing and powerful influence on all subsequent historical development.

Egypt, whose food supply was assured by the regenerating waters of the Nile, could have survived without external trade. Sumer, working the almost exhausted soil of Mesopotamia, could not. Nor, more than two thousand years later, could Greece, whose frail natural resources were to be so swiftly destroyed by that very civilization which had such a seminal influence on the minds of later generations. The Greeks depended for their life on food imports. It was they who, following those professional traders, the Phoenicians, opened up much of the early world around the shores of the Mediterranean, establishing footholds in southern France and Italy, and pushing east to the rich country bordering the Black Sea. They imported copper, tin, textiles and glass; exported olive oil and wine. But grain was the urgent need which stimulated much of their enterprise.

As with Greece, so with Rome, where for many centuries the wheat supply played a dominant role in shaping administrative, economic, and international policies. The imperial frontiers, along much of their length, came to be closely aligned with the borders of the wheat-growing regions of the Classical world.

Wheat was a factor not only in the territorial expansion of the Roman empire, but in the history of seafaring. The price of a bulky low-value commodity could be doubled in the course of a land journey, because draft cattle might take a week to haul a ton or two of grain a hundred miles. But ships carrying a thousand tons, given fair winds, could make the 300-mile journey from North Africa to Ostia, port for the city of Rome, in four days or less, the 1000-mile one from Alexandria in thirteen.[1] Docks and lighthouses were built specifically for the grain ships, and even Britain was not too far away to become an imperial granary.

As Rome became more sophisticated, an increasing demand grew up for spices. For hundreds of years, these Eastern luxuries had found their way to Greece and Rome through the agency of the Arabs, who controlled the key points on the trade routes from Asia. But at the beginning of the first century A.D., Rome began to break the Arab monopoly by building ships large enough to sail from the Egyptian Red Sea coast all the way to India.[2] The journey was long and dangerous, and spices at first remained scarce, pepper at one stage reaching the astronomical price of

Loading up a Roman merchant ship.

£50 or $125 per Roman pound (12 ounces).[3] By the middle of the century, however, Western mariners had discovered the monsoon winds, which carried them to south India and back in less than a year. Soon, "the beautifully built ships of the Yavanas [foreigners]" became a common sight at the port of Muziris in Malabar. They "came with gold and returned with pepper, and Muziris resounded with the noise."[4] As Rome began to drain India of her spices, Indian merchants in turn had to look for supplies beyond their own frontiers, to the lands of southeast Asia, to such places as Takkola ("market of cardamoms") and Karpuradvipa ("camphor isle").[5]

The sea routes between West and East were thus stabilized before the long and difficult land route—the Silk Road—which was to be opened up more by the efforts of the Han emperors of China than by those of imperial Rome. Pirates were only a minor hazard at sea, but the warlike nomads who infested the wastes of Central Asia seriously inhibited land trade until the military power of the Han was able to police the area. With trading conditions eased, Rome's avidity for the luxuries of China became insatiable. By the second century A.D. caravans regularly left the Chinese city of Lo-yang with silk, ginger, cassia (a type of cinnamon) and *malabathrum* (cassia leaf),[6] winding their way over the hundreds of miles by Tunhuang, Lop Nor and Kashgar to the Stone Tower, a great meeting point somewhere north of the Pamirs. There, in the wilds of Central Asia, exquisite Chinese silks and exotic spices were bartered for all that Rome could provide in exchange—glassware, pottery, asbestos cloth, coral beads, intaglio gems, grape wine for the emperor, and, above all, gold and silver.

Even before the monsoon winds were discovered or the Silk Road opened, Pliny estimated that Rome was losing the equivalent of roughly £10 million or over $25 million of today's money to Asia every year.[7] Later, the drain of gold increased considerably and when, in the fourth century, precious metals became scarce in the West, there was a full-scale financial crisis.* The subsequent drift back to the barter economy of a thousand years earlier helped to ruin not only international trade but the Western Roman empire as well. The Eastern half of the empire, Greek-

---

* Money was so seriously devalued that a measure of wheat which, in Egypt, had cost six *drachmai* in the first century A.D., cost two million shortly after A.D. 344.[8]

speaking, with a fragile unity imposed by hundreds of years of economic interdependence, survived to become the empire of Byzantium.

After the fall of the Roman empire in the west, the Alans and the Ostrogoths, the Visigoths and the Franks brought a breath of fresh air into the stifling atmosphere of the Romanized world and, on a more earthy level, sponsored an increase in stockbreeding which was to have incalculable effects on the future of Europe. The Franks, once no more than a confederation of particularly troublesome barbarians on the northern frontiers of the empire, expanded until in A.D. 830 their dominions covered most of western Europe. But the attempts of even their greatest emperor, Charlemagne, to repair the structure of trade in his dominion had only limited success.

Long-distance, large-scale trade in foodstuffs had become, in inland and northern Europe, almost non-existent. It was inhibited by poorly maintained roads and clumsy transports, by rivers which served only restricted areas, and by a reduction in the number of towns large enough to create demand on a commercial scale. *Multum in parvo* became the undeclared motto of the merchants—for the commodities that were really profitable were those which were high in price and small in dimensions. Basic foodstuffs did not meet these criteria, and although spices did, their cost was so formidable that merchants offered them only in the richest markets.

Not until the end of the first millennium A.D., when Europe north of the Alps became a force to be reckoned with, was there a revival in trade to match the needs of a suddenly expanding population.

In the millennia between 3000 B.C. and A.D. 1000, in the area covered by the Roman empire at its widest extent, many developments took place in food and diet.

The agricultural revolution had already converted man from a predominantly meat to a predominantly grain diet. This was a far-reaching change, for it tended to immobilize large numbers of people, to keep them tied to the land they farmed, and to increase their communal awareness of boundaries and frontiers—the first step toward national consciousness. Those peoples who remained

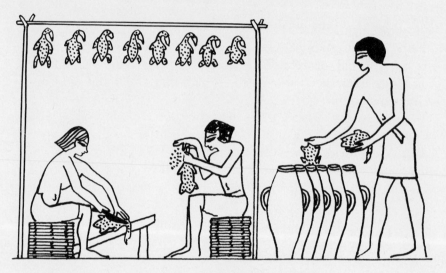

The Egyptians preserved game birds by salting.

herdsmen rather than land cultivators had a different concept of frontiers, one most closely linked to natural topographical features, to plains, watering-holes, and mountain barriers. The result was constant friction between settled grain-eaters and nomadic meat-eaters. The meat-eaters, full of protein energy, frequently came off best.

During the course of the neolithic revolution, the phenomenon of fermentation had been discovered, and when the first civilizations appeared on the historical scene, they came fully supplied with mead, wine, and beer. In Egypt, knowledge of fermentation and the development of new types of grain was to lead to the discovery of raised, or leavened, bread, while the unexacting demands of agriculture in the Nile region gave leisure to develop comparatively advanced methods of salting and drying fish and poultry.

In Greece, poor land for livestock, animal fats were scarce, and the Greeks cultivated olives for the sake of their oil and played a key role in popularizing the olive throughout the Mediterranean area. Greece, too, helped to make grape wine a common drink instead of one reserved, as it had been before, for noble households and temple rituals.

The part played by Rome was one mainly of establishment and

encouragement. Bread, for example, was established as being more desirable than grain-pastes and porridges. Spices were established as an essential of refined cooking. Because Rome was such a sizable market, her very existence had the widest repercussions. Her demand for spices gave an impetus to the whole trade of south Asia; her fondness for hams from Gaul encouraged the French *charcutier* to widen his scope; orchards expanded in North Africa to provide her with exotic fruits. When Rome fell, and many areas were thrown back on their own resources, the production of local specialties faltered. But the memory remained—to be revived when the world and its trade opened up once more.

3.
The First
Civilizations

Cities are the index of civilization, admired for their palaces and temples, art and aqueducts—but not, as a rule, for their granaries. Yet the whole magnificent structure of the world's first great civilizations—Sumer and Egypt—rested on those granaries and the men who worked to fill them.

During seven thousand years of experiment, man had discovered which crops he was best able to grow, and how best to grow them. Slowly and painstakingly, he had evolved a few basic tools which enabled him to cultivate the light soil of the Near East. These were the hoe, the harrow, the rake, and the mallet. The hoe, which scraped a shallow groove in the surface of the earth, soon developed into a scratch-plow pulled by one man while another walked behind, forcing into the soil the tip of the hooked branch from which the plow was made. When, during the third millennium B.C., oxen were harnessed to the plow, it became possible to drag the tip more deeply through the ground. Deeper plowing helped to slow down the process of soil exhaustion.

The armory of the Sumerian agriculturist also included a harvesting tool which had been invented in the early days of grain gathering, one which was so well designed that it could scarcely be improved on. This was the sickle, a curved instrument made from wood or horn, fitted with flint teeth, and bearing a strong resemblance to that most functional grass-cutting mechanism, a sheep's jaw.[1] The flint-toothed sickle was not to be superseded until tempered metal blades came into use.

Farming technology did not stop at tool design. By 2500 B.C., the accumulated expertise of the centuries had been codified in the Sumerian "Farmer's Almanac," one of the world's earliest surviving works of reference. "When you are about to plow your fields," says the Almanac, "keep your eye on the man who puts in the barley seed. Let him drop the grain uniformly two fingers deep . . . use up one shekel of barley for each *garush* [a strip of land roughly six to seven yards long]. If the barley seed does not sink in properly, change your coulter, the 'tongue of the plow.' " * [2]

By modern standards, the tools and technology of Sumerian and Egyptian agriculture may seem very primitive. But they were the product of a long period of trial and error, and so well adapted to the conditions for which they were devised that in some places they remain useful today. It is salutary to realize that land sown with grain in Egypt in 1000 B.C. yielded as rich a crop as it does in the twentieth century A.D.[3]

FOOD IN SUMER

Sumerian records are not expansive on the subject of food, but seven thousand years of farming had proved that a given acreage of land put down to wheat or barley filled more stomachs, more quickly and more cheaply, than the same land given over to livestock. For "civilized" man, grain had supplanted meat as the mainstay of the diet.

The raw materials of the Sumerian diet were barley, wheat and millet; chickpeas, lentils and beans; turnips; onions, garlic, leeks; cucumbers; and fresh green lettuce, cress and mustard. By early Babylonian times, a kind of truffle had been discovered which was regarded as a great delicacy and dispatched to the king by the basketful.[4]

Everyday meals probably consisted of barley paste or barley bread, accompanied by onions or a handful of beans, and washed down with beer. Variety was provided by the fish which swarmed in the rivers of Mesopotamia. Over fifty different types of fish are mentioned in texts dating from before 2300 B.C.[5] A few cen-

* The Almanac's translator uses the word "plowshare" toward the end of this quotation, but "coulter" is more accurate and has therefore been substituted here.

Goats, sheep, and cattle in Sumer, c. 2500 B.C.

turies later, although the varieties of fish had diminished, there were still to be found among the stalls in the narrow, winding streets of such cities as Ur, vendors of cooked foods who offered short-order fried fish to the hungry passerby, as well as onions, cucumbers, and freshly grilled meat. In the hot weather, a slaughtered animal had to be consumed almost immediately if it was not to spoil, and because of this, meat was probably eaten more often in the cities, where the number of potential customers was large, than in the countryside.

Beef and veal were popular with people who could afford them, though most cattle were slaughtered only at the end of their working lives, by which time they would be tough and stringy. In fact, "old oxen"—according to a palace inventory of about 2400 B.C—were frequently used "to feed the dogs." [6]

Mutton was more common, perhaps because the dynamic incomers who seem to have been responsible for putting the Sumerian state on its feet had originally been sheep herders. In the surviving vocabulary of Sumer there are two hundred words describing types and varieties of sheep—specially fattened sheep, mountain sheep, and fat-tailed sheep among them.[7] The fat-tailed sheep, first described by Herodotus, was for many centuries regarded by scholars as no more than one of that geographer's more imaginative flights.[8] But the breed turned out to be perfectly genuine, the tail—a great delicacy, rich in high-quality fat —accounting for as much as ten pounds out of a total carcass weight of sixty pounds.[9]

Goat was another acceptable meat, and pork had not yet been rejected by the peoples of the Near East. It is often said that the prohibition on eating pork—in the Jewish and Muslim religions, for example—had its origins in medical doctrine. Certainly, pork is a dangerous meat in a hot climate, and this must have been taken into account when dietary regulations were being formulated. Nevertheless, although the peoples of the Near East knew all about pork and its dangers, no taboos appear to have been placed on it until somewhere about 1800 B.C.[10] This was the time at which Indo-Aryan nomads were ranging great areas of eastern Europe and western Asia. Sheep, goats and cattle were the livestock to which the nomads were accustomed in their home territory, and they appear to have had an almost pathological dislike of the pig—a contrary animal, with little stamina and a constitutional objection to being herded. Half a dozen pigs gave far more trouble. than a hundred sheep. The Indo-Aryans were responsible for spreading many new ideas and techniques through the lands they invaded; it is possible that they also spread their loathing for the pig and that this was the stimulus which converted a general wariness of pork into a full-scale prohibition.

THE ORIGINS OF BEER

Greek tradition has it that the god Dionysus fled from Mesopotamia in disgust because its people were so addicted to beer—or, more correctly, ale, for the bitter preservative herbs such as hops which are used in true beer were not introduced until the very end of the Middle Ages. Certainly, it appears that forty per cent of the Sumerian grain yield was used for beer production. An ordinary temple workman received a ration of about 1.75 Imperial or 2.2 American pints * a day, and senior dignitaries five times as much, some of which they probably used as currency.[11]

In Sumer, eight types of barley beer seem to have been made, another eight from an early type of wheat, and three from mixed grains. The goddess Ninkasi, "the lady who fills the mouth," was in charge of beer production; it was she who baked "with lofty shovel the sprouted barley." [12]

Beer preparation may first have evolved from a particular method of breadmaking. The neolithic housewife had learned how to make raw grain digestible by leaving it to sprout.† But she

* When liquids are measured by volume, British (Imperial) and American measures are different, the British being based on the 20-ounce pint and the American on a 16-ounce pint. With dry ingredients, however, volume measures are the same on both sides of the Atlantic.

† This is the important factor in modern brewing, where the method is, briefly to allow barley to germinate, then to dry it, pound it lightly, soak it in hot water, and leave the strained-off liquor to ferment. When the broken grain is first put to soak in the hot water, it produces a thick, porridge-like substance—not unlike a dilute version of the neolithic grain-paste. Such a "porridge" may well have been a delicacy in early times. Given the right conditions, left-overs in a pot could have fermented to produce a rough type of beer—thick and dull, perhaps, but still mildly stimulating.

had gone on to discover that bread made from sprouted grain which had been dried and then pounded kept better than bread made from conventional flour, and by the early Egyptian period beer-making was specifically related not to raw sprouted grain but to baked bread. A special dough was made from sprouted, dried grains, and partially baked; the "loaves" were then broken up and put to soak in water; and the mixture was allowed to ferment for about a day. After this, the liquor was strained off [13] and the beer was ready to drink. By the end of the third millennium B.C., Egyptian brewers were making differently spiced and flavored "beer breads" and their customers had a correspondingly wide range of brews to choose from.[14]

Until about 1500 B.C., brewing remained a hit-or-miss affair. The presence of the micro-organisms which cause fermentation was largely fortuitous, although brewers were observant enough to realize that their old beer jars (full of cracks and crevices which were a splendid home for bacteria) produced better beer than brand-new ones. But until pure yeasts became available, most drinkers must have felt a quiver of trepidation whenever they broached a fresh jar.

Brewers in the early world were usually women, who sold the beer from their homes. The Code of Hammurabi, dated at just before 1750 B.C., strikes a very familiar note in its condemnation of ale houses and their under-strength, over-priced beer,[15] while an Egyptian papyrus of about 1400 B.C. gave advice to drinkers which has remained good ever since. "Do not get drunk," it recommended, "in the taverns in which they drink beer, for fear that people repeat words which may have gone out of your mouth, without you being aware of having uttered them." [16]

In Egypt the type of beer most commonly drunk was known as *haq* and was made from "the red barley of the Nile." [17] It appears to have been fairly mild, though some other Egyptian beers are said to have achieved an alcohol content of about twelve per cent, and to have been so sweet and aromatic that they were very little inferior to wine. According to Athenaeus, that polymath of the Classical world, it was reported that "those who drank this beer were so pleased with it that they sang and danced, and did everything like men drunk with wine." [18]

Beer continued to be the favored drink on the Nile, but in

Mesopotamia—as irrigation soured the soil and grain became ever more difficult to grow—the time came when there was not enough barley to spare for beer. At that stage, the Sumerians' successors changed their drinking habits and took to date wine.

THE DATE PALM AND THE FIG

In some regions, the date palm had flourished as far back as about 50,000 B.C., and developing man must always have found it useful —though not, in an era of primitive technology, quite the universal provider it is today, when it is said to have 360 different uses. Even the stones can be used as camel fodder, or reduced to charcoal for the fire.

The network of irrigation canals in southern Mesopotamia provided ideal conditions for palm cultivation. The palms clung to the canal banks, leaving the open land free for other crops. So productive were these palms * that dates were cheaper than grain, forming a staple food of the poor. The fruits could be eaten fresh and whole, or the juice could be pressed out and allowed to evaporate into a thick syrup which was used for puddings and sweetmeats, as a general alternative to honey for sweetening (sugar was not yet known in the Near East), and as an ingredient in fermented and soft drinks. In winter, dried compressed dates were much used, sometimes being chopped up and mixed in with a barley-paste. Xenophon, in the early fourth century B.C., remarked on the size and succulence of the dates he ate during the Persian expedition. "Their color was just like amber," he said, and the Babylonian villagers dried them and kept them as sweets.[19]

The date palm had other contributions to make to the diet. In Babylon, apparently, the new foliage sprouting from the crown of an old tree was eaten as a vegetable. This "cabbage" had a "peculiarly pleasant taste," though it was apt to cause headaches.[20] Since the tree died when the "cabbage" was removed, it must only have been palms well past their prime that were so treated. In fact, the "cabbage" may have been a byproduct of the final toddy-tapping. The crown of the date palm was often tapped

* An average date palm produces about one hundred pounds of rich, sugary fruit every year for sixty years or more, and a good tree half as much again.

for its sugary sap, which could be fermented to make palm toddy, or boiled down into a thick syrup. The tapping had to be carried out with moderation during the useful life of the tree, but when it had passed its peak of fruitfulness a great deal more sap could be drawn off. The people of Babylon, wishing to clear the ground for new young palms, may have disposed of the old by stripping the "cabbage," draining the tree of sap, and leaving it to die of its own accord.

Figs, another fruit with a high sugar content, were also very popular in the Near East and throughout many of the hotter parts of the Mediterranean. The fig tree, however, did not have the multitudinous virtues of the date palm, and it seems likely that in lands where the date would grow it was always preferred. In Greece—where palms refused to fruit satisfactorily—the fig was valuable in the diet of rich and poor alike,[21] particularly in winter in its dried form.*

In Egypt, whole baskets of figs have been found among the tomb offerings of dynastic times. There may have been more than one reason for this. As a people, the Egyptians were much preoccupied with their digestions, believing that most illnesses had their source in the alimentary canal. As a result, they made a habit of fasting, and dosed themselves with emetics at regular intervals. The fig, with its mild laxative properties, must have appealed to them as a food which was not only delicious, but good for them, too.

EGYPT   AND   THE   DISCOVERY   OF
RAISED   BREAD

It was in Egypt, reputedly, that the art of making bread was first discovered, although the evidence is elusive and the date even more so. However, conditions in Egypt in early historical

---

* "Nothing is sweeter than figs," said Aristophanes,[22] exaggerating slightly, but the fame of this fruit certainly spread far beyond the lands in which it grew. It is recorded that in the third century B.C., Bindusara, king of the Maurya dominions in India, wrote to the West asking for some grape syrup, some figs, and a philosopher. The reply he received was courteous. Figs and grape syrup would be sent to him with pleasure, but it was "against the law in Greece to trade in philosophers." [23]

times were much more favorable to such a discovery than in Mesopotamia, where wheat had become scarce.

One of the first requisites for leavened bread was wheat, and a particular kind of wheat. Barley and millet, because of their chemical composition, are unsuitable for leavening; so, too, are oats—which were, in any case, unknown in the Near East. Rye, the best alternative, was also unfamiliar in the civilized world before the first millennium B.C.

The starchy endosperm of wheat contains gluten-forming proteins. Yeast, under favorable conditions, produces carbon dioxide gas. When the two ingredients are brought together in a bread mix, the result is a spongy mass consisting of minuscule gas bubbles contained in an elastic framework of dough. The subsequent application of heat changes the nature of the gluten-forming proteins so that they become firm instead of elastic, and this is what "sets" the bread. But if the crucial proteins have been subjected to heat *before* they are brought into contact with the yeast, their nature has already been changed; instead of being elastic, they have become hard and unable to respond to the leavening action of the yeast.

Gathering figs in Egypt, c. 1900 B.C.

Since most of man's early grains had to have a preliminary toasting before they could be satisfactorily threshed (see page 35), raised bread was an impossibility until new types of grain were developed. By the beginning of the dynastic period in Egypt, however, a wheat had been produced which parted readily from its chaff and could therefore be threshed without the application of heat. For a very long time this wheat appears to have been rare; it may have been grown only on a limited scale to provide bread for the rich, while most fields continued to raise the old-fashioned wheat for use in old-fashioned ways. This is no more than speculation, but it is difficult to explain in any other way the fact that products made from the new bread wheat did not become common in Greece until the fourth century B.C.,[24] although the Greeks had been in regular trade contact with Egypt since the seventh century B.C. and in equally regular need of imported grain.

The discovery of raised bread was probably made when some favorable micro-organisms drifted into a dough made from the new wheat. The dough, left aside for a while before baking, would rise—not very much, perhaps, but enough to make the baked bread lighter and more appetizing than usual. As so often in the ancient world, inquiring minds set about the task of re-producing, deliberately, a process first discovered by accident. Fermentation was clearly involved, so known ferments were probably introduced into the dough.

The leaven used for bread came from various sources. The Gauls and Iberians, said Pliny the Elder, skimmed beer foam for the purpose; this, he said, was why they had "a lighter kind of bread than other peoples." The Greeks and Italians, who were not beer drinkers, used millet flour, dipped in grape juice and then kneaded and kept until it fermented. Wheat bran steeped in white wine was also used, as was wheat flour made into a kind of porridge which was then left to go sour. "Manifestly," Pliny commented, "it is natural for sourness to make the dough fer-

An Egyptian bakery-brewery, c. 2000 B.C.

ment." [25] But the commonest method was to keep a piece of dough from the previous day's baking and incorporate it in the new mix. The "sourdough starter," in fact, has continued to be used ever since, for despite the fact that it has now been generally superseded by commercially produced block or dried yeasts, it still makes the best leaven for really good bread.

The discovery of leavened bread, which kept better than the old flatbread and whose texture was a great improvement on grain-pastes, did not mean that the ancient world instantly began to make nothing else. The worn teeth of surviving Egyptian skulls show quite clearly that the average Egyptian went on chewing flat bread made from the old flours, thick with bran and rough with fragments of chaff and straw.[26] The demanding process of making leavened bread, and the fact that it worked only with particular types of grain, made it a restricted food for very many centuries. Even in the Middle Ages in northern Europe, it was still uncommon.

EGYPTIAN FOOD

Bread, beer and onions probably formed the basic diet of the peasant in dynastic Egypt. By the twelfth century B.C., there were bread stalls in the village streets where it was possible to buy the commonest kind of flatbread, known as *ta*.[27] But nobles and priests could choose among as many as forty different types of bread and pastries. Some were raised, some flat; some round, some conical, some plaited; some varieties were made with honey, others with milk, some with eggs. Rich Egyptians, in fact, probably ate quite well. Among the relics excavated from a tomb dated at early in the third millennium B.C. were dishes of barley porridge, cooked quail, kidneys, pigeon stew, fish, beef ribs, wheaten bread, cakes, stewed figs, fresh berries, cheese, wine and beer—enough food to keep the deceased going until she reached the other world.[28]

The Egyptians were very serious about the organization of their food supply. Until about 2200 B.C. they persisted in trying to domesticate a wide variety of animals, among them probably the ibex, oryx, antelope and gazelle. When this proved unrewarding,

they turned more of their attention to the large areas of marsh-
land preserved for hunting, fowling, fishing, and the gathering of
wild fruits and such vegetables as wild celery, papyrus stalks, and
the lotus root. Small birds were very popular, said Herodotus.
Some of them were pickled in brine for a few days and then eaten
raw.[29] And Hipparchus, in the second century B.C., turned a jaundiced eye on a place where, he said, they were "forever plucking
quails and slimy magpies." [30] The Nile marshes and canals contained eel, mullet, carp, perch, and tigerfish, as well as many other
aquatic species which have not been identified. Egypt soon developed a thriving trade in dried and salted fish, which were
exported to such regions as Syria and Palestine.

Hunting wildfowl in the Nile marshes, c. 1450 B.C.

4.

*The Food of
Classical Greece*

Although by 3000 B.C., the peoples of the Tigris-Euphrates and
Nile valleys had adapted their diet to fit their farming, in Greece
—according to Homer—animal husbandry was still the decisive
factor two thousand years later. Antiphanes might afterward complain that Homer's idea of a good meal was woefully dull,[1] and
Athenaeus that the epic heroes knew nothing of even such commonplace delicacies as "entrées served in vine leaves," [2] but
Homer drew on a sound tradition, not only for his characters'
exploits but for their food. The warriors of Greece in the twelfth
century B.C. had ancestral ties with the nomad pastoralists of Central Asia and, in all probability, still lived a life not too far removed from theirs. When Achilles played host to Odysseus outside
the walls of Ilium, he gave him a meal which might have been
offered by any nomad chief for a thousand years before, or two
thousand years after, the Trojan wars.

Patroclus "put down a big bench in the firelight, and laid on it
the backs of a sheep and a fat goat and the chine of a great
[wild] hog rich in lard. Automedon held these for him, while
Achilles jointed them, and then carved up the joints and spitted
the slices. Meanwhile, Patroclus, the royal son of Menoetius, made
the fire blaze up. When it had burned down again and the flames
disappeared, he scattered the embers and laid the spits above
them, resting them on logs, after he had sprinkled the meat with
holy salt. When he had roasted it and heaped it up on platters,
Patroclus fetched some bread and set it out on the table in hand-

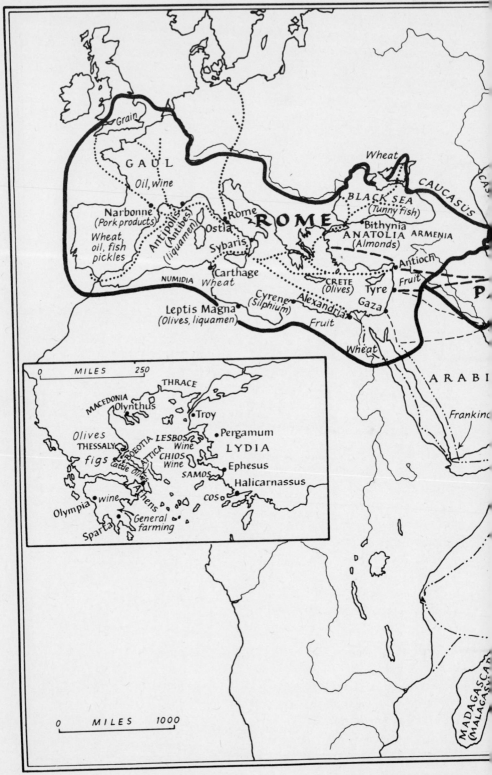

2. THE CLASSICAL WORLD

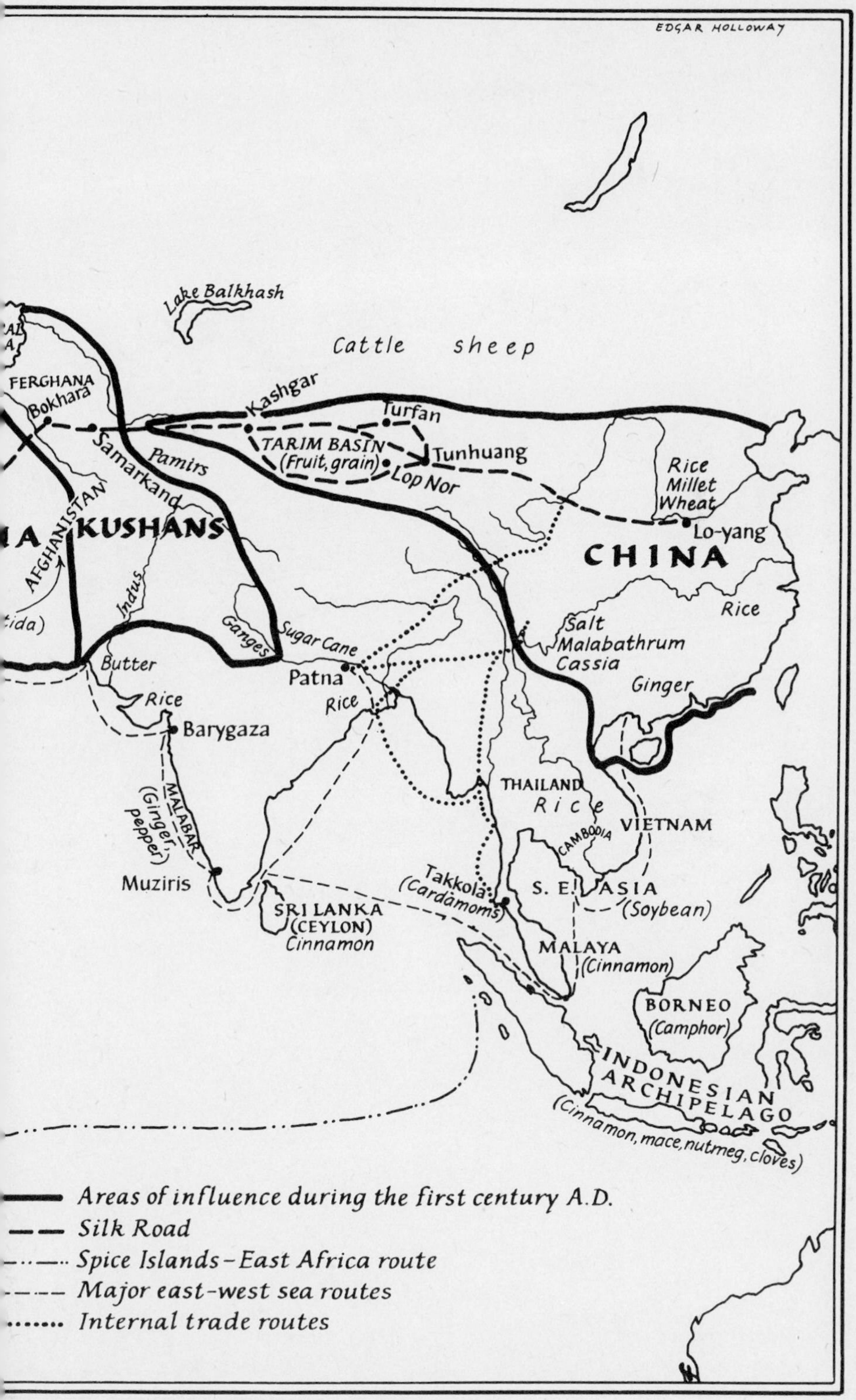

EDGAR HOLLOWAY

Lake Balkhash

Cattle   sheep

FERGHANA
Bokhara
Kashgar
Turfan
Samarkand
Pamirs
TARIM BASIN
(Fruit, grain)
Tunhuang
Lop Nor
AFGHANISTAN
KUSHANS
Indus
Ganges
Sugar Cane
Butter
Rice
Patna
Rice
Barygaza
MALABAR
(Ginger,
pepper)
Muziris
SRI LANKA
(CEYLON)
Cinnamon
Takkola
(Cardamoms)
S. E. ASIA
(Soybean)
MALAYA
(Cinnamon)
THAILAND
Rice
CAMBODIA
VIETNAM
Rice
Millet
Wheat
Lo-yang
CHINA
Rice
Salt
Malabathrum
Cassia
Ginger
BORNEO
(Camphor)
INDONESIAN
ARCHIPELAGO
(Cinnamon, mace, nutmeg, cloves)

— Areas of influence during the first century A.D.
- - Silk Road
-·- Spice Islands – East Africa route
- - - Major east-west sea routes
······ Internal trade routes

some baskets; and Achilles divided the meat into portions." [3]

This heroic predilection for roast meat was not to survive the problems set by the landscape of Greece. In the early days, wild boar were still there for the hunting, and a few settled communities were able to feed the domestic pig on acorns and beechmast from the trees which clothed the lower levels of the mountain ranges. But the long narrow valleys of the interior and the slender ribbons of fertile plain around the coasts set an irrevocable limit to stockraising. Only in a few areas, such as Boeotia—whose name, in fact, means "cow land"—were there plains wide enough for pasturing cattle.

While the human population was small, the farmer and his family lived off the land in modest comfort. They grew a little wheat or barley, tended their olive and fig trees and a few vines, reared pigs, and kept a goat to provide milk and cheese. If they were rich, they might have a small flock of sheep, or a pair of oxen or mules.

By about 650 B.C., however, many peasants in such areas as Attica were leading a marginal existence on marginal land. As the population increased, good land became scarce. The hillsides had been denuded of many of their trees to provide the timber needed

The Homeric heroes preparing a meal.

Gathering olives,
sixth century B.C.

for houses, for the ships on which the Greek states depended for trade and transport, for the charcoal which was being swallowed up in ever-increasing quantities by the demands of metalworking. Tree-felling at first seemed beneficial. Not only did it provide valuable timber; it also cleared new land for cultivation.

But the light soil of Greece, no longer fed by dead leaves or held together by living tree roots, began to be washed away in the torrential rains of winter. Formerly, the rains had been valuable. Filtered through the branches, they had soaked slowly and gently into the soil and then down to the limestone below; from the limestone they drained gradually to the plains. Now, instead, the rains became destructive, pouring down on the naked hills too heavily to be absorbed, and then thundering on to flood the plains. Gradually, the hills lost their soil and the valleys their fertility.[4]

The peasants who attempted to carry on traditional, self-sufficient farming on the increasingly barren lower levels of the hillsides plunged deep into debt. In the old days, a family short of grain in the lean period before the harvest had been able to borrow a sack or two from a neighbor. But after money was introduced into Greece in 625 B.C., things changed.[5] Instead of borrowing grain, the peasant had to borrow enough money to buy it at high pre-harvest prices. When the time came to repay, he either had to raise the cash by selling his own produce at low post-harvest prices, or hold on until the market began to improve, paying punitive rates of interest in the meantime.

THE OLIVE

At the beginning of the sixth century B.C., Solon forbade the export of any agricultural produce other than olive oil. It was a well-meant gesture, but it struck the fatal blow at the Greek landscape.

Such fibrous-rooted trees as remained were felled for the sake of the olive, whose deep-striking tap root soaked up the moisture far down in the limestone and did nothing to knit, conserve or feed the topsoil. By the fourth century B.C., Plato was gloomily contrasting the bare white limestone of the Attic countryside he knew with the green meadows, woods and springs of the past.[6] The pure and brilliant light which is so startling a characteristic of Greece today had been bought at the expense of the trees which had once kept the land fertile. It took thousands of years for the neolithic revolution to desiccate the flat countryside of Mesopotamia, but only a few hundred in the topographical context of Greece.

Cultivation of the olive seems to have originated six thousand years ago at the eastern end of the Mediterranean. The straggly, spiny wild plant, poor in oil, was widely distributed even before this time, but it needed the agricultural and mercantile genius of the Syrians and Palestinians to develop the thornless, compact, oil-rich variety which was to spread all along the shores of the Mediterranean.

Oil was everywhere in demand in the ancient world, for food, lighting and medicine, as well as for the lustrations of Egypt and the perfumed unguents with which the early Mediterranean peoples anointed their bodies. The olive was by no means the only provider, though it was the richest known during the Western bronze age. In Greece, oil was also extracted from the walnut and the opium poppy; in Mesopotamia and Africa, from sesame; from almonds in Anatolia; flax and radish seeds in Egypt; flax and cameline in northern Europe. South, Central and western North America had, respectively, groundnut, maize, and sunflower-seed oil, while in Asia the soybean and the coconut palm were probably the richest early sources.

In Crete, the olive was under cultivation at least as early as 2500 B.C., and the island soon waxed fat on exporting oil as well as the timber that had to be felled to make way for the new groves. The palace of Nestor at Knossos has yielded to archeologists great numbers of stirrup jars which once contained expensive and much-prized oil perfumed with aromatic herbs from the hillsides.[7] But dependence on the olive in a small country brought, as a natural sequel, dependence on external trade for the necessities of life and a resultant defenselessness in wartime. Crete discovered this, and Athens was to do so too.

During the century and a half after Solon, Athens gréw rich on silver from the mines of Laurium and the smooth green-gold oil of the olive. But as first the olive and then the vine—supplemented by fig and nut trees—took over the Attic landscape, livestock became few and wheat and barley virtually disappeared. The trade of Greece, and the Greek empire itself, expanded to meet the country's urgent need for basic food supplies.

VINTAGES OF THE GREEK WORLD

The olive was the first great export crop of Greece, but it was closely followed by the product of the vine. From about the fifth until the latter part of the first century B.C., Greece and the islands were, to the Mediterranean world, the home of fine wines.

There are many picturesque tales about the origins of wine, but what almost certainly happened was that at some time in prehistory a containerful of grapes was left neglected in a corner; that they fermented; and that some inquisitive person tasted the fermented juice—and found it good.

The wild vine flourished in the Caucasus, and it was probably there that the plant was first brought under cultivation. By 3000 B.C. it had reached Mesopotamia—whose rulers seem from then on to have taken a very personal interest in it—and Egypt, where wine was first used almost entirely for temple rituals. It was not, apparently, until Greek influence began to be felt in Egypt in the first millennium B.C. that private vineyards became common and wine found its place as a popular drink. But Egyptian temple vintners had become expert long before then, and it is possible that the Greeks simply re-exported to secular Egypt the knowledge that they had earlier imported from priestly Egypt.

In the Mediterranean during the Greek golden age, many countries produced their own *ordinaires,* but the rich insisted on importing the scarce and expensive vintages of Lesbos and Chios. The great growths appear to have been sweet, and it has been suggested that the most famous wine of antiquity—the Pramnian so frequently mentioned by Homer—may have been as rich as Tokay.[8] Since both Greeks and Romans followed the Egyptian custom of drinking their wines well diluted with water, the finer vintages were often kept until they were as thick and sticky as honey.

The wine was fermented in vats smeared inside and out with resin, which gave it a characteristic tang, and then filtered into goatskins or pigskins if it were intended for local consumption, or into clay amphorae for export. Fermentation was not a scientifically controlled process, and the wines of the ancient world did not keep well unless special mixtures were added. Each region had its own formula. One consisted of adding a brew of herbs and spices which had been mixed with condensed sea water and matured for some years, while a later Roman recipe favored the addition of liquid resin mixed with vine ash to the grape juice before fermentation. Filled wine jars were often kept to mature in the loft where wood was seasoned and meat smoked, but although reasonable smoking was thought to improve a wine,[9] all Romans with pretensions to good taste were united in vilifying those French vintners who over-smoked their wines in order to make them appear older than they were.[10]

Greek wines were to go out of international fashion after the first of the great Italian vintages, the Opimian, appeared in 121 B.C.[11] In the centuries that followed many other Italian wines, including Falernian, became household names and the competition turned out to be too stiff for Greece. Italian vineyards were able to produce over 1600 Imperial, or 2000 American, gallons an acre [12]—far more than those of Greece, which were never very productive and always old-fashioned in their methods. Also, as the power of Rome expanded, the taste for Italian wine—even the vine itself—was carried to many new lands.

GREEK   FOOD   AND   COOKING

The Greek peasant never saw much of the profit from his olives or his vines, but while there was peace he and his family could rely on a solid, if monotonous, sufficiency of food.

Sir Alfred Zimmern's frequently quoted definition of the Attic dinner as consisting of two courses, "the first a kind of porridge, and the second a kind of porridge," was unduly severe.[13] The Greek word *maza*, like the Latin *puls*, is usually translated—rather indiscriminately—as "cakes" or "porridge," but in fact both *maza* and *puls* were terms which almost certainly included unbaked grain-pastes in the neolithic tradition (see page 36). The word *maza*, for example, implies kneaded things *other than bread*,[14] while *puls* seems to have been a more general term which included pastes made from lentils and beans as well as from grain. From the elder Pliny's recipes for Greek and Italian barley *puls*, it is clear that the result must have been an oily, highly seasoned paste rather than a porridge.

The Greeks, said Pliny, "soak some barley in water [probably for a few days] and then leave it for a night to dry. Next day they dry it by the fire and then grind it in a mill . . . When it has been got ready, in the mill they mix three pounds of flax seed [which produces linseed oil when warmed and pounded], half a pound of coriander seed, and an eighth of a pint of salt, previously roasting them all." Italians, on the other hand, first baked their barley without steeping it in water, and then ground it "into fine meal, with the addition of the same ingredients, and millet as well." * [15]

It was still one of the virtues of the grain-pastes, even in these

---

* It is interesting that while the Greeks seem to have favored a mixture made from sprouted and dried barley the Italians used the other traditional method of making the grain digestible, and precooked the unsprouted seeds.

late and sophisticated forms, that they remained palatable for a considerable time. For long-term storage, Pliny recommended packing the *puls* into a container and covering it with a layer of flour and bran.

In Classical Greece, the peasant ate not only barley-pastes but barley gruel and barley bread. With this basic fare, he would have a handful of olives, a few figs, or some goat's milk cheese. Occasionally there would be salt fish as a relish. The meal was washed down usually with water or goat's milk, sometimes with wine.

Meat was a rarity except at times of religious sacrifice and feasting. On such occasions the officiating priest, after paying due heed to the portents indicated by the shape and condition of the sacrificial animal's liver, would divide the carcass into three parts— one (not usually the best) for the god, one for the priest, and one for the donor or donors.[16] While the god's portion reduced itself to cinders before the altar, the priest exercised his culinary skill in preparing and roasting the donors' ration, watched by his audience in a silence compounded of equal piety and anticipation. None, it may be assumed, would have dared be as greedy as the later Roman emperor Vitellius, who, according to Suetonius, "thought nothing of snatching lumps of meat or cake off the altar, almost out of the sacred fire, and bolting them down." [17]

Until the middle of the fifth century B.C., the diet of rich and poor in Greece probably did not differ very radically. The rich would drink less water and more wine; they would eat goat, mutton or pork more frequently; and such game as deer, hare, partridge and thrushes might lend variety to the menu. But in country and city alike, early Greece was an outdoor society and its cuisine was correspondingly plain. Morning and midday snacks were taken outdoors, or at the corner of a table, and the more substantial evening meal was equally unceremonious. The symposium or banquet so dear to literary tradition was a type of dinner party at which the food was disposed of rapidly before the real business of the evening—talking and drinking—began.

Some idea of the style of cooking in Greece in about 450 B.C. can be gathered from a passage in Telecleides' *The Amphictyons*, in which the author reconstructs life in an imaginary golden age. "Every torrent ran with wine, and barley-pastes fought with

A soothsayer consults the liver of a sacrificed animal.

From inscribed clay models—such as this of a sheep's liver—
soothsayers learned what deductions to draw.

wheaten loaves to be first to men's lips . . . Fish would come to
the house and bake themselves, then serve themselves up at
table. A river of broth, swirling along hot pieces of meat, would
flow by the couches; conduits full of piquant sauces for the meat
were close at hand for the asking . . . On dishes there would be
honey cakes all sprinkled with spices, and roast thrushes served
up with milk cakes flew down a man's gullet." [18] Though it may
sound appetizing, it was essentially a plain cuisine.

The average Greek was no great gourmet, but even he shud-
dered at the diet favored by the earnest Spartans, whose "black
broth"—reputedly made of pork stock, vinegar and salt—was in-
famous throughout the civilized world. Indeed, Athenaeus reports
that a sybarite who went to Sparta was invited out to dine. "As
he lay on the wooden benches and ate with them he remarked
that he had always before been astounded to hear of the Spartans'
courage; but now . . . he did not think they were in any respect
superior to other peoples." For, concluded Athenaeus gleefully,
"the most cowardly man in the world would prefer to die rather
than endure living that sort of life." [19]

The contrast between the food of the rich and poor became
more pronounced in Athens during the period of Athenian great-
ness. The city became a center of magnificence, self-assured and
very conscious of its intellectual eminence. It would have been
strange if this state of mind had not struck an echo in the Greek
kitchen. Although no recipe books remain, titles and extracts
have been preserved in other works. There appear to have been
at least a dozen culinary *vade mecums* with the title *The Art of
Cooking*, and such authors as Glaucus of Locris, Mithaecus,
Heraclidus, Hegesippus, Eristratus and Euthydemus wrote treat-
ises on *Gastronomy, Pickles, Vegetables, Sicilian Cooking*, and
similar subjects.

The father of all Greek writers on cooking, and self-styled in-
ventor of "made dishes," was Archestratus who, in the fourth century B.C., "diligently traversed all lands and seas in his desire . . .
of testing carefully the delights of the belly." [20] In the historical
record, Archestratus was the first in that long line of gastronomic
pedants, half ludicrous, half irritating, wholly familiar even in the
twentieth century, whose pronouncements on *haute cuisine* have
so successfully obscured the realities of everyday eating. While

most Athenians who liked tunny fish had to put up with the dried or salted variety from the Black Sea, Archestratus busily insisted that none but the fresh kind from Byzantium would do, and that it should be eaten only "in the autumn, what time the Pleiad is setting." [21]

As the decades passed, Athenian tastes became more exotic. A pig which had died of over-eating was regarded as a great delicacy, and geese were painstakingly fed on moistened grain to fatten them for the table. The eggs of the peacock—a rare and much admired bird, bred in the gardens of the rich—were claimed to be highly superior. "Fox-goose" eggs ranked second, and hens' eggs a distant third. The domestic hen was common in the Mediterranean by the fifth century B.C. and almost every Athenian had one—which may explain the rather poor gastronomic rating of its eggs.[22]

By the third century B.C., Athens had developed the original

A Greek fishmonger tops and tails a fresh tunafish.

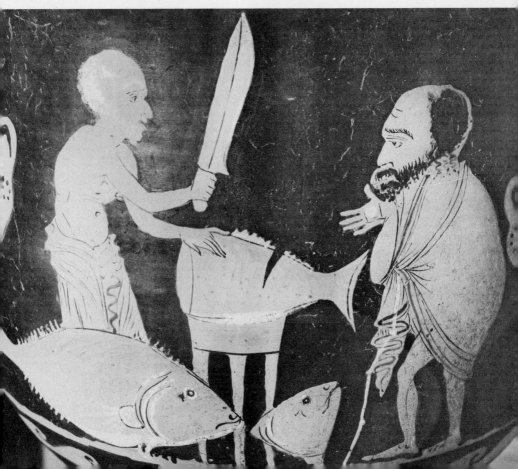

hors d'oeuvre trolley, an innovation which other Greeks stigmatized as evidence of a miserly disposition. Lynceus, in *The Centaur*, complained that an Athenian dinner was little short of revolting, especially to a hungry man. "For the cook sets before you a large tray on which are five small plates. One of these holds garlic, another a pair of sea urchins, another a sweet wine sop, another ten cockles, the last a small piece of sturgeon. While I am eating this, another is eating that; and while he is eating that, I have made away with this. What I want, good sir, is both the one *and* the other, but my wish is impossible. For I have neither five mouths nor five right hands. Such a layout as that *seems* to offer variety, but is nothing at all to satisfy the belly." [23]

Satisfaction was a relative term. The Peloponnesian wars of the latter part of the fifth century B.C. had wrought havoc in the Attic countryside. Within the walls of Athens, Sophocles, Euripides and Aristophanes produced works of genius; outside the walls, villages were razed and crops ruined. Recovery was to be, at the least, agonizing, at the worst, impossible. It takes three or four years for a newly planted vine to produce a worthwhile crop, thirty years in the case of the olive. Ultimately, the small peasant sold out to the speculators and left the countryside—as so many peasants in so many countries have done, before and since—for the doubtful haven of the city.

The poet Alexis of Thurii, in the fourth century B.C., described the fare of an impoverished family of five who existed mainly on pulses, greens and turnips, varied with iris rhizomes, beechnut, lupin seeds (reported to be sour but very nutritious), an occasional grasshopper, wild pears, "and that god-given inheritance of our mother country, darling of my heart, a dried fig." If there was enough food for more than three of the family, it was unusual. As a rule, the other two had to make do with a mouthful of barley-paste.[24] But though sporadic attempts were made to help the Athenian poor, it was to be left to the Romans to embark on the first massive—and, in the end, self-defeating—social welfare project.

5.

Imperial

Rome

The population of Rome, said the historian Fronto in the second century A.D., was "absorbed by two things above all others, its *annona* and its public spectacles." [1] Or, as Juvenal had put it forty years earlier, by its bread and circuses.[2]

The *annona*, the distribution of free grain by the authorities, had originated in attempts to relieve poverty, but had grown into a massive general subsidy which seriously distorted both the economic and the social structure of the state. From as early as the sixth century B.C., Rome had been troubled by occasionally serious shortages and famines, but it was only in 123 B.C., when the cost of living rose to a seemingly impossible level, that Gaius Gracchus set a precedent by allowing all citizens to buy from public granaries at a price below that ruling on the market.[3] By 71 B.C., *free* grain was being dispensed to forty thousand adult male citizens of Rome.[4]

In the decades that followed, the number of people receiving free grain increased so greatly that Julius Caesar felt he had done well in cutting the public assistance queue back to a mere 150,000.[5] In the days of Augustus, it crept up again to 320,000— which was just under one third of the estimated total population of Rome.[6]

Politics inevitably played a part in the administration of the *annona* system. Early in the third century A.D., Septimis Severus ingratiated himself not only with the city plebs but with the people of his native Leptis Magna in North Africa, then suffering

In the wheatfields of North Africa in the second century A.D., Romans still used cattle and horses for threshing grain.

a trade recession, by buying up their oil for free distribution in Rome.[7] Thirty years later, Severus Alexander decreed that ready-made bread should be distributed instead of grain.[8] Aurelian increased the daily ration to almost 1½ pounds and added pork fat to the list of free foodstuffs.[9] So as to use up the wine paid as taxes-in-kind by the growers, he gave it, too, away to the plebs. When he proposed that this should form a permanent feature of the *annona*, a scandalized official exclaimed: "Before we know where we are, we will be giving them chickens and geese as well." [10] But in the latter days of the empire money became scarce, even for emperors, and free food distributions ceased, though many basic foodstuffs were still made available at an uneconomically low price.

The quantities of wheat required to feed the people of Rome were considerable. It has been estimated that in the time of

Augustus it was necessary to import fourteen million bushels of grain a year—the produce of several hundred square miles of wheatfields—to ensure supplies for the city alone.[11]

One third of this came from Egypt, and most of the rest from North Africa. When Rome defeated Carthage in the second century B.C., she tore down the city and, rather melodramatically, plowed its very foundations into the soil. But there was no question of destroying its valuable wheatfields. To safeguard her own hold over them, Rome first became suzerain of the Numidian kingdoms, and then subdued the semi-nomadic tribes of the hinterland. In the first century B.C., Cyrenaica and Egypt also submitted, and Rome held all the cultivable land north of the Sahara.

The city of Rome had first call on the wheat of Egypt, North Africa and Sicily. Transport of grain for official distribution was subject to the strictest security precautions. Wheat was handed over in its country of origin to shippers who were required to carry it to Ostia by the shortest possible route—or, after Ostia silted up, to the adjacent artificial harbor of Portus—and were forbidden to put in to land at any intervening point on pain of death or deportation.[12] The plebs of Rome knew as well as the authorities the importance of grain ships and the times at which they were due in. On at least one occasion, in A.D. 70, when the ships were late, the result was a full-scale panic in the city.[13]

On reaching port, the grain was unloaded and checked, for quality as well as for quantity; a sample of the shipment was usually sent separately, in a sealed bag, as insurance against adulteration or fraud.[14] Afterward, barges by the hundred carried the grain up river on the last three-day stage to Rome, where it was distributed to the millers.

GRAIN INTO FLOUR

In the beginning, millers were responsible mainly for pounding and cleansing grain, and sometimes for turning it into flour.

Grinding grain had never been an easy task. It demanded both patience and physical stamina.

At the beginning of the neolithic era, the people had used a device developed long before for pounding berries and dyes. This consisted of a large saucer-shaped stone and a smaller bun-shaped rubbing-stone. In time, this design was replaced by the "saddle quern." The miller knelt at one end of a slanted, rectangular base stone, and pushed his rubbing-stone (now shaped like a rolling pin) back and forth over the angled base. The next development affected only the rubbing-stone, which became squarer in shape to accommodate a central slit, through which whole grain could be trickled to the grinding surface. This saved lifting up the rubbing-stone every time another handful of grain was added.

For thousands of years, the grinding motion had been backward and forward, but at some time in the fifth century B.C. it was discovered that a side-to-side action eased the task considerably. In this case, the use of a lever and the momentum of the rubbing-stone itself reduced the physical effort demanded of the operator. It was the introduction of full rotary motion, however, which gave the professional miller an advantage over the housewife by making large-scale, semi-mechanical grinding possible. It had never been possible to drive animals backward and forward to match the jerky action of the old millstones, but it *was* possible to drive them around and around in a circle. With a large rotary mill and a couple of donkeys, the professional miller found himself—profitably—in business. In the second century B.C., millers also became bakers.[15] There is no record of why this happened, but it may have had something to do with the introduction into Italy of leavened bread, a product beyond the scope of most private kitchens in the early Classical world.

The Roman miller-baker became one of the first mass producers in the food industry, but he was not always to be depended on. In the first century A.D., for example, the mills of Rome ground to a halt when Caligula commandeered all the animals which powered them.[16] Again, in the sixth century, flour production came to a standstill when the invading Goths cut off the water supply, on which many Roman mills by then depended.[17] Against such contingencies as these, most households kept a saddle quern or a small rotary quern which could be brought into use for grinding grain, as well as for a great many other culinary purposes.

The saddle quern, as used in Egypt in about 2500 B.C.

A Central American version of the saddle quern. (It can be seen in use in the illustration on page 249.)

Base stone with slotted rubber, or "hopper rubber."

Side-to-side, lever-operated hopper rubber.

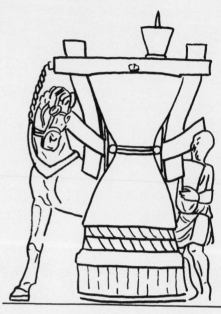

Rotary quern, domestic size. The central peg was a pivot, and the other peg a handle used to force the upper stone around. (Shown here in use in nineteenth-century India.)

Roman donkey mill. The upper half of the hourglass was a hopper, the lower half a revolving millstone which grated against an inner cone. The flour was channeled out through the grooves at the bottom onto a circular platform.

Early water-powered mills ground to a halt when the level of the river fell, but this was overcome by mounting the mills on rafts or boats which rose and fell when the water did. (Shown here in action in fourteenth-century Paris.)

ROMAN BREAD

The ancient world had very definite views on the dietetic value of different types of flour and bread. The writer on hygiene Diphilus of Siphnos declared that "bread made of wheat, as compared with that made of barley, is more nourishing, more digestible, and in every way superior. In order of merit, the bread made from refined [thoroughly sieved] flour comes first, after that bread of ordinary wheat, and then the unbolted, made of flour that has not been sifted." [18]

Methods of cooking were also regarded as important. Galen, the great physician whose pronouncements were to remain the foundation of Western dietetic medicine for almost fifteen hundred years, said that "bread baked in the ashes is heavy and hard to digest because the baking is uneven. That which comes from a small oven or stove causes dyspepsia and is hard to digest. But bread made over a brazier or in a pan, owing to the admixture of oil, is easier to excrete, though steam from the drying makes it rather unwholesome. Bread baked in large ovens, however, excels in all good qualities, for it is well flavored, good for the stomach, easily digested, and very readily assimilated." [19]

In his discussion of breads ancient and modern, native and foreign, Athenaeus throws out an endless list of names for what must have been the Scotch baps, *croissants*, Parker House rolls, and *churros* of the Classical world. Many can no longer be accurately identified, though it is safe to say that the general term "bread" was also used to cover what are nowadays called cakes, pastries and cookies. Honey-and-oil bread, suet bread, and griddle cakes are there, along with cheese-bread, the large and gritty Cilician loaves, and rolls baked on a spit (a military speciality). There was a soft, salty, raised bread known as Cappadocian, and a mushroom-shaped loaf covered with poppy seeds. Wafer bread, thin and crisp, had wine, pepper and milk among the ingredients, while *dice* were square loaves seasoned with anise, cheese and oil.[20]

Bread in the modern sense might have been discovered, but the concept of bread and butter was still very far distant. Greece and Rome relied on the olive, and butter was to them mainly a food of

A baker's shop at Pompeii.

barbarian cattle herders—"your butter-eating gentry," as Anaxan-
drides called them.[21] Generally, the plain breads, raised or flat,
were probably eaten dry as an accompaniment to meat, or dunked
in wine or goat's milk for a quick snack. The flavored breads would
be regarded as a meal in themselves, to be eaten with water, milk
or wine as a *prandium*, or midday snack.

FOOD, THE RAW MATERIALS

The basic diet of the Roman poor consisted of grain-pastes or
coarse bread bristling with chaff,* and a polenta-like porridge made
from millet. Water was the usual drink. Cooking was primitive
because equipment was primitive, fuel a problem, and the fire
risk high in the tall, narrow, overcrowded *insulae*, or tenement
houses, which accommodated so many of the people of Rome.[22]
As a result, the poor avoided cooking whenever possible. Sometimes, they might buy a slice of roast pork or some salt fish from
one of the "grimy cookshops" whose wares were spread half
across the public streets.[23] More often, probably, they ate olives,
raw beans, figs or cheese with their bread or grain-paste.

The food of the rich was very different, and it is difficult not
to be curious about the flavors—the finished effect—of a cuisine
which many people believe to have been one of high sophistication. The range of ingredients was certainly remarkable. A
modest man like Juvenal might content himself with dining simply, on "a plump kid, tenderest of the flock," with "more of milk
in him than blood"; some wild asparagus; "lordly eggs warm in
their wisps of hay together with the hens that laid them"; and
grapes, pears and apples to end with.[24] Others regarded a costly
and ostentatious table as a proof of status. Ostentation might
take the form of elaborate presentation, as in that standard text
of gastronomic literature, Trimalchio's Feast,[25] where guests were
offered a hare tricked out with wings to look like a Pegasus, a
wild sow with its belly full of live thrushes, quinces stuck with
thorns to look like sea urchins, roast pork carved into models of

* The general quality of bread may have improved in the third century A.D. when
the *annona* began distributing professionally made loaves instead of grain.

fish, songbirds, and a goose.* This kind of display would be unlikely to ruin a man of means, but the fashion for exotic foreign
foodstuffs was another matter. The only pike worth eating may
have come, conveniently, from "between the two bridges" at
Rome [26]—from the stretch between the Tiber island and the
cloaca maxima (the main sewer)—but pickles had to be imported
from Spain, ham from Gaul, wine from the Jura, pomegranates
from Libya, oysters from Britain, and spices from Indonesia. Snails
had to be bred and fattened on milk until they were too plump
to retreat into their shells; dormice to be fed on nuts, and confined in an earthenware jar until they were fleshy enough for the
table; pigeons to be immobilized by having their wings clipped or
their legs broken, and then fattened on chewed bread. The acme
of extravagance was to be found in such dishes as that dedicated
by the emperor Vitellius to the goddess Minerva, which rejected
the flesh of several rare and expensive species—"collected in every
corner of the empire from the Parthian frontier to the Straits
of Gibraltar"—in favor of what must have been a very cloying
mixture of pike liver, pheasant brains, peacock brains, flamingo
tongues and lamprey roe.[27]

Fortunately for the economy, perhaps, Rome knew nothing of
the Americas, and comparatively little of the more distant parts
of Asia. Otherwise, gourmets would have been compelled to send
even farther away—for the chocolate, the potatoes, the butter
beans and "French" beans of South America; the tomatoes, maize,
and turkey, of Central America; the limes and bananas of India;
the oranges, rhubarb and tea of China.

THE PROBLEM OF TEXTURE

The nearest thing to a Roman cookbook which survives today is
that bearing the name of the first-century gourmet Apicius, who
is reported to have poisoned himself when he realized that he had
no more than ten million sesterces left (equivalent to just under
three-quarters of a ton of gold bullion), on which he estimated
that it would be impossible to maintain his standard of living.[28]

---

* Trimalchio's Feast, of course, satirizes the exhibitionism of the *nouveaux riches*.
As a reflection of the truth about food it must be treated with the utmost discretion.

Reclining at table.

By no means all the recipes in the book, which was not compiled until at least three centuries after Apicius' time, can be attributed to the master himself. Some were certainly later, and a few of these were extracted from manuals of dietetics—fortunately, since writers on diet sometimes specified quantities (a practice not adopted by food writers until the fifteenth century). One recipe in the Apician cookbook, for a sauce for roast meat, lists a quarter of an ounce each of pepper, lovage, parsley, celery seed, dill, asafetida root, hazelwort, cyperus, caraway, cumin and ginger, plus a little pyrethrum, 1 Imperial or 1¼ American pints of *liquamen* (see pp. 96-99), and 2½ fluid ounces of oil.[29] There is, however, no indication of how much meat this potent brew was intended to be sprinkled on—or to drown. Since the correct number for a full dinner party in Roman times was nine (the Greeks, according to Archestratus, had a preferred maximum of five [30]) it is possible that quantities were generally given for nine people, in which case there would be five or six tablespoons of comparatively thin but highly flavored sauce for each diner.

Although surviving recipes may remain cryptic about the texture of food, the Roman style of dining suggests a number of possible conclusions. The nine guests were usually accommodated on three couches arranged in a "U" shape round a table. The diners reclined at three-quarters length, propping themselves on their left forearms and stretching for food and drink with their right hands. Forks were as yet unknown, knives and spoons only occasionally used. Most Romans simply ate with their fingers—a messy procedure if the meat were served already sauced. Although they did use fingerbowls, and sometimes napkins which they spread out over the edge of the couch to catch the drips, the most convenient food must have been a dry-cooked meat, pieces of which might be dipped into a sauce as thick as a good modern mayonnaise. Many of the sauces in Apicius are, in fact, thickened with wheat starch, some with crumbled pastry. Thin sauces were probably mopped up separately with pieces of bread, while pastry cases had a double function, acting as both dish and food. They could also be used to make the most of a fine sauce. One character in Petronius, describing a cold tart served "with a mixture of some wonderful Spanish wine and hot honey," tells how he took "a fat helping of the tart and scooped up the honey generously." [31]

LIQUAMEN AND SILPHIUM

The problem of taste is more complex than that of texture, partly because Roman recipes are uncommunicative about quantities, and partly because they include ingredients which are not only unfamiliar today but impossible to reconstruct with any guarantee of accuracy.

Rich Romans certainly appear to have had a rooted dislike for natural, unadulterated flavors and customarily gave meat, fish and vegetables an entirely new complexion with sauces consisting of at least a dozen strong ingredients.

Perhaps the most commonly used seasoning was *liquamen* (or *garum*). This was so popular that it was factory-produced; towns such as Pompeii, Leptis Magna, and Antipolis (Antibes), were famous for the quality of their product.

There were several recipes for *liquamen*, but that used at

Bithynia on the coast of the Black Sea appears to have been the canonical one. "It is best to take large or small sprats, or, failing them, take anchovies, or horse-mackerel, or mackerel, make a mixture of all and put into a baking trough. Take two pints of salt to the peck of fish and mix well to have the fish impregnated with salt. Leave it for one night, and then put it in an earthenware vessel which you place open in the sun for two or three months,* stirring with a stick at intervals, then take it, cover it with a lid and store away. Some people add old wine, two pints to a pint of fish." [32] If the sauce were made from especially fine fish, or from shellfish—shrimps, for example—the result was a refined, expensive, gourmet product. But whatever the ingredients or fermentation time, the *liquamen* was usually a clear golden fluid which kept well in a bottle or jar, and added a distinctively salty, slightly fishy, slightly cheesy flavor to any dish.

There was also a quick-brew *liquamen* which was very simple to make. "Take brine and test its strength by throwing an egg into it to try if it floats; if it sinks the brine does not contain enough salt. Put the fish into the brine in a new earthenware pot, add oregano, put it on a good fire until it boils . . . Let it cool and strain it two or three times, until it is clear." [33] This must have been a very feeble substitute for the real thing, even if it were afterward left to mature. (The recipe does not mention fermenting, but possibly this step was so obvious to contemporaries that it did not need to be specified. Without fermentation, the liquid was no more than a salty fish stock.) The nearest modern equivalent to *liquamen* is probably the fermented fish sauce popular in southeast Asia. It is known in Thailand as *nam pla*, in Vietnam as *nuoc mam*, and in Cambodia as *tuk trey*. Ten million gallons a year are said to have been consumed in what was formerly known as French Indochina in the 1950s, the last period for which statistics are available. [34] In the West, the liquid from salted anchovies might today be used as a stand-in for *liquamen*.

The scene at the great *liquamen* factories of antiquity may have been very similar to that in Eastern ports today, where a chain of laborers passes baskets of fish up from the boats to a foreman who levels the fish out in great wooden vats partially open to the

---

* If the sauce were made with larger fish, the two to three months' exposure might stretch to as much as eighteen months.

King Arcesilas of Cyrene supervises the weighing and storing of silphium.

air. A layer of fish is covered with a layer of salt until the vat is full. After a few days the liquid is drained off from below and tipped back in on top of the heap; this process is repeated several times. Finally, a wicker lid is placed on the vat and weighted down, and the fish are left to ferment and mature for several months. The resultant sauce is nutritionally very valuable, and a few spoonfuls a day—supplemented by vitamins from some other source—are said to give almost a full quota of the nutrients required by the human body.

If the fish were fermented *without* preliminary salting the end product would have a different flavor. Salt inhibits bacterial action, and prevents development of the full cheesiness which results when certain materials ferment; in *liquamen*, the inclusion of salt maintained a balance between fishiness and cheesiness. Twentieth-century Eskimos, however, sometimes store the fins, heads, tails and guts of fish in underground pits. After a few months; these decompose into a homogenized paste which tastes like strong cheese, with virtually no flavor of fish.[35] It is possible that the Romans numbered similar preparations among their general "fish pickles."

Clearly, *liquamen* was something of an acquired taste. But it was so commonly used that its absence from a dish may have been more noticeable than its presence—as in the case of salt, for example, in modern Western cooking.

Not quite as ubiquitous as *liquamen*, but just as necessary in the Roman kitchen, was the herb silphium, which came mainly from the former Greek colony of Cyrene (Cyrenaica) in North Africa. Cyrene's main exports were silphium and horses, and life in the colony revolved around them to such an extent that the dramatist Antiphanes, in the fourth century B.C., made one of his characters groan: "I will *not* sail back to the place from which we were carried away, for I want to say goodbye to all—horses, silphium, chariots, silphium stalks, steeple-chasers, silphium leaves, fevers, and silphium juice!" [36] As a result, it seems, of overcropping, silphium disappeared at about the time of Nero, and Romans had to use Persian asafetida as a substitute. This, as its name suggests (Persian *asa*, mastic; Latin *foetida*, stinking), was a rather pungent resin, and in some cases the Classical world seems to have taken a perverse delight in adding inhalatory insult to exhalatory injury. "If you want an onion," said a character in Athenaeus, "just consider what great expense it takes to make it good. You must have cheese and onion and sesame, oil, leeks and vinegar, and asafetida to dress it up with." [37]

Both silphium and asafetida were expensive. The Apician cookbook even gives a recipe for making an ounce of silphium last longer, by keeping it in a jar of pine nuts which it impregnated with its flavor (very much as a vanilla pod flavors a jar of sugar). When a recipe required silphium, a few of the pine nuts could be used.[38] A microscopic drop of asafetida concentrate still gives an indefinably pleasant taste to fish dishes, but it is no longer possible to judge how discreetly the Romans used it.*

SPICES

As well as *liquamen* and silphium, Roman cooks used large quantities of spices. The spice trade was of considerable antiquity. Imported cinnamon had been known in Egypt from as early as 1450 B.C., but the full flood of the spice trade did not come until the first century A.D.

Most of the cinnamon bark used in Classical times travelled westward either by the Silk Road from China (Chinese cinnamon, known as cassia, had a sharper "bite" than true cinnamon), or from Malaya and Indonesia. The Malayan product made a long and dangerous journey, first over 4500 miles of open sea in Indonesian double outrigger canoes to Madagascar and the African mainland, and then up the coast of East Africa to the Red Sea.[39]

For centuries, the Arabs monopolized much of the traffic with the East, and did their best to protect their middleman's profit by confecting ingenious myths about the origins of spices. Herodotus, in one of his believe-it-or-not passages, records the Arab way of "collecting" cinnamon bark. "Where it comes from and what country produces it, they do not know," he says. "What they say is that the dry sticks, which we have learned from the Phoenicians to call cinnamon, are brought by large birds which carry them to their nests, made of mud, on mountain precipices which no man can climb, and that the method the Arabians have invented for getting hold of them is to cut up the bodies of dead oxen, or donkeys, or other animals, into very large joints which they carry to the spot in question and leave on the ground near the nests. They then retire to a safe distance and the birds fly down and carry off the joints of meat to their nests, which, not being strong enough to bear the weight, break and fall to the ground. Then the men come along and pick up the cinnamon, which is subsequently exported to other countries." [40] There were equally grip-

---

* Asafetida was favored as a seasoning not only in Classical Greece and Rome. Indians have always used it (under the name of *hing*), sometimes in such quantity that supplies have had to be imported from Afghanistan.

Black pepper.

ping tales about frankincense and cassia, which entailed fighting off flying snakes and belligerent bats.[41]

Cassia leaf, known as *malabathrum*, was also used in the Roman empire. It was transported in tightly balled bundles from China to an important market at the mouth of the Ganges, and shipped from there to other parts of India and to the West.[42] Apicius, strangely, mentions *malabathrum* only three times, and cinnamon bark not at all. But there is scarcely a single recipe in his book which does not make use of pepper.

Pepper was the spice *par excellence* of the Classical, as of the modern, world. It was already fairly common in Greece by the fifth century B.C., although used for medicine rather than in cooking. Hippocrates recommended it, combined with honey and vinegar, for use in the treatment of feminine disorders,[43] and Theophrastus as an antidote to hemlock or, mixed with vinegar, as a potion for reviving a victim of suffocation.[44] In many cases, spices were to remain as important in medicine, drugs, ointments, perfumes, cosmetics and incense as they were in food. One formula for the compound Egyptian incense known as *kuphi*—literally, "holy smoke"—included twenty-six different spices in all.[45]

It is some indication of the Roman demand for spices that, by the first century A.D., they accounted for forty-four of the eighty-six classifications of goods imported to the Mediterranean from Asia and the eastern coast of Africa. (The others included elephant trainers and eunuchs, parrots and palm oil, cottons and cooks).[46]

THE FLAVOR OF FOOD

What did Roman food really taste like? Attempts to recapture its flavor in a modern kitchen offer little guidance. It is a matter not only of inadequate recipes and unfamiliar ingredients, but of fundamental differences in the quality of raw materials. How fatty, for example, was Roman pork in comparison with the meat of the modern pig, bred for lean flesh? How would the old, semi-wild spices, sun-dried and carried on camel back and in foul-smelling, leaky ships for many long months, compare with the carefully cultivated, hygienically packed, and swiftly transported spices of today?

The fact that no one knows what Roman food was even intended to taste like has never, of course, acted as a bar to speculation. There are two main schools of thought. The amateur gourmet is revolted by an Apician recipe which recommends serving cold chicken with a sauce of dill, mint, asafetida, vinegar, dates, *liquamen,* mustard, oil, and boiled-down grape juice—forgetting that what went into last night's excellent duck *à l'orange,* if set down in the same random and unquantified fashion, would sound scarcely more appetizing.* The second, more sophisticated view is that the ingredients listed in Roman recipes, if judiciously balanced, can produce a very acceptable result. But from this perfectly tenable position, apologists for Roman cooking too often go on to imply that the food *served on Roman tables in classical times* would be acceptable today. An unwarrantable assumption. "Balance" and "acceptability" are matters of taste—and who is to

---

* Arrowroot, vinegar, carrot, port, salt, orange juice, giblets, duck fat, butter, pepper, sugar, bayleaf, orange rind, onion.

say what a modern cook's taste has in common with that of a chef in a Roman villa?

It is, however, possible to make certain deductions from what might be described as the atmosphere of Roman recipes, and to integrate them with what is known about Roman life and attitudes of mind.

The very size of the city of Rome undoubtedly influenced the cuisine. In Sumer, Egypt and Greece, even the greatest centers of population were comparatively small, intimately linked with the countryside which continued to provide many of their basic, perishable foodstuffs. But Rome expanded until it covered an area almost a quarter as large as modern Paris.[47] The countryside receded. Transport was slow. "Fresh" foods had to be stockpiled in warehouses. There was no refrigeration. Disguising rancidity must have been one of the cook's major preoccupations; another, to find some way of giving character to the grindingly monotonous dried, salted and smoked foods which took on increasing importance as "fresh" foods became more suspect.

The curiously competitive ambience of Roman society must also have played a part in shaping the cuisine. What was expensive, or rare, had to be good. Rome's foreign trade was based, it is said, on five "essential luxuries"—Chinese silk, African ivory, German amber, Arabian incense, and Indian pepper. The first four were easy enough to display, but the man of fashion would

The domestic hen was common in Roman times. Horace reported that a fowl **drowned to death** in wine had a particularly fine flavor.

have to be sure that his expensive spices rose triumphant over the more commonplace ingredients.

Nevertheless, strongly flavored sauces may first have found favor in more modest households, where bread, grain-paste or beans formed the staple diet. A powerful sauce, even in tiny quantities, can transform quite large amounts of starchy food. The most intense of the world's repertoire of sauces—the soy mixtures of China, the curries of India, the chili blends of Peru—are all designed, fundamentally, as seasonings for bulky carbohydrates, which both absorb and dilute the sauce. Only when the rich get to work—the people who can afford a full meat or fish dinner every day—are such sauces eaten with flesh foods rather than with grain. Meat and fish dilute sauces scarcely at all, so when the latter are transferred from starch to protein foods the whole essence of the cuisine changes.

One other, recently advanced, theory about Roman society and its decline seems to reinforce the idea that distinctively flavored foods would have more appeal than mild ones. The American sociologist Seabury Colum Gilfillan has suggested that the Roman aristocracy suffered acutely from lead poisoning.* [48] Among the symptoms—many of which fit the Roman situation with almost startling precision—are loss of appetite and a metallic taste in the mouth. Chronic sufferers, it may be supposed, would go to considerable lengths to find dishes which would stimulate their appetites and kill the taste of lead.

But whatever the truth about the flavor of Roman food, it was a fitting irony that the barbarians who materialized outside the gates of the city at the beginning of the fifth century A.D. should have demanded as tribute not only land, subsidies, and military titles for their chiefs—but three thousand pounds of pepper.

* Lead may have found its way into the Roman system by a number of routes. Wine merchants, for example, often added to their wine a preservative syrup which had been boiled in lead-lined pots. Rich households used lead cooking pots or pewter vessels made from an alloy of seventy per cent tin and thirty per cent lead.

6.
The Silent
Centuries

When the barbarians overran Europe in the fifth century A.D., it was, said Sidonius Apollinaris, "the funeral of the world." [1] He was unduly pessimistic. The Goths, Vandals, Gepids, Alemanni and Franks who had milled around the frontiers of the Roman empire for so many centuries before they finally reached the Mediterranean were frugal men, living principally on milk, cheese and meat, driven on toward expansion by population pressures, nomad incursions from the East, and the pursuit of year-round grazing for their herds. The barbarian tribes conquered not, in the main, because they were numerically superior—in Spain, for example, there were only 200,000 Visigoths in relation to an estimated native population of six million [2]—but because they were more mobile and more dynamic, and their needs were imperative.

One of the more immediate effects of the barbarian invasions was to accelerate that return to the land which had begun in the previous century. Prudent citizens deserted the towns and cities— a natural magnet for invaders—and settled again in the countryside. Townsmen, of course, had never been more than a small minority, contributors to that particular urban life-style which is the nucleus of "civilization." In Classical Europe, as almost everywhere until the full flood of the Industrial Revolution in the West, ninety per cent of the population was directly engaged in agriculture.[3] The life of this silent majority is ill documented in comparison with that of the monarchs and merchants, aristocrats and abbots, who have always formed the visible tip of the social ice-

Trapping hares.

berg, but it is salutary to remember what a large proportion of the world's population was responsive to rural rather than urban conditions.

Rural conditions were uneasy in the fifth century. The currency crises which had for so long bedeviled imperial Rome had brought about a widespread return to a barter economy and the final disintegration of the Western empire led to the dislocation of such organized trade as survived. These economic factors, more than the direct impact of the barbarian invasions, had a repressive effect on rural life—and on the rural kitchen.

The diet of the European peasant in the so-called dark ages was certainly not as monotonous as the usual catalogue of "bread, porridge, herbs and roots" would suggest. Many peasants were able to fatten their pigs on the acorns and beechmast in the local forests. The domestic fowl pecked for provender in every hamlet. Only the most incompetent countryman would fail to bring home (legally or illegally) an occasional rabbit or hare for the pot. Rivers and lakes supplied fish to local inhabitants, and coastal communities probably continued to gather molluscs, as they had always done. Turnips, radishes, onions and leeks, carrots perhaps, and an undeveloped form of parsnip were among the root crops common in Europe during the first millennium A.D., while "herbs" included cabbage, spinach and cress, green turnip tops, and the early sprouts of nettles, thistles, and a number of other leafy plants.

There was, therefore, quite a variety of foods available, differing according to region and climate. But many of these foods were markedly seasonal as well as limited in quantity. A pig of the scraggy, slow-to-fatten medieval breed was nothing like as prolific as its plump little Chinese counterpart. The hen, though not the reliable egg factory she is today, was still more valued for her output than for her meat. Herbs and roots had to be cultivated or gathered, and if the women of the house were preoccupied with weaving the tribute of cloth demanded by the lord of the estate, they might have no time for such tasks.

Even in prosperous years, there was always a barren period in the last months of winter when nothing grew, when man and animal languished and sickened because their diet lacked essential vitamins. At such times as these, the best meal a peasant housewife could produce might add up to no more than bread and ale, with perhaps a piece of salt pork or, more probably, some stewed winter cabbage or kale or onion.

EARLY MEDIEVAL COOKING

In those countries (particularly around the Mediterranean) which had felt the full force of Roman influence, Roman cooking persisted, although it suffered considerably when trade flagged and deprived the cook of *liquamen*, asafetida and spices. This may not have been so serious in the north, where it is unlikely that Roman cooking was ever generally adopted.

There is a popular conception that most nations have the cuisine they deserve—a proposition much favored by gourmets of one country when they are being derogatory about the food of another. But it is a matter of historical fact that good plain cooking in any specific country, at any specific time, is—within the limits of contemporary technology—intelligently and logically adapted to the materials, equipment, and fuel available. Trade influenced the availability of many materials used in northern and southern kitchens; fuel had much to do with differences in cooking styles.

Around the Mediterranean, a roaring fire was not only undesirable but progressively more difficult to maintain. Metalworking needed charcoal, charcoal was made from timber. The Iron Age of Greece and Rome swallowed up the forests of southern Europe at a perilous rate. But scarcity of fuel encouraged the development of simple, enclosed charcoal stoves, and these made it possible for the southern cook to become expert with a frypan.

In the north, however, there was no shortage of timber,* and the great halls of the nobility—built, until the eleventh century, more often of split logs than of stone [5]—were warmed by blazing fires in the center of the room, where cauldrons boiled, spits were turned, and hotplates sizzled at the side. When there was no fire in the hall, cooking took place outdoors or in a separate kitchen building.

What was cooked in the cauldrons which hung almost permanently over the fire, in peasant huts as in lordly manors, remains a matter for conjecture. There is a serious hiatus in detailed European food records between Roman times and the twelfth

---

* Even when the forests of the north and west began to show signs of exhaustion at the end of the first millennium A.D., as the result of a great expansion in land cultivation, the German successors of the Frankish empire were able to push east across the Elbe and tap the seemingly limitless forests of the Slav hinterland.[4]

Cauldrons for the larger household were no light weight.

century, and, for once, the food of the rich is almost as inadequately documented as that of the poor. The emperor Charlemagne "almost hated" his doctors, "because they advised him to give up the roast meat to which he was accustomed, and eat boiled instead." [6] His main meal of the day "was served in four courses only, exclusive of the roast, which the hunters used to bring in on spits." [7] Contemporary literature has little more to say about cooking styles in the early Middle Ages.

From other sources, however—administrative archives, inventories, and ecclesiastical records, for example—there emerges a picture of a plain-living society, scattered over much of Europe north of the Alps, dining on most days of the year on bread, water or ale, and a *companaticum*—"that which goes with the bread"— from the cauldron.* The cauldron, probably, was the original stockpot, or *pot-au-feu*, providing an ever-changing broth enriched daily with whatever happened to be available, and very rarely cleared out except in preparation for the meatless weeks of Lent.

A rabbit, hen or pigeon would give the broth a good meaty flavor. The taste of salty pork or a cabbage would linger for days. But except in really hard times there would generally be something hot and filling in the pot—a soup thick with the shreds of past dinners, a piece of pork or game, or substantial dumplings of rye flour and pea meal.

Savory puddings, too, could be cooked in the cauldron, if they were tied in a flaxen cloth and suspended from a pot hook. Pease pudding, that mess of dried legumes which went so well with the boiled salt meat that was the commonest flesh food of the Middle Ages, may have been cooked in this way. The old rhyme:

> Pease pudding hot, pease pudding cold,
> Pease pudding in the pot, nine days old

suggests that the dish had keeping qualities which endeared it more to the housewife than to her family.

In addition to the cauldron, most households probably had a pan of some kind for special dishes. Though an egg might, at a pinch, be boiled in the stockpot, it could hardly be fried or scrambled. Left-over meat hashed with legumes and crumbs would

* The peasant's bread was frequently cooked (either by decree or by choice) in the bakehouse belonging to the lord of the manor.

Fish and coarse bread were standard fare near coasts and rivers.

taste quite different made into pan-fried croquettes instead of boiled dumplings. Fresh fish or eels, when available, may have been cooked separately "in their own brew."

For frumenty, that milky jelly made by soaking husked wheat in hot water for twenty-four hours, the housewife needed only a sturdy earthenware dish placed in a corner of the hearth. Frumenty could be eaten cold with milk and honey—a very nourishing combination—or reheated and mixed with fragments of meat or vegetable from the stockpot for a savory main dish.

It seems possible that more frumenty than bread was made from the wheat grown in northern Europe during the Middle Ages. Rye, which had originally been a weed of wheatfields, was by now the main crop over a wide belt of the continent. The flour from it, sometimes mixed with pea flour and a little barley, made the ordinary everyday brown bread. Many farmers persisted in planting wheat, but what usually came up in cooler areas was a mixed crop of wheat and rye. The two had to be harvested together, and the flour made from them—known as maslin, or, in French, as *miscelin*—was used for good-quality bread and, in sophisticated households, for pastry.* [8] But though the northern housewife was rarely, if ever, able to make pure wheaten bread, it may have been possible for her to gather an occasional armful of mixed wheat and rye grasses, and to sort out from them enough wheat for a dish of frumenty.

The *batterie de cuisine* in the average early medieval household in northern Europe added up to a sharp knife or two, a ladle, a cauldron, a pan, perhaps a trivet (a three-legged iron pot stand), and a spit. In time, the *rachyncroke* ("racking crook") was developed, a double-ended pot hook which, by means of a ratchet device, permitted the cook to raise or lower the cauldron over the fire. In time, too, the spit was improved with a jack which allowed for semi-mechanical turning. But the cauldron remained the central feature of the northern kitchen until the eighteenth century, and it was the cauldron which dictated how most food should be cooked.

During the centuries after the fall of Rome the peasant housewife's cooking was largely circumscribed by the raw materials to be found near her home. In inland and northern Europe long-distance trade in foodstuffs had become almost non-existent. She may or may not have had an extensive repertoire. She may or may not have inherited recipes from her grandmother. But—certainly—she had no cookbooks, no imported delicacies, no commercially preserved exotica, and her knowledge of nutrition was wholly empirical. Some tenth-century families may have been consistently well fed. For others, salt pork may have been the forerunner of today's ubiquitous hamburger, pease pudding the medieval equivalent of French fries.

ABBOTS AND EMPERORS

In an era when many communities had to be self-supporting, monasteries and royal courts evolved their own methods of dealing with the problem. As the centuries passed, bishops became as adept as kings at persuading the devout or the dutiful to bequeath

* Pure rye flour made a pastry that was too soft to handle, and barley one that was too brittle.[9]

to them desirable vineyards or productive olive groves which would remedy the deficiencies of their local estates.

Transporting wine or oil back to monastery or court was a purely administrative matter, solved with the aid of relays of tenants, but it was another question with perishable goods. From the countryside through which they passed, however, on the way to inspect their various estates and benefices, kings and bishops were usually prepared—indeed, anxious—to accept tribute or taxes-in-kind. One eighth-century English village, for example, was required by the laws of King Ine of Wessex to supply for royal consumption three hundred round loaves, ten sheep, ten geese, twenty chickens, ten cheeses, ten measures of honey, five salmon, and one hundred eels,[10] and in A.D. 844 Charles the Bald of France decreed that a bishop could requisition, at each halt in his pastoral progress, fifty loaves, ten chickens, fifty eggs, and five suckling pigs [11]—a heavy burden on the community if the bishop chose to halt in a tiny hamlet.

Sometimes, the arrival of a king posed wholly unexpected problems to his host. Once, when Charlemagne was on his travels, he was offered a cheese which was rich, creamy, and had a firm outer skin. Charlemagne discarded the skin and fell to on the heart of the cheese. Pained, his host said: "Why do you do that, lord

The medieval pedlar—about to be robbed, in this illustration from a fable, by a pair of apes—was to many hamlets the only purveyor of trinkets, gossip, and exorbitantly priced spices.

emperor? You are throwing away the very best part!" The emperor tried the skin, and admitted that his host (a bishop) was right. He then added: "Be sure to send me every year to Aix two cart-loads of just such cheese." Each year for the next three years, the unfortunate bishop conscientiously scoured the countryside for two cartloads of cheese in perfect condition, until Charlemagne finally took pity on him and released him from the duty, reward-ing him with "an excellent estate, rich with grain and wine." [12]

The monks and minor nobles who remained at home while their masters made their gastronomic tour of the countryside had their own ways of varying the menu. The nobles went hunting, while the monks—less strenuously—merely exacted rent or tribute from adjacent villages. In the ninth century, for example, St. Riquier in Picardy provided the local monastery with one hundred loaves, thirty gallons of fat or tallow, thirty-two gallons of wine and one of oil each week, as well as sixty gallons of ale a day.[13]

Vegetables and herbs were usually grown within the walls of the monastery itself. According to a plan drawn up between the years A.D. 820 and 830 for St. Gall in Switzerland (but never put into execution), the ideal was to have a physic garden close to the doctor's house, planted with sixteen medicinal herbs; a kitchen garden with nine large beds each devoted to a different kind of food plant; and, in the cemetery, fifteen fruit trees planted between the graves. There were also pens for sheep and other domestic animals.[14]

Monks were allowed to eat meat only on a limited number of days in the year, and although one property belonging to the Bavarian abbey of Staffelsee could, in the early ninth century, list among its stores "twenty smoked porkers with sausages," [15] fish was a more usual item of diet. To ensure a regular supply, many monasteries had their own *vivaria*, ponds where fish were kept alive until needed. Conveniently, frogs and beavers were counted as fish, and it may have been medieval monks who first domesti-cated the rabbit—for the sake of its feti. Unborn or newly born rabbits, once a favorite delicacy of the Romans, were classified (like eggs) as "not meat." * [16]

* Later in the medieval period, the church became subject to attacks of extreme asceticism—brought on, very often, by the sight of too many plump abbots—and at such times not only eggs, meat and rabbit feti were banned on fast days, but milk and butter as well.

St. Riquier, in Picardy.

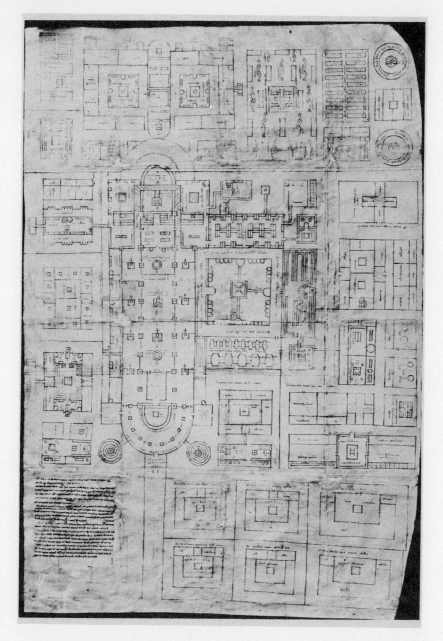

A large monastery was a complex community—farm, trade school, and commercial center as well as religious foundation. In this ninth-century plan for St. Gall, the designer incorporated a physic garden, a kitchen garden, and (at the foot) enclosures for live-stock.

A monastery, with fish vivarium in the foreground.

THE YEARS OF FAMINE

For the peoples of northern and western Europe, there were many black years in the ninth and tenth centuries. The Scandinavians erupted suddenly and destructively into history, reduced churches and monasteries to smoking ruin, razed crops and carried off cattle. In the Rhine valley, too, in A.D. 857, came the first serious recorded outbreak of ergotism, in which thousands of people died, poisoned by their daily bread.[17] Rye is susceptible to a particularly virulent fungus, known as ergot, which contains twenty poisons including lysergic acid diethylamide—the hallucinogen LSD.[18]

If the rye is badly affected, eating bread made from it leads either to intense abdominal pain, delirium, gangrene and death, or to that acute inflammation of the skin which in the ninth century, drove sufferers to insanity and gave ergotism its common name of "Holy Fire." In the hundred years following A.D. 857, Europe endured twenty "grievous famines"—some of them lasting for three or four years in succession.[19]

The south did not escape, any more than the north. There had been wars there, too, between the all-conquering Arabs and the Byzantines, and in their triumphal progress along the Mediterranean the Arabs had carried with them a single small bush which was to bring havoc to the agriculture of southern Europe. Until the early Middle Ages, the deadly black stem rust which can lay a whole harvest to waste had been almost unknown in the west. With the advent of the barberry bush, however, which plays host to the rust parasites during certain stages of their development, disease began to ravage the wheat fields.[20] As the

The medieval farmworker, a bunch of leaf vegetables slung over his shoulder, dog and sheep on a leash at his heels.

barberry spread, valued for the curative potion which could be extracted from its stems and for the brilliant berries which made a refreshing conserve, so did wheat rust, flourishing wherever there were warm rains, fogs, or heavy dews. By the early part of the tenth century Spain was suffering from appalling failures of the wheat harvest, which may well have been due to rust, and which (notably in A.D. 915 and 929) brought famine in their wake.[21]

Where there was famine, there was also cannibalism. What was said of India a few centuries later was probably equally true in tenth-century Europe. "Life was offered for a loaf, but none would buy; rank was to be sold for a cake, but none cared for it . . . Destitution at last reached such a pitch that men began to devour each other, and the flesh of a son was preferred to his love." [22] Demand produced supply. In some of the more isolated regions of central Europe killer bands roamed the countryside, waylaying travelers, cooking their flesh, and selling it to the highest bidder. Purchasers may have been told the meat was pork (which cannibal communities of the modern world have said it resembles), or mutton—even "two-legged mutton," which was what the Chinese called it when there was a famine in the northern provinces in the twelfth century.[23] Cannibalism was to persist in Bohemia, Silesia and Poland until the end of the Middle Ages, an actuality which helped to lend color to legends of werewolves and vampires.

Nevertheless, during these dark and often despairing years, new developments in agriculture were taking place which were soon to have a revolutionary effect, not only upon the food of western Europe, but on the whole of society.

PART THREE

Asia Until the
Middle Ages,
and the Arab World

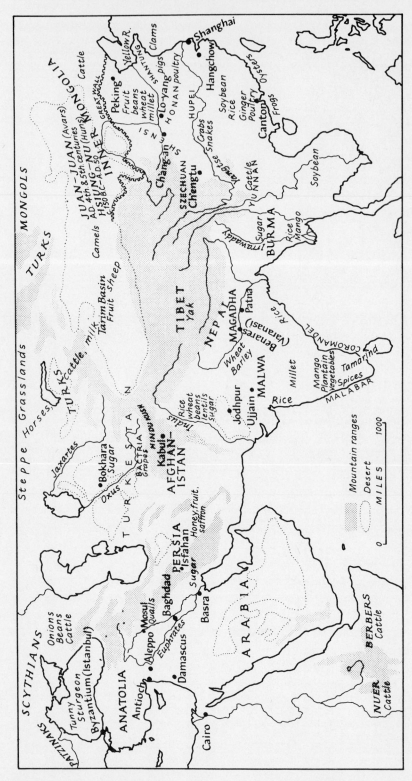

3. ASIA, A.D. 200–1200

INTRODUCTION

The Influence
of the Nomads

The influence of the Roman empire had stretched over a wide arc from Britain to the Near East. But in the ancient world there was another arc of influence, no less decisive, which was centered on the heart of Asia and reached from the borders of China in the east to Rumania in the west.

Historians have so far been defeated in their attempts to piece together the story of the nomadic herdsmen who ranged this Eurasian heartland. They appear to have left no writing to be deciphered, no great settlements to be excavated, and the earliest burial sites which have been discovered—some of them including superb examples of nomad art among the grave goods—cannot be dated at earlier than 1000 B.C.[1] But long before then the nomads had made a radical contribution to other peoples' history and culture.

The nomads of the Eurasian steppes were neither relics of a remote past nor rebels against an ordered present. Toward the western end of the steppes, it seems probable that an earlier hunting way of life had developed logically into a stockbreeding economy, better adapted to the terrain than settled agriculture.*

Farther east, some of the tribes may also have been directly descended from prehistoric hunters, but others appear to have gone through an intermediate stage as unsuccessful farmers.[2]

---

* The Aryan, or "Indo-European," tribes who erupted into Anatolia in 1900 B.C. and into Greece and India about two hundred years later are thought to have come from this region.

During the neolithic revolution, many cultivators had inevitably been crowded out of the good land onto marginal land which became steadily poorer under the assault of primitive agricultural techniques, and in the end, whole families and clans seem to have moved off with their herds to become nomads of the steppes. A highly complex organizational system was developed to serve the needs of this mobile society. Pasture land was too important for its boundaries to be settled by the ancient law of survival of the fittest, and a fair allocation of grazing had to be ensured. Ultimately, the steppe economy came to resemble a vast and intricate square dance, in which at a pre-ordained moment nomads scattered over thousands of miles of territory moved according to an almost ritual pattern. In a landscape of dark clouds and pale grass, the tribes lived in black felt tents, plastered, perhaps, like those of the later Mongols, with tallow or sheep's milk to keep out the rain.[3] When drought exhausted the waterholes and withered the grass, the herds sickened and died. The nomads, dependent on their livestock for food, came near to starvation.

Hunger on the steppes of Asia sometimes had far-reaching effects, reverberating all the way across the Eurasian landmass. In the first century A.D., for example, there was an extended drought, which sent a number of tribes from the Chinese border off to the west, there to join up with Iranian herdsmen and Mongols from the forests of Siberia to become the people known to Europe as the Huns.[4] In the middle of the fifth century, under the leadership of Attila, these Huns swept right across Europe as far as France, with devastating effect.* A hundred years later, a new tide of Central Asian invaders, the Avars, followed the first.[5]

Although China, at times, was able to manipulate the nomads of Central Asia, there were long periods when the fiery, black-browed horsemen of the steppes—well nourished on animal protein foods —overcame their more stolid carbohydrate-fed neighbors. When there was a strong dynasty in China, such as the Han (202 B.C.- A.D. 220) or the T'ang (A.D. 619-907), the nomads were usually held at bay, but during the intervening periods they frequently

---

* It seems to have been the first impact of the Huns on the borders between Asia and Europe which helped to impel the barbarian tribes of Europe to cross the imperial frontiers of Rome.

raided and sometimes occupied the northern provinces. When the Sung dynasty (A.D. 960-1279) attempted to reunite the empire, one nomad tribe was permitted to settle inside the Great Wall of China. This was the Ch'i-tan or Khitai tribe, from whose name the word Cathay was to be derived.[6] The Sung dynasty achieved exquisite heights of culture, but its army was inefficient and its administration corrupt. By 1138 the court had taken refuge at Hangchow, on a coastal inlet about a hundred miles southwest of modern Shanghai.

In 1167, the great Genghiz Khan was born, son of a minor leader of the wild but not wholly uncivilized Mongols.[7] When he died sixty years later much of north China was in Mongol hands, and in 1276 Hangchow itself finally submitted to Genghiz Khan's grandson, Kublai—the "Great Khan" of Marco Polo's time. The campaigns of the preceding 150 years had reduced the population of China from one hundred million to less than fifty-nine million.[8]

For almost fifteen hundred years, since the beginning of the Han period, as well as for the thirteen hundred years of recorded history preceding it, China had rarely been one, united country. In most senses—social, political, topographical, ethnic—it was more like three. And the same was true of its cuisine.

Because of the configuration of northern China, the nomads who so drastically influenced its history had only a limited influence on its food. The Chinese terrain could not accommodate herds of cattle.

In India, it was another matter. Domesticated animals had already been common there at the height of the Indus valley civilization, though meat did not form the mainstay of the diet. With the collapse of Harappa and Mohenjodaro in about 1750 B.C., and the arrival of the Aryan nomads from the Eurasian steppes, livestock—and cattle in particular—assumed greater importance. The Aryans' food was mutton and beef, milk and curds, and the cooking medium was *ghi*—clarified butter which, unlike fresh butter, can be kept for months even in a hot climate. What the Aryans seem to have introduced into India was not an increase in meat eating, but a heavy dependence on dairy products. This dependence, reinforced by the precepts of the *Vedas* (the religious epics of the Aryans), led to the slow diffusion throughout the subcontinent of a belief in the sacredness of the cow and the sanctity of her products. It was to be many centuries before Aryan influence and religion became established in the south, a region largely cut off from the rest of the country by the mass of the Vindhya mountains, but in the north by the middle of the first millennium B.C. the impositions of the *vedic* system had become so heavy as to provoke a strong social reaction. Fundamental to the two new religions which then arose—Buddhism and Jainism— was a belief in the sanctity of all life, and a resultant advocacy of vegetarianism.

In the three or four centuries after 1000 B.C., the spread of dairy products seems to have been paralleled by the general spread of rice cultivation. Rice had been known at the time of the Indus valley civilization, but it appears first to have become important on the other side of India, in the region of the river Ganges.[9]

During the first millennium A.D. India, like China, was sometimes one state, sometimes several, sometimes rich, sometimes poor. The diet of the nobility responded to changing conditions, absorbing foreign foods and foreign cooking techniques in sudden surges of innovation. But the food of the peasant had already taken on an air of permanence.

Very different from the nomads of the Eurasian steppes were the Arabs, who were to have such a far-reaching influence on European civilization from the seventh century A.D. onward. During the first millennium B.C., the peoples of the arid peninsula between the Red Sea and the Persian Gulf had discovered the benefits of trade, and had profited greatly from the incense they alone were able to produce, as well as from their role as middlemen in the east-west spice traffic. But there was constant friction between the tribes, until, in the early part of the seventh century A.D., the religion preached by the prophet Muhammad gave a sense of unity to the Arab peoples.

Under the banner of Islam, the Arabs swept along the Mediterranean coasts and over the Persian empire. In A.D. 763, the Abbasid caliphs built a new walled capital at Baghdad on the Tigris, in the still fertile valley where Kish and Babylon, Seleucia and Ctesiphon had once flourished.[10] Outside the walls of this "Round City" gathered an extraordinary medley of peoples, not

Zucharum.

Sugar, carried to Sicily and Spain by the Arabs, was to become an important trading commodity—retailed in small and expensive quantities in the north —until the seventeenth-century expansion of sugarcane production in the New World.

only Arabs but Syrians, Persians, and Turks, a population in whose veins ran the blood of Greeks, Parthians, Sassanids, even of Romans.

The Arabs who had lived the austere life of the desert for so many centuries took to the civilized, cosmopolitan luxury of Baghdad with whole-hearted enthusiasm. Arab colonial administrators, enchanted by the tinkling waters and green gardens of the irrigated valley of the Tigris, were soon creating similar oases in the sunbaked lands of Spain and watering them with the aid of a greatly improved system of canals. Yearning for the fresh tang of the citrus fruits they had so recently discovered and the bland crispness of almonds, they planted them wherever they would grow in newly conquered lands. Men who were exiled to far countries took with them rice grains and cuttings of the sugar cane the Persians had introduced from India, foods that it was more practical to plant than to import. They took saffron, too, and its golden glow soon suffused the food of the West. As the centuries passed, many of the foods carried west by the warriors of Islam for their own enjoyment became commercial crops, the financial support of later generations.

From Baghdad itself innumerable caravans set out to bring back foods from afar. There were Arabs and Rhadanite Jews who ventured as far as China for cinnamon and rhubarb, or to India for coconuts; others who traveled to Bactria for grapes; to Isfahan, for honey and quinces, apples, saffron and salt; to Mosul for quails; or to Hulwan for pomegranates, figs or vinegar sauces.[11]

But whatever their motives, personal or commercial, during the three hundred years of their most concentrated achievement the Arabs succeeded in introducing into the cooking of most Mediterranean countries, not only a great number of new raw materials —many of them originating in Asia—but also several new and refined cooking techniques.

7.
Central Asia

Herodotus described the Scythians as "a people without fortified towns, living . . . in wagons which they take with them wherever they go, accustomed one and all to fight on horseback with bows and arrows, and dependent for their food not upon agriculture but upon their cattle." [1] The Scythians probably led a more comfortable and sociable life than the majority of nomad herdsmen. They ranged the fertile lands around the Caspian and the Black Sea, supplemented the products of their herds with tunnyfish and sturgeon, onions, garlic, and beans, and traded for luxuries with the prosperous towns of the Classical world. Hippocrates characterized them as being, in general, a fat and humorous people.[2]

This could hardly have been said of their fellow nomads at the Chinese end of the steppes, harsh, energetic men, bow-legged from constant riding, with large heads, blazing eyes, and massive chests built to withstand the freezing nights and parching days of the Gobi desert,[3] where, "gazing on all sides as far as the eye can reach in order to mark the track, no guidance is to be obtained save from the rotting bones of dead men, which point the way." [4]

But however different the temperament of the various tribes, and however dissimilar the landscape in which they lived, their grazing needs were much the same, and so, too, were their food habits.

Central Asian nomad,
possibly a Scythian.

THE DIET OF THE ASIAN NOMADS

Their flocks and herds supplied most of the nomads' needs, whether felt for their tents, hide for their armor, or meat for their stewpots.

Most of the meat was probably mutton, but when the larger livestock were breeding well, or when a horse had become too old for its strenuous life, the nomads undoubtedly relished a sirloin of beef, a roast hump of camel, or a cup of rich horse broth.

Roast camel's hump was (and is) a great delicacy, the stewed feet or braised paunch scarcely less so, while horse is in many ways superior to beef. In some parts of the Western world, horse-eating is regarded with almost as much revulsion as cannibalism, although attempts to improve on the inadequate diet of the poor in nineteenth-century France by popularizing horse-flesh did have a measure of success. In 1855, one M. Renault, director of a veterinary college, held a "comparative tasting" of horse versus beef. A twenty-three-year-old horse suffering from incurable paralysis was slaughtered and its meat was cooked in the same way as similar cuts of beef. The panel of tasters, all dedicated gourmets, concluded that horse bouillon was superior to beef bouillon, and that roast fillet of horse was appreciably better than roast fillet of beef. Boiled horse, though not quite as good as the best boiled beef, was still better than beef of ordinary quality.[5] In England, on the other hand, horse-flesh found no supporters even when, in 1868, a dinner was held in London at which were offered such poetic creations as roast fillet of Pegasus, patties of Bucephalus-marrow, and lobster with Rosinante-oil mayonnaise.[6]

The nomads of Central Asia may have been able to eat horse-flesh more frequently than beef, camel, or yak. Very little is known about the type of livestock herded on the steppes, but in the wilder areas cattle were probably rare; the cow is none too well adapted to a rigorous life. Camels, which produce no more than a single foal at intervals of three years, would be uneconomic to

The sheep and goat, essential animals in the steppe economy, drawn by a Chinese scholar at the court of the nomadic Mongols.

kill for food, while the rich and abundant milk of the yak also made it more valuable alive than dead.

BLOOD AS FOOD

One of the most characteristic nomad foods was the blood of living animals. Marco Polo gives a detailed description of how the Mongol armies of the thirteenth century provisioned themselves when they had to move far and fast. To allow for frequent changes of mount on a ten-day journey, each man had a string of eighteen horses and mares. They traveled "without provisions and without making a fire, living only on the blood of their horses; for every rider pierces a vein of his horse and drinks the blood." [7] Half an Imperial or ⅝ American pint every tenth day could be taken from each animal, enough to sustain the rider without impairing the efficiency of his mounts.

The great advantage of blood as food was that it did not need special transport, preparation or cooking. Fire was often a problem for the men of the steppes, either because fuel was scarce or because the flames of a cooking fire could be seen for many miles around. William of Rubruck, emissary to the East of Louis IX of France, said when he was describing his experiences in Central Asia forty years before Marco Polo's time: "Of hunger and thirst, cold and weariness, there was no end . . . Sometimes we were compelled to eat flesh half sodden, or almost raw, for want of fuel to boil it, especially when we lay in the plains or were benighted before we came to our journey's end, because we then could not conveniently gather together the dung of horses and oxen, for other fuel we found but seldom, except, perhaps, a few thorns in some places." [8]

Blood drinking, in one form or another, appears to have been common in pastoral communities throughout recorded history. Arabs before the days of Islam enjoyed a dish composed of camel hair and blood, mixed together and then cooked on the fire.[9] In the ninth century, a Chinese traveler to the Berber country south of the Gulf of Aden recorded that the people "often stick a needle into the veins of cattle and draw blood, which they drink raw, mixed with milk." [10] The eleventh-century Byzantine scholar

Michael Psellus said of the Patzinak tribes that, if they were thirsty and there was no water available, "each man dismounts from his horse, opens its veins with a knife and drinks the blood . . . After that they cut up the fattest of the horses, set fire to whatever wood they find nearby, and, having slightly warmed the chopped limbs there on the spot, they gorge themselves on the meat, blood and all." [11] In seventeenth-century Ireland, a critical French traveler noted that the peasants "bleed their cows and boil the blood with some of the milk and butter that came from the same beast; and this with a mixture of savory herbs is one of their most delicious dishes." * [12] In the counties of Tyrone and Derry, the blood was even preserved; it was allowed to coagulate in layers, each layer "being strewn with salt until a little mound was formed, which was cut up in squares and laid by for use as food in the scarce time of the year." [13]

Today, the Masai of Tanzania tap the jugular vein of cattle or sheep by shooting a special arrow—which has a stop below the point to prevent it from penetrating too far—into the neck, draining off as much blood as they need and then closing the wound with a plug.[14] The Masai drink the blood fresh, but the Nuer tribe of the Upper Nile either boil the blood to thicken it, or allow it to coagulate into lumps which can be roasted in the embers of the fire.[15]

ANIMAL MILK PRODUCTS

The nomad herdsmen of the first millennium A.D. also made use of more conventional dairy products. Where horses were numerous, as they were over the entire belt of the steppe lands, mare's milk was of supreme importance—and may well have been a decisive factor in the nomads' exuberant good health.

From the high proportion of meat in their diet, the nomads were well supplied with protein, fat, and vitamins A and B. But, except in Scythian territory, their access to the essential vitamin C appears to have been limited. Fresh fruit and vegetables were very rare on the steppes, and, by rights, the nomads ought to have

---

* This is a version of the "drisheen"—a kind of blood pudding—still known in County Cork and elsewhere today.

died like flies from the vitamin-C deficiency disease of scurvy—or, at the very least, to have shown signs of the laziness and lethargy which are characteristic of the disease. Indolence was not, however, one of their more striking characteristics, and the reason for this was almost certainly their high consumption of mare's milk—which has twice as much vitamin C as human milk, and four times as much as cow's milk.[16] If they were accustomed to drink large quantities of mare's milk every day, they would be adequately supplied with vitamin C from this source alone.

From the milk of their other animals, the nomads probably made a number of foods of the curd or yogurt type. Curdled products must have been discovered almost as soon as man learned about milking at the beginning of the neolithic era. A container of milk, left to stand for a few hours, would soon curdle in the climate of the Near East. Depending, among other factors, on temperature and on the type of bacteria floating in the air, the curds might be fine or they might be coarse. The fine variety would develop ultimately into the kind of sharp, refreshing product represented today by the yogurt of the Balkans, the *taetta* of Scandinavia, the *dahi* of India. Coarse curds, strained off, made the first soft, fresh cheese, and cheeses with an individual character emerged when man discovered how to precipitate curdling by adding certain types of vegetable juice, or putting the milk into a leathern container made from a young cow's stomach. (The lining of a calf's stomach contains an enzyme, rennin, which produces rennet, the curdling agent.) Curds pressed into basketry molds, or perforated earthenware dishes, could afterward be left to ferment and mature.

Butter, the other major dairy product, must have developed in cooler lands; the churning which produces it may have been accidentally discovered when a traveler carried a container of milk with him on a journey. In time, it was found that the palatable life of butter could be extended by heating it, evaporating the water, and straining off the impurities, or simply by adding salt in the making.

Curds, cheese, yogurt and butter were all useful methods of preserving milk that was surplus to man's immediate requirements. So, too, was dried milk. Marco Polo described how the Mongols made it and how they used it. "First they bring the milk to the

The Chertomlyk Vase, made in the fourth century B.C. This is, in fact, a *kumiss* jug with four spouts ending in animal heads. *Kumiss* sometimes throws a flaky deposit, and filters were therefore fitted in the neck of the jug and in the spouts.

boil," he said. "At the appropriate moment they skim off the cream that floats on the surface and put it in another vessel to be made into butter, because so long as it remained the milk could not be dried.* Then they stand the milk in the sun and leave it to dry. When they are going on an expedition, they take about ten pounds of this milk; and every morning they take out about half a pound of it and put it in a small leather flask, shaped like a gourd, with as much water as they please. Then, while they ride, the milk in the flask dissolves into a fluid, which they drink. And this is their breakfast." [17]

KUMISS

As well as using mare's milk fresh or dried, the nomads converted it into another drink which was both nourishing and pleasurable— the fermented liquor most commonly known by its Mongol name of *kumiss*. The camel-milk version is called *kephir*, and that of the yak, *airan*.

A quantity of fresh mare's milk, reported William of Rubruck, was poured into a great bag which was then beaten "with a piece of wood made for that purpose, having a knot at the lower end like a man's head, which is hollow within; and so soon as they beat it, it begins to boil [or froth] like new wine, and to be sour, and of a sharp taste; and they beat it in that manner till butter comes." [18] Although William does not mention it, the milk was allowed to begin fermenting before churning started, and the churning went on sporadically for about three or four days, which is a length of time still favored by the Kazak peoples who still make *kumiss* in Russian Turkestan today.[19] William was, however, able to report that "after a man hath taken a draught, it leaves a taste behind it like that of almond milk, going down very pleasantly, and intoxicating weak brains, for it is very heady and powerful." [20]

---

* Marco's mention of bringing milk "to the boil" is misleading. Milk, in which the cream had already risen to the surface, was probably put in shallow containers and heated slowly to a few degrees below the boiling point. The cream would then become thick and crumpled, easy to skim off when it cooled. This is, in fact, what is known today as "clotted cream" or "Devonshire cream"; it is not unlike butter, even without churning. If the Mongols had failed to skim off the cream before drying their milk, the powder would have turned rancid very quickly.

When William of Rubruck arrived at Karakoram, he discovered that a far-flung French goldsmith, one Guillaume Boucher, had built for the Mongol prince, Mangu Khan, a silver fountain with four spouts which dispensed, respectively, *kumiss*, wine, mead, and rice wine.

At some unrecorded stage in history, the Asian nomads made improvements on their *kumiss*. When, in the nineteenth century, interested Europeans began to inquire into the *Pen Ts'ao*—the Chinese pharmacopoeia—they discovered many "wines" which certainly had their origin in wild rather than settled lands. Among those listed were deer wine, tiger bone wine, tortoise wine, snake wine, dog wine, and mutton wine. (The latter four were, respectively, good for bronchitis, palsy, lassitude, and strengthening the stomach, kidneys and testicles.[21]) Among the ingredients for a number of these "medicinal" drinks was *kumiss*, loosely translated by the Victorians as "cow's milk whiskey."

In a spirit of scientific inquiry, the Reverend J. Gilmour—a British missionary—asked his Chinese lama, or teacher, to instruct him in the making of mutton wine. The recipe ran as follows: "1 sheep, 40 catties* of cow's milk whiskey, 1 Imperial or 1¼ American pints of skim milk, soured and curdled, 8 oz brown sugar, 4 oz honey, 4 oz fruit of dimocarpus, 1 catty of raisins, and half a dozen drugs weighing in all about 1 catty. The sheep must be two years old, neither more nor less, a male, castrated." [22] The brewing process was complex, and the end product, which smelled strongly of mutton, had an alcohol content of 9.14 per cent.†

SUBSTITUTE   MILKS

The nomads can never have gone short of animal milk, but in other societies substitutes were extensively used.

Nuts were one of the major sources of substitute "milk," and though they were not, generally, as nutritious as the animal product, they still fulfilled a useful purpose. India and southeast Asia made great use of the coconut, draining off the clear natural liquid from immature nuts and infusing the grated flesh of ripe

---

* The catty was a somewhat variable measure of weight, though theoretically equivalent to 1⅓ pounds.

† Though this recipe may not sound very appealing, it should not be dismissed out of hand. Eighteenth-century English and American cookbooks gave instructions for making a "cock ale"—ingredients 10 Imperial or 12½ American gallons of ale, one large and elderly cock, raisins, mace and cloves [23]—which was not, in principle, much unlike the mutton wine of the Mongols, while at least one modern English work on home winemaking [24] speaks in eulogistic terms of the excellent flavor given to beer by the addition of a cockerel to the ferment.

ones in water. From hickory nuts and pecans, the North American Indians extracted a milky liquid which they used for gruels or in making maize cakes.

In Europe, walnuts and almonds, blanched, pulverized, and soaked in water, provided the staple milk of many households until at least the end of the eighteenth century. Most almonds at the time were imported from Italy and Provence, to which trees had been introduced by, or as a result of, the Arab conquests.

A milky fluid could also be extracted from beans and other pulses, simmered, reduced to a purée with some of the cooking liquid, and then strained. Bean milk was used in many parts of the world, notably in China, for the Chinese, unlike their Central Asian neighbors, relied scarcely at all on grazing livestock or the dairy products they supplied.

8.

China

Every now and then, scientists engaged on research into modern nutritional problems come up with a suggestion that has interesting historical implications. Recently, the fact that many adult Asians and Africans are unable to digest fresh milk, suffering severe discomfort if they drink more than a small quantity, has led researchers to inquire more closely into the relationship between milk and the digestive processes.[1] The result could throw new light on the history of dairy products in Europe and America, as well as in Asia and Africa.

All new-born babies, it seems, regardless of nationality, produce an enzyme (lact*ase*) which allows them to digest the milk-sugar (lact*ose*) in their mother's (or any other) milk. But if, after they are weaned, they stop drinking fresh milk—as they do in countries where the climate is hot or milk-giving animals few—they also stop producing the enzyme necessary for digestion, because it no longer serves a useful purpose.

In the towns and cities of the Western world, physicians spent hundreds of years lamenting the fact that fresh milk was indigestible. It now seems that this need not have been wholly due to the dubious quality of the milk itself. But in the West there were always enough cattle to ensure that a proportion of the rural population, at least, continued to drink fresh milk. The milk-drinking habit was therefore maintained, and when pasteurization was developed and good fresh milk became generally available, most European and American children went on from breast milk to cow's milk, and so continued to produce the lactase enzyme into adult life.

But in such countries as China, where milk-giving animals were always few and far between, dairy products never had a place in the diet—although it must be stressed that milk was neither wholly unknown nor wholly rejected. The great T'ang emperor T'ai-tsung, for example, was quite prepared to swallow a decoction of "long" pepper—a particularly potent variety—simmered in milk, to cure an intestinal disorder,[2] and a later emperor of the same dynasty enjoyed, in the hot weather, a frosty dish of rice cooked with cow's milk and two preparations of camphor— "dragon's eyeball powder" and "dragon's brain fragments."[3] In the mid-thirteenth century, too, a Chinese writer describes coconut flesh as being of a "jade-like white, and of an agreeable taste, resembling that of cow's milk."[4] None of this suggests any deep revulsion at milk *per se*. Nevertheless, milk was a rarity in China, and something of an acquired taste.

The general absence of dairy products from the diet of the mass of the Chinese people is frequently attributed to a national hatred for the cattle-raising nomads who so often brought destruction to the northern provinces—an argument which is unsound on all levels. The nomads first began to trouble China in about the third century B.C., and north China has been either occupied or ruled by nomad or nomad-originated dynasties for almost one third of the two thousand and more years which have elapsed since then— a very long time for the Chinese to cherish a hatred for the food of their conquerors. Furthermore, there is no point in being a conqueror if one has to submit to the prejudices of the conquered, and the nomads who settled in the northern provinces would be unlikely to give up their familiar dairy products merely because the Chinese disliked them. In effect, if dairy products had been widely available, clear of religious taboos, and dietetically acceptable, they *must* have been adopted in China.

There appear to have been no religious taboos, but because of the intensive crop-farming of the Yellow river heartlands grazing livestock were scarce and so were dairy products. The result must have been a vicious circle—since they did not drink fresh milk regularly, the people of China would find it indigestible, and this would in turn discourage them from expanding the stock-farming which would, in the end, have overcome the allergy.

If, however, the Chinese had been prepared, like other peoples, to make use of soured-milk products, they would have solved at least some of their problems. In the process of souring, the indigestible lactose, or milk sugar, undergoes a chemical change, with the result that a consumer who may suffer acute discomfort when he drinks fresh milk has no difficulty at all in digesting yogurt, curds, or cheese.

The Chinese, however, appear to have developed strong views on hygiene at a fairly early stage,[5] and if knowledge of milking in fact came to China as late as 2000 B.C., the date usually suggested, soured-milk products may immediately have been classified as unclean, or tainted, by those who dictated the pattern of life. (If so, they were wrong, for the chemistry of soured-milk products makes them unusually hygienic.)

EARLY   CHINESE   FOOD

The beginnings of the distinctive Chinese and east Asian cuisine are by no means clearly defined. There are no literary sources before the first millennium B.C.,* and political upheavals in China throughout the present century have, until recently, gravely hampered scientific archeology.

The earliest surviving Chinese text is the *Shih ching*, the "Book of Songs," a collection of traditional ballads and fragments gathered together sometime after 600 B.C. Feasting and farming both find a place in the *Shih ching*, which describes the life and occasionally the food of the warrior-farmers of the northwestern highlands of Shensi.

In winter, the men hunted animals for their furs and cut and stored ice for use in the summer months. In early spring, after the land was plowed, there was held the rite of expiation, the sacrifice of a lamb which even then, almost three thousand years ago,

---

* When a modern Western book on Chinese cooking claims that "in 2000 B.C., I Yin wrote: 'In making a mixture you must judge what is sweet, sour, bitter, sharp, and salt,' " what the author really means—whether he knows it or not—is' that at some time between 500 B.C. and A.D. 100, scholars engaged on collecting ancient traditions heard tell of a sage, who was said to have lived in the time of the (probably legendary) Hsia dynasty, whose name was reputedly I Yin, and who was believed to have spoken of the importance of the Five Flavors.

Shooting game birds and cultivating grain in the highlands of Szechwan.

was aromatically seasoned with garlic before being cooked on a bed of fragrant southernwood.

> High we load the stands,
> The stands of wood and earthenware.
> As soon as the smell rises
> God on high is very pleased:
> "What smell is this, so strong and good?" [6]

In summer there were plums and cherries, and the people boiled beans and mallows (a plant with leaves similar to spinach) for their evening meal. In the last month of the working year, the rice wine was set to ferment, millet, beans and wheat were brought indoors, rats were smoked out of the houses, windows and doors blocked up against the weather to come, and roofs rethatched with newly gathered reeds. Finally:

With twin pitchers they hold the village feast,
Killing for it a young lamb.
Up they go into their lord's hall,
Raise the drinking cup of buffalo-horn:
"Hurrah for our lord; may he live for ever and ever!" [7]

Traditionally, the *Shih ching* is said to have been compiled by Confucius himself, and there is further information on early Chinese food in the *Lun Yü* (or "Analects"), a collection of his sayings, supplemented by the reminiscences of disciples and extracts from traditional non-Confucian texts. One of the latter describes how a man ought to prepare himself before he makes a sacrifice to the spirits. His behavior, his clothing, and his food, must all be ritually "correct."

"There is no objection to his rice being of the finest quality, nor to his meat being finely minced. Rice affected by the weather or turned he must not eat, nor fish that is not sound, nor meat that is high. He must not eat anything discolored or that smells bad. He must not eat what is overcooked nor what is undercooked, nor anything that is out of season. He must not eat what has been crookedly cut [which might cook unevenly] nor any dish that lacks its proper seasoning.

"The meat that he eats must at the very most not be enough to make his breath smell of meat rather than of rice. As regards wine, no limit is laid down; but he must not be disorderly. He may not drink wine bought at a shop or eat dried meat from the market. He need not refrain from such articles of food as have ginger sprinkled over them; but he must not eat much of such dishes." [8]

On the basis of this text—highly informative on the Chinese view of what constituted pure, hygienic food—some writers optimistically claim that Confucius himself was particular in his tastes, a gourmet of no mean order. What it really shows, however, is that the Chinese were well aware of the causes (and effects) of digestive upsets. The spirits to whom a man proposed making a sacrifice could hardly be expected to look kindly on his plea if he were so disrespectful as to dress badly or behave badly,[9] and would be revolted by a supplicant who reeked of garlic or ginger, belched in their presence, or treated them to the sound and scent of what Dr. Johnson disarmingly described as "an ill wind behind." [10]

Among the spirits who expected deference were "the ancestors," and when a man reached the age at which his death and conversion into an ancestor seemed imminent, he was treated with the greatest consideration, not only by his family but by the state.

In the *Li-chi*, a handbook of ritual compiled during the Han era (202 B.C.-A.D. 220) but containing earlier material, recipes were given for the Eight Delicacies which were to be prepared for the aged on ceremonial occasions. The meat of the ox, sheep, elk, and two kinds of deer were all regarded as suitable for these dishes, if tenderized by pounding, marinating, or mincing. Three of the recipes, however, deserve fuller quotation.

One was a savory fry-up of pre-soaked rice and crisp morsels of

By the second century B.C., the pig, duck, goat, and hen were China's primary food animals.

the fat from a wolf's breast. Another entailed wrapping the liver of a dog (a commonplace meat animal in China) in a thin casing of its own fat, moistening it, and then roasting it. To give it a crackling finish, it was seared at the last minute directly on the flame. But the *pièce de résistance* among the Eight Delicacies must have been the suckling pig stuffed with dates.* After stuffing, the pig was encased in a coating of wet clay and roasted until the juices were sealed in, the skin soft, and the clay dried out. The shell was then broken off, and the skin removed and pounded with rice flour and a little liquid. The resulting paste was either added to the stuffing or, more probably, used to coat the piglet again (the surviving text is vague on this point). Next, the whole animal was deep-fried to a crisp golden brown. Finally, the meat was cut into slices which were placed on a bed of herbs in the upper part of a kind of *bain marie*. After three days' immersion in delicately scented steam, the suckling pig was ready—soft as butter, no doubt, and exquisitely aromatic.[11]

Rich Chinese ate a great variety of foods; if they were rich enough, they could even afford to eat beef. A number of luxuries were listed in the third century B.C. poem "The Summons of the Soul."

All kinds of good food are ready:
Rice, broom-corn, early wheat, mixed all with yellow millet;
Bitter, salt, sour, hot and sweet: there are dishes of all flavors.
Ribs of the fatted ox cooked tender and succulent;
Sour and bitter blended in the soup of Wu;
Stewed turtle and roast kid, served up with yam sauce,†
Geese cooked in sour sauce, casseroled duck, fried flesh of the great crane;
Braised chicken, seethed tortoise highly seasoned, but not to spoil .the taste;
Fried honey cakes of rice flour and sugar-malt sweetmeats;
Jadelike wine, honey flavored, fills the winged cups;
Ice cooled liquor, strained of impurities, clear wine, cool and refreshing.[12]

---

* More probably, jujubes—*Zizyphus jujuba*, sometimes known as the "Chinese date," though it seems to have originated in Syria.

† A sauce or purée made from the true yam (probably *Dioscorea opposita*), not the sweet potato, which was not cultivated in China until about the sixteenth century A.D.

The concept of the Five Flavors—bitter, salt, sour, hot and sweet—seems to have been established comparatively early in Chinese *haute cuisine*,* and the cooking of other countries would certainly have been much improved if they, too, had had the wit to realize that contrast is the essence of good menu-planning.

Exotic foods and elegantly balanced flavors were for the rich, but it is possible that the style of cooking nowadays regarded in the West as being "typically Chinese" may have evolved in the peasant kitchen.

As Chinese society developed, it became the custom for all those who worked on the land to move out from the villages in early spring to live in temporary huts in the fields until the harvest in September or October.[14] During this period of comparative isolation, the peasants were thrown back on limited resources, although there may have been some communal organization of essential supplies. Fuel was one obvious problem. When the full agricultural economy developed on the plains of the Yellow river, fields broken only by dykes must have stretched as far as the eye could see. In summer, the bushes and scrub which topped the dykes would be too green and sappy to use, and the field laborer must have had to depend on wood or charcoal brought from a distance, or on the dried dung of a few draft animals. It seems probable that the situation was ripe for the evolution of that cooking style which, though requiring maximum preparation time, also takes minimum cooking time—the stir-fry method, by which wafer-thin fragments of vegetables or meat, fragile pancakes of millet meal or wheat flour, are cooked in no more than a few moments. Supplies of boiled rice, which reheats well (or could be eaten cold) would perhaps be brought up from the village every two or three days.

It is possible that noodles were also a development of the peasant kitchen, though there is no evidence either way. But at least until the sixteenth century they were regarded as coarse and vulgar food, not acceptable to refined palates.[15]

* By the fourth century B.C., they were so well entrenched as to become an element in philosophical debate. The *Tao te ching*, the most important work of the Taoist school of thinkers, argued that the Five Flavors actually ruined the sense of taste—because using any sense to the full would finally dull it.[13]

THE   SOYBEAN

Just as stir-fry cooking means "Chinese" in the West today, so too does soy sauce, now made from the bean *Glycine max*,* although northern China probably made similar sauces from other kinds of bean long before the *Glycine max* variety was introduced from the south during the second century B.C.

To make the sauce, the beans are simmered and reduced to a purée, after which the "milk" is strained off. This, when boiled, throws a sediment that can be dried to make the bland, digestible and nourishing bean curd which, eaten with cabbage, remains as fundamental to Chinese home cooking as sausage-and-mash used to be to English. The drained purée is shaped into loaves and carefully put away for the winter to ferment in a cool, dark place. Afterward, the fungoid coating which develops is scraped off and the loaves are soaked in brine for a few weeks. The briny liquid, when strained, is soy sauce, and the debris of the loaves is made into a thick, flavorful "cheese" (now partially blamed for the high incidence of stomach cancer in Asia).[17]

The soy bean, all in all, is a remarkably versatile food. As well as "milk," curd, sauce and "cheese," it yields an oil which can be used in cooking, can be converted into a flour with an unusually high protein and low carbohydrate content, and can also (like many other beans and peas) be left to germinate in the dark for a week, when it produces the crisp little sprouts so much used in Chinese cooking.

IMPORTED   DELICACIES

Despite the centuries of disruption which succeeded the fall of the Han dynasty, trade with Persia and the outward-looking atti-

---

* The common name of soy is, confusingly, a Japanese corruption of the Cantonese expression for "salted beans." [16] Possibly, this variety of bean responded particularly well to preservation by salting; possibly, "salted beans" is merely descriptive of any briny bean sauce.

A merchant caravan leaving one of the walled settlements on the Silk Road.

tude of India during the age of the Guptas combined to sustain, in China, an awareness of the world beyond her frontiers. When the T'ang dynasty came to power in the early seventh century A.D., she began to take a more active part in the trade of that world.

When the warlike Turkish nomads of the steppes became, for a short period, allies of the new empire, China's two capitals, Ch'ang-an and Lo-yang, responded by whole-heartedly adopting Turkish fashions. They invested in Turkish-Chinese dictionaries, wore Turkish clothes, set up elegant sky-blue tents in the heart of the city. The emperor's son even camped in the grounds of the imperial palace, and with his own sword hacked off slices of boiled mutton for his dinner.[18]

More refined foods were also adopted from foreign parts, little cakes fried in oil becoming particularly popular. The recipes for these (even the cooks themselves) may have come from India, as did the "light and high" wheat-paste which was steamed in baskets.[19] The latter may have been a raised bread—and it is interesting that the Chinese still steam bread today (baking ovens being wasteful of fuel). Wine was imported from the Tarim basin, that fertile oasis toward the western end of the Silk Road, as were cuttings of a wine vine destined to be planted in the imperial park. The king of Nepal sent some spinach plants, a "vinegar leaf vegetable," and what appears to have been garden celery. There were kohlrabi, which came from Europe by way of the Silk Road, and pistachio nuts brought from Persia. Indian pepper was not as essential in T'ang China as in imperial Rome

—the Chinese had their own milder variety, called *fagara*—but seems to have been almost as expensive. "Stone honey" was another imported luxury. This was the juice of sugarcane boiled and then dried in the sun. The whitest sugar loaves came from Bokhara, where careful skimming of the liquid and the addition of milk contributed to the snowy beauty of the finished product.

THE FOOD OF THE POOR

As in all societies, there was a world of difference between the food of the rich and that of the poor. Most of China's population would never even hear of, far less see or taste, the "brahmin bread" or the "Western plate" meat dishes for which Indian black pepper was the required seasoning. Nor would they sit at leisure around the mat, dining off a morsel of this and a fragment of that. They ate, probably, in the manner of the Japanese carpenters who appeared so extraordinary to Sei Shonagon, the great court lady of eleventh-century Kyoto. "The moment the food was brought, they fell on the soup bowls and gulped down the contents. Then they pushed the bowls aside and polished off all the vegetables. I was wondering whether they were going to leave their rice; a second later there wasn't a grain left in their bowls. They all behaved in exactly the same way and I suppose this must be the nature of carpenters." [20] It was the nature of the hungry peasant, in Japan as in China, never entirely sure when his next meal would appear. The poor man's bean curd soup or bowl of rice is a recurring symbol in literary sources, sometimes as a reflection of poverty, sometimes as a factor in the virtuous simple life. But what did the poor build on these foundations? Throughout China, they certainly made use of any available vegetable materials— onions, bamboo shoots, and beans in particular—and probably dressed them with soy sauce. Fish was of the greatest importance —sturgeon, bream or tench—and it seems likely that the large fat carp, which thrives in muddy water and can be fed on kitchen refuse, may have been domesticated at an early date.[21]

Vegetables and fish were usually lightly cooked, sometimes not cooked at all. The eighth-century Buddhist traveler I-ching preferred Indian food to that of his native China because there, he complained, "people of the present time eat fish and vegetables mostly uncooked." [22] Learned doctors inveighed against this habit, pointing out that a number of diseases arose "because raw or cold things have been eaten, or greasy food, or uncooked fish soaked in wine." [23] Learned doctors, however, did not have to worry about where the fuel for tomorrow's rice was coming from. But even those who ate raw fish probably ensured that, when they had meat (synonymous with pork), they also had enough fuel to cook it. Simple observation must have established the dangers of undercooked pork at a very early period.

In different parts of the country there were local foods which sometimes found their way to the imperial kitchens in the form of tribute. Since regional specialities often grow out of superfluity, it is possible that what was regarded as a rare delicacy in Ch'ang-an was so commonplace in its native village that even the poor could eat it frequently.

There was a wide range of these local dishes, for China has great diversity of climate and vegetation. Indeed, the history of Chinese food is much complicated by the fact that what is now called "China" originally had—and to some extent still has—at least three separate cultures. The first of these was in the crowded north—according to the T'ang census of A.D. 754, about seventy-five per cent of the total population of China lived north of the Yangtse river.[24] Ch'ang-an had two million inhabitants, and more than twenty-five other towns well over half a million.[25] The

A Chinese kitchen during the T'ang period.

peasants of the north may have been able to enjoy Venus clams, the "sugar crabs" of the Yangtse river, the dried flesh of the "white flower snake" (a type of viper found in Hupei), and the cherries and pickled melons of Shensi.

To the south, the people were closer to southeast Asia than to heartland China. Only as late as the last two centuries B.C. did the Han empire begin to colonize the south, and for a long time the colonists remained isolated in a strange land. There, however, rice was plentiful, and there were frogs and dried oysters to lend it savor.

To the west, in the enclosed valleys of Szechuan and the mountains of Yunnan, the people were different again, independent, self-sufficient, often cut off from the rest of the country. There was a dash of nomad in their ancestry as well as in their food. When Marco Polo passed through Yunnan in the thirteenth century, he found that they ate their mutton, beef, buffalo and poultry raw. "The poorer sort go to the shambles and take the raw liver as soon as it is drawn from the beasts; then they chop it up small, put it in garlic sauce and eat it there and then. And they do likewise with every other kind of flesh. The gentry also eat their meat raw." [26] In view of Marco's occasionally indiscriminate use of "Tartar" as a synonym for "Chinese," it is arguable that the modern *steak tartare* may have had its origins in Yunnan.

MARCO POLO'S CHINA

The Hangchow of Marco's day was a teeming, cosmopolitan city, a jewel set among rivers and lakes, outlined against a background of strangely shaped mountains and deeply cleft valleys—the land-scape of the great Sung painters. This Chinese Venice was visited by innumerable ships bringing spices from the Indies and carrying away silks for the Levant. There were Arab merchants there, and Persians, and Christians; the shops overflowed with precious goods and transactions were carried out with paper money—unheard of in Marco's native Italy.

To feed all these hurrying people there were restaurants, hotels, taverns and tea houses, each with its own specialty. Famous restaurateurs went each morning to market for the materials for their renowned iced delicacies, their honey fritters, or fish soups.

The sweetmeat vendor who sold cakes and candied fruits from his bamboo stall.

The fish market was an impressive sight. Every day "a vast quantity of fish is brought upstream from the ocean, a distance of twenty-five miles. There is also abundance of lake fish, varying in kind according to the season, which affords constant occupation for fishermen." Marco Polo thought it worth noting that these fishermen were full-time professionals. So many fish were on sale at the market that "you would imagine that they could never be disposed of. But in a few hours the whole lot has been cleared away." * 27

* It should be remembered that Marco Polo was no open-mouthed backwoodsman, awestruck at his first sight of a great town. Far from it. He had come from the busiest and most cosmopolitan city in the Western world—Venice.

At the Cat Bridge, Wei-the-Big-Knife was famous for his cooked pork. Between 1 A.M. and dawn he had probably paid a visit to the main pork market off the Imperial Way where hundreds of pigs were slaughtered every day. Other eating-house keepers, too, would go to one of the ten principal markets of Hangchow for the silkworms or shrimps from which they made pies to serve with their drinks, or the oysters, mussels or bean curd sold to the poorer classes. There were even short-order restaurants for customers in a hurry, which served quickly-cooked snacks, probably of the *chia-tzu* ("wrapling") or "spring roll" type—little packages of thin dough stuffed with a savory mixture of vegetables and soy sauce.

The residents of Hangchow were gourmets as far as rice was concerned. Rich families had their own specially selected varieties imported daily into the city. It is difficult for Westerners to appreciate the infinite subtleties of rice in Asia, where it plays a central rather than a supplementary role. China had, among other types, pink rice, white rice, yellow rice, mature rice, and winter rice. All had their own characteristics, and many had a quite individual, almost flower-like fragrance. The Chinese custom of serving rice and other foods all in separate bowls made it possible for fine rice to be savored as it deserved to be.

Rice, vegetables and pork were the mainstays of Chinese cooking, although the economical peoples of the countryside, like the French of later times, made use of all possible edible materials—among them "brushwood eels" (snakes), "brushwood shrimps" (grasshoppers), and "household deer" (rats). But European travelers constantly exclaimed over the quality of the best Chinese foodstuffs. Friar Odoric de Pordenone—a fourteenth-century visitor—was dazzled by cheap ginger and plump geese. "Here you can buy three hundred pounds of fresh ginger for less than a groat! The geese too are bigger and finer and cheaper than anywhere in the world. For one of them is as big as two of ours, and 'tis all white as milk . . . And these geese are as fat as fat can be, yet one of them well dressed and seasoned you shall have there [in Canton] for less than a groat." [28]

The people of Hangchow ate three meals a day, one at dawn, one at noon, and one at sunset. Their total rice intake is said to have worked out at the almost incredible average of 37 ounces per head per day.[29] Not all of this, of course, was consumed in whole-grain form. Some of it must have gone into the various dishes which used rice flour, and much probably also went to make rice wine, of which fifty-four different varieties were recorded in Marco Polo's time.

For important banquets, Chinese hosts would call in a professional caterer, few households being equipped to produce the numerous dishes required. Friar Odoric reported that, in Honan, anyone who wished to give a dinner to his friends went to "one of the hostels which are established for this very purpose, and saith to the host thereof: 'Make me a dinner for such a number of my friends, and I propose to expend such and such a sum upon it.' Then the host does exactly as ordered, and the guests are better served than they would have been in the entertainer's own house." [30]

A grand banquet in thirteenth-century China probably consisted of about forty dishes of stir-fried, grilled, and roasted meat or seafood; the same number of fruits and sweetmeats; half that number of vegetable dishes; close on a dozen rice dishes, differently prepared and flavored; up to thirty pungent variations on dried fish; and a wide choice of refreshing drinks which performed the same function as the sorbets of later French entertainments —cooling the palate and reviving the appetite between courses. The National Palace Museum of Taiwan has recently tarnished this luxurious image a little by alleging that much of the food served at imperial banquets not only remained uneaten at the end, but was not fit to eat in the first place. Many of the dishes were apparently stale leftovers, set before the guests in order to keep up appearances.[31] (Probably, they were placed well out of reach.) Diners would not, in any case, expect to sample almost one hundred and fifty offerings. Then, as now, the Chinese meal consisted of a number of different dishes designed to ensure that each guest would find at least something to enjoy. Until the nineteenth century, the same civilized custom was followed at European tables, where, though one course might consist of a dozen dishes, only the most gluttonous diner would try some of everything.

9.

India

When the Aryans arrived in India in the second millennium B.C., they brought their own cattle with them, but these were gradually superseded by the breed native to India and better adapted to the climate.

Tropical cattle, however, gave less (though creamier) milk than the *primigenius* type, and as the indigenous peoples of India adopted dairy products with enthusiasm, there probably came a time when too many consumers were chasing too few supplies.

It seems clear that, as the Aryans spread over the country, they found it advisable to guard the cow with the fullest protection of religious law. Even as early as the *Rig-veda*, the text which relates to the first period of the Aryans in India, goat, horse, sheep and buffalo are all mentioned as food, but only *barren* cows.[1] A fertile cow's milk, like a fertile hen's eggs, can feed more people than its carcass. By about 1000 B.C., the *Atharva-veda* was declaring that to eat meat was to commit an offense against one's forefathers.[2] Even barren cows were now forbidden. They were to be given away to mendicant brahmins, the priests of the Aryan hierarchy.

As time passed, the law against cattle slaughter began to relax (as such laws so often do) and by about 700 B.C. it was generally accepted that cattle could be killed to meet the laws of hospitality, or in sacrifice to the gods and spirits.[3] Soon, however, the brahmin priests were demanding more and more cattle from their local communities for ritual sacrifice. The drain on the farmer's valuable draft and milk animals became intolerable and, partly in revolt against these impositions,[4] two new religious leaders arose —the Buddha and Mahavira.

THE PRINCIPLE OF VEGETARIANISM

Both the Buddha and Mahavira founded sects which were opposed to the Aryan divisions of caste, to violence, and to animal slaughter. The Buddha contented himself, in the latter case, with advising his followers not to permit animals to be specially killed for them, but Mahavira forbade his disciples (the Jains) to eat even fruit or vegetables without first making sure that they contained not even an insect. This was the product neither of fastidiousness nor of a sentimental belief in kindness to animals, but of an opposition to ritual sacrifice and to caste (with its pre-ordained social exclusiveness) which was given constructive shape in the doctrine of transmigration of souls.

This highly sophisticated idea, which may have had its seeds in the early resurrection myths, holds that, when a living thing dies, if it has lived its life well its soul is afterward reincarnated at a higher level; if badly, at a lower one. Even the lowest of men, therefore, may by virtuous living during a number of incarnations rise to the highest level, and then achieve the paradise of release from the cycle of rebirth. Even an insect, therefore, is inhabited by what may have been, and may again become, a human soul.*

Buddhism and Jainism thus gave religious sanction to a vegetarian diet. Coincidentally, they also restated the old prohibition on cow killing. So influential was their anti-slaughter campaign that by the first century B.C. even the brahmin priests of the orthodox *vedic* faith had come around to prescribing rituals which involved no animal sacrifice. All three of India's major religions —that of the *Vedas*, Buddhism, and Jainism—now agreed either directly or by implication that the cow was sacred.

Vegetarianism in India was often a matter of necessity, only sometimes an expression of virtue. Even if religion had not been involved, there would, in the countryside, have been a natural reluctance to kill the large and productive cow for food.

* A somewhat similar doctrine was being preached at much the same time, if for different reasons, by the followers of Pythagoras in Classical Greece.

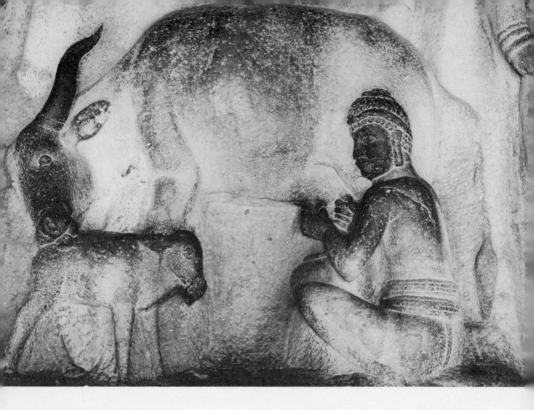

Cows and cowherds were under the protection of the Hindu god Krishna.

Some communities kept goats as meat animals, but not sheep—which were unrewarding in tropical areas—and not pigs, which, although known and eaten at the time of the Indus valley civilization, seem in the main to have disappeared from the Indian diet soon afterward. Throughout most of the subcontinent, therefore, the only protein food which occasionally interrupted the vegetarian routine of the peasant table was that of the hen, or, in areas around the coasts, fish and seafood.

As an expression of virtue, vegetarianism flourished in the northern areas, where Buddhism and Jainism held strongest sway. But it also became important in south India through the agency of the brahmins. By the time these priests laid the heavy hand of orthodoxy on the south, they themselves had adopted vegetarianism. Toward the end of the first millennium A.D., when this came about, the south was thus introduced not only to a matured faith but to a faith which equated vegetarianism with a meritorious life. Perhaps because of this, south Indian vegetarian cooking can still be counted today among the world's most distinguished cuisines.

THE SACRED COW

Even in the cities and princely courts, where religious prohibitions had less real force than in the countryside, the cow continued to be protected. The rich had many other kinds of meat—products of the hunt, strong or delicate—but no other animal could provide the dairy products which had become so essential to Indian cooking. Tropical goats gave very little milk, and although buffalo milk might well have been used, the higher castes then, as now, probably had an aversion to the rich, greenish liquid with its highly distinctive flavor.

The cow's sacredness did, however, continue to move in cycles. The original, and basically practical, Aryan commandment had been restated by the Buddhist and Jain religions. When, in the natural course of time, these pressures began to lose some of their force, they were reimposed by the fundamentally secular demands of territorial expansion in about the fifth century A.D. New lands were being settled, and groups of pioneers were sent out equipped with the necessities of life and accompanied by a handful of cattle and a brahmin advisor who knew all about the calendar, the mysteries of planting, the techniques of sowing, and the breeding of cattle. Cattle were so few in relation to the stretches of territory involved, and conditions frequently so difficult, that it was necessary once again to place an absolute ban on cow slaughter. Wherever the brahmin went—and he went everywhere as large parts of the country were opened up—the cow's sacredness was emphasized.

The Muslim invasion of India in the Middle Ages (a conquest by foreigners whose religion permitted them to eat beef) helped to crystallize and confirm the Hindus' own attitude toward the cow, and the Muslim conquest was followed by that of another beef-eating people, the British. In 1857, the British were to precipitate an explosion in northern India by disregarding the strength of Hindu feeling on the subject of the cow; with rare genius, they also succeeded in alienating the Muslim inhabitants of the country.

The occasion was the introduction of the new Enfield rifle, whose cartridges, partially coated with grease, had to be bitten open before loading. Soon the rumor flew through the ranks of the Indian sepoys that the grease was either beef or pork fat. For a caste Hindu to bite on the fat of the sacred cow was an inconceivable sin; * to a Muslim, the fat of the unclean pig was insufferable pollution. The men's British officers denied the rumor, "but nothing was easier than for the men belonging to the regiments quartered near Calcutta to ascertain . . . that the assurances of their officers were not in accordance with facts." [5] Though a deep social unease had made the Indian Mutiny inevitable, it was the matter of the greased cartridges which set it in motion.

DAIRY PRODUCTS

A very fair picture of the important elements in the Indian diet is given in the *Puranas*, or "Ancient Stories," a curious compilation of legend, religious instruction, and obscure geographical information dating from somewhere in the early centuries of the present era.

The human world, it was said, formed a series of concentric circles around Mount Meru—a succession of ring-like continents separated from one another by seven oceans. The ocean immediately surrounding Mount Meru was composed of salt; the next of *jaggeri*, a very coarse, sticky, dark brown sugar; the third of wine; the fourth of *ghi* (boiled and clarified butter); the fifth of milk; the sixth of curds; and the seventh of fresh water.†

Of these seven magical oceans, representing the staple needs of mankind in India (other than grain), no less than three were of dairy products. *Ghi* was the essential cooking medium, although

* Many sepoys in the Bengal Army were brahmins, i.e., of the highest caste. If they were guilty of sacrilege, it meant they would have to struggle, again, through many lifetimes, before they once more came in sight of release from the cycle of rebirth.

† This picturesque view of the world was to appear highly comical to later Western minds. Nevertheless, when the nineteenth-century English explorer John Hanning Speke first discovered the sources of the Nile, he took with him a map drawn by a fellow officer according to geographical information in the *Puranas,* and found that it showed local names in the interior of Africa with startling accuracy. [6]

Curds seller in an Indian market.

the poor had to make do with oil from sesamum or mustardseed, and the very poor with that of the safflower. Milk, though sometimes used fresh, was more often boiled until it reached a thick consistency, when it was used to make a gruel with whole grain or toasted barley meal. Curds, one of the most popular of all foods, had a slight tartness which was very refreshing in a hot climate; the curdling process was often hastened by adding to the milk pieces of a creeper called *putika* or of the bark of the *palas* (gold mohur) tree.[7]

As the cow became progressively more sacred, its products began to assume more than their face value. The higher castes of Indian society went in ever-present danger of ritual pollution, and here, *ghi* came to the rescue. Anything cooked in it was automatically purified.

HYGIENE

By the middle of the first millennium B.C., religious laws had begun to list a discouraging large number of "impure" items of diet—so many, in fact, that rigid adherence to the laws would have been almost impossible for the poorer peasant. (And it must be remembered that the high-caste brahmin, extremely sensitive to threats of pollution, could be just as poor in financial terms as the lowest of outcaste sudras.) It was therefore accepted that the defiled section could be removed from a prepared dish, and the remainder purified by sprinkling it with water or pouring curds or *ghi* over it.

"Unclean food" included meat which had been cut with a sword, dog meat, human meat, the meat of carnivorous animals, of locusts, camels, and hairless or excessively hairy animals. Rice which had turned sour through being left to stand overnight, readymade food from the market, dishes which had been sullied by insects or mice, or sniffed at by a dog, cat, or human were all regarded as unfit for eating.[8]

By the last century B.C., market regulations specifically forbade traders to sell the meat of an animal that had died of natural causes. Only specially slaughtered meat, freshly killed, was to be offered to carnivorous customers.[9]

Although most of these edicts carried the weight of religious sanction, they were fundamentally laws of simple hygiene and, as such, reflected conclusions which had also been reached in other countries. A first-century A.D. Chinese physician said: "If rats have run over rice baskets, throw it all away and don't eat it," [10] and in the following century another warned against eating the meat of animals which had died spontaneously.[11] The general Chinese corrective for doubtful food appears to have been cooking, or re-cooking—rather more effective remedies than sprinkling with water or clarified butter. However, faith has probably saved as many lives through the centuries as hygiene, and it is in fact possible for the human system to tolerate a surprising number of bacteria once it is accustomed to them.

Preoccupation with hygiene in India extended to plates and dishes as well as to the food itself. If someone ate from an earthenware dish, the laws stated that it had to be broken afterward so that it could not be used again. Most Indians avoided the issue by using thick, unabsorbent leaves for plates. A tenth-century Arab merchant who visited the country reported that it was the custom for princes and nobles to have placed before them each day "tables made with interlaced leaves of the coconut palm; with these same leaves they make kinds of plates and dishes. At mealtime the food is served on these interlaced leaves and, when the meal is finished, the tables and leaf plates are thrown into the water with whatever may remain of the food. They disdain to have the same things served up the next day." [12]

FOOD AND COOKING

In the early centuries of the first millennium A.D. Indians apparently ate two meals a day. They were advised that each meal should consist of thirty-two mouthfuls, and recommended to visualize their stomach as divided into four separate parts. The aim should be to fill two of these parts with food, one with liquid, and to leave the fourth part empty to allow for the movement of wind.[13]

It was a wife's task to prepare her husband's food and serve it to him; she herself ate later. Seated cross-legged on a stool, the

Dining off leaf plates.

man of the house might first be offered an appetizer of one or two pieces of ginger and some salt. After this came boiled rice and bean soup and hot butter sauce, then cakes with *ghi* and fruit, and finally a piece of sugarcane to chew. If he were very poor, he would eat stale boiled rice with half-cooked gourds or other vegetables, or a grain porridge mixed with plenty of mustard stalk, washing it down with an alkaline liquid which reputedly tasted like the water from a salt mine [14] (it may have been the half-fermented water in which rice had been boiled). If he were comfortably rich, he would have golden broth, shining white rice, curries, savory meat dishes, curds, milk rice, sweets, and water perfumed with camphor imported from Borneo.

As in China, the daily diet really depended on the part of the country in which a man lived.

Wheat and barley could be grown in winter in the south, and at almost any time of the year in the cooler parts of the north. In plains where there was natural or artificial irrigation, rice was a standard crop; in the drier areas there was millet. Gourds, peas, beans and lentils were to be found throughout the country, as were sesamum and sugarcane. Pepper, cardamom, and ginger were sent all over India from the southern plantations and entrepôts, and fruits such as the mango, the banana-like plantain, and the pod-bearing tamarind—sharp-flavored and refreshing—were widely grown.

But a list of raw materials gives little idea of Indian food, for India has almost as great a diversity of regions as Europe. To talk of "Indian food" is as inappropriate as to talk of "European food"; to link Punjabi *haute cuisine* with the diet of the Naga hills as incongruous as to bracket the food of Paris with that of an Albanian village. The raw materials may have something in common but the finished products are worlds apart.

On the Malabar and Coromandel coasts during the first millennium A.D., Indian food was subject to many outside influences. Malabar was the spice country, in trade with the Arab world and Rome. Coromandel faced east to the islands of Asia and, through them, to contacts with China. To increase the repertoire of spices already used in south Indian cooking, nutmeg, mace and cloves were imported from the Indonesian archipelago during the early part of this period, while coriander and cumin were introduced from the eastern Mediterranean through the agency of the Arabs. Rice, spices, vegetables and fish were the foundations of south Indian cooking.

In northwestern India, the effects of foreign contact were more profound. Through the passes of the Hindu Kush had come, over a period of two thousand years, a succession of invasions and infiltrations—of ideas, attitudes and techniques—Aryan, Persian, Greek, and Central Asian. These were absorbed into the heritage of the Indus valley civilization to produce a culture which was a strange, but not unharmonious, mixture. Because the land was fertile and many of the foreign influences nomadic, meat was more commonly eaten here than anywhere else in India.

"Made" dishes formed only part of an Indian meal, often a comparatively minor part. A surviving menu for a royal banquet given at the end of the first millennium A.D. shows clearly how much more varied (and refreshing) was Indian food than that either of China or Europe. The Chinese scarcely used dairy products; Europeans were highly suspicious of fruit. But in India great use was made of both.

King Srenika's banquet began with pomegranates, grapes and jujubes. Oranges, perhaps of the sweet variety which had been introduced from China during the first centuries A.D., and mangoes, with their peach-colored flesh and plentiful juice, came next, with finger lengths of tender young sugarcane. Then there were cooked dishes—vegetable or fish mixtures probably, since Srenika appears to have ruled in the south. At a northern banquet, there would have been *kosali*, delicate mouthfuls of spiced roast meat rolled first in a purée of raw meat and then in rice, and cooked briskly over the fire,[15] or *mandaliya*, a kind of sausage made from entrails stuffed with spices and marrow and then roasted on charcoal.[16] After the cooked dishes there were sweet cakes, then spicy boiled rice, then a light soup to refresh the palate. At this stage the plates were removed and the royal hands washed. Perfumed dishes of curds followed, and the royal hands were washed once more. The final course was a rich liquor made from milk thickened by boiling, then sweetened with sugar and honey and tinted golden with saffron.[17]

CURRY

The true Indian curry bears very little resemblance to the parodies of it so frequently served in the West today. For Indians, curry is a sauce designed to add relish to rice or the pliable wheaten pancakes known as *chapatis*. A little of it goes—and is meant to go—a long way. A single *brinjal* (aubergine, or eggplant), with a couple of onions or a handful of lentils (*dal*), would be cooked in a little *ghi* or vegetable oil, flavored with spices (among them cardamom, coriander, cumin and turmeric for a mild blend, white pepper and mustardseed for a hot one *), and diluted with coconut milk or the soured-milk product *dahi*, to make a traditional curry which, with rice and *chapatis*, provided a substantial meal for several people.

Although quite a number of generalized recipes for early Indian food are known, and although at least one work even specifies quantities, it remains difficult to identify the true nature of the cuisine. Working from the *Code of Manu*, a compilation of laws dated to about the first century A.D. and relating to a small district in the area of modern Bangladesh, scholars have calculated today's equivalents for such measures as the *prastha* and the *pala*.[18] Unfortunately, when these equivalents are applied to slightly earlier recipes from the same region, the results are alarming. One recipe for a curry to accompany rice seems to require 27 ounces *each* of meat and spices, which are to be mixed with insignificant quantities of fat, salt and sugar, and a mere 10½ ounces of curds.† [19]

The original south Indian *kari*, from which the word "curry" is derived,[20] seems to have been of a fairly liquid consistency; when Europeans first encountered it they usually described it as a broth or soup, poured over the rice. There were other types, however, with other names; some were like a spicy stew of vegetables, fish or meat, some drier still almost as if the ingredients had been grilled.

---

* Only in the sixteenth century were chili peppers and cayenne introduced to India from their native tropical America. These are the searing ingredients that give character to hot curries today.

† Possibly the *dharana*, the measure used for spices, was as variable in practice as the southeast Asian catty.

With their rice, ordinary peasants would have one curry. The rich had several, liquid ones first, dry ones last. With spices freshly ground, individually blended, their flavors amalgamated and smoothed out by the addition of coconut milk or *dahi*, it was possible to produce a very wide range of different sauces to ring the changes on the basic grain foods of India.

DRINKS

The most common drinks in India in the first millennium A.D. were water, milk, and whey, but mango syrup and lime juice were readily available in many parts of the country, and there was a wide range of fermented liquors. Grape wine, imported first from Rome and later from Kapisi, north of Kabul, was a luxury only kings could afford, but lesser men made stimulating drinks from "sugarcane juice, jaggeri, honey, molasses, the juice of the rose-apple, and the juice of the breadfruit, infused with a decoction of *mesasringi* [the bark of a tree] and long pepper, kept for one month, six months or a year [and then] mixed with two types of cucumber, sugarcane stalk, mango fruit, and myrobalan [21] [an astringent fruit which, according to the Chinese pharmacologist Su-kung, produced a notably "hot" liquor [22]]."

Rice beers were also made. Toddy and arrack were fermented from the sap of the palmyra and talipot palms. And there was a special ceremonial brew—which may, or may not have been intoxicating—made from sugar, *ghi*, curds, herbs and honey. This was given to guests, to suitors about to ask for a young woman's hand in marriage, and to women who were five months pregnant. It was also used to moisten the lips of a newly born first son. The name for this drink was *madhuparka*.

HONEY AND SUGAR

The first syllables of *madhuparka* mean "honey," and it is possible that knowledge of honey was first brought to India by the Aryan invaders. There is, in fact, a universality about Eurasian words relating to honey that suggests that honey-collecting techniques, familiar in the Near East since prehistoric times, were diffused throughout the landmass by one group of tribes or peoples. The Sanskrit word *madhu* and the Chinese word *myit* are related to the *mit* of the Indo-Europeans (Aryans),[23] the *medhu* of the Slavs, and the *mead* of the English.[24]

Until the end of the Middle Ages, honey was everywhere the sweetener *par excellence*, although some countries used date syrup, others fig syrup, still others grape juice. Clearly these were alternatives and were recognzed as such. The *Arthasastra*, for example, defines honey as "that made by bees and the juice of grapes."[25]

Honey was originally collected by smoking bees from their nests, a method illustrated in Egyptian tomb reliefs of the third millennium B.C. but certainly dating back to very much earlier times. Having discovered the pleasant flavor and energy-giving properties of the sweet, clear syrup, man soon found that it had other virtues. Honey is almost pure sugar, and ferments very readily. If the debris of a honeycomb were left neglected in water

Honey collecting
in the Stone Age.

for a few days—perhaps to soak out the last drops of syrup—the result would be a delicious and mildly intoxicating liquid. Honey ale—generally known as mead—was to be popular for thousands of years, particularly in countries where the grape did not grow and grain was not widely cultivated. In England, mead did not lose its hold until the monasteries—where bees were kept for their wax (used to make votive candles) and the honey was only a commercially valuable byproduct—were dissolved in the sixteenth century.

But in India, honey was valued for its flavor rather than its sweetening properties. Sugarcane had been introduced early into the subcontinent, and was of considerable importance by the fifth century B.C., perhaps before. It spread westward very slowly. Though the Greek geographer Strabo reported that in 325 B.C. an admiral on the staff of Alexander the Great had mentioned Indian reeds "that produce honey, although there are no bees," [26] sugar remained a rarity in Europe, imported only in its processed form for use in medicine. It was not until the eighth century A.D., when Islamic rule spread along the Mediterranean, that cultivation of sugarcane began on the shores of North Africa, in Sicily and in Spain, and another eight centuries were to pass before sugar became at all common in Europe.

10.
*The Arab
World*

While the T'ang ruled in China and the Rashtrakutas in India, the Arabs sallied out from the desert lands which had so long contained them and tore great areas of the Near East and Mediterranean from the grasp of Persia and Byzantium. For centuries, Arabs and Byzantines were to fight for economic control of the Mediterranean, and the Arabs often emerged victorious. When, in the seventh century A.D., they diverted Egyptian wheat from Byzantium to the holy cities of Islam, Byzantine administrators took their custom north to the Balkans and southern Russia.[1] When a Byzantine economic blockade placed sentence of death on the old Syrian and Egyptian trade route to the East, the Arabs moved their capital from Damascus in Syria to Baghdad in Mesopotamia.[2] Baghdad became the great entrepôt for Asian wares.

BYZANTINE FOOD

The emperors of Byzantium and the caliphs of Baghdad, despite their continuing animosity, had at least one problem in common —the varied nature of the peoples they ruled. When the Roman empire was finally split into western and eastern halves in A.D. 395, the eastern emperor, based in Constantinople (later Byzantium), had bequeathed to his confrère in the west the hungry and demanding plebs of Rome, who had been an even greater drain on the economy than the gluttonous rich.

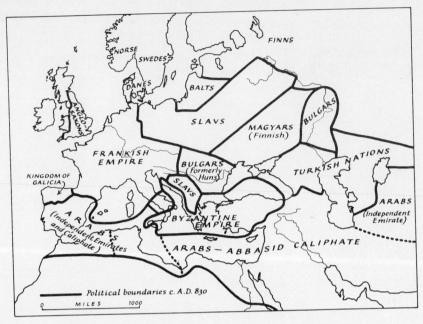

4. SPHERES OF INFLUENCE IN THE WEST, C. A.D. 830

In Byzantium he ruled instead a populace much more capable of fending for itself, both socially and gastronomically. Greeks and Jews, Armenians, Syrians, Macedonians and Italians jealously guarded their own ways of life as well as their traditional cooking styles in face of the Roman cuisine imported by the rulers from the west. Indeed, as the centuries passed, many of the complex Roman dishes favored by the upper ranks of Byzantine society took on—as did society itself—an increasingly eastern tinge. The fermented fish sauces of Classical times were still in favor, as were the hams, game birds, and variety meats of the past, but the Near Eastern and Greek fondness for oil, lavishly used, soon began to transform the cuisine.

That the cooking of Byzantium had diverged greatly from that of Italy by the tenth century is clear from the brief but venomous description left by Liutprand, bishop of Cremona, who was offered at the table of the Byzantine emperor Nicephorus Phocas food which he described as "foul and stinking . . . soused in oil like a drunkard's mess and sprinkled with some horrible fishy liquid." * [3] Liutprand was hardly an unprejudiced witness, but it is apparent

* Liquamen?

that his dislike of the food stemmed as much from its unfamiliarity as from his own rancorous dislike of all things Byzantine.

THE COURT OF THE CALIPHS

In all probability, the bishop would have been just as revolted by the food of Baghdad, redolent of mutton fat and combining, with a fine free hand, meat and fruit, nuts, vegetables and poached eggs, all in a single dish.

The Arabs, who had once lived on mutton and barley, dates and sheep's milk, discovered that, in Baghdad, there was no place for the spare austerity which had characterized life in the desert. Surrounded by the luxurious debris of the Persian empire, they

A banquet for the desert Arab. A camel is slaughtered by ritual throat-cutting, and drained of blood. In the foreground, the cook fills a platter which is then carried off by a servant.

appreciated what they found and adapted it to their own needs and instincts. Baghdad became a symbol of power and riches.

The banquets given at the court of the caliphs were renowned not only for the extravagance of the dishes but for the poetry and gastronomic erudition of the conversation. The tenth-century caliph Mustakfi, for example, gave a banquet at which all the guests were expected to discuss the different varieties of food and the poetry that had been composed about them. One guest recited the verses written by Ibn al-Mu'tazz, describing a tray of *hors d'oeuvre*.

> Here capers grace a sauce vermilion
> Whose fragrant odors to the soul are blown . . .
> Here pungent garlic meets the eager sight
> And whets with savor sharp the appetite,
> While olives turn to shadowed night the day,
> And salted fish in slices rims the tray . . .

The caliph instructed his cooks to prepare all the relishes described while another of the company declaimed some lines by Mahmud ibn al-Husain al-Kushajim.

> First a roasted kid, a yearling,
> With its innards firmly strung,
> And upon it, well to season,
> Tarragon and mint are hung . . .
> Lemons too, with *nadd* [a mixture of perfumes] besprinkled,
> Scented well with ambergris,
> And, for garnishing the slices,
> Shreds of appetizing cheese . . .[4]

Even the most exalted men at court were expected to have a practical as well as a literary acquaintance with cooking. In the golden age of the caliphate, cookbooks were written by princes of the blood as well as by distinguished philosophers, although the earliest known works to have survived cannot be dated before the thirteenth century.[5] On one occasion, the caliph al-Mu'tasim maliciously set all his boon companions to the task of cooking a variety of different dishes which he then required an unwelcome guest to taste and pass judgment on[6]—a challenge which, in the climate of a city where life was held cheap, must have played as much havoc with the guest's nerves as with his digestion.

Self-indulgence, according to the moral tale illustrated in this picture, was epitomized by a meal of roast kid, white bread, and a flask of wine. It ceased to be a sin as the heirs of Islam expanded their wealth and power.

Despite the Koranic prohibition on fermented drinks, the Arab world had its taverns. At lower right, a representation of the vintage—treading the grapes, the juice running out, and the wine being filtered from a leather bottle into a chalice.

ARAB COOKING

According to the *Koran*, that compilation of the words of Muhammad, pork was impure (a characteristically nomad view), animal blood a pollution (a legacy from Old Testament Judaism), and wine an abomination (some of the Prophet's levies had been found drunk and incapable on the eve of battle [7]), but these were minor prohibitions for Arabs faced with a great richness of alternatives.

There were raisins from Jerusalem, olives from Palmyra, apples from Syria. Wheat from Egypt, millet from southern Arabia, rice from the valley of the Jordan. Sheep and goats from Palestine, fish from Shihr, near Aden, and pigeons from special fattening towers everywhere. There were also spices in quantity, many of them from Asia, and rose gardens in many areas to provide the rose water Arabs loved to use in cooking.

In the kitchen, Arabs remained nomadically prodigal with meat. The tenderer parts were cooked in slices or chunks, the tougher ones finely chopped for meatballs. Even the most complicated dishes were cooked in a single pot. Many examples of one-pot cooking are given in a thirteenth-century work written by an upper middle-class gourmet named Muhammad ibn al-Hasan ibn Muhammad ibn al-Karim al-Katib al-Baghdadi—known for brevity's sake as "al-Baghdadi." Among what he chose to call "simple dishes" was *makhfiya*.

"Cut red meat into thin sliced strips about four fingers long . . . Put the meat into the oil, with a *dirham* [roughly ⅛ ounce] of salt and fine-milled dry coriander, and fry lightly until browned. Then cover with water, adding green coriander leaves, cinnamon bark, a handful of peeled chickpeas, and a handful of onion chopped fine. Boil, and remove the scum. Now mince red meat fine, and make into kebabs [meatballs] with seasonings. Take [hard-]boiled egg, remove the whites, and place the yolks in the middle of the kebabs, and place in the pan. When almost cooked, throw in fine-ground cumin, pepper, mastic, and ginger. Take [additional] eggs and beat well: remove the strips of meat, dip them while still hot in the egg, and return them to the pot. Do this twice or thrice, until the slices have a coating of egg, and finally return them to the pot. When the liquor has all evaporated, sprinkle with a *dirham* of fine-pounded cinnamon, spray with a little rose water, and leave to settle over the fire for an hour." [8]

PERSIAN ORIGINS OF THE CUISINE

The recipes which have survived from the first half of the thirteenth century (before new cooking styles were introduced by the advent of the Mongols) can be assumed to bear some resemblance to the princely cuisine of two or three centuries earlier. Full of spices from India and China, highly complex and time-consuming to prepare, many of them were derived from the court cooking of the caliphs' Persian predecessors.

The Sassanid Persians had been particularly fond of *ahbisa*, which meant any dish with the consistency of a starchy jelly, and from which the modern Turkish Delight, or *Rahat Lokum* (which means "giving rest to the throat"), is clearly descended. They liked, too, sweet-sour sauces. In the Near East, "meat" meant strong, fatty mutton, which benefited greatly from the tang added by the juice of exotic fruits from the oases of Central Asia —pomegranates, apricots and lemons.*

From the Persians, too, the Arabs inherited the custom of using great quantities of powdered almonds, walnuts and pistachio nuts to thicken savory or sweet dishes. This technique, which seems earlier to have filtered through from Persia to Rome, became characteristic of the Arab *haute cuisine* in the great days of the caliphate and was to be carried to western Europe (by the Arabs themselves, as well as by Italian merchants and returning Crusaders), there to become an exotic and then a commonplace feature of the bourgeois table. In tenth-century Baghdad, a dish of meat or poultry and vegetables, such as the popular *harisa*,[9] would be simmered in a liquid thickened during cooking with powdered almonds. By the fourteenth century, the European bourgeoisie, too, was growing fat on rich and appetizing meats bathed in the same creamy almond sauce.

---

* Persian sweet-sour dishes probably resembled those of China and India more than of Classical Rome, for whereas the former used fruit to achieve the required effect, the Romans preferred a mixture of honey and vinegar.

The main asset of the fat-tailed sheep had to be protected from wear and tear.

OTHER INFLUENCES

Despite the princely and Persian heritage, the diet of Baghdad also reflected other legacies. There were dishes of sliced meat cooked according to a recipe from the Caucasus in the north. There were cakes from Egypt, and black truffles from the Arabian desert in the south. There were *couscous*, the steamed grain dish from the Mahgreb, and "Frankish-style" roast lamb, from the west. And *maghmuma*, the ancestor of *moussaka*—a layered dish of mutton, onions, and the aubergines (or eggplants) of tropical Asia—from the east.[10] There were also recipes for rice cooked in milk which strongly suggest Indian origins.

The pastoral peasant society of the Near East contributed the oil in which almost every Baghdad dish was put to cook—*alya*, the fat rendered from the tail of a sheep. Time after time, al-Baghdadi began his instructions with the words: "Cut meat into middling pieces: dissolve tail and throw away the sediment. Put the meat into this oil and let it fry lightly . . ." The popularity of tail fat may have had something to do with the existence of the fat-tailed breed of sheep in this part of the world, though whether as cause or effect is open to question.

The old desert Arab tradition persisted, too, in the constant use of fresh or dried dates, as well as in a few dishes which continued to be popular with the multitude even though they did not appear on the best tables. The nomad origins of *hais*, for example, were betrayed by the fact that in the thirteenth century it was still noted as being excellent food for travelers. In texture, it must have been not unlike the old grain pastes. One pound of dry breadcrumbs was to be kneaded with ¾ pound stoned dates, the same quantity each of almonds and pistachio nuts, and a few spoonfuls of sesame oil. The resulting mixture was shaped into balls and dusted with powdered sugar.[11]

One or two other dishes deriving from the peasant or nomad cuisine featured *laban,* which was probably (as today) a preparation similar to yogurt,[12] and "Persian milk" was another soured product.

THE ARABS AND DIETETIC MEDICINE

Just as the Arab cuisine absorbed recipes from many sources, so the Arab mind was receptive to all the intellectual influences of the known world. Among the many subjects which gripped their interest was that of dietetic medicine, which they studied largely from Greek sources and then transmitted back, in slightly amended form, to a Western world which had forgotten it.

The route by which Classical Greek medicine was carried back to the medieval West was devious. Byzantium, heir to the old Greek learning, had been rent by controversies over Christian dogma, and during the subsequent persecutions a number of learned heretics had been forced to flee to tolerant (if Zoroastrian) Persia.[13] There, at Jundishapur, they met Syrian, Persian and Hindu scholars and, in the interests of science and medicine, translated many important works in Syriac, the new language of learning in the Near East. When Persia fell to the Arabs and the caliphs of Baghdad gave their imprimatur to intellectual curiosity,

An Arab view of Galen supervising the cultivation of medicinal plants. Note the humped cattle, which had spread from India to become common all around the Mediterranean by the sixth century B.C., and the fact that threshing is now done with the aid of an axle fitted with sharp-edged discs.

many works of medicine were translated from Syriac into Arabic
—among them, the vast corpus attributed to Galen.

Meanwhile, at Salerno—located close to the trading ports of
Naples and Amalfi, in a pocket of territory surrounded by Byzantine, Italian and Islamic possessions and open to all the cultural
winds that blew along the Mediterranean—a medical school had
grown up under the aegis of the Benedictine monks of Monte
Cassino. The school was remarkably free from Christian dog-
matism and was noted at an early stage for the eclectic nature of
its teachings.

Late in the eleventh century, there arrived at Salerno a man
who had been born in North Africa and had travelled extensively
in the Near East and India. Known as Constantine the African,
he settled down near the school to devote himself to the translation of great works of learning from Arabic into Latin. The authors he translated included the Greek physician Galen.*

The Greek medicine which was now restored to the Western
world had acquired in its travels a number of Persian and Arabic
glosses, some of them relating to new diseases and drugs which
had been brought to light by the expansion of the known world.
Muslim influence, however, had also injected into it an extra
emphasis on hygiene and diet. This was a product, at least in
part, of Islamic doctrine, which barred the faithful from experiments in dissecting and so deflected Arab research from anatomy
to empirical medicine.

Although Salerno remained un-Muslim enough to dissect pigs
in the anatomy class, and to regard bleeding as a cure-all, it still
adopted Arab dietetics—and agreed, however unwittingly, with
the eleventh-century Chinese physician who maintained: "Experts
at curing diseases are inferior to specialists who warn against diseases. Experts in the use of medicines are inferior to those who
recommend proper diet." [14]

THE SALERNO REGIMEN

At Salerno was developed a Graeco-Arabic-Italian "regimen of
health" which was to be disseminated throughout Europe by re-

---

* The Greek language had lapsed into obscurity in western Europe after the
division of the Roman empire.

turning Crusaders (who visited there to be treated for illness or wounds) and was to form the basis of much of European medicine until almost the end of the sixteenth century.

The Salerno regimen of health was founded on the simple proposition, no less appealing then than now, that it was possible to look younger, live longer, on a balanced diet.

The balance favored by Salerno had nothing whatever to do with the carbohydrates, minerals, protein, fats and vitamins of modern nutrition. Instead it was based on the theory that man and his food contained within themselves the same four elements as made up the cosmos. These—air, fire, water and earth—manifested themselves in the human body in the form of four equivalent "humors"—blood, bile, phlegm, and black bile. Some men, some foods, suffered from excess of one or other of these elements. It was therefore as undesirable for a man of choleric (or fire/bile) temperament to eat "hot" foods as it was for the elderly, who were assumed to suffer from a surplus of water/phlegm, to eat cold or moist foods. The choleric man was advised to stick to cool foods, and the octogenarian to warming ones.

Just as the elderly were assumed always to suffer from an excess of water/phlegm humor, so too were children. Cold, moist fruit was forbidden even to their wet nurses. In that curious composite of myth and medicine which decreed—right up until the nineteenth century—what was to be fed to a baby, the theories of Galen and Salerno merged with beliefs of even greater antiquity. It was generally agreed that children imbibed not only strength, but temperament and morals with their mother's milk. As far back as the first millennium B.C. the Indian *Upanishads* had mentioned that a pregnant woman's diet would affect the *type* of child who would be born, not just its health.[15] In sixteenth-century Florence, careful mothers would not have dreamed of employing a wild Saracen woman to suckle their infants.[16] And even at the beginning of the twentieth century, the authors of a housekeeping manual dedicated to "the English girls to whom fate may assign the task of being house-mothers in our Eastern Empire" felt it necessary to ask what, other than racial prejudice, accounted for fears that "the milk of a native woman should contaminate an English child's character, when that of the beasts . . . is held to have no such power?"[17]

From the modern viewpoint, it was unfortunate that Salerno

Despite dietetic theory, which banned cold, moist fruit for infants, artists continued to show the child Jesus accepting offerings of it. In Christian symbolism, a lemon was not fruit but an emblem of fidelity in love.

should have classified fruit as cold and moist and therefore unsuitable even for the indirect feeding of infants. Mothers who followed such precepts deprived themselves of vitamins which would have done much to give their children a sturdier grip on life.

The scholars of Salerno may have inherited their suspicion of fruit from Galen, who claimed that his father had lived to be a hundred because he never ate it. The prejudice probably arose from the fact that fruit is a food of summer and early autumn, seasons which also bring dysentery in warm climates. Furthermore, fruit eaten in large quantities has, independently, a laxative effect.[18] In Classical times, these facts may have been telescoped so that Galen believed, with reason apparently on his side, that fruit caused the enervating disease of dysentery.

Nevertheless, perhaps because of the intervening Arab glosses, the Salerno regimen did occasionally pay a rather backhanded compliment to fruit—or at least to those fruits which were native to the Near East and Asia.

> Cool damsons are, and good for health, by reason
> They make your entrails soluble and slack,
> Let peaches steep in wine of newest season,
> Nuts hurt the teeth, that with their teeth they crack,
> With every nut 'tis good to eat a raisin.
> For though they hurt the spleen, they help the back.[19]

Salerno's "four humors" were perfectly rational in eleventh-century terms, and were supported by long tradition. In China in the sixth century B.C., Ho the Physician had divided diseases into six classes deriving from excess of one or other of six aspects of *ch'i*[20]—the "breath of life" or "subtle wind"—which was a concept similar to the Greek *pneuma*, and from the layman's point of view just as abstruse.* As time passed, the six elements had been reduced to five—fire, water, earth, wood and metal—

* The confusion it still aroused many centuries later was eloquently demonstrated when a Chinese teacher made the mistake of mentioning to the Reverend Mr. Gilmour (see page 136) that a particular drug was good for treating "inside and outside HEE [*ch'i*]." What, demanded that irrepressible inquirer, was HEE? "Inside HEE," he later reported, "is wind ascending and descending, evidently colic; what outside HEE is I can't discover. After pursuing my teacher over the verge of his knowledge, the old man admitted that he had never seen outside HEE, though he had often suffered from inside HEE."[21]

some of which were classified as yin (cool, moist, contracted, female), and some as yang (hot, expanded, male). Yin and yang were the two most important opposed facets of diet, as of life.

In India by the first century A.D., such medical writers as Caraka had also settled for five as the basic number of elements,[22] but it was the "four humors" theory first propounded by Empedocles in Greece in the fifth century B.C.[23] and later embroidered by Galen which formed the foundation of the Salerno school of medicine.

Even in the early days, the idea of four (or five, or six) humors raised a variety of problems. There was no difficulty in identifying a fire/bile or choleric man. He was hot-tempered, bold, and always hungry. The phlegmatic man, too, was recognizable at a glance—he was solidly built and slothful. But it was not nearly as easy to discriminate between foods, and the Salerno regimen failed to classify all of them.

Throughout the centuries, wherever the humoral doctrine has persisted, so have uncertainties as to which foods are "hot" and which are "cold." The distinction is by no means the simple one that might be drawn by modern nutritionists—that energy-giving foods would be "hot," and astringent or insubstantial ones "cold." In modern India, though meat and strong spices are predictably regarded as hot, butter and honey, wheat flour, rice and sugar are all classified as cold.[24]

It seems probable that, although physicians in Europe did try to follow the rules of Salerno for several hundred years—almost certainly to the detriment of many of their patients—the majority of people simply could not afford to.

> All pears and apples, peaches, milk and cheese,
> Salt meat, red deer, hare, beef and goat: all these
> Are meats that breed ill blood, and melancholy,
> If sick you be, to feed on them were folly.[25]

If all these foods had been dutifully eliminated from the diet, there would have been very little left to eat.

PART FOUR

Europe, A.D. *1000–1500*

INTRODUCTION

The Expansion
of Europe

"The whole of the west and all the barbarians who lived between the Adriatic and the Straits of Gibraltar migrated in a body . . . marching across Europe country by country with all their households . . . Full of enthusiam and ardor they thronged every highway, and with these warriors came a host of civilians, outnumbering the sand of the sea shore or the stars of heaven, carrying palms and bearing crosses on their shoulders." [1] Thus Anna Comnena, daughter of the emperor of Byzantium, described the participants in the First—"the People's"—Crusade.

After the initial victories, the "people" were followed by a vast number of the unemployed sons of the Western nobility, with a rabble of attendant servants and peasants. According to recent estimates, fully half the knights of France set off either for the Levant or for the marginal Islamic territories of northern Spain during the thirty years following 1097.[2]

Even a century earlier, it would have been difficult to conceive of such an enterprise as the Crusades, stimulated as much by population pressure as by Christian zeal or the prospect of loot. But agricultural development north of the Alps had brought a great increase in food supplies, and the result—as so often in history—was a population explosion. In this instance, however, there was an important new element in the equation. More food meant more people, but the agricultural revolution also produced food that gave a better-balanced and healthier diet. In those regions of Europe where the improved system of agriculture had been adopted, the population was not only more numerous but more energetic—dynamic, ripe for action, ideal tools for the aggressive imperialism of the Crusades.

The new system of agriculture also contributed, sometimes indirectly, to a revival of village and of urban life. Formerly, the peasant who worked the land had had no transport other than his own feet or a slow-moving draft animal. Oats, however, were an important crop in the new rotation system, and this was partly responsible for an increased use of the horse—which, in turn, brought a measure of freedom to the peasant. Although the location of towns and outlying villages might continue to conform to the old pattern of a day's walk to market and back,[3] it was now possible to make the journey more quickly, and there-

5. MEDIEVAL EUROPE AND WESTERN ASIA

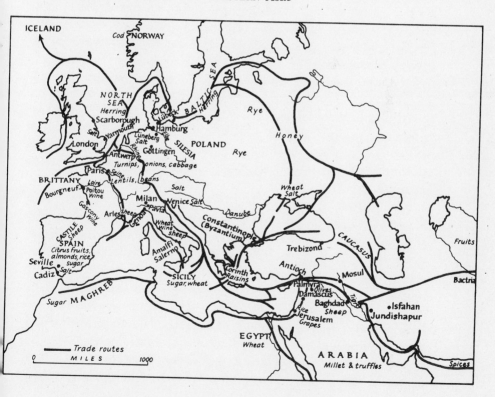

fore more often, whenever the horse could be spared from the fields.

Increased custom for the market led to expansion, and as the market grew, so did the town. Larger towns gave a stimulus to trading enterprise. They also revived many of the problems which had bedeviled the administrators of Rome so many centuries before. The question, once again, was how to feed numbers of people who could not produce food for themselves.

The trade routes of the Western world had been radically changed as a result of the war between Byzantium and the Arabs, for the war had found its expression as much in economic maneuvering as in battles. Spain and Egypt had suffered badly in the contest. The cities of southern France, northwestern Italy, Cyprus and North Africa had been virtually abandoned for a time. The old Rhône valley trade route through France, like the spice route through Damascus and the Red Sea, had faded into insignificance.[4] Much of the Mediterranean had become a backwater. Only its northeastern quarter remained an essential sea link, one that was to prove ever more profitable for merchants who were able to dominate it.

Most European trade with the East was now channeled through Baghdad and Constantinople. The spices and other luxuries still in demand at the courts of the Western world commonly arrived in Baghdad, to be transported from there to Trebizond (Trabzon) on the southern shores of the Black Sea, and then on to Constantinople[5]—this roundabout route being a concession to official Arab-Byzantine enmity.

From Constantinople to Venice they went next—pepper and cinnamon, saffron and cloves, ginger, sugar and cardamom, costly medicines and exquisite silks—and on to Pavia, the crossroads at which the busy highway of the river Po connected with the long-distance land routes over the Alpine passes of the Septimer, Mont Cenis, and the Great St. Bernard, to Germany and northern France.[6] In this thriving city (which began to decline in favor of Milan in the eleventh century), the abbot of St. Gall was among those who found it worthwhile to set up a market to serve the transit trade—the Anglo-Saxon merchants, ceaselessly complaining about the routine at border customs houses, the ingratiating representatives of distant courts intent on their middleman's rake-off, and the great Venetian merchants themselves, every one of whom was annually obliged to buy off the master of the treasury with, among other things, one pound each of pepper, cinnamon, and ginger.[7]

Over the Alps and beyond Switzerland, the cargoes from the East were transferred to the river Rhine, a route opened up first by the Frisians and later taken over by the Vikings. The Rhine connected with the long commercial tentacles which Vikings and Varangians stretched east along the Baltic and westward along the North Sea coasts of continental Europe and England. Amber, furs, fish, tallow, honey, wool and wine were among the important trading commodities of these northern waters which helped to pay for the exotica of the East. As time passed, Scandinavian gave way to German enterprise and the townships which were later to form themselves into the Hanseatic League. By the twelfth century, timber and grain were being floated out by river from the interior of northern Europe in increasing quantity,[8] to meet the ever more pressing needs of expanding economies.

For the last four centuries of the Middle Ages, however, European trade was dominated by the port of Venice, the waist in the hourglass of east-west commerce. Venice had begun to build its prosperity in the sixth century A.D. on the salt from its lagoons, and had improved its trading position over the centuries of discord in the Mediterranean by contriving to sustain an independent but respectful relationship with Byzantium. When the Crusades began, first Genoa, then Pisa, and finally Venice took a hand, supplying transports and warships, arms and siege engines, even the money to subsidize the troops. It was a profitable investment, for the Crusaders repaid them with valuable concessions in the Near East.

The permanent "factories" or trading posts set up by the Italian merchant towns in the ports at the eastern end of the Mediterranean were to be a continuing source of profit, especially to the Venetians. By the fifteenth century, their grasp on the spice trade had become so autocratic that other countries were at last driven into an infuriated attempt to break it. In the process, the Portuguese opened the sea route to India, and Spain discovered America.

The square of St. Mark's, Venice, in the fifteenth century, showing the four bronze horses looted from Constantinople after the Fourth Crusade.

Large numbers of returning Crusaders, dazzled by the warmth and brilliance of the lands they had conquered, carried a taste for new foods, as well as for many other luxuries, back to their northern fastnesses. On to the rootstock of bread and beans, salt meat and dried fish, they grafted imported cooking techniques, the use of pulverized almonds, and above all a fashion (far more widespread than ever before) for spices, which could disguise rancidity in fresh food, reduce the saltiness of salted food, and give character to insipid dried food.

In the beginning, the Crusaders may have displayed their exotic cooking very much as a modern tourist exhibits his souvenirs from abroad. But in the growing towns and cities of the West, where more and more people were condemned to a winter diet of salted and dried foods, spices came to perform a very real function. Ultimately, Europe was to depend so heavily on them that pepper, for example, became a common currency, as negotiable as silver. Today, the phrase "peppercorn rent" is occasionally used to denote "a nominal sum," but in the latter centuries of the medieval world there was nothing nominal about it. A pound of pepper represented the equivalent of two to three weeks' wages for an agricultural laborer.

11.
Supplying
the Towns

The tool which shaped the agricultural revolution of the Middle
Ages was, prosaically enough, a new type of plow. The plow
which had turned the soil since Sumerian times—the "scratch-
plow"—had been improved upon over the centuries, notably
by tipping the point with metal. But it remained, in essence, no
more than a heavy stick which, dragged diagonally over the
ground, cut a shallow furrow with loose earth thrown up at the
sides. Where the soil was light, the scratch-plow worked reasonably well, but on the heavy damp earth of the north it made
little impression.

In the sixth century, however, the Slavs of the northeast introduced to Europe a new heavyweight plow which cut deep into
the soil instead of merely scratching the surface.[1] This, in its fully
developed form, became known as the "moldboard plow." It
had three working parts—a knife blade (the colter), which
slashed vertically into the earth; another (the plowshare), which
cut horizontally through it at grass-roots level; and, behind these
two blades, a shaped board (the moldboard), which turned the
cut slices of turf or topsoil neatly over to one side. A powerful
implement, the moldboard plow took the heavy clay of the
north in its stride, and it became possible to farm great areas of
formerly virgin land, to clear forests, to cultivate waste ground.

Food production increased. So did population. In one part of
Germany, it is estimated that by the end of the seventh century

The
European
scratch
plow.

the population had expanded to four times what it had been in the Roman period.[2] As the centuries passed, the new plow spread gradually over northern and western Europe. But it imposed a new discipline on its users. It was expensive to make and to maintain, and as many as eight oxen were needed to pull it. It functioned splendidly on wide open spaces, but was much too unwieldy for small, individual holdings. Rich men could afford their own plows, but others had to make a radical social adjustment. They began to come together in joint ownership of a plow and its team, and to merge their own patches of land into large, open, jointly worked fields. What a man now and henceforward took from the land was related not, as it had been in the past, to his needs, but to the relative value of what he subscribed toward a corporate enterprise.[3]

CROP ROTATION

Much of the soil which was now tilled for the first time was put to better use than it would have been before. The Greeks and Romans had known that land very soon became impoverished if the same crop was grown on it year after year. But though they also observed that legumes—plants of the pea and bean family—seemed to restore rather than to exhaust the soil, they did not make a habit of alternating legumes with their other crops. This may have been partly because upper-class Greeks and Romans had a peculiarly ambivalent approach toward beans, which some believed to contain the souls of the departed, and others blamed for causing defective vision.* Whatever the reason, and despite the recommendations of such enlightened agronomists as Cato the Elder, the Classical world seems generally to have settled for a simple system of planting half the land with grain in the autumn and leaving the other half fallow; in the following year, the roles were reversed.

Soon after the moldboard plow appeared in the north, however, it became clear that the two-field system of rotation could be improved upon, that a three-field system was, relatively, much more productive.

Using three-field rotation—one field planted at the end of the year with wheat or rye, the second put down in spring to peas, chickpeas, lentils, broad beans, oats or barley, the third left fallow —it was possible to make a given acreage of land productive for two years out of three, instead of just one out of two.

By a fortunate coincidence, farmers who adopted this system produced not only more food but better food. Peas and beans contained amino acids which dovetailed neatly with the elements in grain to produce good, solid, nourishing protein (something which grain alone does not provide). More protein meant better health, increased energy, greater stamina. In the lands of the three-field rotation system—the empire of Charlemagne—society itself became more forceful. As one historian of technology has

* It now appears that broad beans—the type common in early Europe—may be responsible for a disorder of the red blood corpuscles, known as favism, which is rare in most of the world but common among the peoples of the Mediterranean.

The moldboard plow.

Gathering beans.

put it, the people of the north were soon, in every sense, full of beans.[4] The new crop system also led to increased use of the horse, which, first domesticated somewhere in the steppe lands of Eurasia in about 2000 B.C., had been used in early medieval Europe more as a war mount for the knight than a traction animal for the farmer. Its hooves did not stand up well to moist soils. Its strength appeared much inferior to that of the ox. It did not thrive on a diet of hay and grass.

The first problem was solved when heavy nailed horseshoes were introduced to northern Europe,[5] and the second when the farmer discovered that a new-style collar harness—which had filtered through from China—almost quadrupled the horse's draft efficiency.[6] Formerly, the animal had been half choked by the harness strap over its windpipe every time it strained forward to take a load. Now, it proved that it had quite as much strength as the ox, more endurance, and, of course, much greater speed. The answer to its food problem was provided by the three-field rotation system, which gave a regular crop of oats, the best possible food for horses.

Gradually, in many regions, the horse took over the labor of plowing from the ox. Gradually, too, it proved its worth as a transport and a riding animal, helping mankind to become more mobile—and therefore more gregarious—than before.

TOWNS OF THE MIDDLE AGES

Because most of the dwellers in the towns that sprang up during the early decades of expansion were peasants accustomed to working the land, the town not only remained deeply embedded in the countryside but produced much of its own food. There were patches of muddy pasture where a few sheep grazed; neat little areas of garden where the conscientious housewife cherished a few vegetables and the sweet-smelling herbs she strewed on the floors of her home. In wine country, the land immediately beyond the walls of the town would be laid out in individual vineyard plots. Everywhere, the streets would be thick with mud and manure, littered with straw, hay, and refuse. But as more and more people swelled the population, the towns became impossibly cramped and newcomers had to build outside the walls. Their dwellings began to spread ever farther over land that had formerly produced food for the inhabitants.

Until at least the sixteenth century, however, town-dwellers still contrived to keep their own cows, pigs and chickens. Cows were often shackled, and chickens did not wander far, but the scavenging pigs who roamed the streets in search of provender were inclined to trip up pedestrians and tangle up traffic. In twelfth-century Paris, for example, the heir to the throne fractured his skull when a pig ran between his horse's legs. A subsequent edict that there was to be no more pig-rearing in towns was disregarded. Even in the time of Francis I, four centuries later, it was still necessary to empower the public executioner to capture all the stray pigs he could find and take them to the Hôtel Dieu for slaughter. In such cities as Frankfurt and Nuremberg, it seems to have been the pigsties rather than the pigs that were unpopular. In 1481, it was decreed in Frankfurt that pigsties should no longer be located in front of houses on the public streets.[7] But there was no doubt that pigs, in towns, did perform a useful function in addition to providing their owners with meat. In the days before city cleaning departments, the pig cleared the streets of a great deal of waste food that would otherwise have lain and rotted.

GROWTH OF MARKETS

As the towns grew, small markets which had begun for the friendly bartering of produce grew into important trading events, where coinage, spices, wine and silks replaced baskets of apples and day-old chicks as currency. Frequently, so much of a town's prosperity revolved round the market that stringent precautions had to be taken to guard the stallholders against robbery, violence, and the medieval equivalent of the protection racket. A "market peace" similar to that of ancient Greece was established, symbolized in this new Christian world by the cross set up in the market place.

The great cities of France, Germany and England grew with some speed as princes and rulers tightened their grip on the

Street of shops in a small town in northern Europe.

nobility. Formerly, great men had been forced to keep traveling
in order to supervise their estates and their subjects, but the
paraphernalia of administration at last made this impossible.
Armies of clerks and libraries of documents had to be housed
somewhere, and where the records were, there kings and princes
set up their courts. Where the courts were, there merchants and
tradesmen flocked to offer their wares.

Every great city had its great markets, and control over these
soon became, in every sense, a royal headache. Exacting obedience
from the merchants and ensuring the "market peace" were feasible only if the place of sale was subject to regulation. It became
the custom to establish different areas in the city in which different types of merchants could offer their wares.*

But though some regulations were framed primarily for administrative reasons, others grew out of pressures brought to bear on
the authorities by the increasingly powerful merchant associations
and guilds. In early fourteenth-century London, for example, out-
of-town poulterers found it profitable to wander the streets selling
their goods to housewives who had neither the time nor the in-
clination to go to market. The guilds resented this freelance
competition, and in 1345 an edict was passed which flatly pro-
hibited "folks bringing poultry to the City" to sell it in "lanes, in
the hostels of their hosts, and elsewhere in secret," and com-

* This had long been usual in the markets of Asia, and the custom had also been
adopted in Byzantium.

manded them to take it "to the Leaden Hall and there sell it, and nowhere else." [8]

Just as the merchants knew how to force through edicts which suited them, so they knew how to disregard, with impunity, those which did not. In 1369, for example, "Edward, by the Grace of God" informed the dignitaries of the city of London that he had received "grievous complaint" from those of his subjects who lived near the slaughterhouse (or "shambles") of St. Nicholas, concerning "the slaughtering of beasts in the said shambles, and the carrying of the entrails and offal of the said beasts through the streets, lanes and places aforesaid to the said banks of the river . . . where the same entrails and offal are thrown into the water aforesaid." His Majesty pointed out that by "the dropping of the blood of such beasts between the said shambles and the waterside aforesaid—the same running along the midst of the said streets and lanes—grievous corruption and filth have been generated . . . so that no one, by reason of such corruption and filth, could hardly venture to abide in his house there."

Despite an earlier warning from the throne, the mayor, recorder, aldermen and sheriffs had failed to take action by the specified date of the Feast of St. Peter's Chains (August 1), and the king suggested that they would be well advised to get something done by the forthcoming Feast of the Assumption of the Blessed Virgin Mary (August 15). But the city dignitaries paid not the slightest

Small retailers in London's Gracechurch Market, grouped by county.

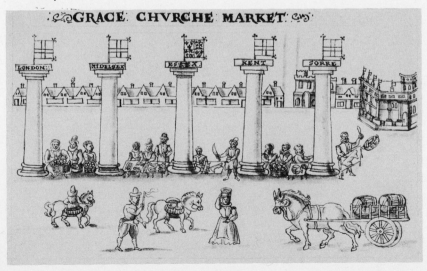

attention. Two years later, the shambles of St. Nicholas were still causing "corruption and grievous stenches and abominable sights," and Edward III was still threatening dire retribution.[9]

In Paris fifty years later, "Charles by the Grace of God" was having much the same kind of trouble. "We have commanded, and we command, so that the air of our said city be not infected or corrupted by these slaughterhouses and knackers' yards, and also that the water of the river Seine be not corrupted nor infected by the blood and other filth of the said beasts falling or being thrown into the said river Seine, that all slaughterhouses and knackers' yards establish themselves outside our said city of Paris . . ."[10] The language was less extravagant, but the message was the same.

QUALITY CONTROL

Though it might be almost impossible, because of the commercial politics involved, to put an end to some of the more blatant offenses against health and hygiene, the authorities worked hard over quality control, and a number of guilds imposed their own standards on members.

In France, officialdom took a close interest in the state of any pork that was to be put on sale. There were inspectors known as *langueyeurs* who examined the pigs' tongues for ulcers, which were thought to cause leprosy in consumers. In Venice, the guilds insisted that all fish be taken to the "tall pole" in the fish markets of San Marco and Rialto to be valued and duty paid before being sold, and the fishmongers' stalls were inspected daily so that stale fish could be destroyed. Nevertheless, it seems likely that Italian "fishfags" still used an old dodge mentioned by Athenaeus centuries earlier. It was not permitted to freshen up fish by sprinkling water over it. One fishfag would therefore knock another down in a fight, whereupon all the bystanders helpfully rallied round and tossed buckets of water over the "unconscious" victim—and, coincidentally, over his fish.[11]

The majority of merchants were probably honest and God-fearing men, but a minority were either inept or corrupt. The archives of most cities are studded with cases brought against offending

A fifteenth-century wine-gauger, or exciseman.

food sellers. Since it was generally believed that bad odors were
responsible for transmitting disease, the medieval nose was peculiarly sensitive to the smell of decay, and for this reason amateur
malefactors were frequently caught. When, for example, John
Gylessone tried to sell the "putrid and stinking" flesh of a sow
he had found dead in a London gutter, he was instantly reported

and brought to trial.[12] Less easy to detect, though still a product of ignorance rather than knavery, was the kind of violation which cropped up in an unusually lurid form in Venice in 1498, when a number of oil vendors were accused of selling cooking oil which had previously been used for bathing sufferers from venereal disease.[13]

The main problem confronting the authorities, however, was deliberate and calculated fraud. While towns remained comparatively small, crooked tradesmen had to be clever. Once a particular trick had been used—and discovered—it was ruled out for years afterward. Wooden nutmegs and juniper berries masquerading as peppercorns were swindles that could only be worked by itinerant pedlars in the countryside. But in the cities there were many ways for a determined miscreant to evade detection, and inspectors spent a great deal of time assessing the quality of such goods as wine, ale, flour and oil—which were particularly liable to adulteration—and investigating what went into sausages and blood puddings.

Catching a wily London baker like John Brid called either for luck on the part of the authorities, disloyalty on the part of the baker's staff, or detective talent on the part of his customers. In 1327, Mr. Brid had a small trapdoor cut in the table on which his customers placed the dough they wanted him to bake for

Punishment of a defaulting baker.

ndam confuetudinem Ciuitas London Debet affari fiep de pane qualiber anno poſt
um ſci andrie p quatuor viros Diſcretos eſſui ad hoc elecos ſceom pporciōem ponder illins

them. While the baker held the customer in conversation, one of his staff, seated below the trapdoor, "piecemeal and bit by bit craftily withdrew some of the dough aforesaid" from the under-side of the loaf. After a few moments, Mr. Brid would pick up the loaf—effectively but not visibly lighter—and pop it in the oven. By this means, said the indictment sternly, he collected great quantities of dough, "falsely, wickedly and maliciously; to the great loss of all his neighbors and persons living near." [14] With it, he made bread for public sale.

As it happened, one of the commonest food crimes in the Mid-dle Ages was selling underweight bread. A loaf's weight was usually fixed in relation to cost. In London in the early fourteenth cen-tury, a halfpenny maslin (wheat and rye) loaf was supposed to weigh twenty-eight shillings. (The shilling, 3/5 ounces, was a standard weight.) If it did not, the baker was drawn through the dirtiest streets in town on a hurdle, with the offending loaf slung round his neck.

PUBLIC COOKSHOPS

Growing towns, in which cooking facilities for the ordinary citi-zen were almost as limited as they had been in the days of Rome, encouraged the proliferation of "baked meat sellers."

Professionally cooked food was, of course, not a new concept. It had been known in Mesopotamia in the time of Nebuchad-nezzar, and the population of the Near East still, in medieval times, preferred not to cook at home but to buy forcemeat balls, roast mutton, fish, fritters, pancakes, and almond-paste sweets from the market. It may, indeed, have been from the Arab world, by way of Spain, that the custom of buying ready-cooked food was reintroduced into Europe, although without the revival of a monetary economy in the West the idea would have made little headway.

In London by 1183 there was a public cookshop, where "accord-ing to the season you may find viands, dishes roast, fried and boiled, fish great and small, the coarser flesh for the poor, the more delicate for the rich, such as venison, and birds both big and little. If friends, weary with travel, should of a sudden come to

A French baker's shop, showing scales and moldboard.

any of the citizens, and it is not their pleasure to wait fasting till
fresh food is bought and cooked . . . they hasten to the river
bank, and there all things desirable are ready to their hand." [15]
Prices in the twelfth century are not known, but in 1363 a leg
of roast mutton was to be had for 1 p., or 2.5 cents (a day's wage
for an agricultural laborer), as were three whole pigeons; a whole
roast pig cost 3.2 p., or 8 cents; ten roast finches no more than
.4 p., or 1 cent; and any customer could have his own capon
baked in a pasty if he paid .6 p., or 1.5 cents, for "the paste,
fire and trouble." [16]

HYGIENE

Though the Middle Ages were aware that disease could be spread by contagion and by airborne infection (which they identified with bad smells), it seems probable that the standard of hygiene in cookshops and in the markets was as casual as in private homes.

Except when a town was in the grip of some epidemic, even the most fastidious housewife—accustomed to sewage in the streets and livestock in the house—may not have thought twice about the perils of the market place. These, in fact, were very much the same as the ones enumerated, long after, by an Englishman in India, who prayed that: "Jones of the club, as he takes the cover off of one of M—'s best entrées, may for once think of the leprous hand that has handled it; Brown may fancy for once he will catch smallpox from his beefsteak; Robinson may think of the dog licking the leg of mutton from which his whack is taken." [17] Such were the hazards of all open-air markets when medical knowledge was a luxury for the few and regulations about hygiene no more than an additional burden for the many.

The very existence of the market sometimes endangered whole cities. The food stores of the great merchants, the waste material of the slaughterhouses, the refuse flung aside by stallholders and householders—all these were breeding-grounds for pestilence, and a haven for the omnivorous black rat which, by the thirteenth century, infested most of the new towns of Europe. When, in the crowded conditions of the market place, a diseased rat paused in the gutter to scratch itself, displaced fleas might find a new home on some passing human. A bite from an infected rat flea could bring plague or typhus, and if the victim already suffered from lice and lived in a lice-ridden community—which fairly described the situation in most medieval towns—a killer epidemic could easily result (lice being transmitters of the typhus virus).[18] When this happened, people died by scores, sometimes by hundreds, occasionally by thousands.

The people who lived on the banks of great rivers also ran the risk of contracting dysentery or paratyphoid from the water. Although some towns, such as Göttingen in central Germany, enforced street-cleaning regulations from as early as 1330,[19] in most places the dirt and refuse in the streets lay there until it was washed away by a good rainstorm—some of it into the wells from which drinking water was drawn, some into the river. Formerly scientists believed that sunlight and the small organisms that feed on bacteria must quickly have purified the sewage in the rivers, but serious doubts have recently been cast on this theory. On the basis of antibodies found in fish, it seems likely that not only the water itself but the fish that swam in it (carefully protected by the authorities, who were determined that the rivers should not be over-fished) must have been potent carriers of disease.[20] Alas for those Parisians who believed that a basket of sand, well washed in Seine water, would improve bitter wine! [21]

Plague and typhus through the agency of rats in the market place, dysentery and paratyphoid from the fish in the river, food poisoning at the hands of the cooked meat vendors—it was hardly surprising that the Dance of Death should have been such a commonplace image in the art of the time. That nightmare pestilence, the Black Death, may have had a no more traumatic effect on the survivors than the steady erosion of family and friends by less dramatic scourges.

GRAIN SUPPLIES

At first, the growth of towns was paralleled by an expansion of cereal production on land increasingly distant from the centers of consumption. But when there was a bad harvest, the lords on their great estates and the peasant cultivators kept what there was themselves, and the townspeople—a new class who owned no land, worked no land, and had no access to land—suffered both shortage and inflated prices. But· if famine struck, landowner and peasant were left to fend for themselves, while the authorities distributed grain to the townspeople who clamored on their doorstep.

It had long been clear to the world's rulers that they could not afford to let their subjects die of hunger—provided, of course, that the cost of keeping them alive was not disproportionately high. The earliest recorded relief works had been designed to help the portionless widow; both the Old Testament and the *Shih ching* mention the custom of leaving ears of grain in the

Kublai Khan distributing grain in time of shortage.

fields for her to glean. Later, the Roman *annona* foreshadowed
not so much famine relief as unemployment benefit. At the end
of the eighth century, Charlemagne did his best to avert shortages
by placing a ban on grain exports from his dominions. But the
Chinese emperor Ying-tsung (1064-67) seems to have been one
of the first to make a systematic attempt to overcome recurring
food shortages when he resurrected an idea originally advanced by
the Han usurper Wang Mang in A.D. 10 and established "regula-
tive granaries." The state bought up surplus grain when the harvest
was good, and released stocks in periods of shortage when the
market price would normally have risen too high for the average
citizen to afford. This method had the double virtue of building
up grain reserves and controlling prices by frustrating speculation.
It did, however, demand a sizable investment by the state, and this
inhibited many rulers from following the Chinese example. Various civic bodies did try to guarantee grain supplies for their cities,
and to insure that prices were kept down to a fair level. Often,
large reserves were kept in specially built granaries, by city ad-
ministrations and by merchant guilds.

The quantities of grain involved were considerable in an era
when bread was a major item of diet in even the richest households. In thirteenth-century England, the domestic economy of
the Earl of Leicester required 300 pounds of grain a day, even
when the master and his sizable retinue were not at home.[22]

Smaller households consumed, proportionately, almost as much. One citizen of Genoa, whose family and servants numbered only ten, still had to buy in roughly five and a half tons of grain to feed them for a year.[23] With consumption running at this level, a town of three thousand people had to be able to call on between 1000 and 1500 tons of grain a year—the produce of about 10,000 acres of land.

Fortunately for the growing towns of the West, a new granary was opened up when the Germans expanded into the Slav countries in the twelfth century. The plains of eastern Europe began to make good the deficiencies of more settled lands.[24] So plentiful, and because of the ease of water transport, so cheap were supplies from the territories fringing the Baltic that there was grain enough and to spare. Hamburg and the Netherlands even used some of it to expand their brewing interests.

The effects were swift. By the beginning of the thirteenth century, great quantities of cereals were being exported by the Baltic route and by the end of the century, in face of this competition, many areas in western Europe had simply given up growing grain. In Gascony and Poitou, the vine took over. Elsewhere, there was a considerable increase in stockbreeding.

SHEEP FARMING

Europe in the later Middle Ages discovered that, of all livestock, the sheep was the most attractive commercial proposition. It supplied milk and meat, the wool that clothed the peoples of the north, and skins which could be sold to the parchment makers who were suddenly doing a roaring trade in manuscript materials.

Less temperamental than the cow and more nimble on rough pastures, the sheep also cropped the grass more closely and was— marginally—more fecund. The small-scale investor looked into the possibilities of sheep farming and found them good. Butchers and burgesses alike advanced cash to enterprising peasants to build up a flock. Sometimes the agreement was confined to sharing the profits; sometimes the stockman was supplied with a flock which he returned to his backer in two or three years, keeping for himself half the number of lambs born in the interval.[25]

Long before, the nomads of Central Asia and the barbarian

tribes of Europe had been equally enthusiastic about the sheep. Harking back even further, perhaps, to the summer-winter migrations which the animals had instinctively followed in their wild state (and which had also kept paleolithic man on the move), the nomads had been accustomed to shift their flocks from summer to winter pastures, and back, at the appropriate seasons. The Visigoths probably took the custom to Spain, where it was well established by the seventh century, and a vital element in the economy by the tenth.[26] Historians today, in fact, believe that the great stimulus which led the northern Spaniards to fight to free the rest of Spain from the Arab invaders was their need to take the flocks south to winter pasture.[27]

In Castile alone there were an estimated 1,500,000 sheep in the year 1300; 2,700,000 by 1467.[28] Moving millions of sheep south or north, over hundreds of miles of territory, during two brief periods every year was an exercise which required considerable organization, and it was hardly surprising that the *Mesta*, the association which supervised the migrations, should have developed into a major power in the land, dabbling not only in national but in international politics.

In France, as in Spain, tens of thousands of sheep were moved annually from the mountains of Provence to winter pasture at Arles,* and in Italy from the Abruzzi to the Apulian plains. Everywhere, there were acrimonious exchanges between the herds-

---

* In Provence in October, communal herds of pigs were also driven across country to fatten on the acorns of Vaucluse and Albion.

Milking sheep in England in the fourteenth century.

men driving their huge flocks and the crop farmers onto whose land the sheep inevitably strayed.

In terms of trade, wool was the sheep's most valuable product. But sheep farming on such a scale also did much to improve the general level of nutrition among the poorer members of many communities, because it meant that mutton, milk and cheese were readily available. The meat was by no means tender, particularly in the migration (or "transhumance") countries where the sheep were kept slim and muscular by their twice-yearly marathons. But there was still protein in the stringy flesh, and many ways of tenderizing it. Mutton could not be regarded as a delicacy, but it was eaten in large quantities. In fourteenth-century Florence, for example, the city's 90,000 inhabitants consumed in a year "4000 oxen and calves, 60,000 mutton and sheep, 20,000 she-goats and he-goats, 30,000 pigs," [29] while in Paris the royal households of Charles VI, his queen and children purchased two hundred sheep every week.[30]

The sheep's second major contribution to the diet was cheese. The thirteenth-century English agriculturalist Walter of Henley estimated that twenty ewes would produce enough milk each week to make 4 Imperial, or 5 American, pints of butter, and 250 pounds of cheese.[31] Since there were eight million sheep in England soon after Walter of Henley's time [32]—several times more sheep than people, in fact—it is easy to see why cheese was so plentiful that it featured on every table.

Nevertheless, within three hundred years and despite a very considerable increase in sheep farming, the English peasant seems entirely to have given up using the sheep's dairy products. It was the cow that people now relied on for what they called "white meats." Surrounded by sheep, they argued their case against the loss of grazing rights by claiming that they needed enough land to keep a cow, for *only* the cow could provide the "butter, cheese, whey, curds, cream, sod [boiled] milk, raw milk, sour milk, sweet milk, and buttermilk" which were so important to their diet.[33] What they really meant was that they had come to prefer the flavor of cow's-milk products. It was the index of a changing society that even the peasant now insisted not only that he had a right to *enough* food—but to enough food of a familiar and acceptable kind.

12.

The Medieval
Table

Although superficial resemblances to the Roman cuisine have tended to obscure the fact, the cooking of northern Europe in the Middle Ages was an acknowledgment of present needs rather than a remembrance of things past. In the towns, particularly, there were long periods of the year when virtually no fresh meat or fish was to be had, when most people lived on foods that had been preserved by salting or drying. Much medieval cooking, therefore, was specifically designed to make something interesting out of materials which, in unimaginative hands, would have had a dismal monotony.

One of the reasons for dependence on preserved foods was that it was difficult to keep animals alive and healthy throughout the northern winter. Beans, dried plant stems, chaff and straw were the usual winter fodder, and on this poor and often scanty fare, only the young and strong could be expected to survive. In October and November, peasants who had bought their draft animals at the beginning of the summer season hastened to sell them again to speculators who could afford to feed them through the winter for resale, in spring, at a healthy profit. The peasant's own stock of fodder might only stretch to keeping a cow and a sow alive. The lord of the manor would do rather better. But any beast of doubtful stamina had to be slaughtered. The end of the year was a time of salting down beef, pork, game, and freshwater fish for the gray days to come, and of feasting on the last fresh meat for several months.

Autumn slaughter in Germany, and the subsequent banquet on fresh meat.

PRESERVATION BY SALTING

There were two time-honored ways of salting food. The first was dry-salting, in which the meat or fish was buried in a granular bed of salt. The results were good, but the labor involved in pounding quantities of the very lumpy salt of medieval times to the requisite state of fineness may have ruled it out for the ordinary family. In noble households, there was often a servant known as·the "powderer" who, with his huge pestle and mortar, was responsible for preparing the materials for dry-salted ("powdered") meat. The second preservation method was brine-curing, in which the meat was immersed in a strong solution of salt and water.

The quality of the meat or fish to be salted was of some importance. If, in the late thirteenth century, for example, a town housewife had to buy, retail, fresh meat which she proposed to cure herself, it would cost her about 2 p., or 5 cents, for 20 pounds.[1] For this weight of meat, she would need something like 2 pounds of salt, coasting another .8 p., or 2 cents.[2] Even without such expensive additions as peppercorns and cloves, therefore, salting immediately added forty per cent to the cost of the raw materials. In many cases, of course—in the country, and in towns where the citizens kept their own pigs—the two costs did not fall together, but the expense of feeding the animal while alive still had to be accounted in the reckoning. With salt at such a high price, the housewife may not have felt justified in preserving any but a fat plump carcass—and this could, in part, explain why comparatively little mutton seems to have been salted. The tough and stringy wool sheep was literally "not worth his salt."

The salting of meat and fish had had a long and somewhat checkered history. Its origins remain obscure, but there was a definite link in early Egypt between the use of salt for embalming the bodies of the dead and its use in preserving food for the living.[3] The Egyptians ran a thriving export trade in salted and dried fish. Strabo, in the first century B.C., reported that the Spanish fish-salting industry was "not unimportant." [4] Gaul was renowned in Roman times for the quality of its salted and smoked hams. But Christianity was to do more for the salting business than even the most optimistic merchant would have had the temerity to expect. Lent, the forty-day fast which preceded Easter, was the most profitable time—fish was essential, and fresh fish was scarce inland. Fridays throughout the year were almost as good, especially in towns. Even as late as the mid-sixteenth century, it was still (theoretically) possible for an Englishman to be hanged for eating meat on a Friday.[5]

The herring was the most important item in the salt fish trade. In the fourteenth and fifteenth centuries, the Baltic and the North Sea swarmed with it. The merchant towns of the Hanseatic League dominated much of the Baltic commerce in salt fish for

Prague merchants were careful to inspect and repack barrels of salt herring imported from the north.

almost two hundred lucrative years, while the busiest individual centers in the North Sea area were Yarmouth and Scarborough on the east coast of England, and Brielle in Holland.

Herring, though plentiful, is a fatty fish whose oils turn rancid very quickly. When it is to be salted, the process has to be begun within twenty-four hours of the catch. This required a high degree of organization in the era of sail, even in the Baltic where the fisheries were usually close enough to land for the haul to be brought in daily. In the North Sea, professional fishermen in the fifteenth century had to process their catch far away from port. The Norfolk doggers which set sail for Icelandic waters at the beginning of the summer carried grain and ale, bacon, salt fish, beef and butter to provision the crew of between five and ten men for several months, as well as over a ton of salt, and either a great many barrels or the materials for making them.[6]

Barrels of herring which had been salted at sea were notorious for having the handsomest fish displayed in the upper part of the barrel, while the small and inferior ones were hidden away in the center. Customers of the Hanse merchants, although they paid more, at least had the assurance that the grading and packing of Baltic herring had been carefully supervised.

TYPES OF SALT

The three main methods of producing salt, in medieval times as today, were by mining the rock-salt residues of ancient seas, boiling down the brine from salt springs, and evaporating sea water in shallow artificial lakes or "pans." The second and third methods were the commonest.

Salt from the springs was much superior to sea salt. The saline content was higher. Production did not depend on continuous sunshine. And the end product was free from the admixture of calcium and magnesium salts which marred the common sea-water type and had such a deleterious effect on preservation processes. Salt from the springs—"brine salt"—was, however, expensive, and supplies were by no means inexhaustible.

Almost as expensive as brine salt, and producing a fine white powder over which the Middle Ages rhapsodized, was what was

Extracting brine from salt springs in China, and sending it through a conduit to the evaporation pans.

known as "peat salt." This was usually made in the Low Countries. Peat impregnated with sea water was burned to ashes, and these— with most of the salt precipitated in them—were then evaporated with salt water over turf fires. The result was excellent, but peat supplies were limited; it could be dug only at certain times of year; and some sunshine was necessary to dry it out before it could be burned. Like brine salt, therefore, peat salt had its limitations.

In the mid-fourteenth century, there was a crisis in north European salt production, partly because of economic conditions, and partly because of the Hundred Years War. In the end, much of the trade was cornered by the salt pans of Bourgneuf Bay on the southern borders of Brittany. Here, unfiltered sea water, generously mixed with grit, debris and seaweed, was used to produce a coarse and heavily polluted salt which was sometimes black in color, sometimes gray, sometimes even green. But it was cheap, and for well over a century great convoys of ships traveled back and forth to the bay in the last months of winter to collect salt for the summer herring season in the north.

As time passed, "Bay salt" came to mean not just salt from Bourgneuf Bay, but coarse salt made by natural evaporation on almost any seacoast. It seems never to have been anything but lumpy and impure, but it cost only half as much as white salt. When its use became common in the latter part of the fourteenth century—replacing the purer products of Lüneberg and Lincolnshire, where many of the less desirable mineral salts were removed by boiling—the quality of salted meat and fish must have deteriorated considerably. Inferior sea salt did not penetrate the flesh quickly enough, and there was time for the inner parts of a fish or a piece of meat to turn rancid before the salt reached them.[7] *

THE IMPORTANCE OF SALT IN HISTORY

Almost since the beginning of time, and certainly since the beginnings of recorded history, salt has been a vital ingredient in man's diet and in the world's economy. As Cassiodorus, the fifth-century Goth administrator, said: "It may well be that some seek not gold, but there lives not a man who does not need salt."[9]

Salt was, and is, not only a stimulus to the taste buds but a biological necessity. When a human being perspires, he loses some of his natural body salts. These have to be replaced by the food he eats. Raw meat is the best provider, cooked meat less good, because salt is usually lost in the cooking process. A diet based on grain and vegetables contains very little salt, and in parts of the world where food is mainly vegetarian it is essential to have a good supply of mineral salt to remedy the deficiency. When

---

* Though this must certainly have worried the housewife, it does not seem to have concerned those who administered criminal justice in seventeenth-century England. When villains were hanged, drawn, and quartered, their heads—before being exhibited in public to discourage others—were first parboiled "with Bay salt and cumin seed—that to keep them from putrefaction, and this to keep off the fowls from seizing on them."[8]

for some reason this is not available, health can suffer quite severely. In 1936, for example, the Chinese communists had to evacuate certain areas south of the Yangtse which they had held for eight years, because the Nanking government blockade had cut off salt supplies.[10] The debilitating effects of salt hunger were more decisive than eight years of military activity.

Although the political role of salt has not often been demonstrated as clearly as this, control of salt pans and salt mines has always been a strong administrative weapon. By the first millennium B.C. it was an essential part of the government administration in China, as it was for the Ptolemies of Egypt and the Seleucids of Persia. Venice built her original trade supremacy on salt, and in eleventh-century Africa the warriors of Islam were assisted in overthrowing the Ghana empire by the Berbers, who had long had their eye on the salt mines of Ankar. In the thirteenth century, France introduced the *gabelle*, or salt tax, as an imposition which none could escape, while in the fifteenth century a whole African nation, the Vakaranga, moved hundreds of miles north from Great Zimbabwe because the salt supplies there had been exhausted.

Even in the twentieth century, salt was still a government monopoly in British India. Indeed, it stimulated one of the greatest political demonstrations of modern times, when in 1930 Mahatma Gandhi marched with a great number of followers on a pilgrimage to the seaside at Dandi, there—illegally—to make salt. His example fired the public imagination so effectively that other Congress leaders were caught unprepared. "We knew precious little about it," confessed Pandit Nehru a few years later, "and so we read it up where we could, and issued leaflets giving directions, and collected pots and pans and ultimately succeeded in producing some unwholesome stuff, which we waved about in triumph, and often auctioned for fancy prices." [11]

PRESERVATION BY DRYING

The second major preservation process in the Middle Ages was drying, used more often in Europe for fish than for meat, although in other parts of the world it was often preferred to salting. Herring could not be dried satisfactorily, but the method was very suitable for less oily fish such as cod, haddock, pollack and ling.

Climatic conditions were important here. In mild, damp countries, the method required not only protection from the weather but limitless supplies of fuel. Where the weather was hot, however, or consistently dry and windy, it was both satisfactory and cheap. In the Near East, from very early times, dates, figs and grapes had been dried by the simple expedient of burying them in the hot desert sand. Meat was beaten with stones to extract the juices and then exposed to the sun. The Scandinavians adapted the latter technique to northern temperatures, and found that clear, crisp air and a cool wind did the job almost as well.

Norwegian *stokkfisk*, cod which were gutted and then hung in thousands to dry on wooden racks, provided the people of the Middle Ages with a cheap and almost indestructible food reserve. It was not perhaps the most restful material for the cook to deal with. A fourteenth-century Paris merchant recommended that, when preparing ten- or twelve-year-old stockfish, "it behoves to beat it with a wooden hammer for a full hour and then set it to soak in warm water for a full two hours or more, then cook it and scour it very well . . . then eat it with mustard or soaked in butter." [12]

COOKING TECHNIQUES

Much of what is known about medieval food comes from the kitchen account books of monasteries or noble households, and from court catering documents. These are informative about raw materials, prices, and quantities. Recipes and general culinary lore, on the other hand, are to be found in a few surviving cookbooks and books of manners.

Most of these sources * have one major historical failing—they relate to the kitchens of great landowners, where there was almost invariably some kind of fresh meat—game, usually—to replace or lend variety to the preserved foods on which lesser households depended in winter and spring. Salt meat and dried fish are in fact

* With the rare and notable exception of a domestic manual composed by the fourteenth-century merchant known as the *Ménagier* of Paris.

very seldom mentioned in the cookbooks. Nevertheless, it is reasonable to assume (even if only because "fresh meat" is specified in a number of recipes) that in most cases fresh or salted ingredients could be used according to availability. Just as early cookbooks rarely bothered to define quantities or give instructions on how to roast a cut of beef, so they assumed that the professional cooks for whom the recipes were designed would know, without being told, how to deal with the preliminaries in the case of salted or dried foods.

Inadequately soaked salt meat must have been a recurring hazard of the dining table in days when there was no domestic water supply, when a casual instruction to "soak in several changes of water" involved some weary scullion in a great many trips to the well. Sometimes, the cook was able to avert disaster while the meat was simmering by suspending in the cauldron a quantity of oatmeal tied in a "fair linen cloth," which absorbed some of the excess salt. But this was not the complete answer. It is clear from

Preparing tripe in a fourteenth-century Italian kitchen.

surviving recipes that the medieval cook brought a whole battery of other weapons to bear.

The simplest and most common method was to cook or serve with the meat an accompaniment which would absorb the salt without itself becoming salty. Where potatoes would be used today, the medieval cook used dried peas, dried beans, breadcrumbs, or whole grain. Puréed beans with bacon was standard fare in poorer households, but the rich demanded something more enterprising. Their kitchen staffs did not neglect breadcrumbs and grain (which also had the property of thickening a mixture) but used, in addition, spices or fruit to offset any residual saltiness, or creamy sauces to smooth it out.

Many medieval recipes look alarming at first, but the reader who blinks at the sight of pepper, ginger, cinnamon, saffron, cloves and mace all in one recipe would remain unmoved if "a pinch of mixed spice" were specified instead. Probably, medieval cooks used a great deal more than a pinch, however—if only because the starchy ingredients and creamy sauces which reduced saltiness also reduced the intensity of the spices themselves. In a number of the more substantial "made" dishes, the spices would have had to be used quite generously if their flavor was to be discernible. "Pumpes," for example, were meatballs in sauce, and were made as follows:

"Take and boil a good piece of pork, and not too lean, as tender as you may; then take it up and chop it as small as you may; then take cloves and mace, and chop forth withall, and also chop forth with raisins of Corinth; then take it and roll it as round as you may, like to small pellets, a two inches about, then lay them on a dish by themselves; then make a good almond milk, and blend it with flour of rice, and let it boil well, but look that it be quite runny; and at the dresser, lay five pumpes in a dish, and pour the pottage thereon. And if you will, set on every pumpe a flower, and over them strew on sugar enough and mace: and serve them forth. And some men make the pellets of veal or beef, but pork is best and fairest." [13]

Plain boiled (or parboiled and roasted) salt meat required a different technique, and was frequently served up with separate dishes of bland, thick mixtures like frumenty, mortrews, or blamanger.[14] These, based on grain, crumbs, or almond milk and rice, were in effect stiffer versions of the anti-salt sauces described above.

Frumenty, by the Middle Ages, had developed into a thick pudding of whole-wheat grains and almond milk, sometimes enriched with egg yolks and colored with saffron. It was the standard accompaniment for venison.

Mortrews, which took its name and character from the fact that the main ingredients were pounded in a mortar, was most simply made by reducing boiled white meat or fish to a paste, mixing it with breadcrumbs, stock, and eggs, and boiling it again until it was stiff. Pepper and ginger were sprinkled on before serving.

For blank mang or blamanger (the scarcely recognizable ancestor of the modern blancmange) shredded chicken was blended with whole rice which had been boiled in almond milk until soft. The mixture was seasoned with sugar and, sometimes, salt, and left to cook until it was very thick. It was garnished with fried almonds and preserved anise seeds.

Roasts of fresh meat or game needed no such special-purpose accompaniments. On the table instead would appear strongly flavored pasties, pies and fritters, and spicy sauces in which to dip each mouthful of the roasts. So popular were these sauces—and so useful with salt meat as well as with fresh meat that had been too well hung—that the professional saucemaker was a familiar figure in Paris by the fourteenth century.[15] From him housewives could buy readymade "yellow sauce," in which ginger and saffron predominated; "green sauce," with ginger, cloves, cardamom, and green herbs; and "cameline sauce," the great fourteenth-century favorite, in which cinnamon was the essential ingredient, the others being variable.

One of the first known cookbooks of modern Europe—*Le Viandier de Taillevent*, compiled in 1375 (probably from an earlier author's work) by Guillaume Tirel, cook to Charles V of France—gives this recipe for cameline. "Pound ginger, plenty of cinnamon, cloves, cardamom, mace, long pepper if you wish, then squeeze out bread soaked in vinegar and strain all together and salt it just right." [16] On the other side of the Channel, cooks were instructed to "take raisins of Corinth, and kernels of nuts, and crust of bread and powder of ginger, cloves, flour of cinnamon, pound it well together and add it thereto. Salt it, temper it up with vinegar, and serve it forth." [17]

Dried fish, that other mainstay of the medieval menu, was a pallid food given zest in ordinary households by the addition of mustard or vinegar. The rich dressed it up with spicy sauces or, for variety, with rich admixtures of fruit. Lenten "ryschewys," for example, were a kind of cooked rissole encased in batter or folded-over dough and then fried. "Take figs," said the recipe, "and boil them up in ale; then take when they be tender and pound them small in a mortar; then take almonds, and shred them thereto small; take pears and shred them thereto; take dates and shred them thereto; and take [dried haddock or ling] that is well soaked and shred thereto." [18] The resulting paste was floured, dipped in batter or wrapped in dough, and fried in oil.

The medieval world had much the same culinary problems as Classical Rome, used much the same meats, spices, fruits, and grains. But any comparison between the two cuisines is unproductive. Too much interpretation is involved, too little fact. Certainly, memories of Roman cooking may have survived despite the lapse of centuries, the long scarcity of spices, and the disappearance of *liquamen* and silphium, while those manuscript copies of Apicius which were in circulation may have been more informative in the fourteenth century than they are now. But if the late medieval cuisine was *directly* indebted to any one source, it

Almonds, wheat, meat, and salt were among the foods which had to be pounded in quantity in the medieval kitchen. In the center, cauldrons do

was to the Arabs, those cultural middlemen of the post-Classical world. From their synthesis of Roman, Persian and nomadic foods, the medieval West borrowed many of the techniques and materials it needed to solve its own contemporary problems.

MEDIEVAL MENUS

In the fourteenth century, as in most other eras, the poor man's meal was in a class by itself. It still consisted of dark bread made from rye, barley, or maslin—sometimes with pea or bean flour mixed in—and a *companaticum* from the stockpot, with some cheese perhaps, or a bowl of curds to round the meal off. Servants in large country households were better fed than the peasant in his hut. Sometimes they might have beef or goose, as well as maslin bread, pease pudding, salt herring, dried cod, cheese, and ale brewed on the estate.

But the individual character of the medieval cuisine is most clearly identifiable in the company dinner given by the middle levels of society—by prosperous town merchants or minor members of the country nobility.

The medieval menu bore very little relation to that of modern times. *Table d'hôte* and *à la carte* were, in fact, the same thing. Each course consisted of a number of different dishes all placed

duty as double boilers. On the right a scullion turns the spit while poultry is basted with an improbably long spoon.

on the table at the same time, and diners made a selection from what was offered. The courses were not divided along the lines of soup, fish, meat and sweet as they are today, but were a more or less haphazard assortment. It was not really until the sixteenth century that a "course" began to imply some degree of unity (see menu, pages 279-80).

In fact, it is the menu rather than the individual dish which divides the fourteenth century so irrevocably from the twentieth. A "meat tile," for example—which consisted of pieces of chicken or veal, simmered, sautéed, served in a spiced sauce of pounded crayfish tails, almonds and toasted bread, and garnished with whole crayfish tails [19]—might find a welcome place on the modern table, if it were preceded by a clear soup, accompanied by a green salad, and followed by fruit. But in the monotonous context of this Parisian menu of 1393,[20] it loses much of its charm.

FIRST COURSE
Miniature pastries filled either
    with cod liver or beef
    marrow
A cameline meat "brewet"—
    pieces of meat in a thin
    cinnamon sauce
Beef marrow fritters
Eels in a thick spicy purée
Loach in a cold green sauce
    flavored with spices and
    sage
Large cuts of roast or boiled
    meat
Saltwater fish

SECOND COURSE
"The best roast that may be had"
Freshwater fish
Broth with bacon
A meat tile (see above)
Capon pasties and crisps
Bream and eel pasties
Blank Mang (see above, page
    219)

THIRD COURSE
Frumenty
Venison
Lampreys with hot sauce
Fritters
Roast bream and darioles
Sturgeon
Jellies

After the meal, sweets and confections were laid out on the board. Either then or later, spiced wines and wafers were served up, and sometimes dry whole spices "to help the digestion."

In country manors, game birds would figure on the menu, probably in place of the pastries, pasties, or fritters.

Cinnamon. A European view of its harvesting and transport in Borneo.

The aristocratic table differed from that of the middle levels of society in quantity rather than in essence. The recipes used were much the same, although where there was a large kitchen staff more ambitious dishes could be produced. There would be more courses, more dishes in each course, and every course would include—in addition to meat, fish, game and blank mang or frumenty—a "sotelte" (subtlety). This was a sweet dish, a jelly or pastry, sculpted or molded by some artist in the kitchen into splendid and fanciful representations of lions, eagles, crowns, or coats of arms. When sugar became commonplace in the sixteenth century, Italian confectioners achieved renown for the intricacy and magnificence of the spun sugar sculptures with which they bedecked the tables of the nobility.

A classic (if post-medieval) example of how cooks met the challenge of a grand banquet on a fish day was that given to Elizabeth of Austria when she made her ceremonial entry into Paris in 1571. Set out in the hall of the diocese were four large fresh salmon, ten large turbot, eighteen brill and the same number of mullet and gurnard (sea-robins), fifty crabs, eighteen trout, nine large and eight smaller pike, nine fresh shad, three creels of large smelts, two of oysters in their shells and one of oysters removed from their shells, one creel of mussels, two hundred pickled and two hundred smoked herrings, twelve lobsters, twenty-four cuts of salted salmon, fifty pounds of whale (probably the salted blubber, which Parisians used in quantity during Lent), two hundred cod tripes, the same number of fat young lampreys and the same number of fat cray-

The swan, an oily and frequently tough bird, was favored more for its looks than for its flesh and was served up in medieval times (and after) with all its plumage re-affixed and a small crown on its head.

Many dishes were placed on the table simultaneously during the medieval period, a custom which persisted until the nineteenth century.

fish, twelve carp a yard long and fifty which were only a third as large, eighteen full-grown lampreys, and a thousand frogs. The purveyor was slightly embarrassed at not being able to supply sturgeon, bream, turtle, or fresh mackerel.[21]

KNIVES AND FORKS

The food served during the Middle Ages fell into one of four main textural categories. There was the plain dry roast. There was the thickly sauced mixture—sometimes a kind of meat custard, like mortrews; sometimes a spicy grain pudding full of meat strips, like venison frumenty. There was the "brewet"—meat, poultry or fish in a thin, creamy spiced sauce. And there was the simple soup, with a few sops, pieces of bread or meat swimming in it.* In a rather different category were pies, pasties and fritters, which consisted of meat, sauce, and plate all in one self-contained package.

Texture was important in medieval eating because of the limited number of eating tools used. Most people carried a knife of the old, general-purpose dagger shape, and spoons were not uncommon. But the dinner fork was an oddity in most of Europe until the eighteenth century.

Forks had been used as kitchen implements for hundreds of years, and in Byzantium small ones were used at table from as early as the tenth century.[23] From Byzantium they traveled to Greece,[24] and from Greece to Italy, a country whose refined manners had once more become the envy of all Europe. But in Italy, for a while, they stuck. A French silk merchant, Jaques le Saige, noted them favorably at a ducal banquet in Venice in 1518. "These seigneurs, when they want to eat, take the meat up with a silver fork."[25] Yet although Catherine de Medici appears

---

* The number of sops in a serving was taken by guests as an indication of their host's meanness or generosity; the more, the better. On one occasion, when the Sieur de Vandy dined at the home of the Comte de Grandpré, "they placed before him a soup in which there were only two poor sops chasing each other around. Vandy tried to take one up but, as the plate was enormous, he missed his aim; he tried again, and could not catch it. He rose from the table and called his valet de chambre.

" 'You there! Pull off my boots.'

" 'What are you going to do?' his neighbor asked him.

" 'Permit me to have my boots removed,' said Vandy coldly, 'and I propose to dive into that plate in order to seize that sop!' "[22]

to have taken not only her cooks but her entire kitchen with her when she went to France in 1533 to marry the dauphin, the fork did not catch on. Seventy years later, the traveler Tom Coryat flattered himself that he had introduced a fashion for forks to the nobility of England.[26] It did not last. For another hundred years, although a few eccentrics used a fork for dining, most Europeans continued to eat with their fingers. Even as late as 1897, sailors in the British Navy were forbidden the use of knives and forks— because they were regarded as being prejudicial to discipline and manliness.[27]

TABLE MANNERS

The absence of the table fork would have had few repercussions on modes and manners had it not been for the way in which the service of food was organized. Usually, only men of the very highest rank had their own dishes, plates, and drinking cups. Other people ate in pairs, one "cover" meaning a serving for two. Each diner, however, had his own trencher, which was originally a thick slice of stale, unleavened bread measuring about six inches by four.[28] This acted as a kind of absorbent plate; sometimes the diner ate his trencher at the end of a meal; sometimes it would be given to the poor; sometimes to the dogs. In about the fifteenth century the bread trencher began to be superseded by a square of wood with a circular depression in the middle.*

When roast meat or game was being served, the carver placed the best pieces on the important guests' trenchers, the rest on platters on the table. The majority of other types of food were placed on the table in dishes containing portions for two, or sometimes, depending on the shape of the table and the proximity of the guests, for four. Some diners might use their knives for eating, but fingers were the customary tools, and the most efficient ones. Knives and spoons were of little help with the unboned chunks of meat and poultry often to be found in brewets and frumenties. Diners usually fished with their fingers in the platters

---

* It is an interesting survival that Scottish students today still give the name "trencher" to the type of university cap known elsewhere as a mortarboard, possibly because of the resemblance in shape, possibly because they once found that upside-down wooden trenchers offered excellent head protection against the rain.

The bread trencher. A pile of extra trenchers was kept handy to replace any that became sodden during the course of the meal.

they shared with their neighbors, conveyed a portion of food to their trenchers, and then to their mouths.

Because of this, the cleanliness of one's neighbor's fingers was a matter of some concern. Indeed, as Giovanni della Casa said: "Before meals it is right to wash your hands openly, even though you have no need to do so, in order that those who dip their fingers in the same dish as yourself may know for certain that you have cleaned them." [29]

It was one thing for a man to wash his hands *before* a meal, quite another to keep them clean during the course of it. In the Middle Ages and the Renaissance a number of "courtesy books" were written in an attempt to instill some decorum into the sprigs of the nobility, and they give a hair-raising picture of the table manners of the time. The fact that authors found it necessary to condemn certain undesirable habits suggests that those habits, though not necessarily common, were certainly not unknown.

"Let thy hands be clean," said Fra Bonvicino da Riva in 1290. "Thou must not put either thy fingers into thine ears, or thy hands to thy head. The man who is eating must not be cleaning by scraping with his fingers at any foul part." [30] By "any foul part," Fra Bonvicino may only have meant spots or stains on the clothing—or he may not. Later writers were more specific. They requested their readers not to blow their noses with their fingers, and not to go scratching at that part of the male anatomy which the Middle Ages and the Elizabethans called the "codware."

Scratching, when fleas and lice were omnipresent, was one of the habits most thundered against in the courtesy books. If it could be done surreptitiously, well and good. But to remove one's fingers from a shared bowl of food and promptly scratch one's head or neck could not be regarded as polite behavior. "If it happen that you cannot help scratching," recommended the fourteenth-century German author Tannhäuser, "then courteously take a portion of your dress, and scratch with that. That is more befitting than that your skin should become soiled." [31] (It also reduced the possibility of transferring a scratched-at louse back to the bowl, adhering to a soupy finger.)

Napkins, like forks, were unused in Tannhäuser's time, but if Della Casa is any guide, they had not done a great deal for cleanliness even by the sixteenth century. After discussing gluttons who dipped their hands into a dish almost to the elbow, Della Casa

Eating with the fingers.

remarked that they made a fearful mess of their napkins. "And these same napkins," he added, "they will use to wipe off perspiration, and even to blow their noses. You must not so soil your fingers as to make the napkin nasty in wiping them; neither clean them upon the bread which you are to eat." * [32]

There were other habits against which writers on etiquette warned their readers. It was, for example, offensive to "poke about everywhere when thou hast meat or eggs or some such dish. He who turns or pokes about on the platter, searching, is unpleasant, and annoys his neighbor at dinner." [33] Some people, too, were inclined, "when they have gnawed a bone, to put it back in the dish." [34] The correct place for such relics was the floor, thoughtfully carpeted with rushes, and strewn with sweet-smelling basil and southernwood. This was the custom even in the most elevated households. When Benvenuto Cellini was a young man, his employer made a "very large vase designed for the table of Pope Clement, into which at dinnertime were thrown bones and rinds of fruit." Perhaps the pope, at least, preferred a boneless floor? But no. "It was made," Benvenuto went on, "rather for display than necessity." [35]

DIGESTIVE WIND

The scene at a medieval banquet must have been one of considerable bustle and activity. Most guests brought their own retainers, who either stood nearby to fetch anything their master required,

* Della Casa's Victorian translator could not here restrain himself from interpolating: "We should hope not!"

or hovered behind his chair ready to pass a delicacy which might be out of reach. Servants scuttled back and forth from the boards set up around the sides of the room, bringing wine, carved meats, sauces, fresh trenchers, sweetmeats. Great nobles had tasters, whose task it was to ensure that the food and drink had not been poisoned. Dogs scavenged among the rushes on the floor. And senior household dignitaries supervised the whole proceedings, keeping an anxious eye on the clearing of one course and the setting of the next, while troubadours and acrobats entertained the guests during the interval.

But despite the noise, the spicy aromas of the food, and the predominant smell of unwashed humanity, the medieval courtesy books still remained adamant on the subject of breaking wind. Then—as before and since—it was not to be tolerated in polite society.

Of all the regulations relating to table manners through the ages, that against breaking wind has had the longest life. Surviving texts are not always specific about which aspect of the subject they are discussing (or perhaps it is simply that translators have too much delicacy to be precise in their anatomical geography), but it is clear that while a delicate burp has usually been acceptable in most societies, the audible release of digestive gases from the nether regions most certainly has not.

Dutiful Chinese were forbidden this relief as early as the sixth century B.C. In India four hundred years later, Kautilya ruled that men appointed to the king's service should "not indulge in bellicose talk, nor make statements that are uncultured . . . nor indulge in loud laughter when there is no joke, nor break wind." [36] It was said that the Roman emperor Claudius "planned an edict to legitimize the breaking of wind at table, either silently or noisily—after hearing about a man who was so modest that he endangered his health by an attempt to restrain himself." [37] (Though the question remains—who had made it illegal in the first place?)

A few eccentrics maintained their independence. When one of the caliphs of Baghdad paid Ibn al-Junayd the signal honor of inviting him to become an official boon companion, he declined, remarking that he preferred less elevated company, "where one can pass gas in this or that direction withou; much fuss being made about it." [38] He would have had the support of Salerno in this matter, for the *Regimen* claimed that:

By the end of the meal, the floor was a paradise for scavengers.

Great harms have grown, and maladies exceeding,
By keeping in a little blast of wind:
So cramps and dropsies, colics have their breeding,
And mazèd brains, for want of vent behind.[39]

It was unfortunate that the three main vegetables of the Middle Ages should have been among the most fartable of all. The modern astronaut knows that he has to lay off beans, cabbage and onions before a flight,* but medieval man was oblivious to cause and effect. He knew only that, despite the odds, he should "always beware of [his] hinder part from guns blasting." [41]

* The Western Regional Research Laboratory of the U.S. Department of Agriculture has, in the course of studying suitable foods for astronauts, developed a system for measuring, in quantitative terms, the "flatus-producing effect" of various substances. [40] Qualitatively, however, they have not yet been able to improve upon the Fartometer attributed to Dr. O. Medary, even though his Camelus windscale would appear to be susceptible to further refinement.

"Scientific researches! . . . or—an Experimental Lecture on the Powers of Air." Digestive wind in 1802.

PART FIVE

The Expanding World,
1490–1800

New Worlds and
New Foods

During the fifteenth century, the spice trade became somewhat chaotic. The Mongols who had ruled many of the land routes from the East were replaced at key points by the inflexible Ottoman Turks. For a time, however, Venice and Florence continued to trade profitably at Alexandria and Damascus. Venice alone brought back to Europe an estimated 2500 tons a year of pepper and ginger, and almost as much again of other spices.[1]

The merchants of the Italian cities were only the last in a long chain of middlemen who all exacted their profit from the trade. What this profit amounted to in the fifteenth century is uncertain, but in 1621 an Englishman reckoned that 3000 tons of spices could be bought in the Indies for £91,041, or $227,603, whereas by the time they reached Aleppo—the buying center at the eastern end of the Mediterranean—the price had soared to £789,168, or $1,972,920.[2]

Clearly, any nation which could bypass the established trade routes by sailing straight to the Spice Islands and buying direct from the producers would find it a profitable enterprise. There were many difficulties, not least those of ship design. But the fifteenth-century development of sturdy merchant ships which could withstand the buffeting of the open sea and had three masts instead of one—an innovation which made supplementary oars unnecessary—overcame the greatest of the practical difficulties.

The psychological turning point came when the last remnant

of the once great Byzantine empire—Constantinople itself—was captured by the Ottoman Turks in 1453. Three years later, Athens, too, the *sanctum sanctorum* of that Classical world which Europe had so recently rediscovered, fell to the assault of the infidel. Men who lived on the Atlantic coasts of Europe, visualizing complete closure of the eastern Mediterranean, looked again at what had been said in the past about the physical shape of the world, and some were convinced that, as the ancient philosophers had claimed, the western coasts of Africa could not be far from the eastern ends of India.

Personal fame, the glory of God, and a share in the spice trade —an unbeatable combination in fifteenth-century terms—all played a part in sending Columbus off on the voyage which was to end in the New World. For the admiral himself, the first prospect was perhaps the most enticing. Luis de Santángel, who lent Queen Isabella of Castille the money to subsidize the voyage, seems to have been more concerned with the second. But it was the possibility of intervening in the highly remunerative commerce in spices which almost certainly swung the balance for Isabella, her exchequer dangerously depleted by the campaign against the last Muslim garrisons in Spain.

When Columbus reached "the Indies" in 1492, he found none of the "powerful kingdoms and noble cities and rich provinces" [3] which one of his advisors had told him he might expect, but merely a "gentle, peaceful and very simple people" to whom he gave "little red caps and glass beads which they hung about their necks, together with other trifles that they cherished." [4] On his second voyage, he thought he had discovered in Haiti "different kinds of wild spices that could be brought to perfection by cultivation, such as fine-colored cinnamon (though bitter to the taste), ginger, pepper, and different kinds of mulberry trees for producing silk." [5] Whatever the "cinnamon" and "ginger" may have been, only the pepper—which was entirely different from the East Indian species—was to prove a useful addition to the spice chests of the Old World.

Vasco da Gama had more success. Arriving at Calicut on the southwest coast of India in 1498, he sent a man ashore to prospect. The emissary was greeted with: "May the Devil take thee! What

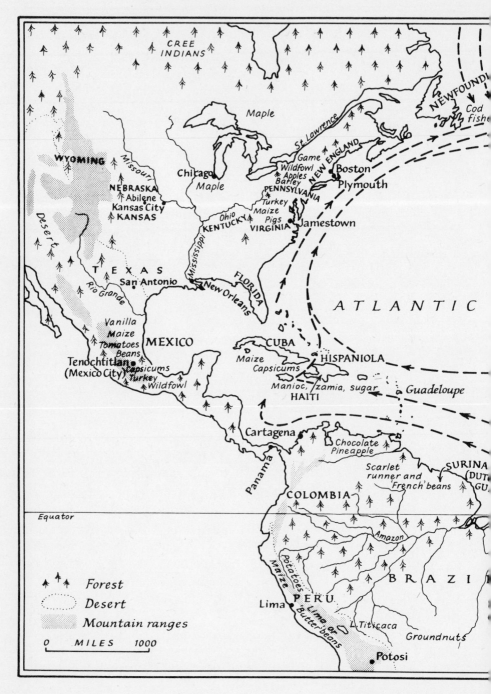

6. The New World

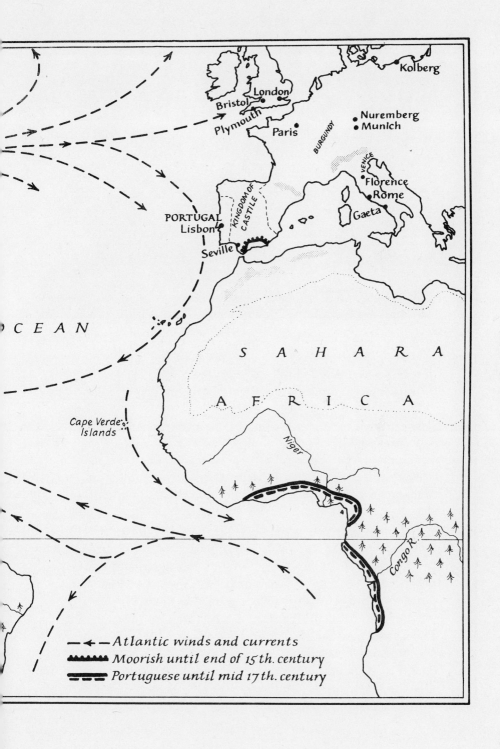

Kolberg

Bristol
London
Plymouth
Paris

Nuremberg
Munich

BURGUNDY

VENICE
Florence
Rome

PORTUGAL
Lisbon
KINGDOM OF CASTILE

Gaeta

Seville

OCEAN

S A H A R A

A F R I C A

Cape Verde
Islands

Niger

Congo R.

— ◄ — *Atlantic winds and currents*
▲▲▲▲▲ *Moorish until end of 15th. century*
▬▬▬▬ *Portuguese until mid 17th. century*

A pepper harvest. This Persian miniature shows the preparation of white pepper, in which the fruits were soaked so that the outer covering could be rubbed off, and then dried. The milder black pepper is produced by drying unripe berries gently in the sun.

brought you hither?" He replied: "We came in search of Christians and spices." [6]

Within twenty-five years, the nations of Europe were complaining just as much over the Portuguese monopoly of spices as they had earlier done over the Venetian. In 1523, a decree issued at Nuremberg commented sourly on the fact that over 100 tons of ginger and almost 2000 tons of pepper had come into Germany from Lisbon alone. And "the king of Portugal, with spices under his control, has set . . . prices as he will, because at no manner of dearness will they rest unsold among Germans." [7]

Later in the century, the Dutch began to whittle away the Portuguese monopoly, and by 1599 the English were so incensed over the fact that pepper had gone up from 15 p., or 37 cents, a pound to 40 p., or $1, that eighty London merchants met to establish the East India Company [8]—and, however unwittingly, the British Indian Empire. Soon, France, Denmark and Austria also contrived to find footholds in Asia, and Spain reached the East Indies by the Pacific route.

The question of imperial rights in unmapped territories had been "settled" by Pope Alexander VI Borgia in 1494 when he drew a line from north to south through the Atlantic, allocating to Spain all new lands west of the line, and to Portugal all those to the east. This, by chance, gave Brazil to Portugal, and it was the Portuguese possession of Africa in the east and Brazil in the west which had much to do with the associated expansion of the sugar and the slave trades.

The New World produced none of the traditional spices that had helped to stimulate the voyages of discovery. But it was to contribute to the diet of the Old World several new foodstuffs which were to be of the greatest importance in the centuries to come.

To Europe came maize or Indian corn, to become a staple food in northern Spain, Portugal and Italy and, later, in the Balkans. Potatoes, which, though an agent of disaster in Ireland, were to be a useful source of vitamin C to many other peoples. Chocolate, peanuts, vanilla, the tomato, the pineapple, "French beans," lima beans, the scarlet runner, red peppers, green peppers, tapioca and the turkey—all widened the horizons of the European cuisine.

Asia benefited by the introduction of pineapples, papaya and the sweet potato, which arrived little more than a century after Columbus's discovery of America. Chili peppers soon gave a new and scorching tang to Indian curries. In the early nineteenth century, potatoes were planted in Nepal, where they later became a staple food of the Sherpas.

From the Americas to Africa went maize, manioc, sweet potatoes, groundnuts and French beans, immensely valuable in supplementing the few subsistence crops of the Dark Continent. In colonial times, administrators were also to introduce pineapples and other exotic fruits to the south.

By the time Australasia came into the orbit of the settled world, there had been a long period of experiment in other lands and it was possible to stock the new territories with every suitable known plant, as well as with cattle, sheep and pigs to swell the range of indigenous livestock, which in most places consisted of no more than dogs, bats and rats.

The traffic in foodstuffs between the Old World and the New was by no means one-way. Columbus himself carried vegetable seeds, wheat, chickpeas, and sugarcane back with him to the Caribbean on his later voyages. The second Spanish governor to arrive in Colombia, in 1543, took with him the seeds of wheat, barley, chickpeas, broad beans and vegetables, as well as the first cows to be seen there—which he sold for 1000 gold pesos each.[9] British settlers introduced the same foods to North America a few decades later. Bananas, rice and citrus fruits—natives of Asia— were all taken to the New World. Yams and cowpeas traveled across the Atlantic with the slaves for whom they had been staple foods in Africa. Coconuts were taken to the Bahamas. Coffee to Brazil. Breadfruit to the Caribbean.

Despite all these exchanges, however, no "international cuisine" resulted. Rather the opposite, in fact, for the European pursuit of empire nourished an increasing awareness of national identities. Formerly, the pattern of eating had been divided horizontally.

Dinner at sea . . .

The food of the rich in Europe, like that of the poor, had a great deal in common, regardless of country. But a vertical division now also emerged, and the cuisines of individual countries began to take on consciously individual characteristics.

The feeling of "separateness" was intensified rather than diminished by the reports of those travelers who began to haunt the highways of the world in the seventeenth century. In the past, explorers, sailors and merchants had all viewed "foreign" food with the eye of the hungry realist. "The world is a bridge, pass over it but build no house upon it." [10] The early venturers erected no theories of racial superiority on the bridge of other peoples' worlds.

But it was to be a different matter when the amateur traveler embarked on those jaunts to foreign parts which were to become so fashionable, especially in the eighteenth century. Books of reminiscence and advice began to appear in growing numbers, and the travel writer, wise in the ways of his world, made the point that no country other than his own had such superb raw materials for its food, such refinement in handling them, or such delicacy in consuming them. His descriptions of foreign food were not only defamatory, but very funny indeed. It was unfortunate that he should also have succeeded in conveying the impression that the use of knives and forks was an index of civilization.*

In Europe—inevitably—the non-traveling man became progressively more certain that the jungle began immediately beyond his own frontiers.

* Chopsticks remained problematical until the nineteenth century, when they were finally condemned.

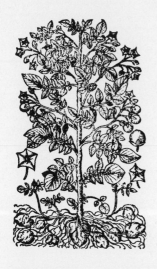

13.
The
Americas

The "gentle, peaceful and very simple people" [1] who greeted
Columbus when he reached America were inhabitants of the
Bahamas, islands "full of green trees and abounding in springs,"
with "gardens that were as beautiful as Castille in May." [2] But
"the Admiral could see that this was not the land he sought; nor
did it offer such promise of riches as to hold him there." [3] In the
months that followed, the Spanish ships cruised south, visiting
many of the islands in the Caribbean—still in search of spices and
gold, but surveying the territory as they went and learning a little
about the people.

One thing they learned was that the people ate many foods
which appeared revolting to Europeans, among them "large fat
spiders, white worms that breed in rotten wood, and other decayed
objects." [4] The peoples of tropical America had, in fact, a long
tradition of eating the plump insects which abounded in those
latitudes, and the agave worm (*meocuilin*) was a delicacy greatly
favored at the Aztec court and still relished in Mexico in the
twentieth century. Since Columbus encountered the Taino tribes
of the islands on friendly terms, the "other decayed objects" probably included a Taino speciality—zamia bread.

This was made by grating the stems of the zamia plant and then
shaping the pulp into balls which were left in the sun for two or
three days until they began to rot, turn black in color, and become wormy. When suitably ripe, the little spheres were flattened
into cakes and baked on a griddle over the fire. "If it is eaten

Production of cassava bread in the Lesser Antilles. 5—Peeling the manioc roots. 6—Pulping them in the large rotary grater. 7—Pulping them on an old-fashioned saddle grater. 8—Pressing out the poisonous juices. 9—Sifting the flour. 10—Cooking the bread on a hotplate. 13 (under the eaves of the right-hand shed)—The bread hung up to dry. (Tobacco preparation is the other activity illustrated in this engraving.)

before it becomes black and is not full of . . . worms, the eaters will die," said the Tainos.[5] They were perfectly right. Unless zamia pulp is fermented or very thoroughly washed, it can be highly toxic.

Far more acceptable to the Spaniards was the bread made in Cuba from an equally poisonous plant, the bitter variety of manioc. The roots of this were peeled and grated, and the unwholesome juices squeezed out under heavy pressure. These, if boiled, could be used to make the harmless cassareep sauce, and also threw a sediment which could be transformed into that innocuous dish known in the Western world as tapioca. The pulp itself was sieved and then shaped into flat cakes, which were cooked slowly on a griddle. Soft and flexible when fresh, this bread—cassava—could be dried and kept for two or three years. The Spanish, and later the French, adopted cassava with some enthusiasm. There were even gourmets who claimed that it was superior to wheaten bread.

Manioc was to be introduced into Africa by the Portuguese during the sixteenth century, where it proved a valuable addition to the indigenous food plants. Though deficient in protein, it was highly resistant to attack by the famine-bringers of the Dark Continent—locusts—and could be left in the earth for as much as two years after maturity without deteriorating, so acting as a useful reserve against hunger.

As well as objectionable insects and strange breads, the people of the Caribbean ate many other foods which the European voyagers had never seen before. There were "cooked roots that had the flavor of chestnuts" [6]—probably sweet potatoes. There were beans, in variety. The only domesticated food animal appeared to be the dog, but there were wild birds, fish, and crabs in abundance. In Panama, the people were expert at preserving a special kind of small fish. They wrapped them "in leaves as apothecaries roll electuaries [medicinal powders] in paper, and after being dried in the oven the fish keep for a long time." [7] There were also many fruits, from which fermented drinks were made.

Of all these unfamiliar new foodstuffs, maize was to be the most important in later history. Europe knows this grain by its Cuban name; in North America, seventeenth-century settlers were introduced to it by local Indians and called it "Indian corn" ("corn" being, then as now, a general-purpose European name for any kind of grain).

MAIZE

On his early visits to Cuba, Columbus noted that maize was "most tasty, boiled, roasted, or ground into flour." [8] When he returned to Spain, his most popular exhibits from the New World proved to be a few specimen "Indians" and some handfuls of gold dust, but he seems also to have taken maize seeds with him.

With the aid of the Venetians who carried it to the Near East, the Spaniards were instrumental in distributing maize around the Mediterranean. Less directly, they also introduced it to Asia. When Ferdinand Magellan set out in 1519 to make another attempt on Spain's behalf to reach the Spice Islands by a westward route, he probably took maize with him. It was known in the Philippines soon after, and by 1555 was sufficiently important in parts of China to rate a mention in a regional history of the inland province of Honan. [9]

By 1563, when Arcimboldo painted this personification of "Summer," maize was familiar enough around the Mediterranean to be included in it.

To Portugal, however, belongs the doubtful credit of having introduced maize to Africa, where it was first grown to provide ships' stores for the slave trade. Among history's many ironies is the fact that a food introduced to fuel the slaving ships should have led to a general population increase in tropical Africa which ensured that those same ships would never sail empty of human cargo.*

Maize was accepted willingly in Africa because it grew so much more rapidly than other grains and its cultivation was far less demanding. Although the large, specially bred plants of modern times require a fertile soil and careful tending, this is because heavy crops are the aim, and the same land is worked year after year. In sixteenth-century Africa, however, when one patch of soil became exhausted, the peasant cultivator merely moved on to another. A woman working alone could plant maize, leave it to grow, and harvest it as and when she needed it, or in greater quantity for storage. It was subsistence, not commercial agriculture, but one woman, unaided, could produce enough food to ensure that her family did not go hungry.

In time, the health of those peoples in the Old World who adopted maize as a staple food deteriorated. The peoples of Africa today are still only too well acquainted with "the disease of the mealies" (maize), otherwise known as pellagra. Modern nutritionists have discovered that maize lacks certain important vitamin elements, and over-reliance on it therefore results in deficiency symptoms. In Central and South America, the people who depended on maize ate with it tomatoes, capsicum peppers, and fish (which are unusually rich in the missing elements) and so escaped pellagra, but fruit and vegetables were not much eaten in Europe and Africa until the eighteenth or nineteenth century. Furthermore, vegetables were often cooked in such a way as to destroy their vitamin content, and the most easily available fruits were those—such as apples—with a comparatively low vitamin rating. Fresh fish, like meat, was relatively rare food among the poor in, for example, parts of France and Italy, and it was the poor who adopted maize as a staple grain. As a result, it soon lost much of its

---

* There were occasions when the Portuguese regretted their introduction of maize to Africa, as when they visited the kingdom of Quiteve (inland Mozambique) in the sixteenth century and were entertained with "wine of maize . . . called *pombe,* which they must drink, although against stomach, not to contemn the king's bounty; whence the Portuguese have had some trouble . . ." [10]

initial popularity in Europe, if not in Africa (where the options were fewer), and did not regain it until a more balanced diet became common.

FOOD IN MEXICO

If Cortés and the four hundred Spaniards who discovered Mexico in 1519 had been more concerned with cooking and less with conquest, they might have been able to teach the people of the Old World how to make more nourishing use of maize.

The Mexican, in Aztec as in later times, lived mainly on maize, beans, tomatoes, and capsicum peppers. The mass of the people began their day several hours before they breakfasted, pausing only at about 10 A.M. for a bowl of maize porridge, sweetened with honey or spiced with red pepper. The main meal of the day came at the hottest time, in the early afternoon. Then there would be tortillas to eat, a dish of beans—which were grown in Mexico in great variety—and a sauce made from tomatoes or peppers.

Tortillas were the foundation of the Mexican diet. Dried

A Mexican girl learning to make tortillas. She grinds the boiled kernels on a *metlatl,* or saddle quern, moistening the paste with water from the pot on her right. Afterward the paste will be kneaded and patted into flat cakes and cooked on the *comalli,* an earthenware platter resting on three hearthstones.

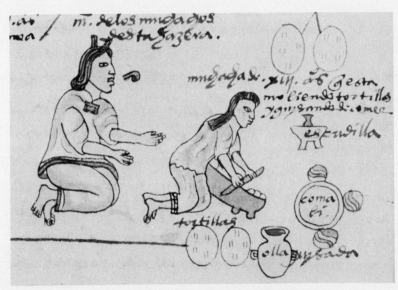

kernels of maize were boiled in water with a little charcoal or lime added to loosen the skins, which were afterward removed by rubbing between the hands. The kernels were then crushed with a stone roller to form a paste, extra water being added if necessary. Finally, the dough was kneaded and slapped into thin round cakes and cooked on a special hotplate, the *comalli*, which rested over the fire. (The grain for these tortillas was thus cooked twice, which made a considerable difference to the finished result; the Old World prepared maize in the same way as its other grains, and finished up with a tough cornmeal which could be used only for a rather stodgy porridge such as *polenta*.)

Beans, which supplied the protein in the diet, were usually boiled, although if young and small they were probably eaten fresh. Aztec Mexico does not appear to have extracted cooking oil from plant seeds, and the meat they used was usually that of wild game, which provided very little fat. The *refrito* so common in the country today, a dish of boiled beans, mashed, fried, and topped with grated cheese, became a feature of the table only after the Spaniards had introduced cows and other domesticated animals to Central America.

Tomatoes, now such a favored ingredient in salads and composite dishes throughout the world, seem to have made their first appearance as weeds in the maize fields. Cultivation had increased the yield and greatly improved the varieties by the time the Spaniards arrived in the Americas. Thin shavings of unripe tomatoes were used in a number of Mexican dishes, while the ripe fruits were often combined with chili peppers to make a tangy sauce for a bland dish of beans. The type of tomato introduced into Europe in the sixteenth century seems to have been yellow in color, hence the name "Golden Apple" by which it was first known. Although the tomato fruit consists largely of water, it is a valuable source of vitamins A and C.

The American pepper, with its very high vitamin-C content, bore no relation to the *Piper nigrum* of India. There are two classifications of red pepper, or capsicum—the large "sweet" type and the smaller "chili." Sweet (bell) peppers can be used as a vegetable while they are still green and unripe; a special type, ripe and red, is dried and powdered to make paprika. Varieties of chili, whose effect can be inflammable, are sometimes cooked in meat dishes, sometimes pickled to make Tabasco sauce, some-

Mexicans cultivating a walled garden in which there are leaf vegetables and fruit trees.

times dried and powdered into cayenne. The people of tropical America used—and still use—capsicums with everything. It was estimated in the early seventeenth century that there were at least forty varieties; [11] in Mexico today there are said to be ninety-two. In early Columbian times, capsicums were incorporated fresh in soups and stews, eaten with fish and flesh, mixed sometimes with salt or tomatoes to moderate their impact. The people dried them, too, and made them into a variety of pickles to take with them on journeys.

Although maize was most often used for plain tortillas, there was one other Mexican dish, featured on special occasions, which combined tortilla dough with a savory stuffing. Here, beans, capsicums, green tomato shavings, and shreds of meat or fish were mixed together and wrapped in a casing of tortilla paste. This, in turn, was wrapped in corn husks or leaves, and the whole was steamed until it was cooked. The result, after the inedible husks were removed, was a tamale, a savory one-dish meal—the Mexican equivalent of England's Cornish pasties, or China's spring rolls.

When the conquistadors ventured into the market of the Aztec capital, Tenochtitlán, they were "astonished at the number of people and the quantity of merchandise that it contained, and at the good order and control that was maintained . . . Each kind of merchandise was kept by itself and had its fixed place marked out." Some stallholders sold "beans and sage and other vegetables and herbs," some "rabbits, hare, deer, young ducks, little dogs [bred for food], and other such creatures," some fruit, some salt, some honey and honey paste, and some "cooked food, dough, and tripe." [12]

The "cooked food" would be stews, spiced maize porridge, or tamales. The dough would be readymade tortilla paste. But the "tripe" was probably not what is known as tripe today—the stomach lining of ruminant animals. The only ruminant animal of Aztec times seems to have been the wild deer, which was unlikely to have been common enough to keep a tripe seller in business. Bernal Díaz, the conquistador whose description this is, may have been using the word "tripe" in the casual sense, where "tripes" are equated with guts or entrails. There would be enough business, and to spare, for a vendor specializing in prepared poultry giblets, for although game animals were rare, there were great seasonal migrations of ducks, geese and other wildfowl, when birds could be trapped in considerable numbers. Even the poorest citizens of Tenochtitlán, who might not be able to eat the birds themselves, could at least afford to buy giblets to include in a tamale stuffing.

Mexicans ate not only wild game, but many—nowadays unusual —foods from the lakes in which the capital was built. These included tadpoles, water flies, larvae, white worms, and a curious froth from the surface of the water which could be compressed into a substance similar to cheese, as well as more conventional pond life, such as frogs and freshwater shrimps. At the court of Moctezuma, *axolotls*, a variety of newt peculiar to Mexico, were considered a great delicacy. So, too, were winged ants, the agave worm (sometimes called the maguey slug), and the iguana, that large tree-lizard which even Columbus's sailors, finding it in the Caribbean, had admitted to be "white, soft and tasty." [13] The agave worm was often served with guacamole, which in Aztec times seems to have been made not only with avocados, or alligator pears—rich in protein, fat, and A and B vitamins—but with tomatoes and the inevitable capsicums.

The only domesticated livestock of Mexico were the turkey and the dog, which was regarded as a useful but inferior food. In meat dishes, "the turkey-meat was put on top, and the dog underneath, to make it seem more." [14] When European cattle were introduced, the dog ultimately disappeared as a food animal. The turkey, by contrast, entered on a wider stage after the Spanish conquest.

THE TURKEY

How the turkey acquired its English name remains, despite energetic theorizing, something of a mystery. The most probable answer seems to be that it was carried to England soon after its first arrival in Europe (in about 1523-24) by the "Turkey merchants" who traded to the eastern Mediterranean and usually touched in at the Spanish port of Seville during the voyage. Not knowing its Mexican name *uexolotl*, or perhaps merely reluctant to make the effort of pronouncing it, the English simply dubbed it the "turkie-bird."

Continental Europe was no less vague on the subject. In France, the name most generally favored was *coq d'Inde* (Indian cock), ultimately corrupted to *dinde* or *dindon*. In Italy, the bird was at first called *galle d'India*; in Germany *indianische Henn*. The sex

Mexican portrait of a turkey.

German portrait of an *indianische Henn*.

of the names might be variable but the principle was the same. At first sight, it seems perfectly reasonable that the bird should have been attributed to India; the New World stubbornly remained the "Spanish Indies" for some time after Columbus's discovery of it. Unfortunately, both the Germans and the Dutch chose to embroider on the Indian theme, producing the *calecutische Hahn* and the *Kalkoen* [15] which so confusingly suggest an origin in Calicut on the southwest coast of India, where da Gama first landed.

The likelihood is that the *calecutische Hahn* was no more than the brain-child of some sales-conscious European breeder, trying to convince his customers that what he had to offer was not just any old *indianische Henn* but the genuine article, all the way from Calicut. India does not, in fact, appear to have played any part in the transmission of the turkey from Mexico to Europe; in the early seventeenth century, the Mughal emperor Jahangir was still having difficulty in finding hen birds to mate with the three cocks he had managed to acquire. What *is* odd is that the Indian name for the turkey comes geographically closer to the mark than most, although it is still a few hundred miles out. The Indians call the bird *peru*. Regrettably, however, the bird was no more indigenous to Peru than it was to Turkey or, indeed, to India.

CANNIBALISM IN THE AZTEC WORLD

What the conquistadors found most reprehensible about the Aztecs was the practice of ceremonial cannibalism. The Spaniards might execute their prisoners and criminals in the most barbarous fashion, but they killed them in the name of Christianity and did not eat them afterward.

Cannibalism appears only to have become an accepted part of Aztec ritual in the fifteenth century. It is, perhaps, difficult for modern man to sympathize with the custom, but the human heart has always appeared to be the finest offering a human being can make to the god or gods he worships. It depends very much on social conditions whether the offering is made symbolically, or in actuality. Given a particular set of circumstances—in which war, overpopulation, and ruthless political leadership often figure—this basic concept has often been expanded to take in a belief that, just as the gods draw strength from an offering of the human heart, man can increase his own strength by absorbing the strength of another man, preferably one who has proved a worthy adversary in battle. The only way of absorbing such an opponent's strength was to eat the flesh and sinew of which it was composed.

The conquistadors were horrified at the sight of the skull racks of Tenochtitlán, relics of apparently numberless blood sacrifices to the sun and subsequent cannibal banquets. The Aztec gods demanded the *living* heart of their sacrifices, so the priests ripped the victims open, alive, with a flint knife, and tore out the still beating hearts. Afterward, the head was hung on a skull rack, one thigh was presented to the supreme council and other choice cuts to various nobles. The remainder of the body was returned to the victim's captor, who took it home and had it cooked into *tlaca-tlaolli*, or maize-and-man stew, which was reverently consumed by all the family.

It was, perhaps, the ritual acceptance rather than the blood which so appalled the conquistadors. As they were soon to prove, they had nothing to learn from the Aztecs as far as torture and death were concerned. Before the time of Cortés, it is estimated that Central Mexico had 25,000,000 inhabitants. Thirty years later, these had been reduced to just over 6,000,000. By 1605, only 1,075,000 remained.[16] War, economic upheaval, exploitation, new diseases to which the peoples of Central America had no resistance —all these combined to produce one of the most comprehensive human catastrophes in the history of the world.

THE INCAS OF PERU

Cortés had gone north from the Caribbean to Mexico. Francisco Pizarro went south on an even more extraordinary voyage of discovery. In Peru, he found the dream of all explorers—a land where emeralds were to be had for the asking, and temples were paneled in gold.

The food eaten by the people of Peru was mainly vegetarian, although there was an abundance of fish along the narrow coastal strip and in the mountain waters of Lake Titicaca, and there would sometimes be a communal game hunt, when deer, wild llamas and guanacos, bears, pumas, foxes, and the large rodent called *vizcacha* were trapped and slaughtered. Guinea pigs, too, were raised in almost every household, and ducks seem also to have been domesticated. The Incas disapproved of eating dogs, but some people still regarded them as a useful item of diet.

Nevertheless, these foods were occasional luxuries. It was maize and potatoes, squash and beans, manioc and sweet potatoes, groundnuts (peanuts), tomatoes, avocados, and chili peppers which made up the bulk of the Peruvian diet. The beans, groundnuts and avocados supplied a good deal of protein. Vitamin A came from winter squashes, tomatoes, and avocados; B from groundnuts and avocados; and C from tomatoes, peppers, and, in smaller quantities, from potatoes.

Groundnuts were already familiar to the Spaniards, who had encountered them in Haiti and were soon to be instrumental in introducing the Peruvian variety to the Malay archipelago, from which it traveled on to China in the early 1600s.[17] But the potato was something entirely new—"a dainty dish even for Spaniards," admitted one of the conquistadors.[18]

Climatically, Peru and the neighboring Andean regions were very different from Mexico and the islands. Maize was the staple food of the lowlands, where it was cooked without much refinement; Peruvians merely ground the dried kernels and boiled the flour to a porridge, instead of using the more troublesome boil-and-bake process favored in Mexico. Above 11,000 feet, however, maize would not grow. It was replaced in most of the highland areas by potatoes, or by oca, quinoa or other tubers which were never to travel beyond their Andean homelands.

The peoples of Peru had discovered how to preserve potatoes by a combined freezing and drying method. When the crop had been harvested, the potatoes were spread out on the ground and left overnight in the biting open air. Next day, great numbers of men, women and children assembled to tread out the moisture from them. The same process was repeated for the next four or five days, after which the potatoes, now freed from much of their water content, were finally dried and stored. These dried potatoes, known as *chuñu*, were of the greatest importance to the people of the highlands.

Digging and
transporting
potatoes
in Peru.

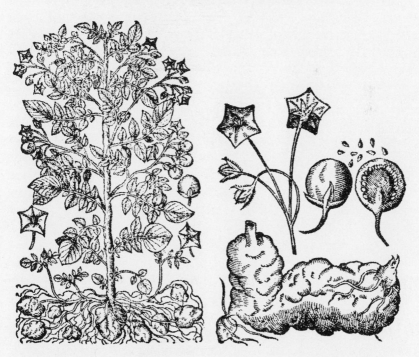

Solanum tuberosum. The potato arrived in Europe in good time for classification according to Bauhinus's new binomial system in 1619.

The conquistadors soon recognized the virtues of the potato, fresh, or in *chuñu* form, as a food for the masses. The slave workers in the silver mines of Potosí subsisted almost entirely on *chuñu,* and before long speculators were streaming across the Atlantic from Spain to buy up supplies from the producers in the mountains, resell them at an inflated price to the mineworkers, and then return home considerably richer from the enterprise.

INTRODUCTION OF THE POTATO TO EUROPE

As soon as Spain began to organize her shipping to carry away the wealth of the Peruvian mines, she adopted potatoes as basic ships' stores. The plant was therefore carried to Europe, and cultivated there, very soon after the conquest of Peru. By 1573, enough potatoes were being grown in Spain for the Hospital de la Sangre at Seville to order in stocks of them at the same time as other provisions.[19] From Spain they found their way to Italy, where by 1601, according to the botanist Jules Charles de l'Ecluse, they were so common that people did not even treat them as a delicacy but cooked them "with mutton in the same manner as they do with turnips and the roots of carrots." [20]

The potato reached England and, from there, Germany by a different route. It seems probable that Sir Francis Drake collected supplies at Cartagena on the Colombian coast in 1586, when he was on his way to Virginia to take off a few starving English settlers and ship them back to Europe. Owing to some confusion in the *Herbal* published by John Gerard in 1597, it was believed for centuries that the potato originated in Virginia, and it was not until the 1930s that the geneticist N. I. Vavilov showed this to have been impossible.[21] Curiously enough, the potato was introduced to Virginia only when English colonists took it back across the Atlantic from Europe, and it was not grown in Mexico until as late as the eighteenth century.

In the early days, the new vegetable became fashionable in some European circles. Dr. Tobias Venner said that the nourishment it yielded, "though somewhat windy," was "very substantial, good and restorative," [22] and William Salmon claimed that it stopped "fluxes of the bowels," was full of nutrients, and cured consumption. "Being boiled, baked or roasted," he went on, potatoes "are eaten with good butter, salt, juice of oranges or lemons, and double refined sugar . . . They increase seed and provoke lust, causing fruitfulness in both sexes." [23] But a great many people remained unconvinced.

In 1619 the potato was banned in Burgundy because the people were persuaded that "too frequent use of them caused the leprosy." This idea persisted in France until well into the eighteenth century, and in other regions other ills were attributed to the vegetable. In Switzerland, where it was eaten in quantity, it was blamed for scrofula.

Where potatoes were not immediately cultivated after their introduction into Europe, people became remarkably obdurate about accepting them in later times. In 1774 the hungry citizens of Kolberg refused to touch them when Frederick the Great of Prussia dispatched a wagonload to relieve famine. In 1795, the American Benjamin Thompson, Count Rumford in the hierarchy of the Holy Roman Empire, during one of his scientific experiments into feeding the poor as well as possible for as little as possible, decided that barley soup was the answer, thickened with potatoes and peas, seasoned with vinegar, and served with snippets of stale bread to encourage that mastication which seemed "very powerfully to assist in promoting digestion." [24] But though Count Rumford favored potatoes in the soup, the poor of Munich most definitely did not, and it was some time before they could even be persuaded to taste it.

Even that energetic advocate Antoine-Auguste Parmentier had an uphill task persuading the French that potatoes were not in fact poisonous. Success came at last, however. In 1806 Antoine Viard published the cookbook *Le Cuisinier Imperial* in which there were several potato recipes, and in 1814 Antoine Beauvilliers regaled the French public with a work extolling such traditional British delicacies as *Woiches Rabettes* (Welsh rarebit), *Plomb-poutingue* (plum pudding), and *Machepotetesse* (mashed potatoes).[25]

BRAZILIAN SUGAR AND THE SLAVE TRADE

Sugar and the slave trade became interdependent very soon after the discovery of the New World, in the Caribbean even before Brazil. As early as 1506, Spain had begun cultivating sugar in the Greater Antilles, that string of islands dominated by Cuba and Hispaniola which rims the north side of the Caribbean. Decimation of the native population had led to a labor shortage, and laboring was not a task for conquistadors. At home in Spain, slavery was commonplace. In the fifteenth century, rich families had owned as many as fifty slaves, some of them Greeks, Russians, Albanians, or Turks bought at the famous slave market of Caffa on the Black Sea, but most of them Negroes from Africa.[26] Almost automatically, therefore, the pioneers of the New World looked to Africa for labor replacements.

Soon, however, the Spaniards became more interested in gold and silver than in sugar, and it was the Portuguese who saw the profit that could be made from combining slaving with sugar production in their newly acquired territory in Brazil. The Portu-

Sugar production in Brazil, from cane to loaves. In the background the juice is pressed from the cane; in the right foreground it is simmered and reduced until crystals form.

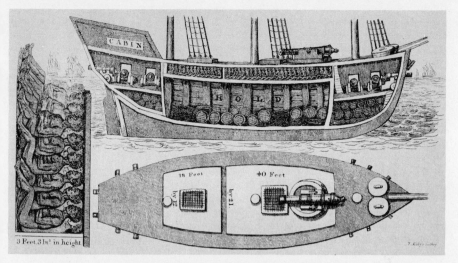

As late as the 1820s, slavers bound for Brazil still packed over five hundred human beings into a space measuring less than nine hundred feet square and just over three feet high.

guese had been able to corner the slave trade with the clearest possible conscience when, in the fifteenth century, Pope Nicholas V had authorized them to "attack, subject, and reduce to perpetual slavery the Saracens, pagans, and other enemies of Christ southward from Capes Bajador and Non, including all the coast of Guinea." [27] As it transpired, the kings and merchants of the Gold Coast were only too anxious to part with slaves in exchange for European cloth, hardware, spirits or firearms.

By 1526, however, even such an ardent Christian convert as Mbemba Nzinga of the Congo was driven to protest to the Portuguese that merchants were "taking every day our natives, sons of the land and sons of our noblemen and vassals and our relatives," kidnaping them in effect, to exchange them for European goods. So great, said the king to his brother monarch in Portugal, was "the corruption and licentiousness, that our country is being completely depopulated, and Your Highness should not agree with this nor accept it as in your service." [28] But the voice of the Congolese ruler was too faint to compete with the demands of the Brazilian sugar producers. More and more slaves were needed to work "for half a year together night and day like horses." [29] In 1550, there were five sugar plantations in Brazil. In 1623, the number had increased to 350.[30]

In 1635, the Dutch began to take a hand in the sugar game

An American Indian town in the 1580s, in what later became Virginia. Top center, a tobacco field. On the right, fields of maize sown at carefully planned intervals to ensure a continuing supply and a choice of green, semi-mature, and mature ears. In the center, a feast laid out.

when they invaded and occupied the whole northern part of Brazil, and a few years later wrested the Gold Coast from Portugal. They were thrown out of Brazil again in 1654, but in the meantime they had learned a great deal about sugar production. The English, French and Danes who had taken possession of a number of islands in the Caribbean soon discovered from the Dutch how to produce good sugar and make a profit out of it.

The demand for slaves to work the new plantations increased enormously. Before 1600, it is estimated that fewer than a million Negroes had been landed in the Americas. In the seventeenth century, the number increased to 2,750,000. In the eighteenth, it reached 7,000,000.[31] By this time, of course, labor-intensive cultivation techniques had proved their worth and had spread to mainland North America. Now it was not only sugar but tobacco and cotton which needed black workers capable of withstanding the combined assault of moist heat and human brutality.

Competition over sugar brought to an end that phase of imperialism which had begun with competition over spices. At the beginning, sugar had been unimportant, a minor luxury. But the development of plantations in America came just when supplies of Europe's traditional sweetener, honey, were falling off, partly as a result of the northern Reformation's campaign against the monasteries, whose need for beeswax candles had placed them among the foremost honey producers. As soon as there was plenty of sugar available, sugar became popular. It became even more popular when it was discovered that fruit could be preserved in it (about 1600) and jam made with it (sometime before 1730).

Sugar became so important to trade that in the 1670s the Dutch yielded New York to England in exchange for the captured sugar lands of Surinam, and in 1763 France was prepared to leave England with the whole of Canada, provided she had Guadeloupe returned to her.

THE SETTLING OF NORTH AMERICA

The potato, the turkey, the tomato, maize, avocado pears, pineapples, lima beans, scarlet runners, "French" beans, chocolate, peanuts, vanilla, red peppers and green peppers—not to mention gold and silver, tobacco, rubber, chewing gum and quinine. What the Americas contributed to the diet of the rest of the world was to add up to quite a formidable list.

Most of these innovations came from Central and South America, however. The North in the early days was to provide mainly fish, furs and timber, though its first explorers continued to hope that it would also disclose a waterway leading to the Pacific, and thence to the Spice Islands of the East. The Spaniards ventured with drastic results into Florida. The French sent Jacques Cartier to have a look at Canada.

The English made a more immediate profit from their early forays. The Cabots had been dispatched in 1496 to "seek out, discover and find whatsoever isles, countries, regions or provinces of the heathen and infidels wheresoever they be, which before this time have been unknown to all Christians." [32] They discovered no heathen provinces within the meaning of the act, but reported the existence of great cod-fishing banks off the coast of Newfoundland. Fishing fleets from England, France, Portugal and Holland haunted the shores of Newfoundland from then on, using the island as a base and a place to dry the catch for transport back to Europe. The abundance of cod within easy range of what was to become New England later gave the infant colonies an excellent start in life.

After two catastrophic attempts to settle Virginia in the sixteenth century, England at last contrived in 1607 to land a number of colonists who proved capable of surviving—though only just. "They chased out a few Indians," reported the contemporary Antwerp agent in London, "and put up a three-sided fort, and planted . . . adjoining land with corn, on which they could live a long time." [33] This highly flattering view of the colonists did not stand up to closer inspection. Two years later, an arriving immigrant discovered that many of them "were dispersed in the savages' towns, living upon their alms for an ounce of copper a day, and fourscore lived twenty miles from the fort, and fed upon nothing but oysters eight weeks space, having no other allowance at all, neither were the people of the country able to relieve them if they would." [34]

The Jamestown settlers were, in fact, an argumentative and incompetent crew, reluctant to work, ill equipped with tools and materials, very conscious of their dignity. The land was rich in game, the waters alive with fish, the woods full of edible berries. But if it had not been for friendly Indians, the colonists would have starved. The Pilgrim Fathers who landed on Plymouth Rock in 1620 seem to have been better equipped and more efficient— if no less argumentative—than their predecessors in the south.

The settlers very soon discovered that they had to learn to make the best of indigenous foods. They had brought wheat and rye seeds with them, but these were difficult to grow in fields still tufted with tree stumps after the colonists' amateurish clearing operations. Maize, on the other hand, was easy. From the Indians they learned not only how to grow it,* but how to cook it in a dozen simple and enjoyable ways—as porridge, flatbread, and as a kind of frumenty. They were pleased, too, to recognize their friend the turkey. True to tradition, there was some confusion over the bird's name, but this time it was very slight. The settlers' turkey was the Indians' *furkee.*

From the Indians, the settlers discovered not only what was edible, but how to cook it. They learned about the seacoast clambake. A pit was dug and lined with flat stones on which a fire was lit. When the stones were white-hot, the embers were brushed away and a layer of seaweed placed on the stones. On top of this went alternate layers of clams and ears of maize, interleaved with further quantities of seaweed. The pit, when full, was covered with a blanket of wet cloth or hide, which was kept moist throughout the hour or so of cooking time. The clams and corn emerged tender, moist and delicious.

Another cooking technique they discovered was the barbecue, which seems to have filtered north from the Caribbean. From about 1610, shipwrecked sailors, runaway bonded servants, refugees from religious persecution, had begun to congregate in the northern regions of Hispaniola, which the Spaniards had never properly settled. They had, however, taken pigs and cattle there, and the wild progeny of these domesticated livestock soon multiplied. The human outcasts of the island learned from surviving Carib Indians how to salt and smoke-dry the plentiful meat on lattices of green wood built over a fire of animal bones and hides. The Caribs

---

* Being from the north of Europe, none of the settlers had seen maize before, although by the seventeenth century it had become fairly common around the Mediterranean.

A barbecue in sixteenth-century Brazil.

called the technique *boucan,* and this passed into French as
boucanier, from which the outcasts' name of "buccaneer" was
derived. In Spanish the greenwood frame was called *barbacoa,*
and this in time became "barbecue." The twentieth-century
barbecue, with its fresh meat and hot or sweet-sour sauces, has
little more than a smoky flavor in common with the technique in
which it originated.

Hominy (mature grains of maize, hulled and used whole or
ground into coarse "grits"), succotash (fresh or dried maize kernels
cooked together with beans and sometimes enriched with fragments of meat), and cornpone (a thick, unleavened maize flatbread, cooked in the embers of the fire or on a griddle) were the
customary grain foods of the early settlers. Venison was so plentiful that they found themselves yearning for a plain joint of mutton, but they were prepared to enjoy shad, terrapin and oysters,
as well as canvasback duck and wild geese when they could catch
them. European domesticated animals were imported as soon as
possible, and the irrepressible pig flourished despite the depreda-

tions of wolves, bears, and North American Indians, who discovered a passion for pork. In Virginia, pigs found the climate
and the foods so congenial that southern larders began to burst at
the seams with pork and hams. Indeed, said William Byrd II
in the 1720s, the people themselves became "extremely hoggish
in their temper . . . and prone to grunt rather than speak." [35]

The success of Columbus and Vasco da Gama sent shoals of tiny ships out upon the oceans of the world. The mariners of western Europe, accustomed to hugging familiar coastlines and putting in for supplies almost anywhere they chose, now pointed their bows out to the open sea and hoped for the best.

When they sighted land, often after many weeks afloat, their first concern was not spices and precious metals but fresh food and water. The ships' logs and journals which survive from the era of sea exploration often include a kind of running catalogue of the supplies to be found in different places. At the Cape Verde islands there were "no fruits nor good fresh water," although "very small" goats were to be had. Off the Pacific coast of South America the islands were more hospitable—"plenty of excellent fat goats, good fish." And among the "Thousand Islands" off Java there was said to be one "where there was abundance of beeves [beef cattle]." [1]

This preoccupation with fresh food was hardly surprising. It took the navigators of the world a long time to understand the pattern of the oceans on which they now embarked, the tangled cross currents, errant gales, unexplained calms. Even the passage from Europe to America—which settled down to a maximum of about ten weeks when the action of wind and waves was fully charted—could last as long as eight months in the early days. When that happened, as on Columbus's fourth voyage, the ship's supplies of food and water ran low. "And what with the heat and the dampness," said the admiral's son, "even the biscuit [dried bread] was so full of worms that, God help me, I saw many wait until nightfall to eat the porridge made of it so as not to see the worms." [2] The fat black heads of the biscuit weevils, the need to eat shark, or rats bought at an extortionate price from the ship's ratcatcher—these were new hazards discovered at the same time as new lands.

CONVENIENCE FOODS

Travelers had known since prehistoric times how to provision themselves when they were away from home. Dried foods, which sustained settled communities in winter, were also the most useful kind for long journeys, since they were light in weight and needed no special care in handling. The Chinese, more than two thousand years ago, regarded dried snake as one of the best convenience foods. Europeans came to favor dried cod. The Indians of Asia, venturing from the coasts into the interior of the subcontinent, carried dried bummelo fish with them—a delicacy now known, for some strange reason, as "Bombay duck." It even seems probable that the unique Tibetan concoction of tea and yak butter —in which dried and powdered tea is mixed with yak butter into

The Tibetan yak provided large quantities of milk which could be made into butter. It could also be ridden (as here, by two British officers in disguise) or used as a beast of burden, when it would carry considerable loads of tea bricks, wool, or skins, as on the right of this picture.

an oily paste—was originally evolved as a convenience food for mountain journeys. The mixing is still done in a section of bamboo, which is then stoppered and slung over the traveler's shoulder to be dipped into whenever necessary. The people of Peru discovered how to dry the meat of game animals to make *charqui* (see page 275). In countries where bread was standard fare, methods were developed of preserving that, too.

But particular difficulties confronted the long-distance *sea* voyager, not least that of storage. The full-rigged ship of the sixteenth century had about 600 tons capacity and had to carry cargo or guns, as well as enough men to handle an increasingly complex system of sails and enough food and water to sustain them for an unspecified period. Unlike land travelers, sailors could not scatter and fend for themselves when supplies ran short, and though they might feed, in extremity, on the fish and seabirds which they hated, their greatest hazard was death from thirst.

The materials of a sailor's food were dictated by two overriding considerations imposed by the construction of the ships themselves. Wooden ships floated because they were built of a substance which absorbed water. This made it almost impossible to keep food dry. Salt (or "barrel") beef and pork were therefore adopted as the staples of long-distance sea voyages, but dried peas and ship's biscuit (or hardtack, or pilot bread) were still carried to provide variety, and to absorb excess salt from the meat. These invariably became alive with weevils, but sailors acclimatized themselves to this as to the many other discomforts of life at sea. Wooden ships also went in constant danger from fire, particularly in latitudes where the sun evaporated moisture from the fabric above the waterline. Because of this, the only fire permitted on board was in the galley, and even that had to be extinguished when the ship was hit by a storm or squall. Sailors had to eat what the ship's cook provided, and at such times it would amount to no more than weevilly biscuit and half-cooked salt pork.

The "biscuit" was made from a flour-and-water dough baked and then dried to such an immortal state of hardness that it was sometimes impossible even to break it with the hands, far less bite into it (although weevils helped by creating a pattern of inner perforations). It remained edible, if not palatable, for as much as fifty years. Sailors did their best with it, soaking it with a little of their water ration into a porridge-like mess which they improved with chunks of salt pork or a dash of vinegar and dignified with such names as skillygolee, lobscouse, or Scotch coffee.[3] Meat was always unpleasantly salty because there was too little fresh water to soak out the excess, and sometimes so gristly that the sailors finished by carving snuffboxes and other trinkets from it. The rest of the foods on the ship's provision list commonly consisted of beer, which soon went sour; butter, which was rancid before the ship even went to sea; and cheese, which more often than not was as tough as old leather.

The shipowners and, later, naval officials responsible for provisioning were as unimaginative as they were parsimonious. Their guiding principle was to ensure a supply of solid, cheap, bulky food which could be expected to remain edible even under unfavorable conditions. Not for the common sailor were the spices and seasonings which gave variety to the food of his betters, although some relishes occasionally found their way on board under the guise of "surgeon's necessaries" for the sick bay. Nor was there any attempt to assuage the sugar hunger which resulted from a diet dominated by salt and starch. Currants and raisins would have helped here, but the authorities regarded these as luxury foods; like that dogmatic traveler William Lithgow, they scorned the "sensual prodigality" of men who could "hardly digest bread, pastries, broth; and (*verbi gratia*) bag-puddings" without such additions.[4]

THE SEAMAN'S DISEASE

The deficiencies of the sailor's diet were not only gastronomic. Indeed, almost every ship which set out from western Europe on a long voyage soon numbered among its crew a high proportion of men who were sick or dying.

Voyages frequently began in early spring when most men who had spent the winter on land were in a poor state of health because of the months without fresh vegetables or fruit. Those who went to sea at this time of year and had to subsist on a diet consisting mainly of preserved foods very quickly began to show symptoms of the vitamin C deficiency disease of scurvy. During Vasco da Gama's first voyage of exploration to the Indies more than half his crew died of it.

Scurvy, even in its early stages, was both debilitating and demoralizing. It could be identified, wrote the sixteenth-century English sailor Sir Richard Hawkins, "by the swelling of the gums, by denting of the flesh of the legs with a man's fingers, the pit remaining without filling up in a good space; others show it by their laziness." [5] Wounds refused to heal. Swollen gums made the chewing of ship's biscuit and tough salt meat a prolonged agony.

Many years passed before the disease was recognized as being related to diet, and it was then blamed not on too little fresh food, but on too much salt food. Western medical men knew by about 1600 that green herbs or citrus fruits could effect a swift cure. The Chinese, as far back as the fifth century, had made it a custom to carry fresh ginger growing in pots on board their vessels, and by the fourteenth century—by purely empirical means—had arrived at some general understanding of the role certain types of food could play in preventing or curing such deficiency diseases as beri-beri. The Dutch, closely involved with the Chinese-influenced areas of southeast Asia, may have learned there of the importance of greenstuffs and citrus fruits in a sea diet and have passed the message on to Europe. When the English East India Company dispatched its first ships to the East in 1601, a chronicler recorded that the little fleet hove to off the southern tip of Madagascar and gathered "oranges and lemons of which we made good store of water [juice], which is the best remedy against scurvy." [6]

But the official mind could see no way of growing sufficient green herbs on board heavily manned ships to protect the crews against scurvy, and citrus fruits were much too expensive for economy-conscious owners or administrators. For two hundred years, physicians and sea captains neglected the only known remedies for scurvy while they attempted to find others which would be cheaper and more convenient. They knew what worked, but not *why* it worked, and so all their many and varied experiments proved valueless. Finally, it was accepted that the juice of citrus fruits was the only medicine which could conquer a disease that was killing more seamen than enemy action.

At the end of the eighteenth century, the British Admiralty decreed that a fixed amount of lemon juice should be issued daily to sailors in the British Navy after their fifth or sixth week afloat.[7] The mortality rate in the Navy declined with startling suddenness.

The citrus juice was usually mixed with the rum ration, whose issue was the highlight of the sailor's day. Since 1740 rum had rarely been dispensed neat. The first commander to dilute the ration was Admiral Vernon, whose nickname of "Old Grog"— which referred to the old cloak of grogram cloth he wore in rough weather—was soon transferred to the watered drink. Subsequent naval officers, finding too many men "groggy" when they were needed for duty, went on reducing the strength of the issue whenever they had the opportunity. After 1795, the Navy's grog was a mixture of rum, water and lemon juice. In the mid-nineteenth century lime juice from the West Indies was substituted for lemon from the Mediterranean. Conservative seamen viewed the innovation with a jaundiced eye, especially when American sailors began to taunt them by calling them "limeys," and lime juice—which has considerably less vitamin C than lemon or orange —did in fact prove to be less effective against scurvy.

THE LAND TRAVELER

Most land travelers expected to live at least partly off the territory through which they moved, and except in vast deserts or the extremes of the frozen north—where explorers on land faced much the same problems and disease as the sailor at sea—they were unlikely to be cut off from all food supplies for any length of time. Nevertheless, they always took a store of provisions with them by way of insurance.

The weight and volume of the food load did not matter greatly on, for example, a military expedition, which usually moved over open terrain where baggage animals and a vast mobile bazaar of camp followers could trail at its heels. But for the solitary ex-

Army camp followers usually included a number of "canteen girls," or drink sellers.

plorer venturing into the thinly populated wilds of the new continents stores had to be light and compact. Often, he would travel on foot and act as his own beast of burden in clinging jungle or over perpendicular mountain tracks.

From the peoples of North and South America, European explorers were to learn the virtues of two sustaining and lightweight meat products, pemmican and *charqui*.

The first of these, pemmican, took its name from the Cree Indian word for fat. Developed in chilly northern regions, it was excellent food for such a climate, its high fat content giving much-needed warmth and energy. It was made by drying thinly sliced lean meat, usually from one of the larger game animals, over a fire or in the sun and wind. After drying, the meat was pounded to shreds and mixed very thoroughly with an almost equal quantity of melted fat, some marrow from the bones, and a few handfuls of wild cherries. Afterward, it was packed in rawhide sacks which were tightly sewn up and sealed with tallow. It was pemmican which sustained the fur trader Alexander Mackenzie during the pioneer journey in 1793 which made him the first European to cross the North American continent from coast to coast. Half a century later, Arctic explorers were to be furnished with a refined version in cans, scientifically prepared by Mackenzie's fellow Scot and successor in Canadian exploration, Sir John Richardson. Richardson found that slow drying over an oak fire improved the keeping qualities of the product, and that top-quality currants or sugar made an acceptable substitute for wild cherries.[8]

Charqui was a convenience food of South America. It may have originated in Peru, as a method of preserving the flesh of game slaughtered at the traditional communal hunts, but once cattle raising was established on the continent, beef came to be more generally used. *Charqui* was made by cutting boned and defatted beef into quarter-inch slices and either dipping these in strong brine or rubbing them with salt. After the meat had been rolled up in the animal's hide for ten or twelve hours to absorb the salt and release some of the juices, it was hung in the sun to dry and finally tied up into convenient bundles. It looked, said one German traveler, like thick pasteboard, and was "just as easy to masticate." [9] When conditions permitted, it was usual to pound the *charqui* energetically between two stones and then cook it in hot water before eating. The "jerked" in "jerked beef" is derived from the word *charqui*.

As well as mass-production items such as pemmican, *charqui*, salt beef and pork, many travelers by land—and sea—were able to take a few small luxuries prepared in their own kitchens. Even one or two containers of potted meat, heavily sealed with fat, helped to postpone the moment of complete reliance on salted or dried food. "Pocket soup" or "portable soup" was invaluable. The ancestor of the modern bouillon cube, it consisted of a concentrated stock made from veal or meat trimmings and pigs' trotters, which set when cold to the consistency of solid glue; it kept for years, and a piece of it could be dissolved in hot water to make a bowl of soup. Ship's biscuit, or hardtack, was as useful on land as at sea, and less infested by weevils. Made in a home kitchen, it was much more palatable than the mass-produced version. Many Americans, however, preferred the dried cornmeal pancake known as jonnycake (or johnnycake), whose name may be a distortion either of "journey cake" or of the American Indian *shawnee*-cake.

All the preservation techniques which were used until the early nineteenth century had been developed over hundreds—in some cases, thousands—of years. Most of them had been evolved for the purpose of storing present surplus against future need. What was "convenient" about early convenience foods was that they were there at all. Only when canning was introduced in the nineteenth century were they to become not only "convenient," but palatable for people who had no access to a properly equipped kitchen.

15.

A Gastronomic

Grand Tour

In the eighteenth century, while explorers were still opening up new lands, intrepid travelers in Europe had begun to venture in increasing numbers on the "Grand Tour"—a pilgrimage to the shrines of established culture. By whichever route these tourists traveled, they ended up in Rome, where they admired the architecture and antiquities of the Classical world and complained bitterly about the food. There might be "raw ham, Bologna sausages, figs and melons," but there was nothing of substance. "No boiled leg of pork and pease pudding," lamented one traveler. "No bubble-and-squeak." * [1]

It would have been possible in the late eighteenth century for a really enterprising traveler to have made a far more stimulating Grand Tour covering much of the known world. If he had been interested in food, and prepared to inquire into developments over the preceding two hundred years, he would have discovered that most major countries now had their own "national cuisines," their own distinctive modes of cooking, or foods which immediately struck the visitor as "characteristic." Some foreign dishes and raw materials would already be familiar to him, because of the explosive expansion of international contacts during two eventful centuries, but others would still be strange.

* A specialty of the British Isles, consisting at that time of boiled salt beef, sliced and fried, served with separately fried chopped boiled cabbage, sometimes with onions and leftover potatoes added.

In such a tour, Italy would have been not an end, but a beginning.

THE FOOD OF ITALY

It had been the Italians who first emerged from the medieval morass of sauces and spices. The riches of the spice trade and the Renaissance rediscovery of the Classical world had at first given back to Italy much of the power and influence of Roman times, but it was to be the *loss* of the spice trade to the Portuguese which transformed Italian tables and, subsequently, those of France. Soon after Vasco da Gama's voyage to the Malabar coast, Italy herself became a prey not only to the territorial ambitions of her fellow Europeans but to those of the Turks. In the uneasy decades of the early sixteenth century, spices became scarce.

The Italians, however, adapted themselves and their cuisine to the exigencies of the time. By 1570, when the cook of Pope Pius V offered his master's guests the following banquet,[2] spices had come to play a comparatively minor role in the armory of the kitchen.

A sixteenth-century Italian kitchen.

First Course

Cold Delicacies from the Sideboard

Pieces of marzipan and marzipan balls
Neapolitan spice cakes
Malaga wine and Pisan biscuits
Plain pastries made with milk and eggs
Fresh grapes
Spanish olives
Prosciutto cooked in wine, sliced, and served with capers,
grape pulp, and sugar
Salted pork tongues cooked in wine, sliced
Spit-roasted songbirds, cold, with their tongues sliced over them
Sweet mustard

Second Course

Hot Foods from the Kitchen: Roasts

Fried veal sweetbreads and liver, with a sauce of eggplant,
salt, sugar, and pepper
Spit-roasted skylarks with lemon sauce
Spit-roasted quails with sliced aubergines
Stuffed spit-roasted pigeons with sugar and capers sprinkled over them
Spit-roasted rabbits, with sauce and crushed pine nuts
Partridges, larded and spit-roasted, served with lemon slices
Pastries filled with minced veal sweetbreads and served with
slices of prosciutto
Strongly seasoned poultry with lemon slices and sugar
Slices of veal, spit-roasted, with a sauce made from the juices
Leg of goat, spit-roasted, with a sauce made from the juices
Soup of almond cream, with the flesh of three pigeons for
every two guests
Squares of meat aspic

Third Course

Hot Foods from the Kitchen: Boiled Meats and Stews

Stuffed fat geese, boiled Lombard style and covered with sliced
almonds, served with cheese, sugar, and cinnamon

Stuffed breast of veal, boiled, garnished with flowers
Milk calf, boiled, garnished with parsley
Almonds in garlic sauce
Turkish-style rice with milk, sprinkled with sugar and cinnamon
Stewed pigeons with mortadella sausage and whole onions
Cabbage soup with sausages
Poultry pie, two chickens to each pie
Fricasseed breast of goat dressed with fried onions
Pies filled with custard cream
Boiled calves' feet with cheese and egg

Fourth Course

Delicacies from the Sideboard

Bean tarts
Quince pastries, one quince per pastry
Pear tarts, the pears wrapped in marzipan
Parmesan cheese and Riviera cheese
Fresh almonds on vine leaves
Chestnuts roasted over the coals and served with salt, sugar, and pepper
Milk curds with sugar sprinkled over
Ring-shaped cakes   Wafers

This was a menu of some finesse, still showing Near Eastern influences, but making considerable use of indigenous materials—the sausages and songbirds of traditional Italian cooking, fruits, and a variety of cheeses—and presenting them in a recognizable form. The whole atmosphere of the menu was simpler than before, depending on materials rather than spices for diversity. It was this revolutionary attitude to food that the Italians were to export to France.

What most travelers took note of in Italy, however, was not its refined cooking but its macaroni.

PASTA

The history of pasta is not easy to disentangle. There are unsubstantiated claims for its existence during Etruscan times, and again during the Ostrogothic period. But the most popular story is that it was introduced into Italy by Marco Polo, who is said to have brought the idea from China. Certainly, the Chinese noodle, developed centuries earlier, was an idea which could be expected to recommend itself in other regions where wheat was grown. It made a change from pancakes and breads, could be eaten hot, and kept its flavor and texture better than many grain products when dried.

At least fifty years before Marco Polo even left Venice on his travels to the East, however, both Indians and Arabs were already eating noodles,* and from the Arab lands to Venice in the later Middle Ages was a very short step. It is possible that pasta may have been introduced to Italy by this route, perhaps as early as the eleventh century. Once established in the great trading cities —Venice, Florence, and Genoa—it may have been spread gradually through the country by the agency of domestic servants. In the late thirteenth and, more particularly, in the fourteenth century, many rich Italian households numbered Mongol (or "Tartar") slaves among their possessions.[5] Sinicized Mongols working in Italian kitchens would have been able, on request, to produce a dish of noodles to grace their masters' tables.†

The most common name for pasta in the later Middle Ages seems to have been "macaroni," although this now means the tubular as contrasted with the flat type. There has always been some confusion in identifying the original Italian forms. The fourteenth-century English *Forme of Cury* gives a recipe for "macrows"—an anglicized plural of "macaroni"—which produces a poached paste of the flat noodle type; the recipe even recommends serving it strewn with morsels of butter and accompanied by grated cheese.[6] But what was the macaroni described by that occasional monk Teofilo Folengo in the sixteenth century, when he said that the artificial language known as Macaronic Latin—a mixture of Latin and Italian—was so called because it

---

* The Indians called theirs *sevika*, meaning "thread."[3] The Arabs called theirs *rishta*, a Persian word which also meant thread.[4] Italians, taking the larger view, were to opt for the word *spaghetti*—derived from *spago*, or string.

† In 1972, at a trade fair in Peking, the Italians returned the compliment by trying to sell the Chinese a spaghetti-making machine. The *New York Times* described this sacrilegious invention: "You put flour, water and tomato sauce in at one end of the machine and five minutes later hot spaghetti, already cooked and prepared and with cheese and sauce on top, comes out at the other end."

Pasta-making in the sixteenth century.

reminded students of Venetian macaroni, "a kind of coarse, rough rustic pudding made of flour, cheese and butter"? [7] Was it merely that Brother Teofilo was fallible on the subject of food, or did the Venetians simmer their pasta in the Arabic fashion (with un-Arabic additions of cheese and butter), using comparatively little liquid and leaving the mass to settle for an hour after cooking?

By the eighteenth century and the days of the pilgrimage to Italy, macaroni was firmly established in European mythology. Middle-class tourists of mature years might scorn it as they scorned most other foreign food, but the adolescent aristocrats who were dispatched, complete with tutor and chaplain, to complete their education, were not so insular. So bored did their less traveled contemporaries become with "Italian" manners, antique busts, sketches of ruins, and poems in praise of pasta that boastful young Grand Tourists became generally known as "macaronis."

FRENCH COOKING COMES OF AGE

When Catherine de Medici arrived from Florence in 1533 to marry the heir to the French throne she took with her a number of Italian chefs and pastrycooks. They, and the staff of Marie de Medici, who went to France at the end of the century as the bride of Henry IV, introduced not only the new Italian style of cooking to that country, but also such vegetables as artichokes, broccoli, and savoy cabbages.

Nevertheless, in 1577, the Venetian ambassador to Paris still could not bring himself to enthuse about French food. The people, he reported, were quite immoderate, eating four or five times a day as and when they felt inclined, consuming very little bread or fruit, but a great deal of meat. "They load the table with it at their banquets," [8] he said. They "ruin their stomachs and bowels by eating too much, as the Germans and Poles do by drinking too much." [9]

By the mid-seventeenth century, however, things had changed for the better, and the Franco-Italian cuisine which had been slowly evolving was codified by Pierre François de la Varenne.*

La Varenne frowned on spices and on thick meat-and-almond mixtures. He recommended sauces based on meat drippings, combined merely with vinegar, lemon juice (still an expensive luxury in France), or verjuice (the juice of sour grapes, or sometimes of sorrel, green wheat, or crab apples). He provided sixty recipes for the formerly humble egg, treated vegetables as food in their own right, made much use of the globe artichoke, described stuffed mushrooms, and even had a kind word to say for truffles.

THE TRUFFLE

Truffles had been known in Babylon as well as in Rome, although the Romans were none too sure about what they really were. Pliny

---

* One of his cookbooks—*Le Pastissier François,* in the edition published in 1655 by the great printing house of Elzevier—is now rated among the most rare and valuable in the world.

the Elder had his own view. "We know for a fact that when Lartius Licinius, an official of praetorian rank, was serving as minister of justice at Cartagena in Spain a few years ago, he happened when biting a truffle to come on a denarius contained inside it which bent his front teeth. This will clearly show that truffles are lumps of earthy substance balled together." [10]

Although the people of medieval Baghdad feasted on truffles from the Arabian desert,* in France they remained sunk in obscurity until the fourteenth century, when they were pickled in vinegar, soaked in hot water, and served with butter. The Italians imported their own native variety for sixteenth-century royal tables, and a hundred years later La Varenne recommended cooking them like mushrooms. But it was not to be until the nineteenth century that the French came to appreciate their true delicacy. Then, truffles became so fashionable, had so many elegies written in their praise, that the demand trebled—and so did the price.

* Desert truffles are not a fiction. The Kalahari Desert, in Botswana, is one of the richest known truffle mines today.[11]

Formality at court in the days of the Sun King. The Grande Mademoiselle dines in state.

A hunt breakfast in the relaxed years which followed the death of Louis XIV.

LA CUISINE BOURGEOISE

Bourgeois food may already have reached a comfortable standard of goodness by the end of the seventeenth century, but it was resistant to new ideas. The French were slow to produce cookbooks for ordinary households.

A new note, however, was heard in cookbook writing when Marin, in *Les Dons de Comus*, claimed that the bourgeoisie could eat like princes if they had proper pots and pans, went to market every day, and knew how to make good bouillon. The acknowledgment that the bourgeoisie even existed was something of a new departure in France, unlike England and Germany, where sensible cookbooks for the ordinary housewife had been available for more than a hundred years. Another French writer of Marin's time, Menon, at first scorned "third-class persons" in his *Nouveau Traité de la Cuisine* in 1739, but mellowed sufficiently as the years passed to admit not only third-class persons to his confidence but third-class cuts of meat to his books.

From about 1660 on, the French had become assured of their superiority in all matters of taste. They might have occasional aberrations, such as the adoption of meat cooked *à l'anglaise*— *rostbif*, for example, and even that interesting variation, *rostbif d'agneau*—but they could find little to admire in the cuisine of other countries. In this they were not alone. One Englishman on the Grand Tour announced categorically that French cooking was "an abomination," and recommended any compatriot who was forced to eat it to "get near enough the door to make his exit suddenly." [12]

CHOCOLATE AND THE SPANIARDS

A visitor to Spain in the seventeenth or eighteenth century would have been struck less by the quality of main dishes than by the

La Halle, the great market of Paris, in 1779.

sweetmeats and drinking chocolate which were a feature of the cuisine.

The food of Spain was a mirror of trade and conquest. The cooking medium, olive oil, had been introduced from the eastern Mediterranean at some time during the first millennium B.C. Production of salt and dried fish had been greatly expanded to meet the demands of Rome. The barbarian invasions had led to a notable increase in sheep farming—and mutton eating. The Arabs had introduced rice, at once a staple foodstuff and an export crop. They also seem to have given Spain a taste for such almond-based sweetmeats as marzipan and nougat. Spain's own victories in the New World brought, in particular, two new foods which soon became fully integrated into the cuisine—the tomato, and the capsicum (whose large, mild variety is known in Spain as the pimiento).

But although many of the new foods from Latin America could be grown in Europe, the tropical cacao tree could not. Spain held most of the lands where the cacao already grew, Portugal the rest, and for well over a hundred years after the conquistadors first discovered the delicious drinking chocolate of the West Indies both production and consumption remained a jealously guarded monopoly.

Drinking chocolate was made by drying cocoa (or cacao) beans and roasting them over a fire. They were then pounded to a paste with water and, sometimes, powdered flowers; by the end of the sixteenth century, sugar seems also to have been added. In Mexico, little cakes of this paste, with spices incorporated, were shaken up with water in a gourd until they frothed. The drink was then gulped down "in one swallow with admirable pleasure and satisfaction of the bodily nature, to which it gives strength, nourishment, and vigor in such a way that those who are accustomed to drinking it cannot remain robust without it even if they eat other substantial things. And they appear to diminish when they do not have that drink." [13]

In Spain by 1631, the preparation of a cup of chocolate had become a major operation. "For every hundred cocoa beans, mix two pods of chili or Mexican pepper . . . or, failing those, two Indian peppercorns, a handful of aniseed, two of those flowers known as 'little ears' or *vinacaxtlides,* and two of those known as *mesasuchil* . . . Instead of the latter one could include the pow-

By the seventeenth century, chocolate drinking was well established in Spain.

der of the six roses of Alexandria [an apothecaries' formula] . . . a little pod of logwood [a dye], two drachmas of cinnamon, a dozen almonds and as many hazelnuts, half a pound of sugar, and enough arnotto [a dye] to give color to the whole." [14]

By the early seventeenth century, a considerable amount of chocolate paste was being exported to Italy and Flanders, but it was not until 1659 that the new drink became widely known in France. At first, the French court was enthusiastic—encouraged by the fact that the Paris faculty of medicine had bestowed its imprimatur on it—but strange tales soon began to circulate, culminating in one of the marquise de Sévigné's finest pieces of gossip. "The marquise de Coëtlogon," she reported, "took so much chocolate, being pregnant last year, that she was brought to bed of a little boy who was as black as the devil!" [15]

Chocolate was regarded mainly as a drink for almost three hundred years after its introduction to Europe. Only in the early nineteenth century was it to be mass-produced in block form for eating.

EUROPE EAST AND NORTH

The overwhelming impression gained by the traveler through the northern regions of Europe would have been one of robust solidity —what an English chef described in 1710 as "substantial and wholesome plenty." [16] Although in the late seventeenth century many northern aristocrats had dispatched their cooks to France to learn about refined cooking, there remained a general feeling that the "quelque chose" (anglicized as "kickshaws") of France were a paltry substitute for real food.

In what was later to become Germany, pork and sausage, cabbage, lentils, rye bread and beer were the staples of the diet. A thick, hearty soup appeared on the table at almost every meal, and a fruit-stuffed goose on high days and holidays. In Russia, though the rich fared well, much of the population subsisted on black bread, soured dairy products, cabbage, and *kasha*, made from buckwheat, and cooked either in whole-grain form to make a dish resembling pilaf or, as groats, into a coarse thin porridge. Poland and Hungary, which had borne the brunt of most of the nomad invasions in history, reflected these incursions in their cuisines. Veal, fermented milks, and pickled cabbage were long established, and the once nomadic Turks who occupied Hungary for much of the sixteenth and seventeenth centuries had introduced maize and capsicums, brought from the eastern end of the Mediterranean. Austria, too, was a clearing house of foreign influences, and nowhere more so than Vienna, whose food included dishes and cooking methods from all over the Hapsburg empire.

In the Low Countries, much food was heavy and fatty, but the Dutch, inspired by their East India Company, had begun to cultivate as many exotic fruits as they could induce to grow.* By 1636, the great still-life artist Jan Davidsz de Heem even went to live in Antwerp because "there one could have rare fruits of all kinds, large plums, peaches, cherries, oranges, lemons, grapes and others, in finer condition and state of ripeness to draw from life." [17]

Across the North Sea, in England, fruit was a feature only of "the tables of the great, and of a small number even among

* Even before the era of colonial enterprise, the Flemish had been notable vegetable growers, and there was a time when they supplied much of Europe with onions and salad materials.

Exotic fruits, as painted by de Heem.

Pancakes were a favorite food with rich and poor in Holland.

them." At the end of the seventeenth century, beef, mutton, fowls, pigs, rabbits and pigeons "infallibly" turned up, the mutton underdone and the beef salted for some days before being boiled and then served up besieged "with five or six heaps of cabbage, carrots, turnips, or some other herbs or roots, well peppered and salted, and swimming in butter." [18] Fifty years later, the situation had improved a little. In 1748, a Swedish visitor remarked that "Englishmen understand almost better than any other people the art of properly roasting a large cut of meat." This, he went on, was "not to be wondered at; because the art of cooking as practiced by most Englishmen does not extend much beyond roast beef and plum pudding." [19]

At their best—and their best was, no doubt, as rarely encountered in the eighteenth century as it is today—many of the standard dishes of northern Europe could be superb, good filling food for a dank climate. But more often they must have been dull, tasteless, as lacking in food value as in savor.

DRINKS

Foods that are heavy in carbohydrates and fats—as most north European foods were—have to be washed down with plenty of liquids, and this may be one of the reasons why Poles, Germans, Dutch and English all acquired a reputation for heavy drinking.

Most countries had their own grain-based beers and ales, and where there was honey there was also mead. These drinks were brewed on the manor during the Middle Ages, and in almost every

A display of sausages, poultry, cheese, pigs' feet, a bowl of lard, fish heads, a side of mutton dripping into the butter—the "substantial and wholesome plenty" of northern Europe.

country household after the collapse of the manorial system. Except in wine-producing areas, and at aristocratic tables, beer was the common drink almost everywhere, at breakfast as well as at other meals. Only when tea, coffee and chocolate became popular did consumption begin to decline.

France was the wine-producing country *par excellence*, and the names of Beaune, St. Emilion, Chablis and Epernay can be found in manuscripts dating from as early as the thirteenth century. The Hansa towns, Flanders and England were among the steadiest markets for the wines of Gascony (Bordeaux), whose pale *rosés*, known as clairet,[20] were drunk only weeks old. But by the end of the Middle Ages, Spanish and Portuguese wines had come into fashion, as had the red *vernaccia* (or "vernage") of northern Italy; Malmsey from Crete, Málaga and, later, Madeira; and Rhenish wines from Germany.

In the sixteenth and seventeenth centuries particularly, immoderate drinking seems to have become a fashion in the north. Giovanni della Casa thanked God that in Italy, "among the many pests which have come to us from beyond the mountains, this vilest one has not yet reached us, of regarding drunkenness as not merely a laughing matter, but even a merit." [21]

Fermented drinks had been known for thousands of years, but the process of distilling seems only to have been discovered in the first century A.D. Fundamentally, this process consists of converting a liquid into vapor through the application of heat, and then of condensing the vapor again. It can be used either to drive liquid off from a partially moist substance, leaving the substance dehydrated, or to extract a pure liquid essence (the condensed vapor) from particular types of solids. (The Arabs, for example, distilled rose petals to provide them with the rosewater they used in their *haute cuisine*.[22])

In the twelfth century, alchemists discovered that distilling could do more than merely separate liquids from solids. With careful temperature control and rapid cooling of the vapor, it was possible to separate one liquid from another. When they tried distilling wine in this way, the result was almost pure alcohol— which vaporizes at a lower temperature than water. Wine contains about one part alcohol to nine parts water. What distilling did, in effect, was to isolate the active ingredient which, in its original dilute form, gave wine its stimulating properties.

A brick still, illustrated
in a book on distilling
published in 1512.

The alcohol produced from distilled wine and, later, from distilled ales, was at first known as *aqua vitae* (water of life), a name immortalized in *eau de vie, akvavit,* and the Gaelic *uisge beatha,* which was corrupted, via the abbreviated *uisge,* to "whisky." In Germany, however, distilled wine was known less poetically as *gebrannter Wein* or *Brandewin* (meaning "burnt" or distilled wine), which was anglicized as "brandy."

By the sixteenth century, spirits were being distilled in the north mainly from fermented grains, and local variants were beginning to appear. There were akvavit, schnapps, and gin in continental Europe—the name "gin" being derived from *genever,* or juniper, with which the drink was flavored—and whisky in Ireland and Scotland. Unblended whisky, drawing its individuality from pale golden grains of malted barley, aromatic peat smoke, and rich brown water from hill burns, comes closest nowadays to competing with Cognac (made from the wines of the Charente) for the favor of the connoisseurs of spirits.

NORTH AMERICA

By the eighteenth century Scots and Irish settlers had introduced whisky distilling to North America. Lacking peat, it was a poor substitute for the real thing, but still preferable—to the accustomed palate—to the early rye whiskey, or the maize version developed at the end of the century by the folk of Bourbon County, Kentucky.

Early Americans, like their contemporaries in Europe, had a built-in resistance to water. This was not altogether surprising, as much "fresh" water within range of human habitation was, if not actually poisonous, very nearly undrinkable. One of the seventeenth-century colonists' earliest concerns had been to organize a supply of fermented drinks. Their initial experiments in growing barley and hops in New England had proved disappointing. Thirst being the mother of invention, however, they soon discovered that very potable brews could be made from pumpkins, maple sugar, and persimmons. The flavor was not the same as that of real beer, but the effect was.

Apple orchards next sprang up in New England and in Pennsylvania, and the cider intake of the colonists rapidly reached gargantuan proportions. Although apples were also valuable for cooking and easy to preserve, their main charm was they could make apple brandy, or another rough and highly potent liquor known as applejack but frequently referred to as "essence of lockjaw." [23] Once Pennsylvania was settled, it proved to be good barley and hop country. Dutch and German immigrants were soon engaged in brewing beer; when the Scots and Irish arrived, whisky followed.

But of all the drinks that warmed the eighteenth-century American interior, rum was perhaps the most important. Just before the War of Independence, it was estimated that the colonists were downing three Imperial, or 3¾ American, gallons of it per head per year, women and children included.[24] Indeed, some historians argue, persuasively, that it was not the British tax on America's tea that precipitated the final schism, but the Molasses

Act of 1733, which imposed a heavy tax on sugar and molasses coming from anywhere .except the British sugar islands in the Caribbean.

The rum trade was founded on molasses, the syrupy liquid which is left after the juice of the sugar cane is boiled once, twice, or thrice, to produce sugar crystals. For some decades, the ship-owners of New England found it profitable to sail with a cargo of rum to the slave coast of Africa and exchange it for slaves, whom they then transported back to the West Indies for sale to ever-eager plantation owners. In the West Indies; the merchants picked up a load of molasses to replace the slave cargo, and took this back home to be distilled into the rum which would provide the capital required for the next round trip. Any restriction on the purchase of sugar or its by-products posed a serious threat not only to the North Americans' own rum supply, but to a whole related trading cycle.

The early North American settlers do not, on the whole, appear to have developed a taste for maize beer, perhaps because they were told that the best way to make it was to include chewed grain to stimulate the ferment. In Peru and Brazil, there were people who hired themselves out as maize chewers.

An eighteenth-century Massachusetts merchant with his bowl of rum punch.

Alcohol in its various forms—the stronger the better—was the great sustainer of eighteenth-century America. It quenched the majestic thirst that resulted from too much salt meat and fish; it was a social ice-breaker in new communities; it even became a political tradition. When George Washington ran for the legislature in 1758, his agent doled out almost three Imperial, or 3¾ American, gallons of beer, wine, cider or rum to every voter. The great man himself was concerned over the extent of this hospitality; he feared that his agent might have been too niggardly.* [25]

When, after the War of Independence, America at last became self-employed, the population began to overflow into uncharted territory in the heart of the continent, and then farther and farther west.

The city lady of the eastern seaboard had her servants, her table silver, her coffee, white bread, imported cheeses, salads, and white loaf sugar. She would have been quite at home in one of the capitals of Europe. Until 1796, even her cookbooks were European, for those which were published under an American imprint before then were no more than special editions of European ones. Only when Amelia Simmons—"An American Orphan"—wrote *American Cookery* did such established national dishes as Indian pudding, slapjack, and jonnycake first make their appearance in print.

On a prosperous eastern farm, the housewife lived almost as comfortably as her sister in the city, though her daily tasks were more demanding. The household had to be supervised, as had food and accommodation for the farmhands. There were dairying, pickling and preserving to be seen to. The smokehouse had to be hung with meat and game for the winter; the root cellar to be filled with bins of potatoes, dried corn, beans, and squash, as well as barrels full of apples.

The poorer farm wife still lived close to American beginnings. She seasoned her stews as often with maple syrup as with salt,

* Washington would, perhaps, have had some sympathy for the Yankee colonel who was to be cashiered during the Civil War a hundred years later for authorizing purchase, for the 1st New York Infantry, of a month's "medical supplies" which included 96 Imperial (120 American) gallons of bourbon whisky, 33.6 Imperial (42 American) gallons pale sherry, 17.2 Imperial (21.5 American) gallons pale Otard brandy, 32 Imperial (40 American) gallons Cabinet gin, and 24 dozen Allsop East India ale.[26]

Prize-winning livestock on a prosperous Eastern farm.

sweetened her pies with molasses, cooked cornmeal mush more
often than bread, broiled fresh meat or fish only when her man
had a good day's hunting. If the soil was poor, the family pulled
up stakes and moved on in search of better. Good housewives
learned to make butter on the march "by the dashing of the
wagon, and so nicely to calculate the working of barm [leaven] in
the jolting heats that, as soon after the halt as an oven could be
dug in the hillside and heated, their well-kneaded loaf was ready
for baking." [27] But most women stocked up on dried corn, jonny-
cakes, pocket soup and preserved meats for their journeys into the
unknown.

What struck visitors to America most forcibly was the variety
of other national cuisines which had found a place on the continent.

As new settlers had arrived in America from various European
countries, they had introduced their own traditional dishes, judiciously adapted when necessary to suit the materials available.
The English brought apple pie. The French introduced chowder
(from *chaudière*, the fish kettle in which the dish was cooked).
The Dutch took cookies (*koekjes*), coleslaw (*kool*: cabbage, and
sla: salad) and waffles. In the end, the American cuisine became
a mirror of history, the names of its dishes reflecting a medley
of peoples, religions, wars, geographical locations, even occupations. There were Ambushed asparagus, Shaker loaf, Burgoo,

Maryland chicken, Snickerdoodles, Spoon bread, Cowpoke beans, Hush puppies, Jambalaya, Pandowdy, Boston baked beans, Philadelphia pepper pot, Moravian sugar cake, Swedish meatballs, Haymaker's switchel, Whaler's toddy . . .

In the backwoods, until well into the nineteenth century, the visitor still found himself eating plain-cooked possums, raccoons and other unexpected animals, but in Philadelphia there were German sauerbraten and sauerkraut, and in New Orleans after the alliance of 1778 a whole range of French specialities was to be had, traditional dishes enlivened by Negro and Spanish influences. Southern slaves on the plantations might have to make do with "soul food," black-eyed peas and leftovers from the house on the hill—turnip tops, ham hocks, and rubbery, tasteless "chitterlings" made from the small intestines of the pig—but once they were able to exercise their talents on more rewarding materials they injected an entirely new gusto into the already circumscribed world of "classical" French cooking.

The European waffle was to become a favorite American food.

SOUTH AND CENTRAL AMERICA

The Spanish conquest had brought radical changes in Latin America—not always to the peasant's disadvantage. There was a very rapid spread of Spanish cattle, which soon ensured that those American Indians who survived had meat to eat, a horse to ride, and a draft animal to work for them. Even the poor benefited, for the goat adapted itself happily to Mexico and to the slopes of the Andes.

Much of the continent to the east of the Andes was suitable for livestock. Sheep and cattle breeders had no particular desire to own land; all they needed was wide-open pastures and permanent quarters for themselves and the hands. But inevitably, they came into conflict with agriculturalists on their settled farms and in the end it became necessary to delimit the ranchers' grazing grounds by fencing them in.[28] In the meantime, however, there had grown up a new breed of mounted vagrants who preyed on the free-ranging cattle. These men were "gauchos,'" part Spanish, part American Indian in blood, and almost wholly lawless. Their life and diet had a great deal in common with those of the Central Asian nomads of a thousand years earlier.

To the European traveler the gaucho was wholly alien, even after serious attempts had been made to civilize him. He fueled his fire with cow dung, held in position with cattle bones which singed but did not burn, and smelled abominable. "And on this material, with its loathsome effluvia, another bone, with some flesh on it, is laid and broiled; and if the gaucho is particularly kindly disposed towards you, he takes the bone for you from the fire, knocks the cinders off on his leg, tears off a morsel with his own teeth, to see whether it is well done; and you, as a polite gentleman, say, with a sickly smile: 'Muchas gracias Señor.' " [29]

In the cities, and particularly those in the north, Europeans found themselves much more at home. Spanish administrators from Europe and the *criollo* aristocracy lived a recognizable if unusually gilded life. What *was* strange to visitors was not the life or the food—not even the food of the peasant, which was

A Mexican butcher in the 1820s—the dirtiest and laziest member of the human race, said the artist who drew this lithograph.

made mainly from materials now familiar in Europe—but the American Indian addiction to chewing coca.

COCA, PAN, AND COLA

Coca was (and is) a leaf that the South American Indians "keep constantly in their mouths, chewing it together with a small amount of ground lime . . . They say that chewing this leaf gives them strength and vigor, and such is the superstition and faith

The areca nut.

Prepared betel quids being offered to the god Krishna.

that they have in it that they cannot work or go on trips without having it in their mouths. And, on the contrary, having it, they work happily and walk a day or two without refreshing themselves otherwise or eating anything." [30]

The coca leaf contains cocaine. In conjunction with powdered dry lime, it deadens fatigue, pain and hunger, makes it easier to breathe at high altitudes—an important factor in Andean regions —appears to sharpen the mind, and enables people who chew it to endure much that would otherwise fall beyond human limitations. Its properties are, in effect, half stimulant, half narcotic.

Historians have yet to agree on the relationship between coca-chewing in Peru, *pan*-chewing in India, and cola-chewing in West Africa. The habit may have developed independently in all three places, or it may have originated in Asia (possibly Malaya) and spread to South America during pre-Columbian times, to be transmitted from there to Africa when the slave trade was in full flood.

Pan-chewing in India is said to go back to before 2000 B.C. Like coca, its effect is partly narcotic and partly stimulating. *Pan* is made by shredding betel nut (the fruit of the areca palm) with powdered lime and spices, and wrapping the mixture in a betel leaf. The effect of chewing it is to reduce hunger, slightly anesthetize the mouth, and create a mild sensation of exhilaration. Indians believe that it sweetens the breath, and women also regard it as having contraceptive qualities.

The similarity between the preparation and the effects of coca and *pan* is remarkable, although coca is stronger and more addictive. In Africa, however, lime does not seem to have been used in preparing the cola quid for chewing. Kernels of the cola nut— from a tree which is also to be found in tropical America—were wrapped "in a thick green capsule" which was "very pleasant, bitter and astringent," and "much esteemed for its stomachic powers." It also had an invigorating effect, since the nut contained not only caffeine but the heart stimulant kolanin. Chewing cola had become habitual in West Africa by the eighteenth century— an "innocent luxury," remarked one contemporary traveler, inaccurately.[31]

CHINA

The voyage from Peru, with its violent contrasts, to the little-known China of the eighteenth century carried the traveler past the Fiji islands, where leaf-wrapped roast human was a familiar dish,[32] and past Australia, still inhabited only by aborigines who feasted on *bogong* moths.[33]

Despite the eulogistic terms in which Jesuit missionaries described the China of the time, the traveler probably expected to be confronted with weird and wonderful food. Most of the population still subsisted on the rice or noodles, the bean curd, pork and vegetables of tradition, but at grander tables these foods were complemented by more exotic dishes. There might be bird's nest soup, for example, much prized for the delicate flavor given by the gelatinous substance, extracted from a type of seaweed, which Chinese swallows used to bind their nests. The best-quality nests came from Java. Or there might be that reputedly aphrodisiac dish made from the dried and smoked sea cucumber (trepang, or *bêche-de-mer*), so popular that it became one of the largest Indonesian exports to China. There would also be more conventional delicacies such as plovers' eggs, sharks' fins, and roasted snails.

It is unlikely that any guest at a Chinese merchant's table would have been offered red-cooked dog or stir-fried cat, though every European visitor until the end of the nineteenth century went in dread of it. Only the poorest of China's millions now ate such meats. But the Westerner's fear of being faced with a plateful of man's best friend was gleefully fostered by generations of humorists, such as the anonymous versifier who claimed that, unable to communicate with his hosts because they had no language in common, he was also unable to identify what he was eating. "Now here, now there, he picked a bit, of what he could not name." But then, the covers were changed:

> . . . he brightened up
> And thought himself in luck
> When close before him what he saw
> Looked something like a duck!

Still cautious grown, but, to be sure,
His brain he set to rack;
At length he turned to one behind,
And pointing, cried "Quack, quack?"

The Chinese gravely shook his head,
Next made a reverend bow;
And then expressed what dish it was,
By uttering "Bow-wow-wow!" [34]

Though they might have doubts about the food, most travelers in Asia were impressed by the way the Chinese ate it. Chopsticks had been used since at least the fourth century B.C.[35] and had spread to some of the more strongly Chinese-influenced countries of southeast Asia. Japan, too, had adopted them, as it had so many other aspects of Chinese civilization. Francesco Carletti, an early merchant visitor, described how ingeniously food was conveyed to the mouth with the aid of two slim sticks, "made in a round shape and blunted, the length of a man's hand and as thick as a quill for writing . . . They can pick up anything, no matter how tiny it is, very cleanly and without soiling their hands. For that reason they do not use tablecloths or napkins or even knives, as everything comes to the table minutely cut up . . . When they want to eat it, they bring the bowl it is in close to their mouth and then, with those two sticks, are able to fill their mouth with marvellous agility and swiftness." [36]

TEA

Tea had been a popular drink in China since the T'ang period, possibly before. It was generally believed to have medicinal value and to contribute toward longevity. When Haji Muhammad reported on it to the Venetian geographer Ramusio in 1550, he said that the Chinese believed that "one or two cups of this decoction taken on an empty stomach remove fever, headache, stomach ache, pain in the side or in the joints, and it should be taken as hot as you can bear it . . . And those people would gladly give a sack of rhubarb [a Chinese plant much prized by European apothecaries] for an ounce of *Chiai Catai*." * [37]

Tea may have been introduced to Europe from Japan rather than from China, and seems first to have arrived in Holland and Portugal in about 1610. By the 1630s it had reached Germany and France, but the date at which England first encountered it is not reliably established. (It was listed among other imports, however, during the first decade of the seventeenth century, in a context which suggests it was then numbered among medicinal drugs.[38])

In 1657 there was held the first public tea sale in England, and three years later Samuel Pepys tried his first "cup of tee (a China drink) of which I never had drank before." [39] The tea merchants claimed that the drink was the ultimate panacea—an infallible cure for migraine, drowsiness, apoplexy, lethargy, paralysis, vertigo, epilepsy, catarrh, colic, gallstones, and consumption. At first it was very expensive everywhere but as time passed its cost-per-cup value came to be appreciated. One pound of tea can make almost three hundred cups, a fact which recommended it not only to the housewife but to the merchant who paid the shipping costs. In the ten years between 1770 and 1779, 18,000,000 pounds of tea were consumed annually by the English—almost three-quarters of which was reckoned to be smuggled [40]—and by the end of the century, they were consuming two pounds of it per head per annum. Today, statistics show that the figure has risen to almost ten pounds per head.

The other European nation which later took to tea-drinking on a considerable scale was Russia. Although the court came to favor it as early as the seventeenth century—the khan of Mongolia had presented 100 pounds of it to a Russian embassy—it did not come into widespread use until the nineteenth, when the opening of five Chinese ports to Russia, the cutting of the Suez Canal, the development of Russia's merchant marine, and the opening of the Trans-Siberian Railway all combined to ease the trade situation with the East and make tea so cheap that almost everyone could drink it. If roast beef symbolized the English meal,

---

* From the word *chiai* or *cha*, the English were to derive the slang word for tea, "char."

Drying tea was a carefully supervised operation.

Two Dutch merchants sampling teas in a Chinese warehouse.

and pasta the Italian, the gastronomic emblem of Russia came to be the samovar, that charcoal-heated *bain marie* with a teapot on top which keeps the tea always ready.

None of the new tea-drinking nations, however, quite appreciated what the Chinese had long known—that the quality of the water makes a very great difference to the *finesse* of the infused drink. But China did pass this knowledge on to Japan, and in Tokyo the fact is still commemorated—in the name of a subway station. The Ochanomisu station takes its name from that of a once pure stream which flows nearby. It means "the emperor's tea water."

Nineteenth-century samovar.

INDIA UNDER THE MOGULS

The establishment of a Muslim imperial power in India in the sixteenth century—that of the Moguls—had had far-reaching effects
not only on Indian society but on Indian food. For the best part
of four centuries, followers of Muhammad had been drifting into
northern India, bringing with them their everyday foods and cooking methods. But at the court of the Moguls, a new *haute cuisine*
was introduced into India. "Mughlai"-style cooking was almost
directly derived from that of Isfahan in Persia, a place which was
as much a symbol of splendor to sixteenth-century Muslims as
Versailles to seventeenth-century Frenchmen.

Kebabs, pilaf (or pilau) dishes of rice with shredded meat, the
technique of mixing fruits into flesh dishes, the use of almonds
and almond milk, rose water, the garnishing of all kinds of food
with fragile strips of tissue beaten out of pure gold and silver—
all these were absorbed into the Indian cuisine. Muslims were
quite prepared to eat beef, but their cuisine was based on mutton
and chicken, and non-vegetarian Hindus were therefore able to
adopt it without hesitation.

The region in which Muslim food became most common was
in the north, the heartland of Mogul rule. Even today, the
cooking of the Punjab has almost as many links with the food of
the Near East as with that of traditional India.

One innovation which spread throughout the subcontinent was
the Muslim addiction to sweetmeats. Just as Spain had learned of
marzipans and nougats from the Arabs, so India discovered the
delights of sugar candy. (The word "candy" itself is derived from
the Arabic for sugar.) Confections of all kinds, made from sugar
alone, from sugar and almonds, from sugar and rice flour, from
sugar and coconut, became immensely popular, as did sweet
desserts such as *halwa*.* But although Hindu Indians ate candies
with enthusiasm, it was Muslims who were most expert at their

---

* The *halwa* of modern India, frequently based on pulped vegetables enriched
with sugar and almonds, bears little resemblance to the *halwa* made a thousand
years ago in the kitchens of the caliphs of Baghdad, which was more like an
almond-spiked pulled toffee.[41]

An imperial banquet in the Mogul style.

manufacture. Predominantly Muslim cities such as Dacca and Lucknow became, and have remained, the great sweetmeat centers of the subcontinent.

In the anarchic early decades of the eighteenth century, English, French, Portuguese, Dutch and Danish travelers would all have found a number of their compatriots in India, settled comfortably in trading posts, living in semi-Indian style, eating semi-Indian food, begetting semi-Indian children. They had already embarked on the development of that bogus Hindu-Muslim-European cuisine which has been passed off ever since in the West as "Indian." Punjabi-Muslim food suffered least at their hands, perhaps, for while they loaded their "curries" with meat, poultry and fish which entirely changed the character of the dish, they felt less need to adapt recipes already based on meat.

Among the favorite European dishes at Surat on the northwest coast of India were two which were characteristically Muslim. One was the improbably named "dumpoked fowl" (from the Persian *dampukht:* air-cooked), a chicken stuffed with rice, almonds and raisins, and braised in butter. Another consisted of kebabs—"beef or mutton cut into small pieces, sprinkled with salt and pepper, and dipped with oil and garlic . . . and then roasted on a spit, with sweet herbs put between every piece and stuffed in them, and basted with oil and garlic all the while." [42]

Neither "dumpoked fowl" nor the true kebab was to infiltrate the cuisine of northern Europe until the twentieth century, but "curry" made an early appearance in the seventeenth-century Portuguese cookbook *Arte de Cozinha.* In the eighteenth century, curry recipes appeared in England, too, along with those for mulligatawny soup (whose name was derived from the Tamil for "pepper-water"), a number of chutneys, and a few spicy ketchups or catsups. The latter seem to have originated in China and found their way through the agency of the many colonies of Chinese expatriates in southeast Asia to India, and thence to England. The word "ketchup" itself comes from the Siamese *kachiap.* [43]

The unbiased visitor to India would have been—and sometimes was—shocked at the serious and often successful attempts made by Europeans there to eat and drink themselves to death. Sitting down to dine at one or two in the afternoon, they would spend three hours over an immensely heavy dinner washed down (by

Kebabs cooked over charcoal, in northern India, 1650.

the abstemious) with five or six glasses of imported Madeira. The mortality rates were appalling. Even in the short space of a year, one army contingent which arrived in India in 1756 lost 87 of its 848 men, not from "epidemical nor malignant disorders," but from irreparable damage to the liver resulting from over-eating and alcoholism.[44] A century earlier, alcoholism would have been to some extent understandable—the water was undrinkable, and there were few familiar alternatives. But by the mid-eighteenth century, chocolate, tea and coffee were well known, and the great center of coffee production was not very far away from India —at Mocha, near Aden, at the southern tip of the Red Sea.

COFFEE

Coffee seems to have originated in Ethiopia. On that, all historians are agreed. But how it became established as the favorite drink of the Near East, and particularly of the Turks, remains a mystery. The eleventh-century Arab physician Husain ibn 'Abdullah ibn Sina, known as Avicenna, is said to have mentioned it,[45] but there is great confusion in the early terminology. The word *kahwah* originally meant wine, but was later transferred to coffee, "the wine of Islam." (In later times, careful people gave the name *kihwah* to coffee to distinguish it from *kahwah*, wine.[46])

According to other Arab sources, coffee was not introduced to Aden until the middle of the fifteenth century.[47] From there it spread to Mecca, then to Cairo, to Damascus, and Aleppo, from which it passed to Constantinople, where the first coffee house was established in 1554.[48] During the next half century there were a few imprecise descriptions of it by European travelers, and it was only in 1610 that William Lithgow noted down more details. Although the people of Constantinople commonly drank cool sherbets "composed of water, honey and sugar" and "exceedingly delectable in the taste," they usually honored their guests with "a cup of coffa, made of a kind of seed called coava, and of a blackish colour; which they drink so hot as possible they can."[49] Pietro della Valle, a few years later, observed that "it prevents those who consume it from feeling drowsy. For that reason, students who wish to read into the late hours are fond of it."[50] In the 1620s, Sir Thomas Herbert, encountering it in Persia, described it as "a drink imitating that in the Stygian lake, black, thick and bitter." [51]

Although coffee is said to have been imported into Italy as early as 1580, and although in about 1637 the Englishman John Evelyn knew a Greek in Oxford who was "the first I ever saw drink coffee," [52] it was only when the coffee house was opened in Europe that it gained popularity.

The first coffee house appears to have been opened in Oxford in 1650. People flocked to it to try the new, hot, unintoxicating drink they had read of in travel books. Curiosity may have drawn the first patrons, but it was congenial company which encouraged them to continue to frequent the coffee houses.

In England the coffee house developed into the exclusive club, but elsewhere in Europe it became the ordinary café. Marseilles appears to have had the first coffee house on the continent, in 1671. Paris followed a year later. Vienna eleven years after that.

The astute peoples of the Near East maintained control over the trade in coffee beans for as long as they could. For half a century, the English and Dutch East India Companies had to go to Mocha for their supplies. By 1720, however, the Dutch had discovered that coffee could be grown in their Javanese territory, and they later introduced it into Ceylon. The English found that the bean would grow in the West Indies, and most of their supplies from the mid-eighteenth until the early nineteenth century came from there. When they afterward acquired and began to develop Ceylon, they imported great numbers of Tamil laborers from south India—an expedient which has had continuing repercussions in Sinhalese politics until the present day.*

THE DARK CONTINENT

Tea, coffee and chocolate were the last of the new discoveries brought in to titillate the palate of Europe in the three hun-

* In 1870, the first traces of coffee rust appeared in Ceylon, and as the decade advanced, less and less coffee was harvested. Gradually the disease spread to other areas of southeast Asia.[53] By the end of the century, almost all the coffee plantations in Asia had been given over to tea and rubber, and Brazil and Colombia had become the world's main suppliers.

An English coffee house.

dred years which followed the voyages of Columbus and da Gama. Coffee, which had originated in Ethiopia, and chocolate, initially an American crop, were to become two of the most important exports of Africa in later times.

But in the eighteenth century, slaves were still the most profitable trading specie. Often, they were prisoners captured during wars in the interior, who viewed the journey toward the coast "with great terror." They had a deeply rooted conviction "that the whites purchase negroes for the purpose of devouring them, or of selling them to others, that they may be devoured hereafter." [54] Until the very last years of the eighteenth century, Europe knew almost nothing about Africa beyond the coastal fringes. The traveler on his gastronomic Grand Tour might well have starved to death, for, as Mungo Park reported during his journey to the Niger in 1796, the white man "was regarded with astonishment and fear, and was obliged to sit all day without victuals, in the shade of a tree." [55] When food did come, it might be a fish "half-broiled upon some embers" [56] or a dish "made of sour milk and meal, called *sinkatoo*." [57]

Far away to the south, an expedition to the lands of the Orange river in 1801 found a city of more than ten thousand inhabitants in the territory which is now Botswana. Surrounded by barren deserts, the people relied much on their cattle, "whose flesh, however, they eat but very sparingly; milk is mostly used in a curdled state, which they keep . . . in leathern bags and clay pots." [58] Grain food consisted mainly of millets, and there were also a legume not unlike the pigeon pea, and a small, spotted·type of bean. The people had their own, unique way of dealing with these foods. All kinds of grain and pulse, reported the expedition, "appear to be sown promiscuously and, when reaped, to be thrown indiscriminately into their earthen granaries; from whence they are taken and used without selection, sometimes by [? making into flatbread and] broiling, but more generally boiling in milk." [59]

Ending his Grand Tour on the borders of unknown Africa, the traveling gastronome of the eighteenth century would have had at least one salutary lesson driven home to him—that cooking is an art only where food is consistently plentiful. When shortages are part of everyday life, filling the stomach is the only art.

PART SIX

The Modern World,
1800 Until the
Present Day

INTRODUCTION

Industry,

Science,

and Food

The industrial revolution which gained international momentum in the nineteenth century was to change the face of the earth for a second time. The neolithic revolution of almost twelve thousand years before had brought fields and farms and villages into being; the industrial revolution created machinery, factories, and vast and suffocating cities.

Few observers in the early days could have anticipated that the new god of the machine would number social chaos and environmental cataclysm among its attributes. But industrialization and the associated expansion of scientific knowledge had a sharply divisive effect on society, as well as a destructive effect on natural resources which went far deeper than ever before.

Britain, the first nation to industrialize, suffered in an extreme form all the early benefits and all the subsequent disadvantages of being first in any major new undertaking, and as the nineteenth century drew to its close, other European powers and the United States of America caught up with and surpassed her achievements. Between 1880 and 1900, Germany succeeded in taking the lead in European industry while at the same time—in the hope of maintaining (as Britain had proved unable to do) self-sufficiency in food supplies—putting an additional two million acres under food crops. But nineteenth-century European agriculture, with the best will in the world, could not hope to feed the ever-growing population, which is estimated to have increased from about 188,000,000 in 1800 to 401,000,000 in 1901.[1]

Fortunately, the situation in Europe encouraged an unprecedented expansion of food production in other continents. British factory laborers existed on a diet of bread and tea, with a piece of cheap meat or bacon on Sundays, and it was a recurring miracle to the country's administrators that it continued possible to supply them with even such unambitious food as that. The improvement in transport brought about by the steam engine, however, allowed grain to be shipped from America in huge quantities, and tea to be imported in bulk from China and India.

Canning, freezing and chilling—new developments of the greatest importance—also meant that meat could be brought in cheaply from the wide-open grazing lands of Australia and America.

In America after the Civil War the transformation from a farming to a manufacturing society was well under way, although even as late as 1860 most of the gross national product was attributable to the processing of agricultural output—by flour mills, tanneries, meat packing plants, and breweries.[2]

In other continents, the situation was very different. Those countries which had been first to enter the machine age depended for their survival on selling the products of their machines, and the nineteenth-century quest for empire was partly a quest for overseas markets. The colonial powers maintained those markets by, in effect, retarding the development of industrialization in their overseas possessions—not by legislating against it (indeed, they often made a show of encouraging it), but by preventing their colonial subjects from learning the managerial skills on which industry so much depends. As a result, large parts of Asia and Africa lagged a hundred years behind the West in economic development. This was to have unfortunate repercussions when former colonial territories began to achieve independence in the mid-twentieth century, leading to over-emphasis on the needs of industry at the expense of agriculture.

Countries which were not subject to Western occupation also felt the effects. China was exploited ruthlessly by all the world powers in the late nineteenth century, including the United States, and so torn for the first half of the twentieth—by wars and internal upheavals—that full industrialization had to wait. Japan, by contrast, was quick as always to learn a potentially valuable lesson even from Western barbarians; by 1870, a mere seventeen years after Commodore Perry's "black ships" sailed into Edo (Tokyo) bay and opened up Japan to Western influences, the country was committed to its own industrial revolution.

The nineteenth century was intensely science-conscious. The first real impact of science on diet came when it was discovered in the laboratory that much of the food sold to rich and poor alike was adulterated with dangerous ingredients. The outcome was the first series of modern regulations relating to food purity.

Food preservation, too, owed much to scientific developments. The technique of conserving food in sealed containers, from which air had been excluded, was discovered at the end of the eighteenth century by Nicholas Appert, but it was only when another Frenchman, Louis Pasteur, identified the part played by micro-organisms in the "spoiling" of food that canning became a safe and satisfactory method of preservation. Pasteurization, or selective sterilization by heat, was to be of continuing value in the food industries.

Science's most fundamental contribution to the diet, however, was not to come until the twentieth century. It appeared at first to consist of no more than abstract knowledge, and a knowledge which did not even promise more or better-quality food. Instead, it offered better health. What the scientists had discovered, in fact, was the existence of vitamins. Only after this discovery did it become possible to arrive at worthwhile conclusions about the foods essential to health. Disseminating this knowledge was to be (and remains) a slow process, but governments have been able by a variety of means to influence some sections of the population toward better nutrition.

Having discovered the essential constituents of food, science has inevitably gone on to create them in the laboratory. "Bacon" and "sausage meat" manufactured from soybean protein have already received wide publicity, and there are other equally revolutionary developments which could be translated into commercial practice in the near future.

Bread or potatoes and an occasional mouthful of meat might sustain great numbers of factory workers during the nineteenth century, but the middle ranks of the growing middle classes considered a minimum of six dishes necessary for an ordinary family dinner. Even so, most townspeople ate comparatively little in the way of fruit and vegetables until early in the twentieth century, when canned types became widely available.

The First World War made it clear that an alarming number of European town dwellers were of poor physique, and that this was partly due to an insufficient or nutritionally ill-balanced diet. Afterward, partly as a result of intensive propaganda on nutrition, but even more because of economic conditions, the diet of many Europeans began to improve. The food industries in America and Australasia increased production of canned fruits and vegetables, chilled butter, eggs and bacon, and despite the financial upheavals of the interwar years progressively more workers found that they could afford to introduce some variety into their diet.

At the same time there grew up a customer demand for consistent quality and stable prices, a demand closely linked with expansion in the manufacture and distribution of branded goods and the energetic publicizing of brand names. Until the twentieth century, brand names and "hard sell" had been the prerogative as much of retailers as of manufacturers. The Hartfords' Great American Tea Company (later the Great Atlantic and Pacific Tea Company) of New York, and the grocery empire begun in Glasgow in 1876 by the redoubtable Tommy Lipton, were no less famous in their way than Borden, Swift, and Armour. But mass-production economics, particularly in the field of canned goods, brought more and more manufacturers into the brand-name business. America, always more preoccupied with hygiene than other countries—perhaps because so many of her early settlers belonged to sects which held that cleanliness was inseparable from godliness—also took readily to neatly tailored brand-named packages of other types of food, although in Britain, for example, even in the late 1940s, local grocers were still wielding butter-patters for every individual customer and shoveling sugar, to order, into thick little blue paper bags.

The consistent quality and price which recommended branded goods to the customer was to lead ultimately to a standardization in almost all food products which many people believe has now gone too far. Certainly it has gone a surprisingly long way, penetrating even into France, where the visitor suffers an odd sense of shock at hearing a Frenchman enthuse over the excellence and convenience of the polyethylene-shrouded packs in the new supermarkets. Blunt-ended carrots bred not to perforate the bag. Tomatoes grown not for taste but for a standard weight which is precisely divisible into a pound or kilo (eight tomatoes to the pound, eighteen to the kilo). Miniature india-rubber mushrooms with nothing to recommend them but their looks.

Undoubtedly, the blandness which has been an inevitable result of trying to cater to all tastes has led in the West to the present revival of interest in herbs and spices, as well as in "natural" foods.* If the present scientific revolution, which has persuaded two ears of grain to grow where one grew before, and also knows how to make bread with no grain at all, continues according to plan, the desire for "natural" foods and spices seems unlikely to abate.

* Not new. The Reverend Sylvester Graham elevated "pure food" into a cult in America in the 1830s and 40s.

"Ten minutes for refreshments." A Great American Tea Co. poster, 1886.

16.
The Industrial Revolution

"The people was all roaring out *Voilà le boulanger et la boulangère et le petit mitron,* saying that now they should have bread as they now had got the baker and his wife and boy." [1] The year was 1789, the place Paris, the "baker" King Louis XVI.

Neither high prices nor food shortages had sparked the outbreak of the French Revolution, but once the middle classes had made the first breach in the political defenses of the privileged élite, the ordinary people of France began to take a hand in the game. While the Constituent Assembly discussed the Declaration of the Rights of Man and the abolition of aristocratic privileges, the market women of Paris demonstrated their disapproval of the fact that a four-pound loaf cost 14½ sous, very little less than the effective daily wage of a builder's laborer (18 sous). Food crises and food riots were to bedevil the plans of the revolutionaries and their successors throughout the 1790s. They were also to sound a warning to the governments of other countries, confronted with the problem of expanding towns and an unprecedented increase in population. Between 1750 and 1800, the population of Europe had grown from 140,000,000 to 188,000,000.[2]

The increase may have been partly due to agricultural developments which promised a reliable improvement in food supplies— a promise unfulfilled in France, where there was a series of disastrous harvests between 1773 and 1789.

SCIENTIFIC AGRICULTURE

Many of the new discoveries in farming had first seen the light of day in the Low Countries, where shortage of land had encouraged the Dutch in particular to embark on a system of intensive cultivation. This required that the land be constantly enriched, never allowed to exhaust itself. The regular collection and use of organic fertilizers became an important feature of farming in the Low Countries, and in the Flemish areas a seven-course system of crop rotation was developed. A specialized dairy industry also came into being—cattle provided valuable manure as well as milk—and by 1750 the Low Countries were producing enough milk to enable them to export butter and cheese to neighboring regions.

The rest of Europe learned from this example. When Frederick the Great set about transforming Prussia into productive agricultural land, he turned to Holland for guidance. The seven-course rotation system proved to be over-refined for countries where land hunger was not so intense, but much of Europe compromised with a four-crop version consisting of wheat, turnips, barley, and clover. Clover enriched the soil. The green turnip tops helped to smother weeds, and both crops made excellent animal fodder.

As the early developments of the industrial revolution began to mesh together, it became possible for animal feeding stuffs to be mechanically chopped or pulped, and compressed into convenient feedcakes which enabled farmers to keep their cattle alive through the winter months. Grain yields were greatly increased when Jethro Tull's seed-planting drill—improved by the introduction of gears into the distributing machinery in 1782—came into general use. This not only reduced the amount of seed wasted during planting, but considerably increased the quantity of grain harvested. Eighteenth-century improvements in cast iron also made it possible to mass-produce farming implements according to well-tried designs; this reduced not only the price, but also the farmer's dependence on the often unpredictable local blacksmith.

The revolutionary and Napoleonic wars hurried on the progress of scientific agriculture, particularly in England. Economic blockades meant that more grain and more meat had to be produced at home. War had to be waged not only against the Corsican monster but against the "unconquered sterility" of unused land. "Let us not be satisfied," exclaimed Sir John Sinclair in 1803, "with the liberation of Egypt, or the subjugation of Malta, but let us subdue Finchley Common; let us conquer Hounslow Heath; let us compel Epping Forest to submit to the yoke of improvement." [3]

"Improvement" had been the watchword of England's more thoughtful landowners for some time, although one of the results of their careful study of agriculture had proved highly injurious to the small farmer and the peasant. In the interests of stock management, what had once been open land had to be hedged or fenced, and a great number of peasants whose landlords were more interested in livestock than people found themselves deprived of the little patches of ground where they had been able to grow a few root crops, tether a cow, or raise a pig.

Nevertheless, these experiments in scientific farming were important. Without the increased efficiency they brought, the lonely British stand against Napoleon might have failed and the subsequent history of Europe and the world would—for better or worse—have been very different.

The foods for which Holland was already famous in the eighteenth century —butter, Edam and Gouda cheeses, and dried fish.

THE INDUSTRIAL TOWNS

The pace of urbanization and industrialization in Europe varied, and so did the timing, but everywhere new towns and suburbs were thrown up to accommodate factories and the ever-increasing number of people who labored in them. Manchester in 1800 had 75,000 inhabitants; fifty years later, 400,000. Stockholm, with only 6000 in 1800, had swelled to 350,000 by 1914. Düsseldorf, a town of 10,000 people in 1800, had 360,000 inhabitants by 1910. The number of people living in London multiplied by four in just over a century; in Vienna by five; in Berlin by nine; in New York— that new city in a new country to which so many refugees were to flee from hunger or oppression in Europe—by eighty.[4]

For almost the first time in history, mass urban poverty could be observed by anyone who cared to see. Conditions in the industrial towns were shocking, not only to early nineteenth-century philanthropists—still more accustomed to green fields than the canyons of high-density housing—but to the people who lived in them and paid dearly for the seemingly guaranteed wage that had attracted them there. The factory laborer rarely died of outright starvation, but bad housing, worse food, and non-existent sanitation took a less direct and no less appalling toll of human life.

Both factories and houses were devitalizing and dehumanizing. Bludgeoned during the day by the intolerable clamor of early machinery, suffocated by the laden air of the weaving shed, the working man or woman went home in the 1830s to a cellar, an overcrowded slum, or a flimsy shack thrown up out of half-bricks by some speculative builder. Cooking facilities were, at best, sketchy. The water supply, drawn from rivers and wells which were often contaminated by the seepage from cesspools, was distributed through street standpipes which might be turned on by the authorities for no more than five minutes a day.* Sewage systems were a mockery. Florence Nightingale, in one of her reports on sanitation, acidly quoted the London woman who, when

---

* "It is only," said one contemporary commentator, "when the infant enters on breathing existence, and when the man has ceased to breathe—at the moment of birth and at the hour of death—that he is really well washed."[5]

Children went to work in factories at the age of seven in the early years of the nineteenth century.

asked about drains, replied: "No, thank God, we have none of them foul stinking things here!" [6]

Hundreds of thousands of children died not only from the resultant diseases but from malnutrition. Friedrich Engels, in 1844, described the diet of the poor in the northern manufacturing towns of England. Descending the poverty scale, he said, "we find the animal food reduced to a small bit of bacon cut up with the potatoes; lower still, even this disappears, and there remain only bread, cheese, porridge and potatoes, until on the lowest round of the ladder, among the Irish, potatoes form the sole food." [7] Fifty years later, in London's Bethnal Green district, 83 per cent of children had no solid food other than bread at seventeen out of the twenty-one meals in the week.[8] It was hardly surprising that the people of the industrial revolution suffered chronically from the scurvy that had, until the end of the eighteenth century, been the scourge of seafarers. Rickets and tuberculosis also sapped the vitality of the poor town dweller, the first a product of vitamin deficiency, the second intensified by poor feeding.

THE FOOD OF THE POOR

In Britain in the 1830s and 1840s, a worker might earn anything from 25 p. to £2 (62 cents to $5) a week. In 1840-41, 25 p., or 62 cents, bought neither more nor less than six four-pound loaves —just enough to feed a typical family of two adults and three children.[9] It left nothing to pay the rent, nothing for tea, nothing for that little piece of bacon which was the poor man's substitute for meat.

A "good meal" meant something hot, filling, and quickly cooked —tea and boiled potatoes more often than not, since potatoes cost only about 5 p., or 12.5 cents, for twenty pounds. The man of the house might have a piece of pie or a sausage from a coffee stall at midday, and at the weekend the whole family sat down to a Sunday dinner of broth, stew and pudding. It was a poverty-line diet, but a great many people lived on it—and a great many died because of it.

The weekly budget of a household whose income was 75 p., or $1.87, a week might, in 1841, have looked much as follows: [10]

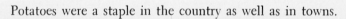

Potatoes were a staple in the country as well as in towns.

5 4-pound loaves	17.5 p.	43.75 cents
5 pounds meat	10.5 "	26.25 "
7 Imperial, or 8.75 American, pints "porter"—a special brew of beer	6.0 "	15.00 "
Coal	4.0 "	10.00 "
40 pounds potatoes	7.0 "	17.50 "
3 ounces tea, 1 pound sugar	7.5 "	18.75 "
1 pound butter	3.5 "	8.75 "
Soap and candles	2.75 "	6.75 "
Rent	12.5 "	31.25 "
Schooling	1.5 "	3.75 "
Miscellaneous	2.25 "	5.25 "
	75.00 p.	$1.87

This distribution of income would be characteristic for a semi-skilled worker at a time of full employment. In bad years, meat, porter and butter would be the first food items to be cut.

There were several "bad years" in the 1840s, just as there had been in the earlier decades of the century, but the climax came with the first failures of the potato crop in 1845. Right across Europe, from Ireland to England, to France, Germany, Poland and Russia, the potato began to rot. In most countries, the diet of the poor was adversely affected, especially when, inevitably, grain and bread prices began to rise. But in Ireland, the result was famine.

THE POTATO FAMINE

The potato had been introduced into Ireland in the 1580s; in the politically stormy centuries that followed, the peasant discovered the advantages of the new root crop. It was not ruined when battle raged over the ground in which it grew. It could remain safely hidden in the earth throughout the winter, even when the peasant's home and stores were raided or fired by English soldiers. A tiny cottage plot could produce enough to feed a man and wife, six children, even a cow and a pig.

Occasionally, there were failures and sometimes even famines, but nothing calamitous enough to wean the Irish from the potato. In 1845, however, in one catastrophic month, plants all over Europe began to wilt and then to rot. Tiny egg-shaped disease spores carried on the winds, beaten down onto the leaves by the rains of a cold, wet summer, devoured the sap and killed the plants. Potato blight had struck in its most acute form.

In Ireland, the potato famine meant more than simple food scarcity for a man and his family. It meant no seed potatoes from which to grow next year's crop. It meant that the pig or the cow which would normally have been sold to pay the rent had to be slaughtered, because there was nothing for it to fatten on. No rent paid frequently meant eviction by a callous or impoverished landlord. Hunger was soon compounded by scurvy, brought on by lack of the vitamin C which potatoes had supplied; later, by failing eyesight and acute nervous debility—sometimes even dementia—because the death of the cow had removed milk, the source of vitamins A and B_7, from the diet.

One result of the Irish potato famine was that the Parliament at Westminster repealed the formerly heavy import duty on grain —one of the first steps toward that doctrine of free trade which was to have such repercussions on the economics of later nineteenth-century Europe. Another was that a high proportion of the Irish who survived the famine left their native land forever, some to go to the growing towns of England, others to flood into the United States. Before 1845, the annual emigration figure had been approximately 60,000. In 1847 it reached over 200,000. There was a pause in 1848 when the potato harvest improved and intending emigrants saved their £3 to £5 ($7.50 to $12.50) for the fare, but by 1851 the annual exodus had reached a quarter of a million.[11] *

---

* Despite these figures, the proportion of Irish among immigrants to the United States—44 per cent—was no higher in the five years following the famine than in those preceding it.[12] This was because food shortages, a severe economic crisis, and extreme political unrest combined to produce an upsurge in emigration from other parts of Europe at much the same time.

Famine in Ireland.

FOOD OF THE RICH

In the first half of the nineteenth century, while the poor struggled to stay alive, the middle classes of industrial England increased in number and in power. The great employers of factory labor needed the services of bankers and insurers, shippers and carriers, engineers and architects, managers and clerks. Growing towns needed more shops, more schools, more medical men, lawyers and clergymen. Some of the new middle classes were very little richer than the factory worker, some very little poorer than the greatest of hereditary landowners. Most of them, however, had some slight margin of income over expenditure, and for that reason they were —in comparison with the majority of factory workers—"rich." They were not forced to eat the food that was cheapest, but were able to exercise choice. And their choice when they entertained, if not necessarily every day, was usually a reflection or an adaptation of what was eaten on the next higher level of the social scale.

On the highest level of all—that of a reigning monarch—the complexities of a dinner menu were considerable, involving not only *potages, relevés, grosses pièces, entrées, assiettes volantes, pâ-tisseries, rôts,* and *entremets,* but the niceties of *service à la fran-çaise, service à la russe,* or *service à la* any one of a number of Franco-Russian compromises.

The somewhat haphazard medieval menu had survived in Eng-land and America until well into the eighteenth century. For example, the two-course dinner for an ordinary household sug-gested in 1727 in *The Compleat Housewife* [13] was still markedly similar in style to the fourteenth-century French menu already described in chapter 12 (see p. 222).

FIRST COURSE

Soup
Ragoût of breast of veal
Roast venison
Boiled leg of lamb with
    cauliflower
with smaller dishes of:
Jugged hare
A marrow pudding
Stewed eels
Stewed carp
A palpatoon, or "pupton," of
    pigeons (a type of hot
    pâté)
A roast pig

SECOND COURSE

Four partridges and two quails
Lobsters
Almond cheesecakes and custards
with smaller dishes of:
Four pocket and lamb stones
    (*animelles* or "lamb's
    fry," i.e., lamb's testicles)
Apricot fritters
Sturgeon
Fried sole
Green peas
Potted pigeons

In France, however, the menu had become not precisely ra-tionalized, but codified. A number of dishes still appeared on the table simultaneously—the grander the household the more there were—but they appeared in groups, each of which had a special name.

For a time, the French dinner appears to have been divided roughly according to these groups into six or eight courses, but the inconvenience, presumably, of having servants clear and reset the table so frequently during the progress of a meal led ulti-mately to a return to three courses, the third being supplied not from the kitchen but from the pastrycook's domain. The first and second courses together, therefore, now included three general types of dish—appetizers, main dishes, and "afters"—each group subdivided into smaller groups.

APPETIZERS
>Soups, thick and clear
>
>*Hors d'oeuvre,* sometimes called *assiettes volantes* or *entrées volantes* ("flying dishes" or "flying *entrées*").* These were platters of mixed delicacies, sometimes slices of salted or preserved meats, sometimes hot preparations of kidney, liver, or other variety meats.
>
>Fish
>
>*Entrées.* These were light "made dishes" which served as an introduction to the more substantial meats that followed.

MAIN DISHES
>Large cuts of meat
>Game birds or poultry
>These formed the *pièces de résistance,* the "solid food" or backbone of the meal. Normally, they were accompanied by salads or garnished with vegetables.

"AFTERS"
>These were usually called *entremets,* "between courses," and were a motley collection of cold meats, delicate aspics, savories, vegetable dishes, and sweet dishes. In medieval times, and after, *entremets* meant an entertainment that kept guests amused while the relics of one course were being removed and replaced with the dishes of the next. By the end of the eighteenth century, the word referred to the food that came between the main meats and the third and final course of pastries and ices.

These three general types of food were set on the table in two courses, each of which was arranged according to a neat and elegant pattern. With the first course, for example, four soups

---

* The word *volantes* is confusing. Many people take it to mean that these were light and insubstantial dishes which flew down the throat almost unnoticed. On the whole, however, it seems more likely that they were true *hors d'oeuvre* (extraneous dishes), foods designed to stimulate the gastric juices, which were not placed on the table but merely passed around once or twice by servants. In later times, the name *assiette volante* came to be applied to dishes such as soufflés which could not be left to stand on a table but had to be served the moment they were ready.

might be placed at the four corners of the table while the *entrées* were ranged tidily along the sides (hence the term "side dishes"). When the soup had been disposed of, the tureens were removed and replaced with four dishes of fish—hence the name "remove" (or *relevé*) for this second installment of the first course.* Then came the *pièces de résistance.*

Toward the end of the eighteenth century, partly under the influence of refugee French chefs, the British began to adopt the

* As the French style of dining was adopted in other countries, chefs attempted to bridge the gap between the French language and the taste of England or Germany. This, in the end, made nonsense of a culinary jargon which was originally precise. Soup and fish might be served at the same time with the result that, when they were taken away, one of the *pièces de résistance* became the "remove." *Entrées,* in the hands of a cook who thought himself above a plain old-fashioned roast, took the place of the *pièces de résistance. Entremets,* as pastrycooks disappeared from the gastronomic scene, came to include the pastries and ices which had once formed the third course; so a word which originally meant "between-courses" was ultimately applied to the last course.

The kitchen of the Brighton Pavilion as it was in Carême's day.

tidier French style of menu planning. They still, however, remained scornful of French kickshaws—made dishes, such as *hors d'oeuvre, entrées* and *entremets*—and because of this the split between courses was made at a different point. Whereas in France both appetizers and main dishes constituted the first course (*entremets* forming the second), in Britain only some of the *pièces de résistance* were incorporated in the first course. Thus a first course of soup, fish, *entrées*, and roast or boiled meats was followed by a second consisting of roast poultry or game birds supplemented by *entremets*. In this ingenious fashion, British diners were able to avoid eating kickshaws altogether, being assured of something plain and substantial in both courses. In fact, the kickshaws usually consisted of "very mild but abortive attempts at Continental cooking, and," remarked one well-traveled diner, "I have always observed that they met with the neglect and contempt that they merited." [14]

This criticism could hardly have been leveled at dinners given by Britain's Prince Regent, later King George IV, when his kitchens were presided over by the distinguished chef Antonin (or Marie-Antoine) Carême, for though Carême certainly made concessions to English taste, he made them with the greatest panache. At the Brighton Pavilion on January 15, 1817, for example, the menu [15] began with the four following soups:

Le potage à la Monglas	A creamy brown soup, Madeira-flavored, made with *foie gras*, truffles, and mushrooms
La garbure aux choux	Rich, flavorful vegetable broth, country-style, full of shredded cabbage
Le potage d'orge perlée à la Crécy	A bland pink purée of pearl barley and carrots
Le potage de poissons à la russe	Fish soup, "Russian-style," probably made with sturgeon

The soups were removed with four fish dishes:

La matelote au vin de Bordeaux	A delicate stew of freshwater fish, cooked in the wine of Bordeaux
Les truites au bleu à la provençale	Plain-cooked river trout with a tomato and garlic sauce

Le turbot à l'anglaise, sauce aux homards	Poached turbot with lobster sauce
La grosse anguille à la régence	A large fat eel, richly sauced, and garnished with quenelles, truffles, and cocks' combs

The fish dishes were followed (the trout and turbot remaining on the table, the *matelote* and eels being taken away) by four *grosses pièces,* or *pièces de résistance:*

Le jambon à la broche, au Madère	Ham roasted on the spit, with Madeira sauce
L'oie braisée aux racines glacées	Braised goose, with glazed root vegetables
Les poulardes à la Perigueux	Truffled roast chickens
Le rond de veau à la royale	Round of veal, enrobed in sauce and extravagantly garnished

These main dishes (with the turbot and the trout) were surrounded by no less than thirty-six *entrées,* of which those listed below form a representative selection.

Les filets de volaille à la maréchale	Chicken breasts coated with egg and breadcrumbs and fried in butter
Le sauté de merlans aux fines herbes	Sautéed whiting with fresh herbs
La timbale de macaroni à la napolitaine	Macaroni and grated cheese, layered with forcemeat, and steamed in a large mold
La noix de veau à la jardinière	Rump of veal garnished with fresh vegetables
La darne de saumon au beurre de Montpellier	Center-cut salmon steak, with a green-tinted spread composed of fresh herbs, egg yolks, butter, capers, anchovies, etc.
Le sauté de faisans aux truffes	Sautéed segments of pheasant with truffles
Le turban de filets de lapereaux	A ring of fillets cut from the breasts of young wild rabbits
Le boudin de volaille à la béchamel	Stuffed chicken quenelles with béchamel sauce

Le sauté de ris de veau à la provençale	Sautéed calf's sweetbreads with tomatoes and garlic
Les galantines de perdreaux à la gelée	Boned, stuffed partridges in aspic
Les petites croustades de mauviettes au gratin	Larks in individual patty cases of oven-toasted bread lined with a creamed chicken-liver mixture
La côte de boeuf aux oignons glacés	Beef sirloin with glazed onions
La salade de filets de brochets aux huitres	Salad of pike fillets with oysters
Le pain de carpe au beurre d'anchois	Carp forcemeat steamed in a mold and served with anchovy butter

There were also five *assiettes volantes* containing fillets of sole, and five of fillets of hazel-grouse (or wood grouse), covered with a béchamel sauce blended with soured cream, and browned in the oven.

This was only the first course. Afterward there were eight majestic set pieces—some made from pastry, with names such as "the ruins of Antioch" and "the Chinese hermitage." Four roasts of game and poultry—cockerels, wild duck, chickens and hazel-grouse. Thirty-two *entremets*—truffles roasted in the embers, lobster *au gratin*, pineapple cream, cucumbers in white sauce, liqueur-flavored jelly, oysters, stuffed lettuce, potatoes in Hollandaise sauce, scrambled eggs with truffles, spongy Genoese cakes with coffee filling, and so on. And another ten *assiettes volantes*, five containing miniature potato soufflés and five containing little chocolate soufflés.

Whether the side dishes were superb, as at tables supplied by Carême, or stodgy and unappetizing, as at most other British tables, no diner was expected to try all of them. Digestively, it would have been difficult enough, but the mechanics of table service made it almost impossible. With *service à la française* (as with the old-fashioned *service à l'anglaise*), when the soup had been disposed of and the covers removed from the fish and *entrées*, "every man helps the dish before him, and offers some of it to his neighbour . . . If he wishes for anything else, he must ask across the table, or send a servant for it—a very troublesome custom." [16] A degree of self-assertion was necessary. The shy or ignorant guest limited not only his own menu but that of others at the table. One young divinity student, for example, when invited to dine by an archbishop who was due to examine him in the scriptures, found himself confronted by a dish of ruffs and reeves, wild birds which, caged and fattened, were a rare delicacy. "Out of sheer modesty the clerical tyro confined himself exclusively to the dish before him, and persevered in his indiscriminating attentions to it till one of the resident dignitaries (all of whom were waiting only the proper moment to participate) observed him, and called the attention of the company by a loud exclamation of alarm. But the warning came too late: the ruffs and reeves had vanished to a bird, and with them . . . all the candidate's chances of . . . preferment." [17]

This type of service also inhibited conversation. A guest might begin to tell a good story about "a farmer of my parish, who used to sup upon wild ducks and flummery; so this farmer—*Doctor Marrowfat, cries his lordship, interrupting him, give me leave to drink your health*—so being fond of wild ducks and flummery—*Doctor*, adds a gentleman who sate next him, *let me advise to a wing of this turkey*—so this farmer being fond—*Hob, nob, Doctor, which do you choose, white or red?*—So being fond of wild ducks and flummery—*Take care of your hand, Sir, it may dip in the gravy.*" [18] At this stage, the good doctor would despairingly abandon his tale.

By the 1830s, however, some of the work at table was being delegated to servants who, "meaning to be very polite, dodge about to offer each *entrée* to ladies in the first instance; confusion arises, and whilst the same dishes are offered two or three times over to some guests, the same unhappy wights have no option of others." [19]

By the mid-nineteenth century, *service à la française* assisted by waiters had begun to merge into *service à la russe*, in which the waiters were supreme. Here, the table contained only decorative set pieces. Serving dishes were laid out on the sideboard, and waiters handed them around to the guests in strict rotation. The first waiter would offer meat to a guest, then would come another with a serving dish of potatoes, then a third with a vegetable, and a fourth with a sauce. To some gourmets, this was purgatory. Even with the most efficient attendants, everything was "provokingly

An American menu which illustrates a transitional stage between *service à la française* and *à la russe*. A dinner which would previously have been served in three courses was now broken into seven—if the boiled meats and entrées were set on the table together, as the design of the menu suggests.

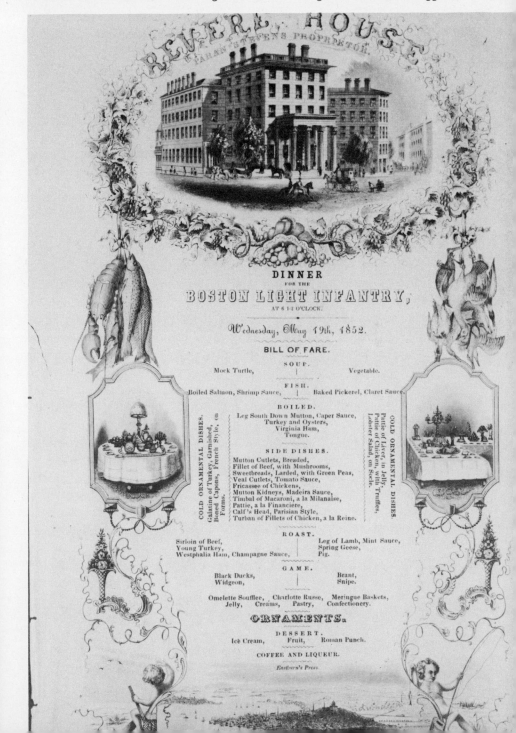

REVERE HOUSE

PARAN STEVENS PROPRIETOR.

DINNER
FOR THE
BOSTON LIGHT INFANTRY,
AT 6 1-2 O'CLOCK.

Wednesday, May 19th, 1852.

BILL OF FARE.

SOUP.

Mock Turtle,　　　　　　　　Vegetable.

FISH.

Boiled Salmon, Shrimp Sauce,　|　Baked Pickerel, Claret Sauce.

BOILED.

Leg South Down Mutton, Caper Sauce,
Turkey and Oysters,
Virginia Ham,
Tongue.

SIDE DISHES.

Mutton Cutlets, Breaded,
Fillet of Beef, with Mushrooms,
Sweetbreads, Larded, with Green Peas,
Veal Cutlets, Tomato Sauce,
Fricassee of Chickens,
Mutton Kidneys, Madeira Sauce,
Timbal of Macaroni, a la Milanaise,
Pattie, a la Financiere,
Calf's Head, Parisian Style,
Turban of Fillets of Chicken, a la Reine.

COLD ORNAMENTAL DISHES.
Galatine of Turkey, Garnished,
Boned Capons, French Style, on
Forms.

COLD ORNAMENTAL DISHES.
Pattie of Liver, in Jelly,
Pattie of Chicken, with Truffles,
Lobster Salad, on Socle.

ROAST.

Sirloin of Beef,　　　　　　Leg of Lamb, Mint Sauce,
Young Turkey,　　　　　　　Spring Geese,
Westphalia Ham, Champagne Sauce,　|　Pig.

GAME.

Black Ducks,　　　　　　　Brant,
Widgeon,　　　　　　　　　Snipe.

Omelette Soufflee,　Charlotte Russe,　Meringue Baskets,
Jelly,　　Creams,　　Pastry,　Confectionery.

ORNAMENTS.

DESSERT.

Ice Cream,　　Fruit,　　Roman Punch.

COFFEE AND LIQUEUR.

Eastburn's Press.

lagging, one thing after another, so that contentment is out of the question." [20] The same, of course, remains true of formal dinners today, when service continues generally to be *à la russe*.

One of the effects of *service à la russe* was to reduce the total number of dishes offered at a dinner. Clearly, servants could not hand around four soups, four fish, four *pièces de résistance*, three dozen *entrées*, ten *assiettes volantes* . . . and so on. What actually happened when *service à la russe* was generally adopted was that the two or three extensive, eat-what-you-please courses of French-style meals were expanded into six or eight obligatory courses that forced *more* food on the diner and yet gave him, effectively, less choice.

BREAD AND MEAT

In industrial England in the first half of the nineteenth century, rich and poor alike still bought the materials for their meals from the same traditional sources.

Grain was still ground, as it had been for five centuries, in small water- or windmills scattered around the countryside. According to the adjustment of the stones and the fineness of the sifter, different grades of flour could be produced, but none of it was very pure, and the oils left in the flour by the stone-grinding

A Paris slaughterhouse in 1890, where ladies went to swallow a medicinal glass of blood.

process turned it rancid in a few weeks. Many women still made their own bread. Others, notably in the industrial towns, bought from the baker. Those few who held advanced views on hygiene were scandalized to see how commercial bread was made—perspiration dripping from the half-naked and not very clean bodies of the kneaders into the dough they were mixing.[21]

Generally, England appears to have lagged behind continental Europe in the matter of bread production, a fact still reflected in the much greater variety of traditional breads and yeast mixes to be found today in, for example, France and the eastern regions of Austria.

In most of the world, however, a city's meat supply still arrived on the hoof and was slaughtered in the shambles. London's Smithfield market in 1845 was "an irregular space bounded by dirty houses and the ragged party walls of demolished habitations." [22] It was estimated that 4100 oxen and 30,000 sheep, as well as unnumbered pigs and calves, could be crammed into this space ready for slaughter and distribution to retailers and restaurants, as well as to the "triperies, bone-boiling houses, gut-scraperies etc." which were located nearby.[23] * Slaughterhouses, anywhere in the world, were a traumatic sight for the innocent meat eater. The butchers who skinned and carved the animals moved placidly about their business, "wading in blood and covered with it all over. Between them lay the skulls and bones, strewed about in wild confusion; the entrails, which were afterwards loaded upon waggons and carried off; and beyond . . . the unborn calves were lying, in a heap of perhaps thirty or forty; near which, boys standing up to their shoulders in blood, were engaged in stripping off the skin of the largest and most matured ones." [24]

ADULTERATION

In the early nineteenth century, one of the first subjects to be placed under the new and improved microscope of the scientific investigator was that of adulteration.

Ingenious retailers had always practiced adulteration whenever

---

* Preparers of tripe, glue manufacturers, and makers of sausage skins all relied on animal by-products for their raw materials.

they could get away with it, but usually on a limited and local scale. The growth of towns and the great expansion of roads and railways, however, brought an organized food industry into being which had to contend not only with handling, transport, storage life and marketing, but with basic problems of the availability of raw materials. If a particular product was scarce and expensive, wholesalers and retailers had to find some way of increasing the quantity and reducing the price, usually by bulking out the genuine article with a cheap additive.

The additive might or might not be harmful. Pepper, for example, had always been adulterated with such comparatively innocuous materials as mustard husks, pea flour, juniper berries, and a commodity known as "pepper dust," which appears to have consisted of the sweepings of the storeroom floor. Tea had also been counterfeited on a grand scale in the days when it had to be brought all the way from China and was liable to a heavy excise duty. There was a flourishing trade in "smouch," a substance made from leaves of the ash tree, dried and curled on copper plates and sold to tea merchants at a few pence per pound for mixing with real tea. In the last decade of the eighteenth century, this trick had become so common in England that an Act of Parliament condemned it not only for diminishing the.revenue, causing "the ruin of fair trade, and the encouragement of idleness," but for the wholesale "destruction of great quantities of timber, woods, and underwoods." [25]

China tea was green, and fake varieties were often produced from thorn leaves by drying them and then coloring them with verdigris—which was, of course, poisonous. But with the introduction of Indian tea, processed by a different method which gave it a warm black tone, easier and cheaper methods could be used. Manufacturers simply bought up used tea leaves from coffee houses, hotels, and the servants of the rich, stiffened them with gum solution, and tinted them with black lead. Even with such additions as verdigris or lead, however, tea was still a healthier drink than some of the "gin" which had been sold a century earlier—compounded, according to one recipe, of ingredients which included sulphuric acid and oil of turpentine.

Just as there had always been adulteration, so there had always been consumers who complained about it. But it was only when

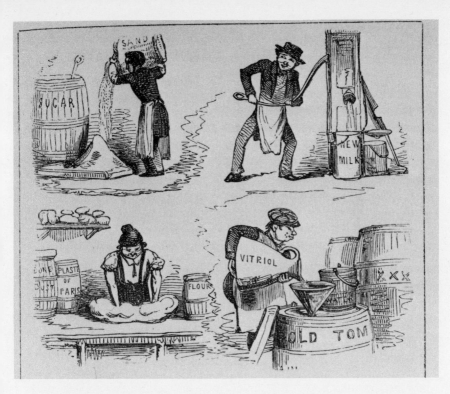

"London Improvements" in 1845—sand in the sugar, water in the milk, plaster of Paris in the bread, and vitriol in the beer.

the German-born chemist Frederick Accum stated the problem in terms of scientific analysis that the public really began to understand how widespread and dangerous the custom had become. Accum's book, A *Treatise on Adulterations of Food, and Culinary Poisons* (1820), revealed to all what was already known in legal and governmental circles. That "crusted old port" was no more than new port crusted with a layer of supertartrate of potash. That pickles owed their appetizing green color to copper. That bitter almonds, which contain prussic acid, were used to give table wine a "nutty" flavor. That the rainbow hues of London's sweets and candies were produced by the highly poisonous salts of copper and lead. That most commercial bread was loaded with alum. And that the rind of Gloucester cheese frequently acquired its rich orange color from additions of red lead. The storm which broke over Accum's head when his book was published ultimately led to his own retreat from England. But although the enraged manufacturers of adulterated food and drink were for the time being victorious, the public had been alerted and listened with attention when later reformers summoned up enough courage to reopen the question.

In England, this time came in 1850 when the medical periodical *Lancet* announced the appointment of an Analytical and Sanitary Commission. Between 1851 and 1854 the two commissioners—Dr. Arthur Hill Hassall, a chemist, and Dr. Henry Letheby, a dietician—published a long series of articles reporting on the extraneous matter to be found in samples of staple foodstuffs bought at random in London shops. Hassall analyzed forty-nine loaves of bread from various sources, not one of which proved free from alum, the mineral-salt whitening agent,* and recorded that coffee was almost invariably diluted with chicory, acorns, or mangel-wurzel (a type of beet). Other researchers soon discovered that publicans put the froth on their beer by doctoring it with green vitriol or sulphate of iron, and that cocoa powder often contained a large percentage of brick dust.

In 1860 the first British Food and Drugs Act was passed. It was drastically revised and strengthened in 1872. But despite subsequent regulations on food purity in almost every country, independent venturers have continued to sidestep the law. Among the more disarming recent cases was that of the Italian gentleman who was charged in 1969 with selling a product described as grated Parmesan cheese—which turned out, on analysis, to consist of grated umbrella handles.

---

* Commercial bread flour today is bleached with chlorine dioxide, which is said to be harmless.

17.
The Food-Supply
Revolution

By the beginning of the 1850s, two dominant facts had emerged about the food needs of an expanding industrial society. An increasing numbers of laborers had to be furnished with more food, more cheaply. And the new middle classes—possessing no landed estates which could supply them with the materials for their *entrées* and *entremets*—were in the market for as wide a variety of socially acceptable foods as the world could provide. It was a situation first defined in Victorian England, but its workings were soon to be observed in the United States of America, as well as in the more advanced countries of Europe.

Once the scale of the challenge had been recognized, many resources were mobilized to meet it. Throughout the course of history, new discoveries, new developments, had always given birth to other discoveries and other developments—but the process had, in general, been slow. What was so startling about the industrial era was the speed of change, the way in which one apparently minor technological improvement in a particular area of knowledge set off an avalanche of progress which swept through many others. Finer-quality glass, for example, coupled with advances in the science of optics, made it possible to manufacture more accurate microscopes, which in turn stimulated research in biology and chemistry and helped to found the science of bacteriology. The repercussions, not only in medicine and public health but in food hygiene and preservation, were to be almost incalculable.

It was the railroad, however, which first influenced both the

[347]

quality and quantity of food in the cities of the industrial revolution. Land transport had always been limited by the size of the load which could be hauled by horses or oxen over narrow, pitted roads, and bulky goods had usually gone by canal, river or sea. In countries which lacked waterways, communications and trade were severely hampered. But a railroad, once built, made it possible to move goods overland far more easily than ever before.

In terms of the food needs of the nineteenth century, the railroad's most immediate value lay in this bulk-carrying capacity, but its speed, too, was to help improve the diet of the city dweller.

In London, for example, meat had customarily been brought in on the hoof—often from considerable distances—for slaughter in the city. By the time the animals arrived, they were lean and weary and their meat was correspondingly inferior in quality. By the 1850s, however, ready-dressed carcasses were being transported to the capital from as far away as Aberdeen, 515 miles distant. Aberdeen, said one contemporary chronicler, had become "a London abattoir. The style in which the butchers of that place dress and pack the carcasses leaves nothing to be desired, and in the course of the year mountains of beef, mutton, pork, and

A dairy, or cowkeeper's shop, in London in 1825.

veal arrive the night after it is slaughtered in perfect condition." [1]

The inhabitants of the capital also found themselves able to buy much better milk than ever before. Until the 1860s, town milk was supplied by local cowmen who housed their animals at first in open green spaces and then, as the buildings closed in, in dank and insanitary sheds open to the street. Many and hideous were the tales told of the milk sold by these dairymen. The thin and watery fluid which was all they could coax out of their ill-nourished and sickly animals was carried through the streets in buckets open to all the germs and dirt of the air, all the mud and manure of the roadways, and was frequently diluted with hot water to support the claim that it came "warm from the cow."

Early attempts to speed fresh milk in from the countryside were not encouraging. Transported, slowly cooling, in an assortment of traditional pots and jars on open rail trucks, it frequently arrived looking very much like grubby cheese. The city cowman's udder-to-doorstep method at least gave the milk no time to turn. By the end of the 1860s, however, a special type of mechanical cooler had been developed, and quick-cooled milk brought in by rail in a new style of metal churn resulted in a marked improvement in the quality of milk available to the Victorian city dweller.

As well as improving food supplies within nations, the railroad eased farm-to-seaport transport and thus gave a stimulus to transoceanic trade. As a result, such foods as tea and grain acquired growing importance on the international mercantile scene. By the last decades of the nineteenth century, tea from the new plantations in India and wheat from the new farmlands of North America were flooding into Europe, and the British factory worker was able to buy the staples of his diet far more cheaply than he had ever done.

GRAIN FROM AMERICA

By the late 1870s, the complex of developments set in train by the American Civil War had turned large areas of the continent into a granary. Between 1860 and 1900 more than four hundred million acres of virgin soil were put under the plow. [2]

Americans had never had to concern themselves with soil con-

The revolutionary McCormick reaper.

servation systems or scientific crop rotation. Land they had in plenty. As Thomas Jefferson said at the beginning of the nineteenth century: "In Europe the object is to make the most of their land, labor being abundant; here it is to make the most of our labor, land being abundant." [3] Although the population of the United States had grown considerably since Jefferson's day, agriculture remained oriented toward labor-saving devices—the McCormick reaper patented in 1834, the Pitts mechanical thresher introduced in 1837, the Marsh harvester in 1858, and the Appleby binder and knotter for grain·sheaves twenty years later. Plows were fitted with steel moldboards, to which prairie soil did not cling. Special types of cultivators were designed to deal with maize. Combine harvesters were developed to sweep vast fields clear of their crops—machines ultimately drawn by as many as thirty horses at a time. In 1860, at the beginning of the era of expansion, there were 6,200,000 draft horses in the United States. By 1900, there were 15,500,000.[4] The total value of tools and machinery on American farms multiplied by fourteen in the years between 1860 and 1920.[5] In 1840, it had taken 233 man-hours to grow a hundred bushels of wheat; by 1920 it took only 87 man-hours.[6]

The transcontinental railroads which opened up the country after the Civil War helped to carry farmers and tools to the new lands, and grain away from them to the ports of the eastern seaboard. Here the grain was loaded into the last of the clippers and the first of the steamships just in time to save the Europe of the 1870s from the results of a series of pitiful harvests.

The overworked soil of Europe was in a bad state. German farming had improved as a result of Liebig's pioneer researches into soil chemistry, but in Italy, agriculture was actively in decline, and in France, torn for many decades by wars and revolutions, only one farmholding in fifteen had even as much as a horse-drawn hoe in 1892, only one in 150 a mechanical reaper.[7]

Cheap grain from America—and from Russia, now expanding rapidly—had much the same effect on the European economy as cheap grain from the Balkans had had in the thirteenth century. It supplied an increasingly urgent need, but at the same time threw the agriculture of other countries into disarray. In Norway, profitability had rested on such a knife-edge that when cheap American cereals began to flood into Europe a great many Norwegians were forced to emigrate. In England between 1870 and 1900 the land devoted to grain shrank by more than a quarter; dairy farming and fruit and vegetable growing increased accordingly (to the benefit of the consumer, if not of the farmer). In Denmark, farmers turned more of their attention to bacon production. From about 1850, they had recognized a large potential market in Britain's industrial towns, and had succeeded in breeding a pig with stable reproduction and growth features which enabled them to produce bacon of consistent quality, cured to suit British tastes. The Danish butter industry also expanded when, in 1877, Gustav de Laval invented a mechanical cream separator

The steam engine used to drive a threshing machine.

The hungry laborers of Europe were served by some of the most elegant ships ever to sail the seas—the fast, slender clippers which fled across the oceans of the world for a few short decades in the nineteenth century.

which greatly reduced operating costs. Of all western European countries, Holland was perhaps least affected by the American wheat influx, since Dutch agriculture had always been more dependent on cattle, dairy products and vegetables.

By the end of the century, American social and economic conditions led to a slackening off in grain exports. But for Europe, the gap was to be filled by increasing supplies from Canada, the Ukraine, and Australia. Except under the special circumstances of total war, the industrialized nations of Europe were never again to go short of the materials for their daily bread.

CANNING

Once the railroad had solved the problem of land transport, it was possible to carry large quantities of grain and tea half across the world. What this did for industrial England was to maintain the *status quo*, to ensure that an increase in population did not mean less food for all. Cheap wheat and cheap tea made it possible for even the poorest factory worker to buy *enough* to fill his stomach, while the less poor found themselves with a tiny budget surplus which could be used for the luxury of bacon or meat.

Bacon, preserved by salting and smoking, had a long storage life and so became an international trade commodity. This was not the case with beef or mutton, which could not be brought cheaply from another country until new methods of preservation were perfected. Most of the salted or dried foods of earlier times were irrelevant to the nineteenth-century situation, not only because processing on a really large scale was difficult and frequently uneconomic, but because the majority of potential customers in the new industrial towns had neither the time, the space nor the cooking equipment to deal with the special problems they presented. Nor could freshly butchered meat be transported over long distances until reliable refrigeration was developed. It was possible to ship live cattle across the ocean—and this, in fact, seems to have been done in the 1870s—but even the toughest-minded merchant seaman must have paled at the prospect.* Fortunately, the technique of canning, developed at the beginning of the century and used initially on a small and specialized scale, proved adaptable to mass production and distribution methods, enabling the new continents to supply Europe with meat as well as with grain.

There had been a hiatus of several centuries in the evolution of preservation techniques, and all that had really been added to the total of medieval experience by the end of the eighteenth century had been the knowledge of how to conserve cooked meats for a limited period by coating them with an airtight layer of fat. Then, however, had come the great breakthrough when Nicholas Appert, in France, developed a method of enclosing meat, fruit, vegetables, even milk, in glass bottles which were subjected to heat and then carefully sealed.

The essential second step, from breakable glass bottles to un-

---

* Passenger ships often carried a few pigs and hens, as well as a milch cow or two, to give variety to the menu on long voyages. The trials of caring for even a few such livestock were clearly implied in the enthusiasm with which a former naval captain described, in 1841, the virtues of canned meat. "Meat thus preserved," he said, *"eats* nothing, nor *drinks*—it is not apt to die—does not tumble overboard or get its legs broken or its flesh worn off its bones by tumbling about the ship in bad weather . . ." [8]

breakable "tin" cans, was taken by Bryan Donkin in England. With an interest in an iron works, he was quick to realize that, if Appert's method could be adapted for use with tinned iron containers, the prosperity of his business would be assured. By 1812, he had set up a canning factory, and six years later it was turning out satisfactory corned beef, boiled beef, carrots, mutton and vegetable stew, veal and soup.

Canned foods were at first more expensive than fresh. For some time they were bought mainly by such customers as explorers, to whom good, convenient, preserved foods were of vital importance. A number of particular delicacies—either canned or in glass—were also dispatched to the farther outposts of the British Empire. As early as the 1830s, truffled hare *pâté* from the Périgord was to be had in Simla,[9] and truffled woodcock in Mussoorie (in the foothills of the Himalayas).[10]

The potential market, however, was large enough to attract an increasing number of manufacturers, and trouble began in Britain when a contractor who was supplying the Admiralty began to use larger cans than before—9 to 14 pounds instead of the common 2- to 6-pound sizes. At this time, producers of canned food believed that it was the expulsion of air from the cans prior to final sealing which had the preservative effect, whereas in reality the heating, which was designed to drive out the air, had the more important result of killing off harmful bacteria. But heating which was capable of sterilizing the contents of a 6-pound can was not so effective with the 14-pound size, and a nest of bacteria was frequently left in the center which caused the meat to putrefy. In 1850, at one naval victualing yard, 111,108 pounds of meat in the large-size cans had to be condemned as unfit for human consumption. The attendant publicity did not do much for the reputation of canned meat in the United Kingdom.

Nor did the quality of the canned mutton imported from Australia during the next two decades. The meat was coarse and stringy, each can containing a lump of overdone and tasteless flesh, flanked on one side by a wad of unappetizing fat, and surrounded by a great deal of gravy.[11] The experienced cook learned to discard the fat, make the gravy into soup, and cut the meat into neat pieces which, egged, crumbed and browned in the oven or over the fire, could be made into an acceptable dish with the aid of an onion sauce.[12] The poorer urban housewife merely served the meat straight from the can, with bread or potatoes on the side. But canned meat from Australia had one great virtue—it cost less than half as much as fresh meat in England, especially after the disastrous epidemic of cattle disease which raged there between 1863 and 1867 and sent the price of home-bred meat soaring. English imports rose from 16,000 pounds in 1866 to 22,000,000 pounds in 1871.[13]

Australia maintained her lead in the canned-meat export market only until America ceased to be preoccupied by the Civil War and its aftermath. Canning factories had been established in the United States as early as 1817. These were soon handling fish as

Baked beans in tomato sauce are rated today as one of the most popular canned foods ever developed. Among the traditional dishes which inspired them was the Bostonians' Sunday dinner of beans long simmered with pork and molasses and eaten with brown bread and homemade ketchup.

well as meat,* and developing a thriving trade in fruit and vegetables—very much an American specialty in the early days of the
trade. During the Civil War, the Union army was able to buy
from its sutlers. American canned meat, oysters, and vegetables,
although the soldiers apparently preferred imported French sar-
dines, salmon and green peas.[15]

From 1868 onwards, when hand-made cans were generally superseded by the machine-cut type, giant canning concerns grew up,
especially in Chicago, where assembly-line processing helped to cut
costs and improve standards. Mass production brought a chain
reaction. Peas, for example, could not be canned economically
while they had to be harvested and prepared by hand. By the end
of the nineteenth century, a mechanical gathering and shelling
device had been devised. Fish, too, at first seemed to present
problems beyond the scope of machinery. In the salmon canneries
of California, Chinese workers were employed to do the cleaning
and boning. But came the day in 1882 when free Chinese immi-
gration into the United States was banned, and it was not long
before the "iron Chink" was invented.

The flavor of canned foods remained open to criticism for
many years. Canned peas, for example, bore only the most distant
resemblance to fresh ones, and the taste of canned salmon was
"rather of oil than fish, with a palpable touch of tin."[16] But
canned peas and salmon were usually sold to customers on the
American prairies or in the urban slums of Manchester, who had
no access to—perhaps had never even eaten—the fresh pioduct.
Even if the gastronomic value of the food was minimal, it gave
life and variety to an otherwise restricted diet. And because canning combines established themselves where production costs were
lowest, customers thousands of miles away were able to buy what
were to them exotic foodstuffs at a highly competitive price.

Canning was convenient, and it was cheap. Once the canning
manufacturers had taken note of Louis Pasteur's discoveries about
the part played by micro-organisms in fermentation and putrefaction—discoveries which were gaining general acceptance by the
late 1860s and the 1870s—and once the Massachusetts Institute

* The "herring boxes without topses" worn as slippers by "My Darling Clemen-
tine" appear to have been the oval cans in which fish were supplied to the Gold
Rush miners of 1849.[14]

of Technology had charted the most satisfactory processing times and temperatures for different foodstuffs (at the end of the century), it became not only convenient and cheap, but safe and reliable as well.

FREEZING AND CHILLING

In the long run, it was to be canned fruit and vegetables rather than canned meat which did most for the diet of the world's industrial workers, because a much more satisfactory method of preserving meat came into use little more than a decade after the first bulk shipments of the canned product in the mid 1860s.

As a conservation process, refrigeration had been known since the ice age. But until the problem of ice in a warmer world was solved, it lagged far behind other processes. The Chinese had discovered how to conserve naturally formed winter ice for summer use as early as the eighth century B.C., by building ice-houses which were kept cool by evaporation. The Mughal emperors of India in the sixteenth century A.D. had sent relays of horsemen to bring back ice and snow from the Hindu Kush to Delhi for their fruit-flavored sorbets, or water ices. The Italians appear to have introduced what is nowadays known as ice cream, using ice from the hills, at some time in the early seventeenth century. And the Americans had mastered the technique of exporting great blocks of "fine clear ice" from Massachusetts to as far away as Calcutta by 1833.[17] But all of these were small-scale enterprises, wholly dependent on climatic conditions and the availability of natural ice.

In the 1830s, however, ice-making machines began to be patented. These were based on newly fashionable scientific principles, and their effectiveness depended either on the expansion of compressed air or on the much older technique of evaporation, applied now not to water but to such highly volatile materials as liquefied ammonia. By the 1850s James Harrison, a Glasgow man who had emigrated to Australia, had designed an improved ether-compressor which made it possible to operate an ice factory, as well as a refrigerating machine which enabled Australian brewers to produce beer even in hot weather. In 1873 a public banquet was held at

Small quantities of ice could be made naturally, even in warm countries, provided the night temperature was low. At Allahabad in India in the 1820s, Europeans ensured supplies by having water ladled into shallow pans when the evenings were cool. At three in the morning, their long-suffering servants chipped the ice out of the pans and rushed it to a heavily insulated icehouse, where it remained until the hot weather began in April.

which guests ate meat, poultry and fish that had been frozen for six months.

But freezing plants that worked on land could not be easily adapted to operate on long sea voyages. Attempts to ship frozen meat from Australia to England met with initial failure. But in 1877, using an ammonia- instead of an ether-compression machine, the S.S. *Paraguay* successfully transported a cargo of frozen meat from the Argentine to France. Three years later, the first load of frozen beef and mutton was successfully carried from Australia to England and, a few months after, the first load of frozen mutton and lamb from New Zealand.

While experiments were being made in transporting frozen carcasses, chilling—cool storage at a temperature of about 30°F.—was also being tried, at first by surrounding the food with a mixture of ice and salt, later by making use of a compressed-air refrigerating machine. Since the voyage from America was short, and since chilling had a less detrimental effect on the quality of

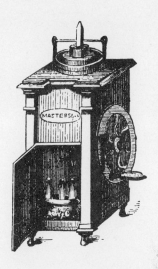

A patent freezing
machine, 1851.

the meat than early freezing, beef from the Americas dominated
the British market from the 1880s until well after the turn of the
century.

Eggs and other dairy products, as well as delicate fruits and
vegetables, proved to respond well to chilling once the packers and
shippers had discovered the conditions best suited to each individual foodstuff. Bananas from the West Indies were one of the
fruits which came to Europe in quantity from the late nineteenth
century onward.

The commercial manufacture of ice played a major part in re-
storing the fortunes of the fishing industry. Pickled herring had
been virtually the only fish available to the poor in the new towns
during the first half of the century, and it was a foodstuff with
limited appeal. In the 1860s and 1870s, however, steam trawlers
were developed which could travel fast and carry stocks of ice in
the hold—the coolest place in the ship. Fish packed in ice at the
moment of catch could be kept chilled throughout the swift return
journey by steam and rail to the city fish seller. One coincidental
effect of the new availability of fresh cod and other fish was the
growth of that British national institution, the fish-and-chip shop.
Who the genius was who first had the idea of marrying batter-
coated, deep-fried fish to sturdy fingers of deep-fried potato remains a matter of sometimes acrimonious debate. There are
claimants from Lancashire, London and Dundee, and the dates
put forward range between 1864 and 1874. But the hot-pie shop

was a well-established institution in Victorian England, and it seems likely that the fried-fish shop (if not the fish-and-chip shop) may have been a natural development. Whatever the truth of its origins, the fish-and-chip shop made a valuable contribution to the protein consumption of the poorer urban worker from the latter years of the nineteenth century until the middle of the twentieth.

MEAT   FOR   THE   MILLIONS

With a vast and expanding market for cheap meat, and the major problems of preserving and transporting it resolved, it was hardly surprising that there should have been an international boom in cattle farming. The period between 1870 and 1890 was the heyday of imperialism, an era of land-grabbing—or utilization of previously acquired land—on the most majestic scale. In those parts of the British empire which lay within the temperate zone, and in the plains inhabited by the North American Indians—the scene of America's own imperial expansion—the cattleman became a force to be reckoned with. The declared enmity between cattlemen and other settlers was a powerful factor in the political equation in almost all the new lands. So, too, was the economic chaos which was to result from over-production.

In the United States in 1871, for example, Texas ranchers drove 700,000 lanky longhorn cattle over the 700-mile Chisholm Trail from San Antonio direct to the stockyards of Abilene, at a rate of about a dozen miles a day.[18] From Abilene they were shipped by rail to the new meat-processing plants in Chicago and Kansas City. But in the late 1860s and early 1870s the Great Plains were being cleared of bison and of the Indians who had depended on them. When the process was complete, the plains were open to range cattle. Now Texans sent their yearlings there on the hoof to be fattened on the northern pastures, and other ranchers went into business on a massive scale, financed by capital which poured into the industry from both American and foreign sources. The profits were considerable. In 1881 the Prairie Cattle Company of Edinburgh (Scotland) was able to declare a dividend of 28 per cent.[19]

In 1880, Kansas had sixteen times as many cattle as it had had

The cattle market at Chicago in 1868.

Buffalo and Indians were cleared from the Great Plains with equal lack of
ceremony. The buffalo were almost exterminated, slaughtered at the rate of
a million a year between 1872 and 1882 for the sake of their hides.

twenty years earlier; Nebraska thirty times as many. In Wyoming alone in 1886 there were nine million head of cattle.[20] The cattle were fatter and of much finer quality than the old Texas longhorns because serious attention had been paid to improving the breeds.

The cattlemen were too successful. Although the industrial towns of America and Europe were very anxious for meat, the price could not be brought down far enough—because of preservation, packing and transport costs—to stimulate any really sharp increase in consumption. Yet, ironically enough, it was to be the fact that many thousand head of uneconomic cattle were killed off by a series of climatic disasters between 1885 and 1887 that was to bring the massive livestock corporations tumbling into liquidation and to deprive a great many ranchers and cattle hands of their livelihood. The margin between success and failure in large-scale cattle raising, as in small-scale agriculture, was very narrow indeed. The new American farmers, cattlemen and grain-growers alike, attempted to improve their lot by taking political action, involving themselves in the Granger and Greenback movements, in the Farmer's Alliances and in Populism—whose agitators in the 1890s urged its members to "raise less corn and more Hell!"

It was not only in the United States that farmers exercised a powerful influence on national politics. The history of much of Australia in the second half of the nineteenth century was shaped by the animosity between diggers (gold miners) and squatters (sheep farmers), while in New Zealand at the turn of the century the "cow cockies," or dairy farmers, dominated the Farmers' Union and turned their dislike of industrial "townies" into an explosive political issue.[21] In Argentina, for many decades, cattle and the economy were indivisible (as, in many ways, they still are). From as early as the 1840s, animal meat was so plentiful that even the chickens and turkeys were fattened on it, while sheeps' skulls were used to fill up quagmires so that roads could be built.[22] By the early years of the present century, ranchers had begun to specialize—as *criadores*, who bred the cattle, or *invernadores*, who fattened them for export. These two groups had great political power. But the economic power was in the hands of the mainly foreign corporations who operated the packing and shipping houses, the *frigorificos*. It was not until the 1930s that the conflict between ranching and packing interests ceased to overshadow the Argentine political scene.

During the first half of the nineteenth century, the industrial revolution had demonstrated the need for a vast increase in food supplies. In the process of fulfilling that need, farmers and stock-breeders began to see themselves, for almost the first time in history, as a separate and important group with separate and specialized interests. The pressure they exerted to have those interests satisfied, combined in almost all the advanced countries with governmental attempts to appease everybody, was to lead in the second half of the twentieth century to a "system" of agricultural economics of almost anarchical complexity.

SUBSTITUTE FOODS

While mass-production techniques were being applied to traditional foods, a few scientists were also engaged in attempting to produce substitutes. The first major success came when it was discovered that sugar could be produced from a root plant which, unlike sugar cane, would grow in temperate climates. As early as 1747, the German chemist A. S. Marggraf had discovered that such commonplace European crops as carrots and beets would yield a small percentage of sugar, but his experiments were of little interest until the end of the century, when France and much of the continent were deprived of supplies from the West Indies and southeast Asia by the success of Britain's naval blockade.

In 1801-02, the world's first sugar-beet factory was built in Silesia, and Napoleon was soon urging similar enterprises on the businessmen of France, Germany and the Low Countries. By the 1840s France had fifty-eight sugar-beet factories producing roughly two pounds per head of population per annum.[23] Germany and Belgium were also well on the way to becoming self-sufficient.

The consumer accepted the new sugar with perfect complaisance, but it was to be another matter when scientists tried to persuade him that margarine was a better buy than the rancid and watery butter he was accustomed to. In the late 1860s a French food technologist, Hippolyte Mège-Mouries, embarked on a series of experiments related to the fat content of milk—and succeeded, as he thought, in producing butter. Suet, chopped cow's udder, and a little warm milk were his ingredients, and the results were probably no worse than what passed for butter in much of Europe at the time. In 1873 commercial production was begun, but the Paris Council of Hygiene ruled that Mège-Mouries' artificial product was not to be sold under the name of butter. Meanwhile, America had been swift to recognize the possibilities, and by as early as 1876 was able to export to the U.K.[24] more than a million pounds of what was called "butterine." Not surprisingly, the producers of real butter fought a strong rearguard action, and many of the hideous rumors which were circulated about the origins of the fats used in butterine can be traced back to their whispering campaigns.

Many years passed before margarine, as it finally came to be called, achieved a really substantial sale. It was not only slanderous rumors which held it back, but the curiously wavy texture and insipid taste of the early types. Manufacturers had to spend enormous sums of money on research—on discovering how to "cream" the artificial product, how to mature it with micro-organisms similar to those which help to create butter, how to utilize vegetable oils, and how to add vitamin concentrates (a development of the 1920s)—before they could even begin to persuade the public to accept margarine, not as a poor man's substitute for butter, but as a middle-class alternative.

In fact, margarine has been making excellent headway in the United States (if not in Europe) in the late twentieth century, partly because butter has become wholly uncompetitive in price, and partly because animal fats are increasingly taking the blame for the high incidence of coronary disease in the Western world.

The human body manufactures cholesterol—a significant ingredient in the mushy deposits which clog the coronary arteries—from a number of raw materials. One of the foodstuffs which reputedly increases cholesterol production is saturated fat, a fat that remains solid at room temperature and has—in chemical terms—hydrogen atoms attached at all available points on its carbon chain. Most saturated fats are animal fats. Fats made from fish, vegetable and seed oils, on the other hand, lack the full complement of hydrogen atoms. They remain liquid at room temperature, and are known as "polyunsaturated fats." Research seems to prove that saturated fats increase the cholesterol level, while polyunsaturated ones do not. Animal fats—including butter —are therefore considered to be more dangerous than the majority of margarines, made (originally for cheapness' sake) from poly-unsaturated fish and vegetable oils.*

THE QUALITY OF COOKING

When Mark Twain toured Europe in 1878 he loathed the food and tortured himself with visions of what he would have to eat when he arrived safely home again. Buckwheat cakes with maple syrup, hot bread, fried chicken, soft-shell crabs, Boston baked beans, hominy, squash—and, of course, "a mighty porterhouse steak an inch and a half thick, hot and sputtering from the griddle; dusted with fragrant pepper; enriched with little melting bits of butter of the most unimpeachable freshness and genuineness; the precious juices of the meat trickling out and joining the gravy, archipelagoed with mushrooms; a township or two of tender, yellowish fat gracing an outlying district of this ample county of beefsteak; the long white bone which divides the sirloin from the tenderloin still in its place." [25] While he was prepared to concede that such foods might not suit all tastes—"the Scotchman would shake his head and say, 'Where's your haggis?' and the Fijian would sigh and say, 'Where's your missionary?' "—he did not go so far as to admit that buckwheat cakes, fried chicken and mighty steaks merited his rhapsodies only when a really first-rate cook had the handling of them. The first might have been stodgy, the second stringy, and the third overdone and greasy.

The poetic language which so often immortalizes good food rarely, in fact, concerns itself with the quality of the cooking—unless the cook happens to be a chef with a talent for publicity. The ability of the cook, however, is at least as important as the quality of the raw materials, and in some ways rather more important than the recipes. A good and experienced cook can overcome the limitations of poor materials and inadequate recipes; a bad cook can ruin the finest and the best.

Because of this, it is almost impossible to generalize about the

* However, though cholesterol-lowering diets (with a minimum intake of animal fats) appear to reduce the incidence of heart disease, they may lay the dieter open to an increased risk of gallstones (see the *New England Journal of Medicine*, January 4, 1973).

quality of food at any period of history. Even today, it is difficult to take seriously writers who are foolhardy enough to pontificate on current improvements (or deterioration) in cooking standards. In the nineteenth century, however, there were three developments which may reasonably be supposed to have brought about an increase in the number of good cooks. These were the expanding range of raw materials, the very considerable improvement in cooking equipment, and the publication (stimulated partly by the growth of the middle classes and partly by the spread of literacy) of large numbers of cookbooks.

After the food adulteration scandals of the mid-nineteenth century, the quality of basic foodstuffs in Britain and, later, in the United States, improved noticeably. And when mass-production techniques took over in the grain and meat sectors of agriculture, smaller farmers turned their attention to dairy products or to fruit and vegetable growing. Milk, cream, butter and eggs began to re-establish, in the town diet, the important position they had once held in the country diet. What the British called "market gardens" and the Americans "truck farms" increasingly supplied local towns with fruit and vegetables in season, while swift refrigerated transport and improved canning techniques introduced tropical and subtropical delicacies to regions which had never known them before. Such foods as these did more than ease the cook's task and lend variety to the menu. As their use became more general, they helped to remedy a number of nutritional deficiencies.

Of more immediate encouragement to the Victorian cook, however, were the new types of stove which became progressively more popular as their price dropped during the century. Until the early years of the nineteenth century, most cooking in western and northern Europe and in North America had been done over an open fire or in a primitive type of enclosed brick oven, heated with coals which had to be raked out before cooking could proceed. Although a great many items of ancillary equipment had been evolved to make the cook's task easier, complicated dishes could only be prepared in large kitchens with large staffs, where it was possible to give undivided attention to each separate stage of preparation. In 1795, however, Count Rumford succeeded in feeding twelve hundred of the poor of Munich for a total sum of £1.37, or $3.44, per day by inventing a stove which economized

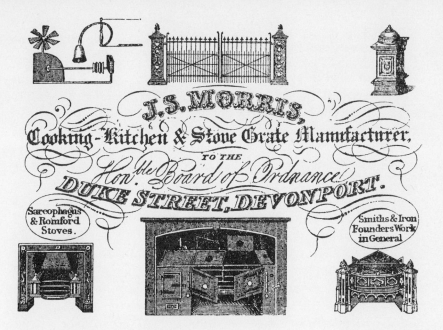

Below center, the Rumford stove.

on fuel.[26] Bending his powerful mind to the problem of cooking for smaller numbers, he ultimately produced a closed-top range which utilized almost all the heat of a small fire and, by means of flues, dampers and metal plates, permitted the heat to be—within limitations—adjusted.

Adjustable heat brought the beginnings of a revolution in food and cooking. Sautés, sauces and soufflés were now within the scope of any household with one of the new ranges. Cooking a meal was no longer searing purgatory, and the adventurous housewife found new horizons opening up.

The iron range came into general use in middle-class homes in the 1860s. Twenty years later, as coal gas became widely available, the gas stove began to supersede the solid-fuel type. (Gas ovens had in fact been used as early as the 1830s in the Reform Club in London.) Once again, the improvement in scope was astonishing. Precision adjustment of heat—one of the major weapons in the good cook's armory—became almost a reality. Although electricity infiltrated the cooking world in the 1890s, it was not to become popular for some decades, partly because the electric range was regarded as unreliable until about 1920. Many cooks still look with disfavor on the electric hotplate which, in the majority of modern stoves, responds too slowly to the cook's commands.

As the nineteenth-century middle classes felt an increasing need to use their tables as an indication of status, they discovered that traditional family recipes were inadequate for the purpose. Cookbooks were necessary—and publishers were only too happy to provide them, in ever-growing numbers.

Sometimes the authors were professional chefs. There was Queen Victoria's Chief Cook in Ordinary, Charles Elmé Francatelli, for example. In *The Modern Cook* in 1845 he tried to cater to all tastes by giving recipes for sheeps' jowls, ears and trotters, as well as venison and reindeer tongues, but still betrayed his *haute cuisine* background by his stress on garnishes.

Sometimes the authors were surprised amateurs. One of the best cookbooks in the English language, *Modern Cookery for Private Families* by Eliza Acton (1845), was written by a lady who would have preferred to be a poet. But her publisher said there was no sale for poems by maiden ladies and told her bracingly that a good sensible cookbook was what she ought to write. She did, and the result was a continuing best seller. The best-*known* English cookbook, however, was written by a young woman journalist with no particular talent in the kitchen. Isabella Beeton's *Book of Household Management* (1861) was encyclopedic in scope; the recipes may have been pedestrian, but Mrs. Beeton made the first serious attempt to include estimates of cost, quantities, and preparation times.

In Germany, as in England, women had competed on equal terms with men in cookbook writing since the early eighteenth century, but in France the gentlemen had reigned almost supreme.* Some of them were chefs, but more appear to have been gourmets.

---

* Some of their works ran through a remarkable number of editions. One of the favorites, *La Cuisinière de la Campagne et de la Ville, ou la Nouvelle Cuisine Economique,* written by Louis Eustache Audot and designed for the modest household, was first published in 1818 and had reached its eightieth edition by the end of the century. *Le Cuisinier Impérial* by A. Viard was published first in 1806. At the restoration, it was reissued as *Le Cuisinier Royal.* In 1848 Louis Napoleon was president of the Republic, and Viard's book appeared as *Le Cuisinier National.* But not for long. Louis Napoleon translated himself into the Emperor Napoleon III and in 1852 *Le Cuisinier National* hastily changed its name back to the *Impérial* of its early days. When the Third Republic was established in 1871, *Le Cuisinier* once more became—and remained—*National.*

The first were inclined to provide recipes beyond the scope of the average kitchen, while the second, brainwashed by too intensive a study of those gastronomic philosophers, Grimod de la Reynière and Brillat-Savarin, frequently overlooked the practicalities of cooking in their attempts to prove that a good meal should be fuel for the spirit as well as for the body.

The same may be said, though in rather a different sense, of certain American writers, who sternly reprimanded the housewife for her ignorance and extravagance and recommended her to look to her morals. "There is no more prolific cause of bad morals," said Mrs. Horace Mann firmly (if somewhat obscurely) in her *Christianity in the Kitchen* (1861), "than abuses of diet." Pork, turtle soup and wedding cake were bad for the digestion and therefore, by extension, immoral and un-Christian. But American housewives were able to learn from other, less dogmatic works. Catharine Beecher, in *Miss Beecher's Domestic Receipt Book* (1846),

Among the special-purpose cookbooks of the nineteenth century were two published in Paris during the siege of 1870 which gave recipes for rats and dogs.

had produced one of the first works to deal with general cooking techniques as well as recipes, and between 1846 and 1896—a notable year in American cooking history—a number of other reliable basic books appeared.

In 1896 came *The Boston Cooking-School Cook Book,* now generally known by its author's name as "Fannie Farmer." * One of the school's founders, Mrs. D. A. Lincoln, had begun to rationalize kitchen measurements, having been offended by the inaccuracy of traditional "pinches of salt" and "nuts of butter," and the inconsistent results such instructions produced. When Fannie Farmer published the *Boston Cook Book,* the precise measuring system which nowadays seems so characteristic of American cooking was well and truly launched. Curiously enough, although it is a sound idea, it has never really caught on in Europe. Despite its major virtue—which is that anyone attempting an unfamiliar recipe for the first time can be sure of achieving something that is at least presentable—most European writers still cling to traditional forms, such as "Add a glass of wine . . ." Claret glass, burgundy glass, or tooth glass? Sometimes even the most experienced cook hesitates.

The vast majority of nineteenth-century cookbooks were designed for middle-class households. They may well have improved the quality of cooking, and by the end of the century they were even encouraging better-balanced menus. This development was long overdue. The Yankee who, in the 1860s, started the day with "black tea and toast, scrambled eggs, fresh spring shad, wild pigeon, pigs' feet, two robins on toast, oysters" [27] may have made no claim to being a gourmet, but the English Colonel Kenney-Herbert, who was by no means lacking in taste, saw nothing wrong with a dinner menu [28] consisting of:

Consommé de perdreaux	Partridge consommé
Matelote d'anguilles	Stewed eels
Poulet à la Villeroy	Chicken pieces sauced, crumbed, and deep-fried
Longe de mouton à la Soubise	Loin of mutton with onion sauce

---

* The Boston Cooking School was mainly a teacher-training institution, and Fannie Farmer was its head.

The baked-potato vendor.

Topinambours au gratin	Creamed Jerusalem artichokes with a coating of melted cheese
Canapés de caviare	Croutons of fried bread coated with caviar and garnished with mayonnaise
Orléans pudding	A chilled custard pudding layered with crushed ratafia biscuits and dried fruits

While the middle-class cook was being urged to try such glutinous menus as this, well-meaning authors also began turning out less ambitious books designed for the laboring poor. Juliet Corson, who had opened one of the first cooking schools in New York, published a string of dull little works in the 1870s with such titles as *Fifteen Cent Dinners for Workingmen's Families.* She may have been spurred on in this way by the success of similar works in England. In 1855, the great chef of the Reform Club, Alexis Soyer—already famous for good works in the shape of soup kitchens for the poor *—had published A *Shilling Cookery for the People.* This sold an impressive 248,000 copies. It would be interesting to know who bought it, and whether they enthused over the great chef's colorless recipes for boiled neck of mutton and sheep's head. It seems probable that this and similar works were in fact bought by the wives of small tradesmen and skilled craftsmen, rather than by the laboring poor for whom they were intended.

No cookbook, however economical, could supply the working wife with time, equipment or fuel. Until well into the twentieth century, the local tripe shop or pork butcher, the hot dog stand, the street whelk seller or oysterman, and the man who sold muffins or sugared waffles did more for the industrial worker's menu than any author.

---

* That usually kindly commentator on the Victorian gastronomic scene, Abraham Hayward, remarked of Soyer that "his execution is hardly on a par with his conception, and he is more likely to earn his immortality by his soup-kitchen than by his soup." [29]

18.
The Scientific
Revolution

Despite the apparent improvements which came about when the second half of the nineteenth century set about redressing the food imbalances of the first, there were a number of as yet unrecognized factors which, to begin with, worsened instead of bettering the diet of the poorest classes. New methods of milk preservation and the production of whiter flours helped to increase, rather than decrease, the incidence of malnutrition.

None of the old techniques of milk preservation had found favor in the eyes of the nineteenth century. Consumers, made wary by recurring adulteration scandals, viewed the sediment in reconstituted dried milk with suspicion. Condensed milk, however, was to have more success. A British patent had been taken out as early as 1835, but it was the American Gail Borden's improved method in the 1850s which first made an impression on the market. Until the principles of sterilization were fully understood, it was not possible to can *un*sweetened condensed milk satisfactorily, but Borden found that if he added sugar—which, in quantity, inhibits bacterial growth—the result was a milk which kept well. Borden's milk had a great success with the army in the American Civil War, and the men carried their liking for it back into civilian life. In some ways, the thick, sweetened milk was far more convenient than fresh—even the really fresh milk beginning to be carried by rail—and it was certainly much more wholesome than milk bought from the old-style town dairyman.

The cheaper brands of condensed milk, however, were made

from skimmed milk, and lacked the fats and vitamins A and D which are among the most nutritious ingredients in the fresh product. As a result, mothers who fed their infants mainly on cheap condensed milk—believing it to be a *whole* food in a pure and hygienic form—were in fact depriving the children of essential nutrients. It seems likely that, in the poorer industrial districts, the incidence of rickets increased.

Whiter bread, too, meant less nutritious bread. A new method of milling flour had been introduced in Hungary in the 1840s, making use of iron rollers which processed the grain much more rapidly than the old stone mills and also gave more consistent quality. The old mills had pulverized the embryo (or "germ") of the grain at the same time as the starchy endosperm. It was the oils from the germ which gave the flour its characteristic yellowish color, and also turned it rancid within a few weeks. The new roller mills, on the other hand, squeezed the grain in such a way that the endosperm popped out of its coating, leaving the germ behind to be sieved off with the bran. Roller-milled flour, therefore, was whiter than the old type, and could be stored for a much longer time without deteriorating. This pleased not only the millers, bakers and shopkeepers, but their customers as well, and with the introduction in the 1870s of porcelain rollers—easier to maintain in good condition than the iron ones—roller-milling became the standard practice. Unfortunately, the discarded wheat germ had been the source of a number of highly nutritious substances, now lost to the people who needed them most—those among the industrial poor to whom bread was the mainstay of the diet.

In Asia, there had been a similar development in grain processing which had a swift and destructive effect on the health of the consumer. To the people of the West, really white bread was alluring. To Asians, white rice seemed no less so. Toward the end of the nineteenth century, it was becoming common to polish the rice to remove its drab-colored outer sheath, and during this process the nutritious germ—similar to the germ of wheat—was torn away and discarded. People who lived on a diet based largely on polished rice began to contract beri-beri, the deficiency disease which attacks the nerves, heart, and digestive system. So concerned were the Dutch over the number of deaths in their colonies in the East Indies that in 1886 they sent out a medical team to investigate. Its researches led to one of the great discoveries in the history of nutrition—the identification of those accessory food factors known as vitamins (from *vita:* life, and *amine:* any chemical compound containing nitrogen; the terminal "e" was later dropped when it was discovered that all vitamins did not, in fact, contain nitrogen).

THE DISCOVERY OF VITAMINS

Mankind had long been aware that different foodstuffs had good or bad effects on health, but it was only at the very end of the eighteenth century that science began to isolate the essential elements in food. Lavoisier then proved that men and animals were heat engines which burned up food for fuel, and by 1846 Justus von Liebig—in his report *Chemistry and Its Applications to Agriculture and Physiology*—was able to describe living tissues (including foods) as being composed of carbohydrates, fats, and "albuminoids," or proteins. Although, during the second half of the century, minerals were added to this list and it was discovered that different types of protein had different biological values, there was still a large and crucial gap in scientific knowledge. If the known food elements were the only ones which existed, then a diet of bread and fatty meat (which supplied all of them) should have been a guarantee of good health—but this was demonstrably not so. It was to be the Dutch researches into beri-beri which isolated the fifth important element.

After three years of research, a member of the Dutch team noticed that hens which had been fed on polished rice developed symptoms of beri-beri; when they were given unpolished rice, or even the "bran" removed during polishing, they rapidly recovered. Abandoning experiments which had been initiated in the belief that beri-beri was an infectious disease, the doctor—Christian Eijkman—turned his attention to the constituents of rice polishings. It was not until 1901 that he identified the importance of the rice germ itself, and even then scientists failed to realize that what had been discovered was, in effect, a whole new class of food components, some of which were essential in themselves,

Liebig's laboratory at Giessen.

and others which had to be present before the human body could, for example, convert carbohydrate into energy, or utilize particular minerals. In 1905 Professor Pekelharing at the University of Utrecht came to the conclusion that some such "unrecognized substances" *did* exist, and in 1909, a German biochemist, Dr. Stepp—without fully realizing it at the time—identified those vitamins which are fat-soluble. Just before the First World War, vitamins A and B_1 were effectively isolated.

For more than a dozen years, the new knowledge scarcely filtered beyond the walls of a few scientific laboratories, but during those years much essential work was done, particularly in Britain. There, the government was both surprised and horrified by the results of a mass medical examination which took place in 1917-18, when 2,500,000 men, theoretically in their physical prime—and from all classes of society—were examined prior to military conscription. Forty-one per cent of them turned out to be not only in poor health but entirely unfit for military service.[1] In most cases, undernourishment was at the root of their weakness. Clearly, nutritional research had become a matter of urgency. To further that research, the Accessory Food Factors Committee set up in 1918 sent a team of scientists off·to Vienna, a city suffering from acute malnutrition as the aftermath of war.

When the British team arrived there in 1919 they found that scurvy was commonplace among infants, and that there had been a serious increase in the incidence and severity of rickets. Austrian doctors knew almost nothing of vitamins. But Dr. Harriette Chick and her colleagues put their experimental vitamin research to work and proved beyond doubt its practical value. They succeeded "in maintaining a large number of artificially fed babies free from [rickets], and . . . were invariably successful in healing children admitted with rickets already developed."[2]

The general pattern of "food values" as it is known today had been established, although there were to be many more years of research and discovery. Indeed, careful scientists are still prepared to admit that all is not yet known about the constituents of food and their nutritional importance.

When war broke out again in Europe in 1939, nutritionists were able to guide governments toward workable rationing systems. In Britain, bread and potatoes were unrestricted, and the consumer even had freedom of choice with food that *was* rationed.* British civilians remained healthy, and so, too, did the armed forces. Cans of American bacon and legs of New Zealand lamb were even floated down by parachute to isolated units in the jungles of Asia.

Many subsequent advances in food technology had their origin in the exigencies of war, although in certain cases—as with dried milk and dehydrated vegetables—there was to be a gap of over twenty years before people who had eaten their fill of such foods

* The choice only too frequently boiled down to corned beef or "luncheon meat," though the Ministry of Food worked hard at publicizing economical and nourishing recipes, many of them—such as oatmeal and cheese soup—of a peculiarly revolting kind.

in the 1940s were able to contemplate them again, even in improved form, with any equanimity.

ADDITIVES

Wartime scientists also took the opportunity of putting back into certain foods what improved manufacturing techniques had taken out of them. In Britain, for example, it was required that all bread flour should contain, either naturally or by deliberate addition, specified proportions of iron, vitamin B_1, and nicotinic acid. These regulations still apply today.

Few consumers would complain about such well-tested additives as these. But the same cannot be said for a number of the ingredients which manufacturers have become accustomed to using in canned, dried and deep-frozen foods in the years since 1945. Despite the watchdog role of, for example, the U.S. Food and Drug Administration, with its "Generally Recognized as Safe" (or GRAS) list of acceptable additives, there has been in recent years a sometimes panicky outcry against a number of the chemical substances used in the food-processing industry. Certainly, the consumer can be forgiven for hesitating over an instant soup mix whose sole ingredients consist of hydrolized plant protein, salt, yeast hydrolysate, monosodium glutamate, sugar, vegetable fat, caramel coloring, spices, onion powder, and calcium silicate.

There are three valid reasons for including artificial substances in processed foods—although the word "artificial" is misleading; many additives are synthetic versions of a natural product, others are themselves natural substances. The first reason is that canning, drying and freezing all have the effect of altering the texture and taste of the original food to a greater or lesser degree. The manufacturer therefore uses improvers (or "taste powders") in an attempt to restore lost flavor. Secondly, many pre-packed foods lose either quality or visual appeal during transport, shelf- and cupboard-life. To overcome this, manufacturers add anti-caking agents to prevent salt, sugar or powdered milk from coagulating into lumps; emulsifying agents, which help to homogenize, or blend, substances which normally tend to separate (such as fat and milk); and sequestrants, which stop trace minerals from causing rancidity in fats and oils, and also prevent soft drinks from turning cloudy. Thirdly, in a world where many people eat more calories than their bodies need, the fashion for slimming has led to a demand for foods in which traditional ingredients are replaced by "non-fattening" ones.

In 1968 to 1970 there was an international furor over two particular additives—the taste powder monosodium glutamate (MSG), extracted from a seaweed which has been used in Asia for hundreds of years to give savor to bland food, and the group of slimming sweeteners known as cyclamates. The latter are synthetic, and have the advantage over the equally synthetic saccharin (which has been known since 1879 but is now also suspect) of leaving no unpleasant aftertaste. Were MSG and cyclamates additives, the public began to ask—or adulterants?

MSG had been proved to raise an allergic reaction in certain consumers—an illness correctly known as Kwok's Disease (after Dr. Robert Ho Man Kwok, who tracked down its source) but often referred to as the Chinese Restaurant Syndrome, since Chinese restaurant cooks sometimes use MSG to excess. Tests in 1969 also led scientists to the discovery that MSG caused brain damage in infant mice. As a result, many baby-food manufacturers said that they would stop adding it to their products, and the New York City Department of Health warned all cooks to use it sparingly.

Equally alarming was the discovery that massive doses of cyclamates led, in the case of rats, to cancer of the bladder, and in embryo chickens to deformity. Some scientists believe that needless fears are aroused by such reports, and that the method of injecting animals with the substance under test is as much to blame for the result as the substance itself. Nevertheless, within a week of the cancer report, cyclamates were ordered off the market in the United States and were banned soon afterward in a number of other countries, including Finland, Sweden, Canada, Japan and Britain. France had never permitted their use in the first place.

Many authoritative sources regard it as foolish to raise a fuss about the comparatively minor and still debatable hazards of such additives as MSG and cyclamates. After all, they say—with perfect truth—salt is far more widely used, and far more dangerous; laboratory research suggests that an ounce of salt a day (a not uncommon dose) can shorten a man's life by as much as thirty years. Too much sugar can lead to obesity—far more dangerous than the side effects of cyclamates, which are consumed in minuscule amounts since they are thirty times sweeter than sugar. Caffeine, the natural stimulant in tea and coffee, is fatal to humans at a dose of about one third of an ounce. Nutmeg can be toxic; so can avocado pears. Onions can cause anemia. Liquorice can result in high blood pressure. Spinach and rhubarb are impregnated with oxalic acid, which builds kidney stones. The pigment carotene, which puts the color in egg yolks, sweet potatoes, mangoes and carrots, can give the consumer jaundice. Even cabbage can help to cause goiter. People have been poisoned by the solanine in green potatoes, the prussic acid in bitter almonds, the cyanide in lima beans. Where, in effect, do health hazards end?

The concerned non-scientist asks the same question, but with a different intonation. If there are so many natural hazards, is it sensible to add artificial ones? MSG and cyclamates may be neither more nor less dangerous than the assorted residues of radioactivity, mercury, and organochloride pesticides which are present—at "well below danger level"—in the human body today. Each, separately, may be a negligible threat. But what about the sum total? Science and scientific knowledge are now so complex that there can be no such thing as a straight answer to the layman's fears. And for as long as governments and manufacturers find it necessary suddenly to withdraw such substances as cyclamates from the market, for so long will the layman continue to view the science of food additives with suspicion.

THE GREEN REVOLUTION

The population of the developed countries can afford to be selective about what goes into its food. But in large parts of Africa, Asia, and South America—continents which accommodate most of that fifty per cent of all mankind which is undernourished and the further fifteen per cent classified as "malnourished" [3]—it is a different matter. There it is the basic volume of foodstuffs which counts. And there, modern science has helped to initiate a revolution.

Enough rice
for the bowl . . .

. . . enough wheat for the *chapatis*. These are the basis of the diet
for well over half the world's population.

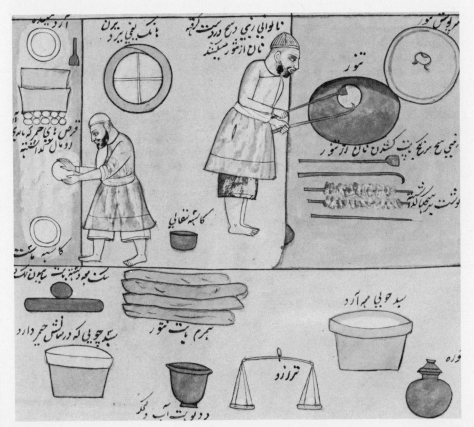

In the 1940s the Rockefeller Foundation embarked, in coopera-
tion with the Mexican government, on a wheat development pro-
gram which in twenty years increased the per-acre wheat yields
of Mexico by 250 per cent. One of the great barriers to improved
grain production in hot countries is that when traditional plants
are heavily fertilized they shoot up to an unnatural height and
then collapse. If they are grown close enough together to prevent
this, one plant shades the other and the yield is reduced. During
the Mexican experiments, however, it was found—after tests involving forty thousand different crossbreeds of plants—that a
short-stemmed grain, if thickly sown at the right depth and
adequately irrigated, could take heavy doses of fertilizer without
becoming lanky, and give spectacularly high yields.

In 1962, the International Rice Research Institute was set up
in the Philippines to try to produce a rice which would parallel
the new Pitic 62 and Penjamo 62 wheats. Rice is the main item
of diet for six out of every ten people in the world. Success came
swiftly, although it was to be only a qualified success. By 1968
a new crossbred variety, IR 8, was being grown on millions of
acres in eighty countries, yielding on average three times as much
rice as traditional plants, sometimes considerably more.

But IR 8 turned out to have disadvantages, needing a great
deal of water and fertilizer, and proving a magnet to the destructive stem-borer insect. Furthermore, though pests liked IR 8,
many people did not. It was too sticky and lumpy for people accustomed to eating with their fingers, though chopstick users had no
objection to it. (Bulk supplies of IR 8 seed have, in fact, been
imported by roundabout routes into China.) Later, however, two
new "miracle rice" plants—IR 20 and IR 22—were developed.
These had more acceptable grain quality, high yields, and an inbred resistance to some of the more destructive pests. There are
reports, too, that Indian scientists are developing a new rice which
will need much less water than other strains.[4] This could be
extremely important in areas where water is scarce or seasonal.

Advances like these lead some participants in the ecological
crystal-ball game to prophesy that, despite the anticipated population expansion between now and the early twenty-first century,
food surpluses are more probable than food shortages. It is here
that scientists and sociologists tend to part company. The labora-

tory researcher has an innocent, almost evangelical faith in the ability of science to solve all problems in the shortest possible time. The social scientist knows that what may look like a solution in the laboratory is not necessarily so in the outside world. Ordinary people often react slowly to new developments, particularly in poor countries which cannot afford the luxury of experiment and possible failure. Even success has its long-term dangers. The "miracle grains" of the Green Revolution, for example, are best suited to large-scale agriculture. The sudden imposition of mass-production techniques in rural areas can—as it is already beginning to do in India—arouse new and potentially violent tensions.

Where time is important—as, in terms of world survival, many authorities believe it could be during the next fifty years—social forces are likely to prove as decisive as scientific advances.

PESTS VERSUS PESTICIDES

A feature of the improved grains which have created the Green Revolution is that unless they have adequate water, rigorous pest and disease control, and abundant fertilizer, they may do less well in poor soil than the lower-yielding traditional varieties.

The last two centuries have seen an explosive increase in the world population not only of people but of plant pests and diseases. This is partly because extensive fields of a single crop—integral to mass-production techniques—have encouraged multiplication of that crop's endemic pests, and partly because the expansion of rail, sea and air communications (as well as deliberate economic policy) has introduced into new lands non-indigenous crops complete with their associated pests, which have acclimated themselves and flourished, often in the absence of those natural predators which in some measure help to control them elsewhere.

Pests and disease take a considerable toll of the world's food output, despite heavy use of pesticides and fungicides. Fungus diseases, for example, are said to destroy, annually, enough food to give 300,000,000 people 2500 calories a day.[5] In storage after harvest, rats and spoilage dispose of sufficient food grains to supply a further 350,000,000 people with an equal number of calories.[6] With a world population currently approaching 4,000,000,000—

sixty-five per cent of them receiving considerably less than the average 3060 calories enjoyed by people in the "have" countries— such crop-loss figures as these are by no means negligible.

If pesticides were banned in America, says Dr. Norman E. Borlaug—who was awarded the Nobel Peace Prize in 1970 for his work in developing the new wheats—the resulting crop losses could reach fifty per cent.[7] Nevertheless, there has been a vigorous (and in the case of DDT, successful) campaign in the United States and elsewhere against chemical insecticides. Residues of DDT—an insecticide which has worked miracles since its introduction in the 1940s—have been found in the human body, in cow's milk, even in the flesh of Antarctic penguins. In the 1950s, an approximately similar pesticide, DDD, was used in heavy doses to kill off the black gnats of Clear Lake, California. The larvae and plankton of the lake also became saturated with the chemical. Fish fed on the plankton, and that graceful bird, the Western grebe, fed on the fish. The grebe population was reduced from a thousand pairs to twenty pairs within the year by a concentration of pesticides occurring at the end of their particular food chain.* [8]

Man's food in the advanced countries is more diversified than that of the grebe, so the dangers may not be acute. But the same is not true in underdeveloped countries, where there is still a great reliance on one or two basic foodstuffs. "Miracle rice," too heavily treated with artificial pesticides and fertilizers, could cause a much swifter build-up of residues in the human body than in the West. Certain unpredictable side effects have also shown up recently in the Philippines. There, as in other parts of Asia, the paddy fields are used to grow not only rice but fish, which supply much of the protein in the local diet. So generous, however, have been the quantities of chemicals fed to "miracle rice" plants that the fish

* Much publicity was given to this ecological tragedy, and the situation has now been reversed. The use of chemicals was given up and a type of small freshwater smelt, the Mississippi silverside, was introduced to the lake to feed on the gnats. The technique proved successful and the grebes have now made a comeback. But the smelts have proliferated furiously on their new diet, so much so that it has become necessary to introduce game fish into the lake to control the smelts. If the game fish also multiply, it has been suggested that all Californians may have to take up game fishing.[9] It is, in fact, much easier to destroy ecological balance than to restore it.

in the paddy fields and in the tributary waterways have died.[10] More rice has therefore meant a reduction in protein.

What thirty years of chemical warfare in agriculture have done is help to demonstrate that mankind is still ignorant of many of the forces involved in the "balance of nature." The sometimes extremist views of modern ecologists serve as a valuable reminder of that ignorance and of the possibly disastrous results of failure to exercise caution.

The fact remains, however, that the underdeveloped countries cannot do without pesticides and fungicides. The still debatable risk of long-term poisoning by chlorinated hydrocarbon insecticides has to be set against the certainty of short-term starvation without them.

Agricultural pests come in all shapes and sizes, only a few of them easy to control. In this photograph, a fence in the center clearly marks the contrast between rabbit-infested and rabbit-free land.

Much research has taken place into alternative methods of pest control. The preferred pesticides are "botanicals," natural poisons extracted from plants rather than from mineral sources. The effectiveness of these is limited, and the farmer often has to spray his crops with a number of different substances to deal with a number of different pests. Cost is therefore a deterrent. Another method which has been developed is biological control (new in practice, though centuries old in theory). Young male insects are raised in a vast laboratory, then sterilized either by radiation or by chemical treatment, and released over an infested area; the female insects with which they mate produce far fewer eggs, most of them sterile, and the pest population is greatly reduced.[11] This method remains, at present, difficult and expensive.

In the case of fungicides, a hopeful start may well have been made with the discovery that bean plants have built-in defenses which enable them to fight off certain diseases (rather as human beings marshal their own special antibodies against infection). It has proved possible to reproduce, synthetically, the natural fungicide involved, and this has been found to give protection to other types of plant.[12]

The anti-pollution movement has undoubtedly helped to hurry along research into these new methods of pest and disease control, but the atmosphere of extreme urgency which has been generated could pose its own dangers—if, for example, new methods were to be introduced without sufficiently rigorous testing. In some ways, too, the fact that the movement's aims are so widely diffused leads to contradictions. In ecological terms, animal manure is infinitely preferable to chemical fertilizers—but cattlemen in America are making intensive efforts to destroy manure, even to reduce the animals' output of it, because run-off from the cattle sheds can cause pollution of nearby rivers and lakes.[13] It is, perhaps, time to rationalize both the objectives and the methods of achieving them.

EPILOGUE

Epilogue

For thousands of years, the search for food has helped to shape the development of society. It has dictated population growth and urban expansion, profoundly influenced economic, social, and political theory. It has widened the horizons of commerce, inspired wars of dominion, played no small role in the creation of empires, precipitated the discovery of new worlds. Food has had a part in religion, helping to define the separateness of one creed from another by means of dietary taboos. In science, where the prehistoric cook's discoveries about the effect of heat applied to raw materials laid the foundations on which much of early chemistry was based. In technology, where the water wheel first used in milling grain was to achieve immense industrial importance. In medicine, which was based largely on dietary principles until well into the eighteenth century. In war, where battles were postponed until the harvest had been gathered in and where well-fed armies usually defeated hungry ones. And even in relations between peoples, where for twelve thousand years there has been a steady undercurrent of antagonism between those whose diet consists mainly of grain and those who depend on animal foods.

In the last analysis, of course, food is not only inseparable from the history of mankind but essential to it. Without food there would be no history, no mankind.

The truth of this—it might be thought, self-evident—proposition is frequently forgotten in a world preoccupied with currency crises, computers, and communications satellites, but if, in the decades to come, population growth and environmental pollution follow the catastrophic course forecast by a number of modern ecologists, acute food shortages could prove a harsh reminder of it.

The debate over whether or not there *will* be a major world food crisis within the next few decades takes the form of a war of opinion, in which the belligerents' weapons are forecasts, not facts. One side believes that scientific advances will ensure a food surplus, the other that there are too many destructive elements in the environment today, too many imponderables in the future, to allow of complacency.

Both sides agree that by the first decade of the twenty-first century the world's population will have doubled from the 3,706,000,-000 of 1971 to over 7,000,000,000 in 2007. Although these figures attempt to take into account a possible reduction in the birth rate brought about by campaigns in favor of birth control, as well as a counterbalancing reduction in the number of deaths which may be expected to result from advances in medical knowledge, they cannot allow for the effects of age-slowing techniques which may emerge in the interim.*

On the present showing of improved wheat and rice plants, however, the optimists appear to be justified when they claim that the food future is satisfactory. If food grains can be trebled while the population does no more than double, and if scientists can produce a sufficiency of manufactured protein and other nutrients—then there would seem to be no problem (except for the gourmet, whose *tournedos Rossini* is probably doomed).

But the pessimist replies that nothing which has to do with food or society is as simple as that, that people are more than computer fodder. What kind, what quantity of food will the 7,000,000,000 people of the year A.D. 2007 want? African and Asian peasants who have had to make do in the past with one meal a day—the majority of the world's population—are now, in the present climate of optimism, beginning to ask for two. And who can blame them. Their demands being met, as they must be, there is another

---

* Biologists believe that large-scale human tests of anti-aging drugs will begin in the 1970s. Anti-aging foods are a possibility, too. Animal experiments have established that if calorie intake is reduced soon after birth to about sixty per cent of normal, the active life span can be prolonged by as much as forty per cent.[1] The calorie-reduction technique would not, of course, begin to affect population figures before about 2050, but anti-aging drugs might have earlier effects.

foreseeable consequence. In Japan in 1962 it was recorded that, as a result of the more balanced and ample diet which became common in the country after 1945, the average junior school student was as tall as the average adult had been in the years between 1868 and 1912.² Two meals a day instead of one. Larger people needing larger meals than before. And, in all probability, two or three thousand million of them. All this could wreak havoc with the comfortable arithmetic of the optimists.

The pessimists are also concerned over the declining fertility of soil that has for centuries been overworked and over-irrigated. About the water supply, steadily being polluted by persistent inorganic chemicals. And about the crop-destroying insects which are proliferating because their natural predators are more effectively killed off by pesticides than the pests themselves.

The simple fact is that either the pessimists or the optimists *could* be right. But it is also a fact that if the pessimists have their way, and prove to have been wrong, comparatively little harm will have been done. If the optimists win, and prove to have been wrong, the results could be disastrous. A few years of famine could mean death for millions of people, and permanent brain damage for many of those who survive.³

Most governments, by their very nature, favor the optimistic view as being less disruptive of the *status quo*; a policy of drift which requires no action other than an apparently forward-looking contribution to research finances, and perhaps a *douceur* to the opposition in the form of some mild legislation against pollution. More than this is needed, however, if only because whether the food supply situation develops well or badly, it is highly probable that it will develop differently from at present. It may in fact be necessary for governments to take a hand in changing the food habits of the people they govern.

What most peoples eat today is the product of thousands of years of dietary choice, the outcome, in effect, of an almost Darwinian process of natural selection. The foods which have survived in different regions of the world have been those best fitted not only to cultivation conditions but to the specific requirements of the inhabitants, requirements originally shaped as much by work and living conditions as by taste and preference. Men who lived in cold damp countries found that rich, fatty foods were not only comforting, but helped to build up a layer of flesh which acted as insulation against the weather. In less extreme climates, the field laborer used up considerable amounts of energy on digging, plowing, hoeing and other agricultural tasks; his need was for calorie-rich starches and sugars to replace that energy. In tropical lands, perspiration, evaporating from the skin, helps to cool the body; strong spices encouraged perspiration and also stimulated a thirst for the liquids which were necessary to replace it. Discoveries such as these—the product of observation and experience, not of scientific analysis—laid the foundations of many food traditions.

During the course of history, however, such logic as there may have been in the origins of food habits has become almost impenetrably complex. It has been distorted by shortages, by surpluses, by the introduction of new foods, and by any number of external developments. Even the commonplace human desire to catch up with those next higher on the social scale has helped to alter adequate diets for the worse.* Only recently, too, has it been appreciated that food preferences are not necessarily the same as food prejudices, that taste and custom are sometimes related to forces † which cannot be readily adjusted by social manipulation.

But however confused, from the modern viewpoint, the logic of food customs may appear to be, history suggests that there has always been a conscious or subconscious attempt to direct food production toward what tradition shows to be the "best" kind of diet for local circumstances.

In any attempt to shape future eating habits, therefore, it would be important to remember just how deeply ingrained certain food traditions are—despite the fact that the late twentieth century is in the process of cutting away the ground on which many of those traditions once rested. Tastes cannot be changed, particularly in peasant societies, simply by taking away one foodstuff

* In Britain's industrial revolution, for example, the assumption that the food of the rich must be "better" persuaded large numbers of the population to live on white bread and tea, instead of the more nourishing brown bread and beer of earlier times.

† Illustrated, for example, by the allergy of many Africans and Asians to milk (discussed on pages 138-40), and the sensitivity of some Asians to barley beer and grape wine.[4]

that is in short supply and replacing it with something else which, theoretically, ought to be a satisfactory substitute. Tradition is against it, and so too are levels of knowledge. In the Bengal famine of 1942-43, great numbers of rice-eating people died because they did not know what to do with the wheat they were given instead—and only the most blinkered optimist would deny the possibility of such a thing happening again, even if on a much reduced scale.

If Brillat-Savarin had been alive today, he might have thought twice before he said: "Tell me what you eat: I will tell you what you are." [5] Certainly, he would have qualified it, for no sane analyst of gastronomic history could be expected to deduce a Liverpool pop singer from yogurt and unpolished rice, or a Manhattan millionaire from black-eyed peas and chitterlings; to connect Scotch whisky with a Frenchman, or French bread with a Japanese. But these apparently wild deviations from the logic of the table—although they have more to do with contemporary social pressures than with food—do reflect a new and more general attitude of flexibility in the prosperous countries of the world and among the richer classes in developing countries.

This flexibility stems partly from the psychological effect of increases in the availability of foreign and "exotic'" foods, canned, frozen, or flown in fresh by air, during the present century; from the impact of foreign travel; from the furious activity, in all the communications media, of experts on cooking; even from the fact that the age balance of the population is currently tipped in the direction of the young, whose ethos includes the need to experiment.

There are also, however, more fundamental influences at work. Men who live in cold damp countries no longer have to eat rich, fatty foods. Many of them work indoors, where the need for warmth and comfort is satisfied by central heating. The field laborer who once burned up calories on reaping and binding grain now drives a combine harvester, which takes rather less energy. In hot lands, perspiration is no longer the only way of cooling the body. Air conditioners make a better job of it.

Central heating, combine harvesters and air conditioning are still the prerogative of the rich, though office workers share in the benefits of the first and third. But food flexibility (as a matter of choice) is in any case usually a characteristic of affluent societies. The nearness of hunger breeds conservatism. Only the well-fed can afford to try something new, because only they can afford to leave it on the plate if they dislike it.

The combined effect of a more open-minded attitude to food and a radical change in living conditions has been to divorce the contemporary diet from contemporary needs. It is nonsensical for a chairbound executive who breakfasted at 8:30 A.M. to lunch in the latest French bistro on a *cassoulet de Castelnaudary* or a *chou farçi à la mode de Grasse*—dishes designed centuries ago to restore farmers who had been hard at work in the fields since dawn. But thousands do it every day, to the post-meridian ruin not only of their mental alertness but of their whole digestive system. Among the lower-income groups, whose food habits tend to be less mobile, the imbalance between diet and need is only slightly less pronounced. Although, in an expanding economy, carbohydrate foods usually lose ground to meat, one lamb chop rimmed with fat contains just as many calories as a slice of white bread and butter. The stomachs of rich and not-so-rich alike, therefore, frequently have more fuel pumped into them than they need or can contend with. Whereas scurvy and rickets were the characteristic diseases of the nineteenth century, over-eating is almost certainly that of the twentieth.

Any attempt to adjust future eating patterns must take account of three essential facts. Familiar food, preferably in a slightly "improved" form, is customarily regarded as "best." There is a willingness to try new foods, but as an extra and *not in place of* the old. And, however little people are aware of it, physiological needs have changed; carefully introduced correctives could help to improve the general level of health.

In effect, the redirection of food habits would present, in the late twentieth century, fewer problems than at any time for many hundreds of years. An intelligent grasp of the situation and serious attention to forward planning are the main prerequisites.

In what direction would people's food tastes have to be turned? The prospect of banqueting on a handful of nutrient pills belongs in the realm of nightmare. What is more probable is that much

of the roast beef of the future will have been woven out of protein made from fuel oil, the bacon from an extract of intensively
grown algae.

Protein, carbohydrates, vitamins and fats can all be created in
the laboratory out of a wide variety of materials. Protein, for example, can be drawn from soybeans, then treated in a coagulating
bath, spun into threads and wound into hanks. These hanks
are next bound with a mixture of flour, gums and other ingredients, passed through a flavoring solution, and then pressed or teased
into a fair imitation of bacon rashers or forcemeat. Protein can
also be extracted from fuel oil, and it is confidently predicted that
natural gas will prove an equally valuable source. Potatoes, molasses, manioc, and many types of green leaves can also be used.

A factory-laboratory of the not too distant future, designed
to serve perhaps fifty thousand people, might run on roughly the
following lines. Dark-tinted water treated with chemical reagents
would be exposed to artificially focused sunlight from which it
would collect energy. The water would then be fed into tanks containing microscopic plants, which would grow at great speed (to
the extent of about one ton per tank per day) by converting
the active ingredients in the water as well as in the high-pressure
atmosphere of the tanks. Some of this plant material would, with
the addition of vitamins and minerals imported from specialized
factories, be fed direct to live cattle, pigs and poultry, to provide
real meat for gourmets and eggs for everyone. Some of it would
be made into flour, oils, carbohydrates, and some processed
through laboratory-grown milk-producing glands, to give milk for
drinking or for conversion into butter and cheese. From some,
protein would be extracted, to be spun and woven into "animal"
muscle—long wrist-thick tubes of "fillet steak," for example, ready
for automatic slicing into tournedos-sized portions. If the factory
had a separate kitchen section, some of the finished substitutes
could be cooked and packaged for distribution as soup, sausages,
bread, TV dinners, and so on. Fruit and vegetables, not catered
for in this system, would probably continue to come from private
gardens and specialist growers.[6]

The standardization which twentieth-century mass production
has helped to bring about—aided and abetted by the Western
housewife, who has preferred reliably mediocre food to food of

erratic quality and price—undoubtedly makes the task of the scientist easier. A steak spun out of artificially produced protein may have considerably less flavor (and, at present, fewer supplementary nutrients) [7] than an Aberdeen Angus entrecôte, but it need not differ much from the enzyme-injected "tenderized" steak which is already familiar. Bread made from carbohydrates which have been manufactured from, say, formaldehyde (a product of natural gas or coal) is unlikely to match the crusty perfection achieved by a good baker using good wheat flour, but neither does the latex foam which passes as bread today. A slice of spun-protein ham may not stand comparison with the genuine article from Bradenham or Virginia, but neither does the pink plastic sheeting of the contemporary supermarket.

Provided that the process of substitution is begun at an early stage and sensibly developed over a period of time, there would not be too much difficulty in persuading a majority of Western consumers to accept the newest offerings of science. Whether the same would prove true of currently underdeveloped countries is another matter. Unless the average income of their inhabitants climbs at an extremely steep rate, the problem here is likely to be as much economic as gastronomic.

Protein from soybeans is cheap, but as yet, insufficient attention seems to have been paid to the cost on a commercial basis of *wholly* manufactured foods. In the case of such a factory-laboratory as has been described above, there would be little differential in the production costs of different types of food, since the same basic materials, the same equipment, and the same complex and probably costly manufacturing control would be necessary for all. This means that a handful of "rice" would cost much the same as a "fillet steak" to manufacture. With factory-laboratories producing, either individually or in collaboration, a wide variety of foods salable over the full range of traditionally differentiated prices, expensive "steaks" would effectively subsidize cheap "grain." This system, however, would not work satisfactorily in places where the diet is limited, as in the rice-eating areas of Asia and the maize-dependent parts of Africa. "Grain" prices could not be subsidized by the sale of more expensive foods unless radical changes in the economy take place in the near future. Furthermore, manufactured foods are relevant only in a monetary

The roast on the plate . . .

Animal?

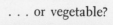

. . . or vegetable?

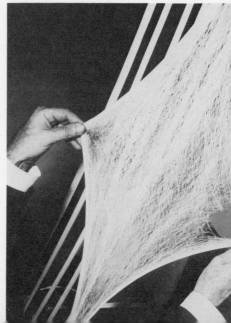

(or paternalist) economy, and there remain comparatively large areas in underdeveloped countries today which still depend on subsistence agriculture.

It is not yet clear whether conventional mass-production economics—the larger the output, the lower the unit cost—would apply in the case of the factory-laboratory. Nor is it clear whether other types of establishment producing "grain" alone—on lines currently being researched—would be an economic or practical proposition.

The need for large quantities of substitute or wholly manufactured foods may never arise, and the world may never see a factory-laboratory of the type described—a type chosen because it is such a classic example of self-sufficiency.* But complete dependence on "natural" food will certainly be out of tune with the times by the end of the present century, and research cannot, in any case, stop short at merely discovering how to manufacture carbohydrates, protein, minerals, fats and vitamins, and how to weave them into eatable foods. It must go on to translate that knowledge into workable reality.

Despite the pundits, developments in the future are no easier to forecast than they have ever been. But it would be well within the historical tradition—a tradition only partially affected by the extraordinary pace at which the world has developed since 1945—if town dwellers in the years to come found themselves living largely on artificial food, while natural foods were consumed in the areas where they were grown.

This would run counter to the present agricultural trend toward specialized and ever larger farming units, because the specialized unit would have a place only in fruit and vegetable production. Diversification would in general be necessary on farms whose role was to provide local inhabitants with a balanced diet.

Such a pattern would have several advantages. It might make it possible for some countries to approach, once again, that position of being self-supporting in food which was destroyed in so

---

* Most other methods of artificial food production currently being advocated make use either of traditional food materials cultivated by traditional methods (and therefore liable to run short in any major food crisis) or of fuel oils, which some—though by no means all—authorities believe will be in dangerously short supply forty years from now.

much of Europe during the industrial revolution, and which could prove critical in any forthcoming world food crisis. Mixed farming, too, would employ proportionately far more farm workers than specialized units, and this could have the effect of reducing that drift to the towns which promises to be one of the more disruptive results of any large population increase. And the contrast between town and country food might even encourage a drift back to the land by those city dwellers whose tongue papillae each contain the statutory 245 taste buds in full working order.

It would be reassuring to believe that the world's governments had given more than cursory consideration to the food pattern of the future. But in recent years thousands of tons of fruit have had to be destroyed, thousands of tons of butter sold off as cattle fodder, furious price wars engaged in for the disposal of surplus grain, millions of hens slaughtered because there is a glut of eggs—and this general climate of world food surplus has encouraged administrators to remain complacent about food and agricultural policies, which are, in most countries, short-sighted, inconsistent, and archaic. It is a situation that must be remedied soon if the next few decades are to be faced with any degree of composure, for the role of food in the future will be no less decisive than it has been in the past.

Bibliography

In order to keep this bibliography within manageable limits, only works of immediate relevance have been included; a full list of books and periodicals consulted would have run to several times the present length. Titles fall mainly into three categories—background material on history, sociology, and anthropology; special studies of subjects related directly to food; and primary sources. Except for one or two key works, cookbooks after 1500 are not listed; K. G. Bitting, André Simon and Georges Vicaire are the standard bibliographies.

Where text notes refer to an edition other than the first, the quoted edition is given in square brackets at the end of the entry. "P" means paperback.

Accum, Fredrick. A *Treatise on Adulterations of Food and Culinary Poisons*. London, 1820.

Adams, D. K., and Rodgers, H. B. *An Atlas of North American Affairs*. London, 1969.

Allchin, Bridget and Raymond. *The Birth of Indian Civilisation*. Harmondsworth, 1968.

Allen, E. Elliston. *British Tastes: An Enquiry into the Likes and Dislikes of the Regional Consumer*. London, 1968.

Allen, H. Warner. *A History of Wine*. London, 1961.

American Heritage Cookbook and Illustrated History of American Eating and Drinking. New York, 1964. (The first half of this work consists of a series of historical essays, on regional food, restaurants, gourmets, etc.)

André, J. *L'Alimentation et la cuisine à Rome*. Paris, 1961.

Annales, economies, sociétés, civilisations. Paris, 1929–   (Since 1961 this journal has been making a sustained and valuable study of the history of everyday life and food, mainly in Europe.)

Apicius. *De re coquinaria/culinaria.* Tr. as *The Roman Cookery Book* by Barbara Flower and Elisabeth Rosenbaum. London, 1958.

Arberry, A. J. "A Baghdad Cookery-Book," in *Islamic Culture*, 13, 1939.

Arciniegas, German. *Latin America: A Cultural History.* London, 1969. ("Culture" here includes food and commerce.)

Ashley, Sir William. *The Bread of Our Forefathers: An Inquiry in Economic History.* Oxford, 1928.

Athenaeus. *The Deipnosophists.* Tr. Charles Burton Gulik. Cambridge, Mass., and London, 1927. A chaotic miscellany on food in the Classical world.)

Atkinson, William C. *A History of Spain and Portugal.* Harmondsworth, 1960.

Austin, Thomas (ed.). *Two Fifteenth-century Cookery Books.* Early English Text Society, Vol. 91. London, 1888.

Avinon, Juan de. *Sevillana Medicina* [1418]. Society of Andalusian Bibliophiles, 1885. (Chapter 14 deals with vegetables; 17 with preserving meat.)

Avi-Yonah, Michael (ed.). *A History of the Holy Land.* London and New York, 1969.

Balsdon, J. P. V. D. *Life and Leisure in Ancient Rome.* London and New York, 1969.

Bardach, John. *Harvest of the Sea.* New York, 1968; London, 1969. (Modern fisheries, power and mineral resources, plankton harvesting, etc.)

Barker, T. C., McKenzie, J. C., and Yudkin, John (eds.). *Our Changing Fare: Two Hundred Years of British Food Habits.* London, 1966.

Barraclough, Geoffrey (ed.). *Eastern and Western Europe in the Middle Ages.* London, 1970.

Barrau, Jacques. "Plant Introduction in the Tropical Pacific," *Pacific Viewpoint*, Vol. I (1960), pp. 1–10.

Basham, A. L. *The Wonder that Was India.* London, 1954; New York, 1959. [1971 P]

Bernal, J. D. *Science in History.* London and New York, 1954. [1969, 4 vols. P]

Best, Henry. *Rural Economy in Yorkshire, being the farming and account books of Henry Best* [1641]. Surtees Society, Vol. 33. London, 1857.

Bhatia, B. M. *Famines in India 1860–1965.* Bombay, 1967.

Birch, Cyril, and Keene, Donald (eds.). *Anthology of Chinese Literature.* New York, 1965. [1967 P]

Bitting, A. W. *Appertizing: or, the Art of Canning: Its History and Development.* San Francisco, 1937.

Bitting, K. G. *Gastronomic Bibliography.* San Francisco, 1939.

Bodenheimer, F. S. *Insects as Human Food.* The Hague, 1951.

Boorde, Andrew. *A Compendyous Regyment, or a Dyetary of Helth.* London, 1542. (One of the earliest English books on diet).

Boxer, C. R. *The Portuguese Sea-borne Empire 1415–1825.* London, 1969.

Bridbury, A. R. *England and the Salt Trade in the Later Middle Ages.* Oxford, 1955.

Briggs, Asa (ed.). *The Nineteenth Century: The Contradictions of Progress.* London, 1970.

Brillat-Savarin, Jean-Anthelme. *La Physiologie du Goût,* 1825. Tr. as *The Philosopher in the Kitchen* by Anne Drayton. Harmondsworth, 1970. (Valuable on the early nineteenth century, but the author's views on history and chemistry must be treated with discretion.)

Brockington, Fraser. *World Health,* Harmondsworth, 1958.

Bronsted, Johannes. *The Vikings.* Harmondsworth, 1960.

Brooks, C. E. P. *Climate Through the Ages.* London, 1926.

Brothwell, Don and Patricia. *Food in Antiquity. A Survey of the Diet of Early Peoples.* London, 1969.

Burkill, I. H. "The Rise and Decline of the Yam in the Service of Man," *Advances in Science,* Vol. 7 (1951).

Burn, A. R. *A Traveller's History of Greece.* London, 1965; New York, 1967 [1966 P].

Burnett, John [1]. *Plenty and Want: A Social History of Diet in England from 1815 to the present Day.* London, 1966 [1968 P].

Burnett, John [2]. *A History of the Cost of Living* (in England). Harmondsworth, 1969.

Calder, Nigel. *The Environment Game.* London, 1967 [1969 P].

Cambel, Halet, and Braidwood, Robert J. "An Early Farming Village in Turkey," in *Scientific American,* 222, March 1970, pp. 50–56.

Carcopino, Jerome. *Daily Life in Ancient Rome: The People and the City at the Height of the Empire.* London, 1941 [1967 P].

Carefoot, G. L., and Sprott, E. R. *Famine on the Wind: Plant Diseases and Human History.* New York, 1967; London, 1969.

Carletti, Francesco, *Ragionamenti,* 1594–1606. Tr. as *My Voyage Around the World* by Herbert Weinstock. New York, 1964; London, 1965. (One of the most literate and observant of travelers.)

Carson, Rachel. *Silent Spring.* New York, 1962 [1968 P]. (The keynote book of the modern environmentalist movement.)

Casson, L. "Grain Trade in the Hellenistic world," *Transactions and Proceedings of the American Philological Association,* 1954, pp. 168–187.

Cave, R. C., and Coulson, H. N. *A Source Book for Medieval Economic History.* Milwaukee, 1936.

Chao Ju-kua. *Chu-fan-chi.* Tr. by Friedrich Hirth and W. W. Rockhill. Saint Petersburg, 1911. (Chinese and Arab trade in the twelfth and thirteenth centuries. A medieval summary of what the Chinese knew about the outside world.)

Chaplin, Raymond E. "Animals in Archaeology," *Antiquity*, Vol. XXXIX (1965), pp. 204–211.

Charlemagne [attr. to]. Capitulary *De Villis*. Translated into French in Guérard, "Explication du Capitulaire 'de Villis,'" Académie des Inscriptions et Belles-Lettres, *Mémoires*, Vol. XXI (1857). (Instructions on the management of the royal estates, etc.)

Cimber, Louis Lafaist, and Danjou, F. *Archives curieuses de l'histoire de France, Louis XI–Louis XVIII*. 27 vols. Paris, 1834–1840. (A collection of historical documents.)

Clark, Colin. *Population Growth and Land Use*. London, 1967. (Valuable statistics on food production, land use, urbanization, and economic development.)

Clark, J. Desmond. "The Spread of Food Production in Sub-Saharan Africa," *Journal of African History*, Vol. III (1962), pp. 211–228.

Cobb, Richard C. *The Police and the People: French Popular Protest 1789–1820*. Oxford, 1970. (Includes material on the influence of food shortages on sociopolitical events.)

Cobban, Alfred. *A History of Modern France*. 3 vols. Harmondsworth, 1968.

Cockrill, W. R. "The Water Buffalo," *Scientific American*, Vol. 217 (1967), pp. 118–125.

Codex Mendoza. Translated by James Cooper Clark. 3 vols. London, 1938. (The tribute rolls of Moctezuma.)

Coles, J. M., and Higgs, E. S. *The Archaeology of Early Man*. London, 1969; New York, 1970.

Collins, J. L. "Antiquity of the Pineapple in America," *Southwestern Journal of Anthropology*, Vol. VII (1951), pp. 145–155.

Columbus, Ferdinand. *The Life of the Admiral Christopher Columbus*. Translated by Benjamin Keen. New Brunswick, 1959; London, 1960.

Columella. *De Re Rustica*. Translated as *On Agriculture* by H. B. Ash, E. S. Forster, and E. H. Heffner. 3 vols. London, 1941.

Coon, Carleton S. *The History of Man: From the First Human to Primitive Culture and Beyond*. New York, 1954; London, 1955 [1967 P].

Cordier, Henri. "L'Alimentation en Chine," *Journal des Debats*, Nov. 19, 1879.

Coursey, D. G. *Yams*. London and New York, 1967.

Crisp, Frank. *Medieval Gardens*. 2 vols. London, 1924.

Critchell, J. T., and Raymond, J. *A History of the Frozen Meat Trade*. London, 1912.

Crossley, E. L. (ed.). *The United Kingdom Dairy Industry*. London, 1959. (A trade publication.)

Curtin, Philip D. *The Atlantic Slave Trade: A Census*. Madison, Wis., 1969. (Statistical analysis.)

Curtis-Bennett, Sir Noel. *The Food of the People, Being the History of Industrial Feeding.* London, 1949.

Curwen, E. Cecil, and Hatt, Gudmund. *Plough and Pasture: The Early History of Farming.* New York, 1953.

Cutting, Charles L. *Fish Saving: A History of Fish Processing from Ancient to Modern Times.* New York, 1956.

Daiches, David. *Scotch Whiskey: Its Past and Present.* London, 1969; New York, 1970. (More present than past.)

Darenne, E. *Histoire des métiers de l'alimentation.* Meulan, 1904.

Darlington, C. D. *The Evolution of Man and Society.* London, 1969; New York, 1970. (A geneticist's view.)

Daumas, Maurice (ed.). *Histoire Générale des Techniques.* 3 vols. Paris 1962–1969.(A French version of Singer [2], below. More up-to-date, and fuller on the Americas, Asia, and the medieval Near East.

Davidson, Alan. *Mediterranean Seafood.* Harmondsworth, 1972 [P]. (Partly a catalog of marine life.)

Davidson, Basil (ed.). *The African Past: Chronicles from Antiquity to Modern Times.* London and Boston, 1964 [1966 P].

Davidson, H. R. Ellis. *Gods and Myths of Northern Europe.* Harmondsworth, 1964.

De Bach, P. (ed.). *Biological Control of Insect Pests and Weeds.* London, 1964.

Deerr, Noel. *The History of Sugar.* 2 vols. London, 1949.

Della Casa, Giovanni. *Galateo, or the Book of Manners* [1558]. Tr. by R. S. Pine-Coffin. Harmondsworth, 1958.

Derry, T. K., and Williams, Trevor I. *A Short History of Technology from the Earliest Times to* A.D. *1900.* Oxford, 1960 [1970 P].

Devambez, Pierre; Flacelière, Robert; Schuhl, Pierre-Maxime; and Martin, Roland. *A Dictionary of Ancient Greek Civilisation.* London, 1967.

Dimbleby, Geoffrey. *Plants and Archaeology.* London and New York, 1967.

Dioscorides. *Materia Medica.* (Book II discusses dietetics, grains and garden herbs.)

Dodge, B. S. *Plants That Changed the World.* London and Boston, 1962.

Douglas, David C. *The Norman Achievement, 1050–1100.* London and Berkeley, 1969.

Drummond, J. C., and Wilbraham, Anne. *The Englishman's Food: A History of Five Centuries of English Diet.* London, 1939 [rev. ed. 1964]. (The standard work, written from the nutritionists' viewpoint.)

Duby, Georges [1]. *Rural Economy and Country Life in the Medieval West.* London and Columbia, South Carolina, 1968. (Exhaustive. Includes a section reproducing ninth- to fifteenth-century documents.)

Duby, Georges [2], and Mandrou, Robert. *A History of French Civilisation.* London, 1965.

Duckett, Eleanor. *Death and Life in the Tenth Century.* Ann Arbor, Michigan, 1967.

Duckham, A. N., and Masefield, G. B. *Farming Systems of the World.* London and New York, 1970. (Contemporary conditions and future planning.)

Dufour, Philippe Sylvestre. *Traitez nouveaux et curieux du café, du thé, et du chocolat.* Lyon, 1685.

Durbec, J. A. "La Grande boucherie de Paris. Notes historiques d'après des archives privées (XIIe–XVIIe siècles)," in *Bulletin philologique et historique*, 1955–56.

Edwardes, Michael [1]. *Asia in the European Age 1498–1955.* London, 1961; New York, 1962.

Edwardes, Michael [2]. *East-West Passage: The Travel of Ideas, Arts and Inventions Between Asia and the Western World.* London and New York, 1971. (Essential antidote to the belief that the world begins and ends in the West.)

Emery, Walter B. *Archaic Egypt.* Harmondsworth, 1961.

Fagniez, G. (ed.). *Documents relatifs à l'histoire de l'industrie et du commerce en France.* 2 vols. Paris, 1898–1900. (Documents in Latin and French from Roman times on.)

Fei, Hsiao-tung. *Peasant Life in China: A Field Study of Country Life in the Yangtse Valley.* London, 1939.

Filby, Frederick A. *A History of Food Adulteration and Analysis.* London, 1934.

Filliozat, J. *La Doctrine classique de la médecine indienne.* Paris, 1949. (Parallels between Indian and Classical medicine.)

Fitz Stephen, William. "A Description of London" (pre-1183). Tr. H. E. Butler, in F. M. Stenton, *Norman London.* London, 1934.

Forbes, R. J. *Studies in Ancient Technology.* 6 vols. Leiden, 1955–58. (Vols. II and III are concerned with food and drink.)

Francis, C. A. *A History of Food and Its Preservation.* Princeton, 1937.

The Forme of Cury. See Pegge, S.

Franklin, A. *Vie privée des français, 12e à 18e siècles.* 27 vols. Paris, 1887–1902. (Rather less woolly than most Victorian histories. Vol. III: *La Cuisine.* Vol. VI: *Les Repas.* Vol. VIII: *Variétés gastronomiques.* Vol. XIII: *Le Café, le thé, et le chocolat.*)

Freyre, Gilberto [1]. *The Masters and the Slaves.* New York, 1946.

Freyre, Gilberto [2]. *The Mansions and the Shanties.* New York, 1963. (Both works relate to social conditions in Brazil.)

Furet, L. "Le Chien comestible chinois," *Bulletin de la Société Nationale d'Acclimatation* (1890), pp. 132, 1159.

Furnas, J. C. *The Americans: A Social History of the United States, 1587–1914.* New York, 1969; London, 1970.

Furnivall, Frederick J. (ed.) [1]. *The Babees Book*. Early English Text Society, Vol. 32. London, 1868. (Includes John Russell's *Boke of Nurture* [c. 1460–1470] and Wynkyn de Worde's *Boke of Kervyng*. The pages overflow with the editor's voluminous notes, all of them informative.)

Furnivall, Frederick J. (ed.). [2]. *A Book of Precedence* [c. 1570], by Sir Humphrey Gilbert. Early English Text Society Extra Series 8. London, 1869. (Also includes extracts from Latini, Fra Bonvicino, Pandolfini, Della Casa, Thomasin of Zerklaere, and the Knight of Winsbeke, as well as Furnivall's characteristic notes upon notes.)

Gamble, Sidney D. *Ting Hsien: A North China Rural Community (1927–33)*. Stanford, California, 1968.

Gellius. *Noctes Atticae* [2nd century]. (Book VI, 16, satirizes the gourmands of the Classical world.)

Gernet, Jacques. *Daily Life in China on the Eve of the Mongol Invasions, 1250–1276*. London, 1962; Stanford, California, 1970.

Gilgamesh, The Epic of. Tr. by N. K. Sandars. Harmondsworth, 1960.

Gottschalk, Alfred. *Histoire de l'alimentation et de la gastronomie depuis la préhistoire jusqu'à nos jours*. 2 vols. Paris, 1948 (Franco-centric.)

Gray, W. D. *The Relation of Fungi to Human Affairs*. New York, 1959.

Griffiths, Percival. *The History of the Indian Tea Industry*. London and New York, 1967.

Grousset, René. *The Rise and Splendour of the Chinese Empire*. London, 1952; Berkeley, 1953.

Harlan, J. R. "A Wild Wheat Harvest in Turkey," in *Archaeology*, 20, March 1967.

Harrison, S. G.; Masefield, G. B.; and Wallis, Michael. *The Oxford Book of Food Plants*. Oxford, 1969. (An essential work of reference.)

Hartley, Dorothy. *Food in England*. London, 1954.

Haskins, Charles Homer. *The Renaissance of the Twelfth Century*. Cambridge, Massachusetts, 1927.

Hatch, John. *The History of Britain in Africa: From the Fifteenth Century to the Present Day*. London, 1969.

Hayward, Abraham. *The Art of Dining: or, Gastronomy and Gastronomers*. London, 1852. (Informative about English middle-class attitudes in the 1830s.)

Helbaek, Hans. "The Domestication of Food Plants in the Old World," *Science*, 130 (1959), pp. 365–372.

Hémardinquer, J.-J. (ed.). *Pour une histoire de l'alimentation*, Paris, 1972. (Articles from the *Annales*. See above.)

Henry VIII. Privy Purse Expenses (1529–32). London, 1827. (Includes details of food expenditure for the royal table.)

Herodotus. *The Histories* [c. 446 B.C.]. Tr. by Aubrey de Sélincourt. Harmondsworth, 1954.

Higgs, E. S., and White, J. P. "Autumn Killing," in *Antiquity*, 37 (1963), pp. 282–89.

Hirth, F. "Notes on the Early History of the Salt Monopoly in China," *Journal of the* [North] *China Branch of the Royal Asiatic Society*. New Series Vol. XXII, Nos. 1 and 2 (1887), pp. 53–66.

Homer. *The Iliad*. Translated by E. V. Rieu. Harmondsworth, 1950.

Hooke, S. H. *Middle Eastern Mythology*. Harmondsworth, 1963. (The development of the creation and fertility myths can be clearly traced here.)

Husa, Vaclav; Petran, Joseph; and Subrtova, Alena. *Traditional Crafts and Skills: Life and Work in Medieval and Renaissance Times*. London, 1967. (Mainly Bohemia.)

Hutchinson, Sir J. B. (ed.). *Essays in Crop Plant Evolution*. Cambridge, 1965.

Hutchinson, R .W. *Prehistoric Crete*. Harmondsworth, 1962.

Huxley, E. *Brave New Victuals: An Inquiry into Modern Food Production*. London, 1965.

Hyams, Edward. *Dionysus: A Social History of the Wine Vine*. London, 1965.

Inama-Sternegg, Carl Theodor von. *Deutsche Wirtschaftgeschichte*. 3 vols. in 4. Leipzig, 1879–1901. (German housekeeping prior to 1400.)

Innis, H. A. *The Cod Fisheries*. New Haven, 1940.

International Action to Avert the Impending Protein Crisis. United Nations Publication, Sales No. E 68 XIII 2. 1969.

Isaac, Erich. "The Influence of Religion on the Spread of Citrus," *Science*, Vol. 129 (1959), 179–86.

Jacob, H. E. *Six Thousand Years of Bread*. New York, 1944. (Exhaustive, but to be treated with care.)

James, Margery Kirkbride. *Studies in the Medieval Wine Trade*. Oxford, 1971.

Jefferys, James B. *Retail Trading in Britain, 1850–1950*. London, 1954.

Jenkins, J. T. *The Herring and the Herring Fisheries*. London, 1927.

Jones, E. L., and Woolf, S. J. (eds.). *Agrarian Change and Economic Development. The Historical Problems*. London, 1969. (International symposium.)

Jones, Peter D'A. *The Consumer Society: A History of American Capitalism*. New York, 1963. [1967 P]

Kautilya. *Arthasastra*. Edited by R. P. Kangle. 3 vols. Bombay, 1960–1965. (Manual of administration, northeast India, c. 1st century A.D)

Keene, Donald. *The Japanese Discovery of Europe 1720–1830*. London, 1952.

Kosambi, Damodar Dharmanand. *An Introduction to the Study of Indian History*. Bombay, 1956.

Kramer, Samuel Noah. *The Sumerians, Their History, Culture and Character.* Chicago, 1964.

Lattimore, Owen. *Inner Asian Frontiers of China.* American Geographical Society Research Series, No. 21. London and New York, 1940.

Lauwerys, J. R. *Man's Impact on Nature.* London and New York, 1969.

La Varenne, François Pierre de. *Le Vray Cuisinier François.* Paris, 1651. (The cookbook that marks the transition from the medieval to the modern table.)

Lee, R. B., and Devore, I. (eds.). *Man the Hunter.* Chicago, 1968. (Papers and discussion at an academic conference held at the University of Chicago in 1966. Part history, part anthropology.)

Lee, T'ao. "Historical Notes on Some Vitamin Deficiency Diseases in China," *Chinese Medical Journal,* Vol. 58 (1940), 314–323.

Lespinasse, René de. *Les Métiers et Corporations de la Ville de Paris.* 3 vols. Paris, 1886–1897. (Reprints a number of original documents.)

Lévi-Strauss, Claude. *The Raw and the Cooked.* London and New York, 1970. Also *Du Miel aux cendres, L'Origine des manières de table,* and *L'Homme nu.* Paris, 1967, 1968, and 1971. (A complex series of analyses of over eight hundred American Indian myths, many of them relating to food. Some of the author's references to the food of more sophisticated societies during the course of history are debatable.)

Lévy, Jean-Philippe. *The Economic Life of the Ancient World.* Chicago, 1967.

Lewis, Archibald R. *Naval Power and Trade in the Mediterranean* A.D. *500–1100.* Princeton, 1951.

Il Libro della Cucina. [14th century] Edited by Zambrini. Bologna, 1863.

Lichine, Alexis. *Encyclopedia of Wines and Spirits.* London and New York, 1967.

Little, E. C. S. (ed.). *Handbook of Utilization of Aquatic Plants.* UN Food and Agriculture Organization publication, 1968.

Livy. *History of Rome.* Translated by W. M. Roberts. London, 1912.

Lloyd, Christopher. *The British Seaman, 1200-1860. A Social Survey.* London, 1968.

Longmate, Norman. *The Waterdrinkers: A History of Temperance.* London and New York, 1968.

Lopez, Robert S., and Raymond, Irving W. *Medieval Trade in the Mediterranean World.* London, 1955. (A collection of documents, informatively annotated.)

Lord, Francis A. *Civil War Sutlers and their Wares.* New York, 1969.

Lutz, H. F. *Viticulture and Brewing in the Ancient Orient.* Leipzig and New York, 1922.

Luzzatto, Gino. *An Economic History of Italy from the Fall of the Roman Empire to the Beginning of the Sixteenth Century.* London and New York, 1961.

Macadams, R. *Land behind Baghdad.* Chicago and London, 1965. (Development of the canal system in Iraq.)

McEvedy, Colin. [1] *The Penguin Atlas of Medieval History.* Harmondsworth, 1961.

McEvedy, Colin. [2] *The Penguin Atlas of Ancient History.* Harmondsworth, 1967.

MacGowan, Dr. "On the Mutton Wine of the Mongols and analogous Preparations of the Chinese," in *Journal of the North China Branch of the Royal Asiatic Society,* New Series VII 1871–72, pp. 237–40.

McNaught, Kenneth. *The Pelican History of Canada.* Harmondsworth, 1969.

Madan Mohan Singh. *Life in North-eastern India in Pre-Mauryan Times (with Special Reference to c. 600 B.C.–325 B.C.).* Delhi, 1967. (Buddhist social background).

Maggs Bros. Ltd. *Food and Drink through the Ages.* Catalogue 645. London, 1937.

Malik, S. C. *Indian Civilisation: The Formative Period. A Study of Archeology as Anthropology.* Simla, 1968.

Mangelsdorf, P. C. *Plants and Human Affairs.* Bloomington, Indiana, 1952.

Mangelsdorf, P. C.; Macneish, R. S.; and Galinat, W. C. "The Domestication of Corn," *Science,* Vol. CXLIII (1964), pp. 538–545.

Marco Polo. *Travels.* Translated by Ronald Latham. Harmondsworth, 1958[P]. [1968]

Marle, Raimond van. *Iconographie de l'Art profane au Moyen-Age et à la Renaissance.* Vol. I, *La Vie Quotidienne.* The Hague, 1931.

Marrison, L. W. *Wines and Spirits.* Harmondsworth, 1957. (Maps.)

Mason, J. Alden. *The Ancient Civilisations of Peru.* Harmondsworth, 1957. [1964 P]

Maurizio, A. *Histoire de l'alimentation végétale depuis la préhistoire jusqu'à nos jours.* Paris 1939.

Meade, J. E. "Population Explosion, the Standard of Living and Social Conflict," *The Economic Journal,* Vol. 77 (1967), p. 233.

Mellanby, Kenneth. *Pesticides and Pollution.* London, 1967.

Mémoires concernant l'histoire, les sciences, les arts, les moeurs, les usages etc. des Chinois, par les missionaires de Pe-kin. 16 vols. Paris, 1776–1814. (Thousands of pages of uncritical but valuable information, compiled by Jesuit missionaries.)

Le Ménagier de Paris [c. 1393]. Edited and translated as *The Goodman of Paris* by Eileen Power. London, 1928.

Miller, J. Innes. *The Spice Trade of the Roman Empire, 29 B.C. to A.D. 641.* Oxford, 1969.

Milne, Lorus and Margery. *The Nature of Life,* London 1971.

Misson de Valbourg, Henri. *M. Misson's Memoirs and Observations in his Travels over England* [1690s]. Translated by Mr. Ozell. London, 1719.

Monckton, H. A. *A History of the English Public House.* London, 1970.

Morettini, A. *Olivicultura*. Rome, 1950.

Moritz, L. A. *Grain-mills and Flour in Classical Antiquity*. Oxford, 1958.

Morris, Ivan. *The World of the Shining Prince: Court Life in Ancient Japan*. London and New York, 1964. [1969 P]

Mossé, Claude. *The Ancient World at Work*. London, 1969; New York, 1970.

Mourant, A. E., and Zeuner, F. E. (eds.). *Man and Cattle*. London, 1963. (Papers from a symposium on domestication.)

Mukerjee, R. *Races, Lands and Food*. New York, 1946.

Mulvaney, Derek J. *The Prehistory of Australia*. London and New York, 1969. (Until the end of the eighteenth century.)

Mumford, Lewis. *The City in History: Its Origins, Its Transformations, and Its Prospects*. London and New York, 1961. [1966 P]

Needham, Joseph [1]. *Science and Civilisation in China*. 4 vols., continuing. Cambridge, 1954–

Needham, Joseph [2]. *Clerks and Craftsmen in China and the West: Lectures and Addresses on the History of Science and Technology*. Cambridge, 1970. (Includes medicine, hygiene, etc.)

Nenquin, Jacques. *Salt, a Study in Economic Prehistory*. Brugge, 1961.

Nye, R. B., and Morpurgo, J. E. *A History of the United States*. 2 vols. Harmondsworth, 1955.

Oliver, R., and Fage, J. D. *A Short History of Africa*. Harmondsworth, 1962. [1968 P]

O'Malley, L. S. *Indian Caste Customs*. Cambridge, 1932.

Oppenheim, Leo. "On Beer and Brewing Techniques in Ancient Mesopotamia," *Journal of the American Oriental Society*, suppl. 1950.

Ostoya, Paul. "La Préhistoire révèle l'origine du maïs," *Science Progrès*, 3353 (1964), pp. 329–335.

Palladius. *On Husbondrie. From the unique MS of about 1420 A.D. in Colchester Castle*. Edited by Rev. Barton Lodge. Early English Text Society, Vols. 52, 72. London 1873, 1879. (A fourth-century manual of agriculture.)

Pan Ku. *Han Shu*. Translated and edited by Nancy Lee Swann in *Food and Money in Ancient China: The Earliest Economic History of China to A.D. 25. Han Shu 24 with related texts Han Shu 19 and Shih-chi 129*. Princeton, 1950.

Parmentier, A. A. *Traité sur la culture et les usages des pommes de terre*. Paris, 1789.

Paske-Smith, M. *Western Barbarians in Japan and Formosa in Tokugawa Days, 1603–1868*. Kobe, 1930.

Pegge, S. (ed.). *The Forme of Cury. A roll of ancient English cookery, compiled, about A.D. 1390, by the master-cooks of King Richard II*. London, 1780.

Pellat, C. (ed. and tr.). *Calendrier de Cordoue*. Leyden, 1961. (The most important of the agricultural calendars surviving from the classical period of Islamic Spain.)

Pendle, George. *A History of Latin America*. Harmondsworth, 1963.

Ping-ti Ho. "The Introduction of American Food Plants into China," in *American Anthropologist*, Vol. 57, 2 i, April 1955.

Pinto, Edward H. *Treen, and Other Wooden Bygones*. London, 1969. (A dictionary/catalogue of wooden relics of everyday life, from prehistoric times onward.)

Pirie, N. W. [1] "Leaf Protein as a Human Food," *Science*, Vol. 152 (1966), p. 1701.

Pirie, N. W. [2]. *Food Resources Conventional and Novel*. Harmondsworth, 1969.

Platina [Sacchi, Bartolomeo de']. *De Honesta Voluptate*. Venice, 1475. (The first printed cookbook. Its author was the Vatican librarian.)

Pliny the Elder. *Natural History* [1st century A.D.]. Translated by H. Rackham. London, 1950. (Book XIV, 5–16: wines; 22: drunkards. XVIII, 27–28: bread. XXII: plants and fruits.)

Pollard, S., and Holmes, C. *The Process of Industrialization 1750–1870*. London and New York, 1968. (Documentary material, translated where necessary.)

Portal, Roger. *The Slavs*. London, 1969; New York, 1970.

Posener, Georges (ed.). *A Dictionary of Egyptian Civilisation*. New York, 1961; London, 1962.

Postan, M. M. "The Trade of Mediaeval Europe: the North," in *The Cambridge Economic History*, Vol. II. Cambridge, 1952.

Postgate, John. *Microbes and Man*. Harmondsworth, 1969.

Prakash, Om. *Food and Drinks in Ancient India*. Delhi, 1961. (A painstaking account from primary sources, up to A.D. 1200. The text is in English, but the extensive quotations are in Sanskrit.)

The Production of Protein Foods and Concentrates from Oilseeds. Tropical Products Institute publication. London, 1967.

Pyke, Magnus. *Man and Food*. London and New York, 1970. (Nutritional knowledge and current research; a valuable summary marred by an abysmal index.)

Renner, H. D. *The Origin of Food Habits*. London, 1944. (An interesting attempt to discover the source of food preferences, although some of the book has been invalidated by recent scientific discoveries.)

Reynière, Grimod de la [Laurent, Alexandre-Balthazar]. *Almanach des gourmands, ou calendrier nutritif*. Paris, 1803–1812. (Published in periodical form.)

Rice, Tamara Talbot. *The Scythians*. London, 1957.

Rich, E. E., and Wilson, C. H. (eds.). *The Economy of Expanding Europe in the Sixteenth and Seventeenth Centuries*. Vol. IV of the *Cambridge Economic History*. Cambridge, 1967.

Richards, Donald S. (ed.). *Islam and the Trade of Asia. A Colloquium*. Oxford and Philadelphia, 1970.

Rickman, Geoffrey. *Roman Granaries and Store Buildings*. Cambridge, 1971.

Riley, H. T. (ed.). *Memorials of London and London Life, 1276–1419.* London, 1868. (A massive collection of documents from the city archives.)

Roberts, John M. *Europe 1880–1945.* London and New York, 1967.

Robinson, Edward Forbes. *The Early History of Coffee Houses in England.* London, 1893.

Robinson, F. P. *The Trade of the East India Company from 1709–1813.* Cambridge, 1912.

Rodinson, Maxime. "Recherches sur les documents arabes relatifs à la cuisine," in *Revue des études islamiques,* 17–18, 1949.

Root, Waverley. *The Food of France.* London and New York, 1958. (A knowledgeably discursive view of French food, mainly modern.)

Rostovtzeff, M. I. *Social and Economic History of the Roman Empire.* 2 vols. Oxford, 1926.

Roux, Georges. *Ancient Iraq.* London and New York, 1964. [1969 P]

Rowntree, B. Seebohm. *Poverty: A Study of Town Life.* York, 1901.

Rumford, Benjamin Thompson, Count. "Of Food: and particularly of feeding the Poor" [1795], in *Works,* Vol. V. London, 1876.

Saggs, H. W. F. *Everyday Life in Babylonia and Assyria.* London and New York, 1965.

Salaman, Redcliffe N. *The History and Social Influence of the Potato.* Cambridge, 1949. (The classic monograph.)

Salerno Regimen. Rhymed English version, *The Englishman's Doctor,* by Sir John Harington. London, 1608.

Scappi, Bartolomeo. "Cuoco Secreto di Papa Pio Quinto," in *Opera di M. B. Scappi.* Venice, 1570. (Early stages of the lighter and more delicate Italian cuisine.)

Schafer, Edward H. *The Golden Peaches of Samarkand: A Study of T'ang Exotics.* Berkeley and Los Angeles, 1963. (Chinese imports in A.D. 618–907.)

Science, Technology, and Development, Volume VI: Health and Nutrition. United States Papers prepared for the United Nations Conference on the Application of Science and Technology for the Benefit of the Less Developed Areas. Washington, 1963.

Scott, J. M. *The Tea Story.* London, 1964. As *The Great Tea Venture,* New York, 1964.

Scrimshaw, Nevin S., and Altschul, Aaron M. (eds.). *Amino Acid Fortification of Protein Foods.* Cambridge, Massachusetts, and London, 1971.

Sheng-han, Shih. *On "Fan Shêng-Chih Shu," an Agriculturalistic Book of China Written by Fan Shêng-Chih in the First Century B.C.* Peking, 1959.

Shih ching [Book of Songs]. Translated by James Legge in "Chinese Classics" series, Vol. IV. London, 1870.

Sigerist, Henry E. *Primitive and Archaic Medicine.* Vol. I of *A History of Medicine.* New York, 1951. [1967 P]

Simkin, C. G. F. *The Traditional Trade of Asia*. London and New York, 1968.

Simmonds, F. J. "The Economics of Biological Control," *Journal of the Royal Society of Arts*, Vol. CXV (1967), p. 880.

Simmonds, N. W. *The Evolution of the Banana*. London and New York, 1962.

Simmonds, Peter Lund. *The Curiosities of Food*. London, 1859. (Interesting material on the author's own time, but untrustworthy on history.)

Simon, André L. *Bibliotheca Gastronomica*, London, 1953.

Simoons, F. J. *Eat Not This Flesh*. Madison, Wisconsin, 1961. (Semite and Jewish taboos.)

Sinclair, Keith. *A History of New Zealand*. Harmondsworth, 1959.

Singer, Charles [1]. *A Short History of Medicine*. Oxford, 1928.

Singer, Charles [2], Holmyard, E. J., Hall, A. R., and Williams, Trevor I. *A History of Technology*. 5 vols. Oxford, 1954–1958.

Smith, Edward. "On the Food of the Poorer Labouring Classes in England." Sixth Report of the Medical Officer of the Privy Council, Appendix No. 6. London, 1863. p 232.

Smith, John. *The General Historie of Virginia*. London, 1623.

Smith, Peter H. *Politics and Beef in Argentina: Patterns of Conflict and Change*. New York, 1969. (Mainly 1900–1930.)

Solheim II, Wilhelm G. "An Earlier Agricultural Revolution," in *Scientific American*, 226, April 1972, pp. 34–41.

Sourdel, D. and J. *La Civilisation de l'Islam classique*. Paris, 1968.

Soustelle, Jacques. *Daily Life of the Aztecs on the Eve of the Spanish Conquest*. London, 1961. [1968 P]

Stamp, L. Dudley (ed.). *A History of Land Use in Arid Regions: Arid Zone Research XVII*. UNESCO, 1961.

Steel, F. A., and Gardiner, G. *The Complete Indian Housekeeper and Cook*. London, 1888 [1917].

Stobart, Tom. *Herbs, Spices and Flavorings*. London, 1970. (History, chemistry, and gastronomy. Both entertaining and erudite.)

Storck, John, and Teague, Walter Dorwin. *Flour for Man's Bread: A History of Milling*. St. Paul, Minnesota, 1952.

Stouff, Louis. *Ravitaillement et alimentation en Provence aux XIVe et XVe siècles*, Paris, 1970.

Stuyvenberg, J. H. Van (ed.). *Margarine: An Economic, Social and Scientific History, 1869–1969*. Liverpool, 1969.

T. de L. [Terrien de Lacouperie]. "Ketchup, Catchup, Catsup," in the *Babylonian and Oriental Record*, Vol. III, 12, November 1889. And "The Etymology of Ketchup," in Vol. IV, 3, February 1890.

Taillevent [Tire, Guillaume]. *Le Viandier* [c. 1375]. Edited by Jérome Pichon and Georges Vicaire. Paris, 1892.

Technology and Scientific Development: A "Scientific American" Book. New York, 1963.

Theophrastus. *History of Plants.* Edited by A. F. Hort. 2 vols. London, 1916.

Thomas, W. J. (ed.). *Man's Role in Changing the Face of the Earth.* Chicago, 1956. (An international symposium.)

Torbrügge, Walter. *Prehistoric European Art.* New York, 1969.

Trevor-Roper, Hugh. *The Rise of Christian Europe.* London and New York, 1965.

Ucko, Peter J., and Dimbleby, G. W. (eds.). *The Domestication and Exploitation of Plants and Animals.* London, 1969. (Papers given at a symposium, some highly technical, others more general.)

Upanishads [c. 8th century B.C.]. Translated in "Sacred Books of the East" series, ed. Friedrich Max-Müller, Vol. I, 15, 1 and 2. Oxford, 1879–1884.

Vaillant, George C. *The Aztecs of Mexico.* New York, 1944 [1956 P].

Vallentine, H. R. *Water in the Service of Man.* Harmondsworth, 1967.

Vavilov, N. I. "Studies on the Origin of Cultivated Plants," *Bulletin of Applied Botany,* Vol. XVI, 2 (1926), pp. 139–248.

Veen, J. Van. *Dredge, Drain, Reclaim: The Art of a Nation.* The Hague, 1962.

Verlinden, C. *L'Esclavage dans l'Europe mediévale.* 2 vols. Bruges, 1955.

Vicaire, Georges. *Bibliographie gastronomique.* Paris, 1890.

Vicens Vives, Jaime. *An Economic History of Spain.* Princeton, 1969.

Villena, Don Enrique de. *Arte Cisoria* [1423]. Madrid, 1967. (Food and manners in the seigneurial household.)

Vogt, Joseph. *The Decline of Rome: The Metamorphosis of Ancient Civilisation.* London, 1967; New York, 1970. (From the viewpoint of the Germanic tribes.)

Vries, Arnold de. *Primitive Man and His Food.* Chicago, 1962. (Mainly travelers' accounts of primitive tribes during the last three centuries.)

Waley, Daniel. *The Italian City Republics.* London and New York, 1969.

Walford, Cornelius. *The Famines of the World: Past and Present.* London, 1879. (Tabulated accounts of dates and causes.)

Wallman, Sandra. *Take Out Hunger: Two Case Studies of Rural Development in Basutoland.* London, 1969.

Ward, Barbara, and Dubos, René. *Only One Earth: The Care and Maintenance of a Small Planet.* London, 1972.

Warner, Richard. *Antiquitates Culinariae.* London, 1791.

Watson, William. *China Before the Han Dynasty.* London, 1961.

Watteville, H. de. *The British Soldier: His Daily Life from Tudor to Modern Times.* London, 1954.

Weatherwax, P. "History and Origin of Corn," in *Corn and Corn Improvement*. New York, 1955.

Weiss, Harry B. *The History of Applejack or Apple Brandy in New Jersey from Colonial Times to the Present*. Trenton, 1954.

Weiss, R. *The Renaissance Discovery of Classical Antiquity*. Oxford, 1969.

White, Kenneth D. *Roman Farming*. London, 1970.

White, Lynn, Jr. *Medieval Technology and Social Change*. Oxford, 1962. [1966]

Willett, Frank. "The Introduction of Maize into West Africa: An Assessment of Recent Evidence," *Africa*, Vol. XXXII, (1962), pp. 1–13.

Willey, Gordon E. *Introduction to American Archeology*, Vol. I. Englewood Cliffs, New Jersey, 1966. (Massive survey of the present state of knowledge on the prehistory of North and Central America.)

Woodforde, John. *The Strange Story of False Teeth*. London, 1968; New York, 1970.

Woodham-Smith, Cecil. *The Great Hunger, Ireland 1845–49*. London, 1962; New York, 1973.

Wright, Lawrence. *Home Fires Burning: The History of Domestic Heating and Cooking*. London, 1964.

Young, Arthur. *Travels in France during the Years 1787, 1788 and 1789*. 2 vols. Bury St. Edmunds, 1792–94.

Younger, William. *Gods, Men, and Wine*, London, 1966.

Yule, Sir Henry [1] (ed. and tr.). *Cathay and the Way Thither*. 4 vols. Hakluyt Society Second Series, Vols. 33, 37, 38, 41. London, 1913–1916. (The travels of Odoric de Pordenone, Vol. II; Ibn Batuta and Benedict Goes, Vol. IV.)

Yule, Sir Henry [2], and Burrell, A. C. (compilers). *Hobson-Jobson: A Glossary of Colloquial Anglo-Indian Words and Phrases, and of Kindred Terms, Etymological, Historical, Geographical and Discursive*. London, 1886. [1903]

Zeuner, F. E. *A History of Domesticated Animals*. London, 1963; New York, 1964. (The standard work on the history of the various animals that have at any time been the subject of domestication.)

Illustrations
and Sources

The present location or source of the illustrations is shown in italics at the end of each entry, followed—where relevant—by departmental or publication references. The author and publishers gratefully acknowledge the permission to reproduce granted by the galleries and collections concerned.

116 Monastery, with fish pond. From a Latin manuscript of c. A.D. 1000. *Staatliche Bibliothek,* Bamberg. MS Patr. 61.

117 Medieval farmworker. Early-fourteenth-century illumination in the *Ormesby Psalter. Bodleian Library,* Oxford. MS Douce 366, fol. 89.

125 Sugar merchant, 1350-1400. From a *Tacuinum sanitatis* manuscript, illuminated in Lombardy. *Bibliothèque Nationale,* Paris. MS lat. nouv. acq. 1673, fol. 81.

128 Head of a Central Asian nomad modeled in stucco, c. A.D. 500. Found at Hadda, near Jallalabad. *Musée Guimet,* Paris.

129 Scroll drawing, ink on paper, of a sheep and goat. By the Sung artist Chao Mêng-fu (1254-1322), who joined the Mongol court at Peking c. 1286. *Courtesy of the Smithsonian Institution, Freer Gallery of Art,* Washington, D.C. Freer Gallery 31.4.

133 Chertomlyk Vase, made in electrum (an alloy of gold and silver) in the fourth century B.C., possibly by a Greek craftsman. *Hermitage Museum,* Leningrad.

135 "Mangu Khan's magic fountain." From Pierre Bergeron, *Voyages faits principalement en Asie.* The Hague, 1735.

141 Hunting, and threshing grain. After a rubbing from a tomb tile of the Later Han Dynasty (A.D. 25-220) found at Ch'eng-tu, Szechwan. *Private collection, Ch'eng-tu.*

143 Chinese plate, painted pottery. Han Dynasty (206 B.C.-A.D. 220). *William Rockhill Nelson Gallery of Art,* Kansas City, Missouri. 34-218.

147 Steppe caravan entering and leaving a fortified enclosure. Wall painting in cave 296, Tunhuang, c. A.D. 600. Photo: Dominique Darbois.

149 Cooking over a brazier. From a manuscript of Chao Lin. Fourteenth-century copy of a seventh-century painting. *Collection C. A. Drenowatz,* Zürich. Photo: Hinz SWB, Basel.

151 "The Sweetmeat Vendor," by the twelfth-century artist Su Han-Ch'en. *By courtesy of the Museum of Fine Arts, Boston. Bequest of Charles B. Hoyt.*

156 Krishna Govardhana relief in the Five Pandavas Cave, Mamallapuram. Seventh century A.D. Photo: Arpad Elfer, London.

.159 Seller of curds in an Indian market. Detail of the wall painting known as "The Wheel of Samsara" in cave XVII, Ajanta. Seventh century A.D.

162 Eating outdoors. Detail from a page of the second book (Ayodhya-Kanda) of the *Ramayana,* illuminated in 1650. *By courtesy of the Trustees of the British Museum,* London. Oriental MSS Add. 15 296, fol. 71r.

167 Honey gatherer. After a rock painting of the Upper Paleolithic period at Cueva de la Araña, Bicorp, Valencia.

171 Camel slaughter. From a manuscript of al-Hariri. *Bibliothèque Nationale,* Paris. MS ar. 5847, fol. 140.

173 Abu Zaid feasting on roast kid and white bread. From a manuscript of al-Hariri. *Oesterreichisches Nationalbibliothek,* Vienna. MS A.F.9, fol.6v.

173 Arabic tavern. From a manuscript of al-Hariri. *Bibliothèque Nationale,* Paris. MS ar. 5847, fol. 33.

176 Fat-tailed sheep. After an engraving in Rudolf the Elder, *New History of Ethiopia,* London, 1682.

177 Galen, with Arab peasants working in the fields. From the *Book of Antidotes* of the pseudo-Galen, A.D. 1199. *Bibliothèque Nationale,* Paris. MS ar. 2964, fol. 22.

180 Paolo Morando, "The Virgin and Child, St. John the Baptist, and an Angel." *By courtesy of the Trustees of the National Gallery,* London.

188 The square of St. Mark's, Venice. From the *Description ou traicté du gouvernment et Regyme de la Cyté et Seigneurie de Venise,* a fifteenth-century manuscript. *Musée Condé,* Chantilly. MS 1344 fol.4v.

191 Scratch plow. From a copy of the ninth-century *Utrecht Psalter* made c. A.D. 1000. *By courtesy of the Trustees of the British Museum,* London. Manuscripts Harley MS 603 fol.54v.

192 Moldboard plow. From the *Luttrell Psalter,* English, c. 1340. *By courtesy of the Trustees of the British Museum,* London. Manuscripts Add. MS 42130 fol.170.

193 Gathering beans. From a *Tacuinum sanitatis* illuminated in Lombardy, 1350-1400. *Bibliothèque Nationale,* Paris. MS lat. nouv. acq. 1673 fol. 44.

196 Market in a small town in northern France or Flanders, c. 1460. From Brunetto Latini, *Le Trésor*, "Dame Philosophie." *Bibliothèque Universitaire de Génève*, Switzerland. MS franç. 160 fol.82.

197 Grace Churche Market. Line and wash drawing from Hugh Alley, *A Caveatt for the City of London, or a Forewarning of Offences against Penal Laws*. 1598. *Folger Shakespeare Library*, Washington, D.C.

199 Wine gauger. From the *Ordonnances de la Prévoste des Marchans et Eschevinaige de la Ville de Paris, 1415*. Edition dated 1500. *Bibliothèque Nationale*, Paris. Imprimés.

200 Punishment of a defaulting baker. Marginal drawing from the *Assisa Panis*, 1266. By courtesy of the Corporation of London.

202 Baking. The month of December from the *Kalendrier des Bergères* engraved by Pierre le Rouge, 1499. *Bibliothèque Nationale*, Paris. Imprimés Reserve V.1266.

205 Great Khan distributing grain in time of famine. From the late-fourteenth-century manuscript known as the *Livre des Merveilles*. *Bibliothèque Nationale*, Paris. MS fr. 2810 fol.137v.

207 Sheepfold. From the *Luttrell Psalter*, English, c. 1340. By courtesy of the Trustees of the British Museum, London. Manuscripts Add. MS 42130 fol. 163v.

210 Autumn slaughter. Detail from a German/Alsatian tapestry altar cloth, fifteenth century, showing the labors of the seasons. *Victoria and Albert Museum*, London. Tapestries 6-1867.

211 Repacking salt herring. From the *Album* of the Prague New Town herring market, 1619. *Archives of the City of Prague*. Photo: Petr Paul, Prague.

213 Chinese brine borehole. After a rubbing from a stamped brick of the Han period (206 B.C.-A.D. 220), from Tse-liu Ching in Szechwan.

217 "Intestina i busecha." From a *Tacuinum sanitatis* illuminated in Lombardy, 1350-1400. *Oesterreichisches Nationalbibliothek*, Vienna. MS ser. nov. 2.644 fol. 81.

220 A Flemish kitchen, 1339-44. *Bodleian Library*, Oxford. Western MSS, MS Bodl. 264 fol. 170v.

223 Cinnamon harvest in Borneo. From André Thevet, *La Cosmographie Universelle*, Vol. 1. Paris 1575. By courtesy of the Trustees of the British Museum, London. Reading Room 568 h 3.

224 David Teniers the Younger, "The kitchen of the Archduke Leopold William," detail. *Mauritshuis*, the Hague. Photo: A. Dingjan, the Hague.

225 Detail from a panel by an unknown artist, sixteenth century, showing a banquet given by Sir Henry Unton. *National Portrait Gallery*, London. No. 710.

228 Banquet scene from a fifteenth-century Flemish manuscript. *Bodleian Library*, Oxford. Western MSS, MS Douce 374 fol. 17.

230 Banquet scene from the *Floreffe Bible*, Belgian, c. 1160. By courtesy of the Trustees of the British Museum, London. Manuscripts Add. MS 17738 Vol. 2, fol.3v.

232 End of a meal. From Christoforo de Messi Sbugo, *Banchetti compositioni de vivande, et apparecchio generale*. Ferrara 1549. By courtesy of the Trustees of the British Museum, London. Reading Room G 2369.

233 "Scientific researches!—New Discoveries in PNEUMATICKS!—or—an Experimental Lecture on the Powers of Air—" Color aquatint by James Gillray, publ. May 23, 1802. By courtesy of the Trustees of the British Museum, London. Print Room Catalogue of Personal and Political Satires, Vol. 8, 9923.

240 Persian miniature of pepper preparation. *Bibliothèque Nationale*, Paris. MS suppl. persan 332 fol. 156.

242 The captain's table aboard the East Indiaman *Clyde* in a heavy swell. Early nineteenth-century aquatint. *National Maritime Museum*, Greenwich.

245 Preparing cassava bread in the Lesser Antilles. From J. B. du Tertre, *Histoire générale des Antilles*, Vol. 2. Paris, 1667. *Bibliothèque Nationale*, Paris.

247 Giuseppe Arcimboldo, "Summer." *Kunsthistorisches Museum*, Vienna. No. 1589.

249 Making tortillas, Mexico, c. 1550. From the *Codex Mendoza* manu-

251 script. *Bodleian Library,* Oxford. Fol. 60.

251 Mexican Indians cultivating a walled garden. From the *Codex Osuna* manuscript, 1565. *Biblioteca Nacional,* Madrid. Doc. VII, fol.500/ 38v.

253 Turkey, Mexico, c. 1550. From the *Codex Mendoza* manuscript. *Bodleian Library,* Oxford. Fol. 16.

253 Jost Amman engraving of a turkey, in Marx Rumpolt, *Ein New Kochbuch.* Frankfurt a/M, 1604. *By courtesy of the Trustees of the British Museum,* London. Reading Room fol. 788 e. 15.

257 Potato cultivation in Peru. From an illustrated Peruvian codex, in F. G. Poma de Ayala, *Neuva coronica y buen gobierno.* Paris, 1936.

257 Botanical illustration of the potato plant. From C. Bauhinus, *Prodromus theatri botanici.* Zürich, 1620.

260 Sugar processing in Brazil. "Brasilise Suykerwerken," from Simon de Vries, *Curieuse Aenmerckingen Der bysonderste Oost en West-Indische Verwonderens-waerdige Dingen,* Utrecht, 1682. *By courtesy of the Trustees of the British Museum,* London. Reading Room 566.e.12.

261 Slave transport in the 1820s. From Rev. R. Walsh, *Notices of Brazil in 1828 and 1829,* Vol. 2, London, 1830.

262 The North American Indian town of Secoton, water color by John White during the 1580s. *By courtesy of the Trustees of the British Museum,* London. Print Room 1906.5.9.1(7).

266 "Comment les sauvages rotissent leurs ennemis." From André Thevet, *La Cosmographie Universelle,* Vol. 2, Paris, 1575. *By courtesy of the Trustees of the British Museum,* London. Reading Room 568 h 4.

269 Two British officers, Moorcroft and Hearsey, in Indian disguise, encounter Tibetan traders on the road to Lake Mansarowar, Tibet. Drawing by Captain Hyder Hearsey, 1812. *Foreign and Commonwealth Office,* London. India Office Library WD 350.

274 "La Cantinière." Engraving by Charles Parrocel (1688-1752). *Bibliothèque Nationale.* Paris. Estampes.

278 An Italian kitchen. Engraving by Giacomo Valesio (1548-87). *By cour-tesy of the Trustees of the British Museum,* London. Print Room Italian Engravings 54ˣ G. G. Valegio 1877.8.11.1053.

282 Detail from an engraving of a sixteenth-century Italian kitchen in the *Opera di M. Bartolomeo Scappi: Cuoco Secreto di Papa Pio Quinto.* Venice, 1570. *By courtesy of the Trustees of the British Museum,* London. Reading Room 1037 h.4.

284 Detail from "Le Repas de la Grande Mademoiselle au Luxembourg," engraved by Jean le Pautre (1618-82). *Bibliothèque Nationale,* Paris. Estampes.

285 J. F. de Troy, "A Hunt Breakfast." *By courtesy of the Trustees of the Wallace Collection,* London. P 463.

286 The market of La Halle, Paris, in 1779, by Nicolas Bernard Lépicié. *Collection Marquis de Ganay,* Paris. Photo: Royal Academy of Arts, London.

288 Chocolate and the American Indian. From Philippe Sylvestre Dufour, *Traitez Nouveaux et curieux du café, du Thé et du Chocolat,* Lyon, 1685.

290 Jan Davidsz de Heem, "Still Life." *By courtesy of the Trustees of the Wallace Collection,* London. P 76.

291 Adriaen Brouwer, "The Pancake Man," c. 1625. *John G. Johnson Collection,* Philadelphia.

292 Pieter Aertsen, "The Butcher's Shop," 1551. *University of Uppsala,* Sweden.

294 Brick still. From Hieronymus Braunschweig, *Buch zu Distillieren.* Strasbourg, 1512.

296 Brazil. "How the Women of the Savages Make Their Drink," from André Thevet, *Las Cosmographie Universelle,* Vol. 2, Paris, 1575. *By courtesy of the Trustees of the British Museum,* London. Reading Room 568 h 4.

297 Wall panel from Moses Marcy House, Southbridge. *Old Sturbridge Village,* Massachusetts.

299 Edward Hicks, "An Indian summer view of the Farm and Stock of James C. Cornell of Northampton Bucks county Pennsylvania. That took the Premium in the Agricultural Society: October the 12, 1848. Painted by E. Hicks in the 69th year of his age." *National Gallery of Art, Washington, D.C. Gift of*

300 *Edgar William and Bernice Chrysler Garbisch.*

300 Fruit, vegetables, and waffles. Engraving, sixteenth century, by J. Maetham. *By courtesy of the Trustees of the British Museum,* London. Print Room Catalogue J. Maetham, Vol. 2, B.167.

302 Mexican butcher. From Claudio Linati, *Costumes civils, militaires et religieux du Mexique,* Brussels, 1828.

303 Areca nut. From Jacobus, *Neuw Kreuterbuch,* Frankfurt am-Main, 1613.

303 The god Krishna offered betel quids. Painting in Basohli style, c. 1710. *By courtesy of the Trustees of the British Museum,* London. Print Room, Oriental 1955-10-8-069.

308 Drying tea leaves. Monochrome drawing, Chinese, early seventeenth century. *By courtesy of the Trustees of the British Museum,* London. Print Room, Oriental Folder 15 Or.9 1878-11-9-159.

308 Tea tasting. Chinese water color. *Victoria and Albert Museum,* London. D.1090-1898.

309 Carved and painted wooden shuttle, nineteenth century. *Historical Museum,* Moscow.

311 Great feast at Hastinapur. Illustration, by the artists Daswant and Bhora, of an episode in the fourteenth book of the *Mahabharata,* in a manuscript of the Persian abridgment (the *Razm Namah*) possibly produced for the Mogul emperor Akbar in the last decade of the sixteenth century. Reproduced from Thomas H. Hendley, *Memorials of the Jeypore Exhibition,* 1883, Vol. IV. London, 1885. *By courtesy of the Trustees of the British Museum,* London. Reading Room K.T.C. 29 b.1.

313 Cooking kebabs. Detail from a painting in the second book. (Ayodhya-Kanda) of the *Ramayana,* c. 1650. *By courtesy of the Trustees of the British Museum,* London. Oriental MSS Add. 15 296 fol. 71r.

316 An English coffee house, anonymous water color dated 1668. *By courtesy of the Trustees of the British Museum,* London. Print Room IIIa 1931-6-13-2.

324 Lithographed poster, 1886. "Ten Minutes for Refreshments." *The New-York Historical Society,* New York.

327 Map vignette, c. 1730. From Gerard Van Keulen's "Die Nieuwe Groote Lichtende Zee-Fakkel." *By courtesy of the Trustees of the British Museum,* London. Map Room c. 8 d. 6.

329 Factory children. From G. Walker, *The Costume of Yorkshire, Illustrated by a Series of Forty Engravings,* London, 1814. *Victoria and Albert Museum,* London.

330 Jozef Israëls (1824-1911), "The Frugal Meal." *Glasgow Art Gallery and Museum.* 737.

333 Funeral during the Irish potato famine. *Illustrated London News,* February 13, 1847.

336 Kitchen of the Royal Pavilion. From John Nash, *The Royal Pavilion at Brighton,* London, 1827. *By courtesy of the Trustees of the British Museum,* London. Reading Room 557 h. 19.

341 Menu for Boston Light Infantry dinner at Revere House, Boston, on May 19, 1852. *The New-York Historical Society,* New York.

342 Blood-drinking as a specific against "consumption," or tuberculosis, in Paris. *Le Monde Illustré,* 1890.

345 "London Improvements"; adulteration of foodstuffs. Engraved by George Cruikshank for K. Ephemerides, *The Comic Almanack for 1845,* London, 1845. *By courtesy of the Trustees of the British Museum,* London. Reading Room C.58 c.7.

348 London dairy in 1825. Water color by George Scharf the Elder. *By courtesy of the Trustees of the British Museum,* London. Print Room 1862-6-14-120.

350 The McCormick reaper, displayed on the American stand at the Great Exhibition of 1851 at the Crystal Palace, London. From the *Official Descriptive and Illustrated Catalogue of the Great Exhibition,* London, 1851.

351 Steam threshing in France at the end of the nineteenth century. Standard motif from the specimen book of the Parisian type founder Deberny & Cie.

352 "The Clipper *Hurricane,*" built by Isaac C. Smith of Hoboken, New Jersey, and painted by Skillet. *Peabody Museum of Salem,* Massachusetts.

355 Trade sign for "Ye Boston Baked Beans," oil painting, 1886, by H.

E. Covill. *The New York Historical Society,* New York. 1937. 459.

358 The ice-making pits at Allahabad, 1828. From Mrs. Fanny Parkes, *Wanderings of a Pilgrim in Search of the Picturesque,* London, 1852.

359 Patent freezing machine shown at the Great Exhibition of 1851 at the Crystal Palace, London. From the *Official Descriptive and Illustrated Catalogue of the Great Exhibition,* London, 1851.

361 "Chicago, Illinois—the Cattle Market," wood engraving from *Harper's Weekly,* October 31, 1868. *The New-York Historical Society,* New York.

361 Lithograph showing a buffalo shoot in the 1870s. *Bibliothèque Nationale,* Paris.

367 Cooking stoves and fireplaces, advertisement in Robert Brindley, *Plymouth, Devonport, and Stonehouse Directory,* 1830.

369 Gustave Doré engraving of Paris besieged in 1871. *Radio Times Hulton Picture Library,* London.

371 The baked-potato man, daguerreotype by Beard from Henry Mayhew, *London Labour and the London Poor,* London, 1861.

376 The teaching laboratory established by Carl Justus von Liebig in 1842. *Deutsches Museum,* Munich.

381 Chinese eating with chopsticks, 1637. From Peter Mundy's *Travels. Bodleian Library,* Oxford. Rawlinson MS A.315.

381 Making *chapatis,* mid-nineteenth century. From a volume of drawings, "Illustrations of the Various Trades in Kashmir." *Foreign and Commonwealth Office,* London. India Office Library Add. Or. 1681.

385 Rabbit-proof fencing. *Australian News and Information Bureau,* London.

396 Beef-flavored granules of spun soy protein made into a "meat" loaf. *General Mills, Inc.,* Minneapolis.

396 Rembrandt, "The Carcass of an Ox," c. 1640. *Glasgow Art Gallery and Museum.* 600.

396 Protein analogue, spun from soybeans. *General Mills, Inc.,* Minneapolis.

TEXT ACKNOWLEDGMENTS

The author and publisher are grateful to the following for permission to quote extracts from copyright works:

George Allen and Unwin Ltd., for Arthur Waley's translations of the *Analects of Confucius* and *The Book of Songs (Shih ching)*; Clarendon Press, for "The Summons of the Soul" in David Hawkes' translation of the *Ch'u Tz'u: The Songs of the South*; Mrs. Anna Evans, for Professor A. J. Arberry's "A Baghdad Cookery-Book"; Miss Elizabeth Rosenbaum, for *The Roman Cookery Book* by Barbara Flower and Elizabeth Rosenbaum, published by George G. Harrap and Co. Ltd.; Rupert Hart-Davis Ltd., for *Tibetan Marches* by André Migot; Loeb Classical Library (Harvard University Press: William Heinemann), for *The Deipnosophists* of Athenaeus and the *Natural History* of Pliny the Elder; Methuen and Co. Ltd. and Random House, Inc., for *My Voyage Around the World* by Francesco Carletti; Penguin Books Ltd., for E. R. A. Sewter's translation of *The Alexiad of Anna Comnena,* Aubrey de Selincourt's translation of *The Histories* of Herodotus, E. V. Rieu's translation of *The Iliad* of Homer, and Ronald Latham's translation of *The Travels of Marco Polo.*

Notes on Sources

Where an abbreviated reference is given below, full details of the work referred to will be found in the Bibliography. Periodical articles and books which are of too marginal relevance to be included in the Bibliography are given in full in the notes.

PART ONE:
THE PREHISTORIC WORLD

INTRODUCTION
The Course of Prehistory
1. A. C. Wilson and V. M. Sarich, in *Proceedings of the Academy of Sciences of the United States,* Vol. LXIII (1969), p. 1088.
2. Watson, p. 23.
3. Brothwell, p. 24.
4. *Arctic and Alpine Research,* Vol. I (1969), p. 1; and Zeuner, fig. 1:3, p. 18.
5. F. Ivanhoe, in *Nature,* Aug. 8, 1970, pp. 227, 577.
6. D. J. M. Wright, in *Nature,* Feb. 5, 1971, pp. 229, 409.
7. Kent V. Flannery, in Ucko and Dimbleby, p. 79.
8. *Ibid.,* pp. 89–91.

9. Edward S. Deevey, "The Human Population," *Scientific American,* Vol. CCIII (1960), pp. 194–204.

1. *Food and Cooking Before 10,000 B.C.*
1. Coles and Higgs, p. 233.
2. *Ibid.,* p. 71.
3. Frank Hole and Kent V. Flannery, in *Proceedings of the Prehistoric Society,* February, 1968.
4. Coles and Higgs, p. 273.
5. Raglan, cited in Darlington, p. 33, and *Sunday Times* (London), April 16, 1972.
6. Singer [2], Vol. I, p. 452.
7. Willey, p. 48.
8. *Arctic and Alpine Research.* See note 4, Intro., above.
9. Quoted in Brothwell, p. 87.

10. Kent V. Flannery, in Ucko and Dimbleby, p. 78.
11. Coon, p. 63.
12. Coles and Higgs, p. 296.
13. In Daumas, Vol. I, p. 43.
14. Henry Walter Bates, *The Naturalist on the River Amazons*, 2 vols. (London, 1863).
15. Willey, pp. 81–82.
16. Vries, p. 29.
17. Herodotus, IV, 60.
18. Francis Galton, *The Art of Travel* (London, 1860), p. 4.
19. Derry and Williams, p. 84.
20. Zeuner, pp. 112–128.
21. E. S. Higgs and M. R. Jarman, in *Antiquity*, March, 1969.

2. *Changing the Face of the Earth*
1. Reported in *Time*, Feb. 9, 1970, and in Wilhelm G. Solheim II in *Scientific American*, April, 1972, 34–41.
2. Halet Cambel and Robert J. Braidwood in *Scientific American*, Vol. CCXXII (1970), pp. 50–56.
3. Kent V. Flannery, in Ucko and Dimbleby, p. 79.
4. J. R. Harlan, in *Archaeology*, Vol. XX (1967), pp. 197–201.
5. B. A. Renfrew, in Ucko and Dimbleby, p. 150.
6. Charles A. Reed, in Ucko and Dimbleby, p. 362.
7. W. Wendorf, R. Said, and R. Schild, in *Science*, Vol. CLXIX (Sept. 18, 1970), p. 1161.
8. Charles A. Reed, in Ucko and Dimbleby, p. 362.
9. *Ibid.*

10. André Migot, *Tibetan Marches* (London, 1955), Harmondsworth, 1957 edn., p. 100.
11. Higgs and Jarman. See note 21, Chap. 1, above.
12. Reed, in Ucko and Dimbleby, p. 361.
13. Dexter Perkins in *Science*, Apr. 11, 1969.
14. Zeuner, pp. 201–40.
15. J. G. Hawkes, in Ucko and Dimbleby, p. 25.
16. Flannery, in Ucko and Dimbleby, pp. 89–91.
17. Quoted in Hooke, p. 39.
18. Wendorf *et al.* See note 7 this chapter.
19. Pliny the Elder, XVIII, xlvii.
20. Oliver and Fage, p. 26.
21. *Ibid.*, p. 37.
22. Harrison *et al.*, p. 120.
23. Willey, p. 82.
24. *Science*, Jan. 5, 1973, and Mason, p. 31.
25. Brothwell, pp. 60–61.
26. *Ibid.*, p. 72.
27. *Ibid.*, pp. 68–69.
28. Vaillant, pl. 2 caption.
29. Allchin, p. 83.
30. *Time* and *Scientific American*. See note 1, this chapter.
31. Malik, pp. 96–99.
32. Reported in *The Times* (London), Sept. 1, 1970, and Dec. 11, 1972.
33. Watson, p. 36.
34. *Ibid.*, p. 39.
35. William Watson, in Ucko and Dimbleby, p. 397.
36. Needham [1], Vol. IV, 2, p. 182.
37. *Time*. See note 1, this chapter.
38. William Watson, in Ucko and Dimbleby, p. 393.
39. Pan Ku, pp. 434–35.

PART TWO:
THE NEAR EAST, EGYPT, AND
EUROPE, 3000 B.C.–A.D. 1000

INTRODUCTION
The Background
1. Balsdon, pp. 226–227.
2. Miller, p. 143.
3. *Ibid.*, p. 201.
4. *Silappadikaram*, quoted in Miller, p. 25.
5. Simkin, p. 23.
6. Miller, p. 123.
7. Simkin, p. 45.
8. Lévy, p. 89.

3. *The First Civilizations*
1. Bernal, Vol. I, p. 93.
2. Quoted in Kramer, p. 341.
3. Posener, p. 40.
4. Saggs, p. 61.
5. Kramer, p. 110.
6. *Ur Excavations*, Vol. III (1947), p. 248.
7. Kramer, p. 110.
8. Herodotus, III, 113.
9. Zeuner, p. 190.
10. Hermann Kees, *Ancient Egypt: a Cultural Topography* (London, 1961).
11. Singer [2], Vol. I, p. 279.
12. Kramer, pp. 110–111.
13. A. Wiedemann, *Das alte Aegypten* (Heidelberg, 1920), p. 299.
14. Singer [2], Vol. I, p. 278.
15. Saggs, p. 137.
16. Quoted in Isaac Myer, *Oldest Books in the World* (London, 1900), p. 132.
17. *Ibid.*, p. 134.
18. Athenaeus, I, 34.
19. Xenophon, *Anabasis* [early 4th century B.C.], translated by Rex Warner as *The Persian Expedition* (Harmondsworth, 1949), II, 3.

20. *Ibid.*
21. Columella, VII, 10.
22. Athenaeus, XIV, 652.
23. *Ibid.*, 653.
24. Needham [1], Vol. IV, 2, p. 181.
25. Pliny the Elder, XVIII, xxvi.
26. M. A. Ruffer, "Abnormalities of Ancient Egyptian Teeth," *Studies in the Paleopathology of Egypt* (Chicago, 1921), pp. 288 f.
27. Posener, p. 32.
28. Emery, p. 243.
29. Herodotus, II, 77.
30. Quoted in Singer [2], Vol. 1, p. 264.

4. *The Food of Classical Greece*
1. Athenaeus, I, 12.
2. *Ibid.*, 9.
3. Homer, IX.
4. Burns, pp. 63–64.
5. *Ibid.*, p. 98.
6. Quoted in Coon, p. 293.
7. Joseph Alsop, *From the Silent Earth* (New York, 1964), Harmondsworth, 1970 edn., p. 87.
8. Lichine, p. 204.
9. *Ibid.*, p. 205.
10. Hyams, p. 105.
11. *Ibid.*, pp. 101–104.
12. Derry and Williams, p. 61.
13. Quoted in H. D. F. Kitto, *The Greeks* (Harmondsworth, 1957 edn.), p. 33.
14. Moritz, p. 150.
15. Pliny the Elder, XVIII, xiv–xv.
16. Devambez *et al.*, p. 397.
17. Suetonius, *The Twelve Caesars*, translated by Robert Graves (Harmondsworth, 1957), Vitellius xiii.
18. Athanaeus, VI, 268.
19. *Ibid.*, XII, 518.
20. *Ibid.*, VII, 278.

21. *Ibid.*
22. Zeuner, p. 450.
23. Athenaeus, IV, 132.
24. *Ibid.*, II, 55.

5. *Imperial Rome*
1. Marcus Cornelius Fronto, edited by S. A. Naber (London, 1867), p. 210.
2. Juvenal, *The Sixteen Satires*, translated by Peter Green (Harmondsworth, 1968), X, 77–81.
3. F. R. Cowell, *The Revolutions of Ancient Rome* (London, 1962), pp. 96–97.
4. Carcopino, pp. 28–29.
5. *Ibid.*, p. 29.
6. *Ibid.*
7. Lévy, p. 96.
8. Mossé, pp. 108–110.
9. Lévy, p. 96.
10. Quoted in Hyams, p. 342.
11. Carcopino, pp. 28–29.
12. Mossé, pp. 108–110.
13. Tacitus, *The Histories*, translated by Kenneth Wellesley (Harmondsworth, 1964), IV, 38.
14. Rickman, p. 189.
15. Moritz, pp. 25–27.
16. *Ibid.*, p. 135.
17. *Ibid.*, p. 139.
18. Athenaeus, III, 115.
19. *Ibid.*
20. *Ibid.*, III, 110–114.
21. *Ibid.*, IV, 131.
22. Carcopino, p. 30.
23. Martial, *Epigrams* (London, 1904), VII, 61.
24. Juvenal, II, 66–74. See note 2, this chapter.
25. Petronius, *The Satyricon*, translated by William Arrowsmith (New York, 1960), pp. 42–76.
26. Balsdon, p. 37.

27. Suetonius, Vitellius xiii. See note 17, chap. 4 above.
28. Lévy, p. 72.
29. Apicius, VII, v, 4.
30. Athenaeus, I, 7.
31. Petronius, p. 72. See note 25, this chapter.
32. *Geoponica*, XX, 46. Quoted in introduction to Apicius, p. 22.
33. *Ibid.*
34. Bardach, p. 139.
35. Vries, p. 29.
36. Athenaeus, III, 100.
37. *Ibid.*, II, 67.
38. *Ibid.*
39. Miller, p. 158.
40. Herodotus, III, 111.
41. *Ibid.*, 108–110.
42. *Periplus of the Erythraean Sea*, translated by W. H. Schoff (New York, 1912), s. 65.
43. Miller, pp. 82–83.
44. Athenaeus, III, 66.
45. Miller, p. 26.
46. *Ibid.*, p. 201.
47. Carcopino, p. 23.
48. Reported in *Time*, Sept. 23, 1966.

6. *The Silent Centuries*
1. Quoted in Edwardes [2], p. 42.
2. Vicens Vives, p. 84.
3. Lynn White, p. 39.
4. Postan, in Barraclough, p. 143.
5. Derry and Williams, p. 172.
6. [Einhard] Eginhard, *Early Lives of Charlemagne*, edited by A. J. Grant (London, 1907), p. 38.
7. *Ibid.*, p. 39.
8. Ashley, pp. 16–20.
9. Best, p. 104.
10. Cited in Duby [1], p. 9.
11. *Ibid.*
12. Einhard, p. 79. See note 6, this chapter.

13. Fagniez, docs. xxix, xxx.
14. Crisp. Vol. I, p. 95.
15. Quoted in Duby [1], p. 365.
16. Zeuner, p. 412.
17. Carefoot and Sprott, p. 24.
18. *Ibid.*, pp. 30–31.
19. Walford, p. 6.
20. Carefoot and Sprott, p. 34.
21. Vicens Vives, p. 108.
22. Quoted in Simkin, p. 173.
23. Gernet, p. 135.

PART THREE:
ASIA UNTIL THE MIDDLE AGES,
AND THE ARAB WORLD

INTRODUCTION
The Influence of the Nomads
1. Karl Jettmar, *Art of the Steppes* (London, 1967), pp. 238–239.
2. Lattimore, pp. 58–61.
3. William of Rubruck, *The Remarkable Travels of William de Rubruquis . . . into Tartary and China, 1253,* in John Pinkerton, *A General Collection of . . . Voyages and Travels* (London, 1808–1814), Vol. VII, p. 28.
4. Simkin, p. 50. Also Jettmar (see note 1, this chapter), pp. 144–145.
5. Grousset, p. 112.
6. *Ibid.*, p. 176.
7. Reuters report, July 27, 1964. of article in *Nedelya* (Moscow).
8. Grousset, p. 236.
9. Allchin, p. 265.
10. Discussed by Saleh Ahmad El-Ali, in Albert H. Hourani and S. M. Stern (eds.), *The Islamic City: a Colloquium* (Oxford, 1970), pp. 93–100.
11. Al-Jahiz, "The Investigation of Commerce," quoted in Lopez and Raymond, pp. 28–29.

7. *Central Asia*
1. Herodotus, IV, 47.
2. Cited in Rice, p. 63.
3. Grousset, pp. 55–56.
4. Fa-hsien, *The Travels of Fa-hsien* [A.D. 399–414], *or Record of the Buddhistic Kingdoms,* translated by H. A. Giles (Cambridge, 1923), p. 2.
5. P. L. Simmonds, p. 100.
6. *Ibid.*
7. Marco Polo, pp. 81–82.
8. Rubruck, p. 49. See note 3, Part Three Intro.
9. Daumas, Vol. I, p. 350.
10. *Yu-yang-tsa-tsu,* quoted in Basil Davidson, p. 121.
11. Michael Psellus, *Chronographia,* translated by E. R. A. Sewter as *Fourteen Byzantine Rulers* (Harmondsworth, 1966), VII, 69.
12. Misson, p. 154.
13. *Ibid.*
14. B. A. L. Cranstone, in Ucko and Dimbleby, pp. 250–262.
15. *Ibid.*
16. *Sunday Times* (London), Nov. 16, 1969.
17. Marco Polo, p. 82.
18. Rubruck, p. 31. See note 3, Part Three Intro.
19. B. A. L. Cranstone, in Ucko and Dimbleby, pp. 250–262.
20. Rubruck, p. 31. See note 3, Part Three Intro.
21. Dr. MacGowan, *Journal of the North China Branch of the Royal Asiatic Society,* New Series VII (1871–1872), pp. 237–240.
22. *Ibid.*

23. Eliza Smith, *The Compleat Housewife* (London, 1727). Also published in Virginia in 1742, under the pseudonym "William Parks."

24. B. C. A. Turner, *The Pan Book of Wine Making* (London, 1965), p. 113.

8. *China*

1. Shi-Shung Huang and E. M. Bayless, in *Science*, Apr. 5, 1968. Also researches at Chiang Mai University, Cambodia, reported in *Nature*, Feb. 22, 1969.

2. Schafer, p. 151.

3. *Ibid.*, p. 168.

4. Chao Ju-kua, II, 19.

5. Needham [2], p. 364.

6. *Shih ching, in* Birch and Keene, pp. 37–38.

7. *Ibid.*, p. 56.

8. Confucius, *The Analects,* translated by Arthur Waley (London, 1938), X, 7–8.

9. *Ibid.*, Introduction, p. 63.

10. Samuel Johnson, *Dictionary* (London, 1755), entry under "Fart."

11. *Li-chi, or Book of Rituals,* translated by James Legge in "Sacred Books of the East" series, edited by Friedrich Max-Müller, Vol. XXVII (Oxford, 1885), p. 467.

12. In Birch and Keene, p. 101.

13. [Lao-tse] Lao-tzu, *Tao te ching,* translated by D. C. Lau (Harmondsworth, 1963), I, xii.

14. Pan Ku, p. 127 n.

15. This point emerges clearly in, for example, the Judge Dee novels, written—on the basis of a wide knowledge of Chinese history and literature—by Rob-

ert van Gulik. Although the stories are set in the T'ang period, Dr. Van Gulik adopted the Ming custom of describing life then as if in the sixteenth century (cf. postscript to *The Chinese Gold Murders*).

16. Yule[2], p. 858.

17. Reported in *Time*, May 9, 1969.

18. Schafer, p. 29.

19. *Ibid.*

20. Sei Shonagon, quoted in Morris, p. 100.

21. Zeuner, pp. 480–482.

22. I-ching, quoted in Schafer, p. 140.

23. Quoted in Needham [2], p. 364.

24. Grousset, p. 171.

25. Schafer, p. 280.

26. Marco Polo, p. 149.

27. *Ibid.*, p. 181.

28. Odoric de Pordenone, in Yule [1], Vol. II, p. 96.

29. Gernet, p. 136.

30. Odoric de Pordenone, in Yule [1], Vol. II, p. 97.

31. Report by directors of the National Palace Museum, Taipei, Taiwan, in *Free China Review,* cited in *Sunday Times* (London), Feb. 16, 1969.

9. *India*

1. Prakash, pp. 15–16.

2. *Ibid.*, p. 18.

3. *Ibid.*, p. 38.

4. Kosambi, pp. 157–158.

5. Field-Marshal Lord Roberts of Kandahar, *Forty-One Years in India, from Subaltern to Commander-in-Chief,* (2 vols. London 1897) 1-vol. edn., London, 1898, p. 241.

6. Kosambi, p. 230.

7. Prakash, pp. 12–15.
8. *Ibid.*, pp. 148–149.
9. Kautilya, II, xxvi, 7–12.
10. Wang Ch'ung, *Lun Hêng,* quoted in Needham [2], p. 364.
11. Chang Chung-ching, *Chin Kuei Yao Lüeh,* in Needham [2], p. 363.
12. Abou-Zeyd-Hassan, in M. Reinaud, *Relation des Voyages faits par les Arabes et les Persans dans l'Inde et à la Chine dans le IXe siècle de l'Ere chrétienne* (Paris, 1845), p. 152.
13. Prakash, p. 158.
14. *Ibid.*, p. 235.
15. *Ibid.*, p. 213.
16. *Ibid.* p. 214.
17. *Ibid.*, pp. 213–214.
18. Basham, p. 505.
19. Kautilya, II, xv, 47.
20. Yule [2], p. 281.
21. Kautilya, II, xv, 17.
22. Schafer, p. 146.
23. E. G. Pulleyblank, "Chinese and Indo-Europeans," *Journal of the Royal Asiatic Society,* (1966), p. 10.
24. Deerr, Vol. I, p. 7 n.
25. Kautilya, II, xv, 16.
26. Strabo, XV, i, 20, quoted in Deerr, Vol. I, p. 63.

10. *The Arab World*
1. Lewis, p. 82.
2. *Ibid.*, pp. 93–97.
3. Quoted in Duckett, p. 171.
4. Quoted in A. J. Arberry, in *Islamic Culture,* 1939, Introduction, p. 22.
5. Daumas, Vol. I, p. 350.
6. A. G. Chejne, "The Boon-Companion in Early 'Abbāsid

Times," in *Journal of the American Oriental Society* (1965), p. 333.
7. Ibn Ishaq, *Life of Muhammad* [c. A.D. 770], expanded by Ibn Isham c. A.D. 820. MS. translation in full by Edward Rehatsek, in the library of the Royal Asiatic Society, London, fol. 1057. (The abbreviated edition published in London in 1964 omits this material.)
8. Arberry, p. 194. See note 4, this chapter.
9. *Ibid.*, p. 27.
10. *Ibid.*, p. 39.
11. *Ibid.*, p. 214.
12. Maxime Rodinson in *Revue des études islamiques,* (1949), p. 151.
13. Bernal, Vol. I, p. 262.
14. Quoted in Needham [2], p. 358.
15. *Brhadaranyaka Upanishad,* VI, iv, 18.
16. J. Lucas-Dubreton, *Daily Life in Florence in the Time of the Medici* (London, 1960), p. 108.
17. Steel and Gardiner, p. 176 n.
18. Drummond and Wilbraham p. 68.
19. *Salerno Regimen.*
20. Quoted in Needham [2], p. 267.
21. In MacGowan. See note 21, chap. 7, above.
22. Prakash, p. 132.
23. Bernal, Vol. I, p. 188.
24. G. Morris Carstairs, *The Twice-Born: A Study of a Community of High-Caste Hindus* (London, 1957), p. 84. Also L. I. and S. H. Rudolf, *The Modernity of Tradition,*

Political Development in India (Chicago, 1967), p. 214.
25. *Salerno Regimen.*

PART FOUR:
EUROPE, A.D. 1000–1500

INTRODUCTION
The Expansion of Europe
1. Anna Comnena, *Alexiad*, translated by E. R. A. Sewter (Harmondsworth, 1969), X, v.
2. Duby [2], pp. 101–102.
3. Elisée Reclus, cited in Mumford, p. 361.
4. Lewis, p. 130.
5. *Ibid.*, p. 123.
6. *Ibid.*, p. 124.
7. Al-Jahiz, p. 58. See note 11, Part Three Intro. above
8. Postan, in Barraclough, p. 157.

11. *Supplying the Towns*
1. Lynn White, p. 53.
2. Cited *ibid.*, p. 54.
3. *Ibid.*, p. 56.
4. *Ibid.*, p. 76.
5. Derry and Williams, p. 195.
6. *Ibid.*, p. 202.
7. E. Belfort Bax, *German Society at the Close of the Middle Ages* (London, 1894), p. 206.
8. 19 Edward III, Letterbook F, fol. cii, ccii. In Riley.
9. 43 Edward III, Letterbook G, fol. ccxxxiii. In Riley.
10. Royal edict of August 1416. In Lespinasse.
11. Athenaeus, VI, 5.
12. 22 Edward III, Letterbook F, fol. clii. In Riley.
13. P. G. Molmenti, *Venice, Its Growth to the Fall of the Republic* (London, 1906–1908), Vol. II, p. 135.

14. Assisa Panis (suppl.), fol. 79v. In Riley.
15. William Fitz Stephen, in F. M. Stenton, *Norman London: An Essay* (London, 1934), p. 28.
16. 2 Richard II, Letterbook H, fol. xcix. In Riley.
17. *Madras Athenaeum*, quoted in P. L. Simmonds, p. 108.
18. Hans Zinsser, *Rats, Lice and History* (New York, 1965 edn.), p. 166.
19. Singer [2], Vol. II, p. 532.
20. W. A. Janssen and C. D. Meyers, in *Science*, Feb. 2, 1968.
21. Ménagier de Paris, p. 241.
22. Cited in Burnett [2], p. 29.
23. Duby [1], p. 66, n. 6.
24. Postan, in Barraclough, p. 162.
25. Duby [1], pp. 149–150.
26. Vicens Vives, pp. 88–89.
27. Sanchez Albornoz, cited in Vicens Vives, p. 131.
28. Vicens Vives, p. 252.
29. "The Chronicle of Giovanni Villani," quoted in Lopez and Raymond, p. 73.
30. Ménagier de Paris, p. 222.
31. Duby [1], p. 145.
32. *Ibid.*, p. 146.
33. Quoted in Drummond and Wilbraham, p. 29.

12. *The Medieval Table*
1. Burnett [2], p. 30.
2. Bridbury, p. 29.
3. Forbes, Vol. III.
4. Quoted *ibid.*, p. 180.
5. Christopher Hibbert, *The Roots of Evil, A Social History of Crime and Punishment* (Harmondsworth, 1966), p. 37.
6. E. E. Power and M. M. Postan,

Studies in English Trade in the Fifteenth Century (London, 1951 edn.), p. 172.
7. Bridbury, p. 8.
8. Quoted in Hibbert, p. 43. See note 5, this chapter.
9. Quoted in Molmenti, Vol. I, i, pp. 14–17. See note 13, chap. 11 above.
10. Lattimore, p. 43.
11. Jawaharlal Nehru, *An Autobiography* (London, 1958 edn.), p. 213.
12. Ménagier de Paris, pp. 272–273.
13. Austin, p. 31.
14. Recipes for variations on all three dishes may be found in Austin and the *Forme of Cury.*
15. Menagier de Paris, *passim.*
16. *Taillevent*, pp. 32–33.
17. *Forme of Cury*, p. 66.
18. Austin, p. 43.
19. Ménagier de Paris.
20. *Ibid.*, p. 228.
21. "Devis et marchés passés par la Ville de Paris pour l'entrée solennelle d'Elisabeth d'Autriche," in *Revue Archéologique* (1848–1849).
22. Gédéon Tallemant, Sieur des Réaux, *Historiettes* [17th century] (Paris, 1834).
23. Henry Havard, *Dictionnaire de l'Ameublement*, 4 vols. (Paris, 1887–1890). See "Fourchette."
24. A late-fourteenth-century representation of a knife and fork, used as a place setting, can be seen in the Greek icon "Hospitality of Abraham" in the Benaki Museum, Athens.
25. *Chy sensuivent les gistes . . . [de] m. J. L. S.*, quoted in Havard. See note 23, this chapter.

26. Thomas Coryat, *Coryat's Crudities: Hastily gobled up in Five Moneth's Travells in France . . .* [1611] (London, 1905), Vol. II.
27. James Morris, *Pax Britannica* (London, 1969), p. 248.
28. Ménagier de Paris.
29. Della Casa, p. 102.
30. Fra Bonvicino, in Furnivall [2].
31. Tannhäuser, in Furnivall [2].
32. Della Casa, in Furnivall [2].
33. Fra Bonvicino, in Furnivall [2].
34. Tannhäuser, in Furnivall [2].
35. Benvenuto Cellini, *Life*, translated by Miss Macdonell (London, 1907), p. 35.
36. Kautilya, V, iv, 9.
37. Suetonius, Claudius xxxii. See note 17, chap. 4 above.
38. Quoted in Chejne, p. 332. See note 6, chap. 10 above.
39. *Salerno Regimen.*
40. Pyke, p. 226.
41. Furnivall [1], p. 136.

PART FIVE:
THE EXPANDING WORLD, 1490–1800

INTRODUCTION
New Worlds and New Foods

1. Michael E. Mallett, *The Florentine Galleys in the Fifteenth Century* (Oxford, 1967), pp. 115–116.
2. T. M. [Thomas Mun], *A Discourse of Trade, from England unto the East-Indies: Answering to diverse Objections which are usually made against the same* [1621], in *East Indian Trade, Selected Works, 17th Century* (London, 1967), p. 11.
3. Quoted in Columbus, p. 47.

4. *Ibid.*, p. 78.
5. *Ibid.*, p. 154.
6. Da Gama's log, quoted in Basil Davidson, pp. 133–134.
7. Quoted in Bax, Appendix A. See note 7, chap. 11, above.
8. Edwardes [1], p. 23.
9. Juan Rodriguez Freile, *El Carnera* [c.1630], translated by William C. Atkinson as *The Conquest of New Granada* (London, 1961), p. 59.
10. Inscription by the Mogul emperor Akbar in 1602 on the Gate of Victory, Fathpur Sikri.

13. *The Americas*
1. Columbus, p. 78.
2. *Ibid.*, p. 80.
3. *Ibid.*
4. *Ibid.*, p. 87.
5. William C. Sturtevant, in Ucko and Dimbleby, pp. 179–193.
6. Columbus, p. 85.
7. *Ibid.*, p. 245.
8. *Ibid.*, p. 86.
9. Ping-ti Ho, *American Anthropologist* (April 1955), pp. 191–201.
10. João dos Santos, quoted in Basil Davidson, p. 162.
11. Barbara Pickersgill, in Ucko and Dimbleby, p. 447.
12. Bernal Díaz del Castillo, *The True History of the Conquest of New Spain*, translated by J. M. Cohen (Harmondsworth, 1963), p. 232.
13. Columbus, p. 83.
14. Fr. Bernardino de Sahagún, *Historia general de la cosas de Nueva España* (Mexico, 1938), Vol. II, p. 372.
15. Yule [2], p. 944.
16. Vicens Vives, p. 386.

17. A. Krapovickas, in Ucko and Dimbleby, p. 434.
18. Juan de Castellanos, quoted in Salaman, p. 102.
19. Salaman, p. 143.
20. *Ibid.*, p. 90.
21. *Ibid.*, pp. 52 ff.
22. *Ibid.*, p. 104.
23. *Ibid.*, p. 106.
24. Rumford, p. 403.
25. Beauvilliers, Vol. I, p. 5, and Vol. II, p. 213.
26. Vicens Vives, p. 214; and Postan, in Barraclough, p. 132.
27. Quoted in H. A. Wyndham, *The Atlantic and Slavery* (London, 1935), p. 221.
28. King Affonso of Congo (Mbemba Nzinga), quoted in Basil Davidson, pp. 194–195.
29. John Ogilby, *America* (London, 1671), pp. 503–505.
30. A. J. R. Russell-Wood, *Fidalgos and Philanthropists: The Santa Casa de Misericordia of Bahia 1550–1755* (London, 1968), pp. 53–54.
31. Oliver and Fage, p. 120.
32. Quoted in McNaught, p. 20.
33. Quoted in Philip L. Barbour (ed.), *The Jamestown Voyages under the First Charter 1606–9* (2 vols., Hakluyt Society, Cambridge, 1969), Vol. II, p. 273.
34. Gabriel Archer, quoted *ibid.*, p. 282.
35. Quoted in Furnas, p. 170.

14. *Food for the Traveler*
1. *Cowley's Voyage Round the Globe*, in Captain William Hacke, A *Collection of Original Voyages* (London, 1699), pp. 7 ff.
2. Columbus, p. 240.

3. Lloyd, p. 256.
4. William Lithgow, *The Totall Discourse of the Rare Adventures and Painefull Peregrinations of long Nineteene Yeares Travayles from Scotland to the most famous Kingdomes in Europe, Asia and Affrica* [London, 1632] (Glasgow, 1906), pp. 58–59.
5. Quoted in Drummond and Wilbraham, p. 138.
6. *True and Large Discourse of the Voyage of the whole Fleete of Ships set forth the 20 of Aprill 1601 by the Governours and Assistants of the East Indian Marchants in London, to the East Indies* [London, 1603], reprinted in *East Indian Trade, Selected Works, 17th century* (London, 1968), p. 6.
7. Drummond and Wilbraham, p. 270.
8. Sir John Richardson, quoted in P. L. Simmonds, p. 15.
9. Frederick Gerstäcker, *Gerstäcker's Travels* (London, 1854), p. 97.

15. A Gastronomic Grand Tour
1. Peter Beckford, *Familiar Letters from Italy to a Friend in England* [pre-1787] (London, 1805), letter XXV.
2. Scappi, p. 392.
3. Prakash, p. 204.
4. Arberry, p. 45. See note 4, chap. 10 above.
5. I. Origo: "The Domestic Enemy. Eastern Slaves in Tuscany in the 14th and 15th centuries," *Speculum*, Vol. XXX (1955).
6. *Forme of Cury*, p. 46.
7. Quoted in Ernest Hatch Wilkins, *A History of Italian Literature* (London, 1954), p. 205.
8. Girolamo Lippomano, *Viaggio* [1577], in M. N. Tommaseo, *Relations des Ambassadeurs Vénitiens sur les Affaires de France au XVIe Siècle* (Paris, 1838), Vol. II, p. 569.
9. *Ibid.*, p. 487.
10. Pliny the Elder, XIX, xi.
11. *The Times* (London), May 18, 1968.
12. William Hazlitt, *Notes of a Journey through France and Italy* (London, 1826), pp. 16–17.
13. Carletti, p. 53.
14. Antonio Colmenero, quoted in Franklin, Vol. XIII, pp: 161–162.
15. Marie de Rabutin-Chantal, Marquise de Sévigné: *Lettres*, edited by Monmerqué et Mesnard, 16 vols. (Paris, 1862–1875), letter of Oct. 25, 1671.
16. Patrick Lamb, *Royal Cookery: or, the Compleat Court-Cook* (London, 1710), p. 41.
17. Joachim von Sandrart, *Der Teutschen Academie* (4 vols., 1675–1679), Vol. II, p. 313.
18. Misson, p. 314.
19. Pehr Kalm, *Kalm's account of his visit to England on his way to America in 1748* (London, 1892), p. 15.
20. Younger, pp. 273–274.
21. Della Casa, in Furnivall [2].
22. E. J. Holmyard, *Alchemy* (Harmondsworth, 1957), p. 51.
23. Only one name among several, equally colorful, quoted in Lichine under "Applejack."
24. Lichine, p. 459.

25. *Ibid.*, p. 397.
26. Lord, p. 45.
27. Quoted in *American Heritage Cookbook*, p. 58.
28. Vicens Vives, p. 395.
29. Gerstäcker, p. 78. See note 9, chap. 14, above.
30. Carletti, p. 46.
31. Thomas Winterbottom, quoted in Basil Davidson, p. 244.
32. A. P. Rice, in *The American Antiquarian*, Vol. XXXII (1910).
33. Mulvaney, p. 55.
34. Anon. [W. C. Hunter], *The "Fan Kwae" at Canton, before Treaty days, 1825-1844, By An Old Resident* (Shanghai, 1911 edn.), pp. 41–42.
35. Needham [1], Vol. IV, 2, p. 58.
36. Carletti, pp. 110–111.
37. Quoted in Yule [1], Vol. II.
38. Quoted in Filby, p. 31.
39. Samuel Pepys, *The Diary and Correspondence of Samuel Pepys Esq. FRS* [1659–1703], edited by Lord Braybrooke (London, 1825), entry for Oct. 25, 1660.
40. F. P. Robinson, p. 127.
41. Arberry, p. 210. See note 4, chap. 10, above.
42. Ovington, quoted in Hilton Brown (ed.), *The Sahibs. The Life and Ways of the British in India as Recorded by Themselves* (London, 1948), p. 50.
43. T. de L. [Terrien de Lacouperie], in the *Babylonian and Oriental Record* (November, 1889), pp. 284–286; (February, 1890), pp. 71–72.
44. John Corneille, *Journal of my Service in India* [1754–1757] (London, 1966), p. 84.
45. Prosper Alpinus, *Historia Ae-gyptiae. Naturalis et Rerum Aegyptiarum Libri*, 3 vols. (1755), Vol. II, p. 36.
46. Yule [2], p. 232.
47. *Ibid.*
48. *Ibid.*
49. Lithgow, p. 136. See note 4, chap. 14, above.
50. Pietro della Valle, *Viaggi* [1614–1626] (Brighton, 1843), Vol. I, pp. 51, 74–76.
51. Thomas Herbert, *Some Yeares Travels into Africa and Asia the Great. Especially Describing the Famous Empires of Persia and Industant.* (London, 1638), p. 241.
52. John Evelyn, *Diary*, May 10, 1637.
53. Carefoot and Sprott, pp. 109–114.
54. Mungo Park, quoted in Basil Davidson, p. 316.
55. *Ibid.*, p. 315.
56. *Ibid.*
57. *Ibid.*, p. 312.
58. John Barrow, quoted in Basil Davidson, pp. 276–277.
59. *Ibid.*, p. 277.

PART SIX:
THE MODERN WORLD, 1800
UNTIL THE PRESENT DAY

INTRODUCTION
Industry, Science, and Food

1. Derry and Williams, p. 278.
2. P. d'A. Jones, p. 91.

16. *The Industrial Revolution*

1. Thomas Blaikie, *The Diary of a Scotch Gardener at the French Court at the end of the eighteenth century*, edited by F. Birrell (London, 1931), p. 74.
2. Derry and Williams, p. 278.

3. Quoted in Elie Halévy, *A History of the English People in 1815* (Harmondsworth edn., 1937), Vol. II, pp. 45–46.
4. F. Bédarida, in Briggs, p. 119.
5. Quoted in J. L. and Barbara Hammond, *The Bleak Age* (West Drayton, 1947), p. 67.
6. Florence Nightingale, "Observations by Miss Nightingale on the Evidence Contained in Stational Returns sent to her by the Royal Commission on the Sanitary State of the Army in India," in The Royal Commission on the Sanitary State of the Army in India: *Report of the Commissioners*, preface to Vol. I (London, 1863).
7. Friedrich Engels, *The Condition of the Working Class in England in 1844* (1845).
8. Drummond and Wilbraham, p. 331.
9. Burnett [1], p. 52.
10. S. R. Bosanquet, *The Rights of the Poor and Christian Almsgiving Vindicated* (London, 1841), p. 91.
11. Salaman, p. 315.
12. Furnas, p. 384.
13. Eliza Smith, pl. 3. See note 23, chap. 7, above.
14. R. H. Gronow, *Reminiscences and Recollections* (2 vols., London, 1892), Vol. I, p. 51.
15. Quoted in full in Roger Fulford, *George the Fourth* (London, 1935), pp. 178–180.
16. Pückler-Muskau, *Tour in England, Ireland, and France . . . in 1829 . . . by a German Prince* (4 vols., London, 1832), Vol. III, pp. 83–87.
17. Hayward, p. 105.
18. Oliver Goldsmith, *The Citizen of the World* (1762), letter LVIII.
19. Hayward, pp. 90–91.
20. Thomas Walker, quoted in Hayward, p. 87.
21. Burnett [1], p. 141.
22. Andrew Wynter, quoted in E. Royston Pike, *Human Documents of the Victorian Golden Age, 1850–1875* (London, 1967), p. 58.
23. *Ibid.*
24. Gerstäcker, p. 61. See note 9, chap. 14, above.
25. Quoted in F. P. Robinson, p. 129.

17. *The Food-Supply Revolution*

1. Andrew Wynter, quoted in Pike, pp. 59–60. See note 24, chap. 16, above.
2. Derry and Williams, p. 680.
3. Quoted in P. d'A. Jones, p. 74.
4. W. M. Hurst and L. M. Church, U.S. Department of Agriculture Misc. Pub. 157 (1933).
5. P. d'A. Jones, p. 186.
6. *Ibid.*
7. Derry and Williams, p. 686.
8. Captain Basil Hall, "Food," in *Encyclopaedia Britannica* (1841).
9. Victor Jacquemont, cited in Philip Woodruff, *The Men Who Ruled India, The Founders* (London, 1953), pp. 234–235.
10. Anon. [Mrs. Fanny Parkes], *Wanderings of a Pilgrim in search of the picturesque* (2 vols., London, 1852), Vol. II, p. 230.
11. Drummond and Wilbraham, p. 322.
12. Wyvern [A. H. C. Kenney-

Herbert], *Culinary Jottings* (Madras, 1891 edn.), p. 340.
13. Drummond and Wilbraham, p. 322.
14. Furnas, p. 690.
15. Lord, p. 43.
16. "The Police-Wallah's Little Dinner," in Aliph Cheem [Walter Yeldham], *Lays of Ind: Comical, satirical and descriptive poems illustrative of English life in India* (Calcutta, 1875).
17. Fanny Parkes, Vol. I, p. 82. See note 10, this chapter.
18. David Lavender, *The American West* (Harmondsworth, 1969 edn.), p. 407.
19. P. d'A. Jones, p. 170.
20. *Ibid.*, p. 169.
21. Sinclair, pp. 189–212.
22. Gerstäcker, p. 48. See note 9, chap. 14 above.
23. H. Colman, *The Agricultural and Rural Economy of France, Belgium, Holland and Switzerland: from Personal Observation* (London, 1848), pp. 168–174.
24. Drummond and Wilbraham, p. 306.
25. Mark Twain [Samuel Langhorne Clemens], *A Tramp Abroad* (Hartford, Conn., 1894), pp. 572–575.
26. Rumford, p. 404.
27. William Howard Russell, *My Diary North and South* (2 vols., London, 1863), Vol. I, p. 48.
28. Kenney-Herbert, p. 457. See note 12, this chapter.
29. Hayward, p. 77.

18. The Scientific Revolution
1. Burnett [1], p. 283.

2. Quoted in Drummond and Wilbraham, pp. 441–442.
3. Dr. Norman Borlaug, speech at FAO meeting in Rome, November, 1971. Reported in *Time*, Nov. 22, 1971.
4. Report in *Sunday Telegraph*, Apr. 5, 1970.
5. Carefoot and Sprott, p. 10.
6. U.S. President's Science Advisory Committee report: *World Food Problem*, Vol. II, p. 554.
7. Dr. Norman Borlaug, reported in *The Times* (London), Nov. 9, 1971.
8. Carson, pp. 56–59.
9. Report in *Time*, Dec. 5, 1969.
10. *Ibid.*, Nov. 22, 1971.
11. Carson, pp. 244–246.
12. Reported in *Sunday Times* (London), Mar. 5, 1972.
13. Reported in *Time*, Sept. 9, 1970.

Epilogue
1. Discussions at Duttweiler Institute conference of biologists, reported in *Sunday Times* (London), Sept. 4, 1971.
2. Hiroshi Takeuchi, "Taller and Broader," *Japan Quarterly* Vol. IX, 1 (January–March, 1962).
3. Dr. John Dobbing, reported in *The Times* (London), Sept. 10, 1969. See also *British Medical Journal*, Jan. 20, 1973, and *Lancet*, Feb. 24, 1973.
4. *Science*, Jan. 28, 1972.
5. Brillat-Savarin, Aphorisms IV.
6. A compressed account of the factory-laboratory described in Calder, pp. 129–131.
7. Dr. Michael Crawford, reported in *Sunday Times* (London), Jan. 1, 1971.

METRIC EQUIVALENTS OF MEASURES USED IN THE TEXT

Weights

⅛ ounce = 3.5 grams
¼ ounce = 7 grams
⅗ ounce = 17 grams
1 ounce = 28.35 grams
3 ounces = 85 grams
4 ounces = ¼ pound = 113 grams
8 ounces = ½ pound = 227 grams
10½ ounces = 298 grams
12 ounces = ¾ pound = 340 grams
16 ounces = 1 pound = 454 grams
1⅓ pounds = 605 grams
1½ pounds = 681 grams
1 11/16 pounds = 27 ounces = 766 grams
2 pounds = 907 grams
2 3/16 pounds = 1 kilogram
2 5/16 pounds = 37 ounces = 1.05 kilograms
3 lb. = 1.36 kilograms
4 pounds = 1.81 kilograms
5 pounds = 2.27 kilograms
6 pounds = 2.76 kilograms
9 pounds = 4.08 kilograms
10 pounds = 4.54 kilograms
14 pounds = 6.35 kilograms
20 pounds = 9.08 kilograms
40 pounds = 18.16 kilograms
50 pounds = 22.7 kilograms
60 pounds = 27.24 kilograms
100 pounds = 45.4 kilograms
112 pounds = 1 hundredweight = 50.8 kilograms
150 pounds = 68.1 kilograms
250 pounds = 113.5 kilograms
300 pounds = 136.2 kilograms
2000 pounds = 908 kilograms
2240 pounds = 1016 kilograms
2500 pounds = 1134 kilograms
3000 pounds = 1362 kilograms
16,000 pounds = 7264 kilograms
111,108 pounds = 50,443 kilograms
1,000,000 pounds = 454,000 kilograms
18,000,000 pounds = 8,172,000 kilograms
22,000,000 pounds = 9,988,000 kilograms

Volumes

1 Imperial pint = 568 milliliters
1 American pint = 454 milliliters
⅛ pint (Imperial) = 2½ fluid ounces = 71 milliliters
½ Imperial, ⅝ American pint = 284 milliliters
1 Imperial, 1¼ American pints = 568 milliliters
1¾ Imperial, 2⅕ American pints = 1 liter
4 Imperial, 5 American pints = 2.28 liters
7 Imperial, 8¾ Americans pints = 3.99 liters
8 Imperial, 10 American pints = I Imperial, 1¼ American gallons = 4.5 liters

10 Imperial, 12½ American gallons = 45.5 liters
22 Imperial, 27½ American gallons = 100 liters = 1 hectoliter
30 Imperial, 37½ American gallons = 1.36 hectoliters
32 Imperial, 38 American gallons = 1.45 hectoliters
60 Imperial, 75 American gallons = 2.73 hectoliters
1600 Imperial, 2000 American gallons = 7280 hectoliters

22 Imperial gallons = 2.75 bushels = 1 hectoliter
100 bushels = 36.37 hectoliters
14,000,000 bushels = 5,091,800 hectoliters

Linear Measures

1 inch = 2.54 centimeters
4 inches = 10.16 centimeters
6 inches = 15.24 centimeters
1 foot = 30.48 centimeters
1 yard = 0.914 meters
1 mile = 1.609 kilometers
11,000 feet = 3666 yards = 2.08 miles = 3.3 kilometers
25 miles = 40.2 kilometers
300 miles = 482.4 kilometers
515 miles = 828 kilometers
1000 miles = 1609 kilometers
7000 miles = 11,263 kilometers

Land Measures

1 square mile = 640 acres = 259 hectares
31 square miles = 19,840 acres = 8029 hectares
2,000,000 acres = 809,360 hectares
400,000,000 acres = 161,872,000 hectares

Index